The Jurassic Park Book

The Jurassic Park Book

New Perspectives on the Classic 1990s Blockbuster

Edited by
Matthew Melia

BLOOMSBURY ACADEMIC
NEW YORK • LONDON • OXFORD • NEW DELHI • SYDNEY

BLOOMSBURY ACADEMIC
Bloomsbury Publishing Inc, 1385 Broadway, New York, NY 10018, USA
Bloomsbury Publishing Plc, 50 Bedford Square, London, WC1B 3DP, UK
Bloomsbury Publishing Ireland, 29 Earlsfort Terrace, Dublin 2, D02 AY28, Ireland

BLOOMSBURY, BLOOMSBURY ACADEMIC and the Diana logo
are trademarks of Bloomsbury Publishing Plc

First published in the United States of America 2024
Paperback edition published 2025

Copyright © Matthew Melia and contributors, 2024

For legal purposes the Acknowledgments on p. xiii constitute an
extension of this copyright page.

Cover design: Eleanor Rose
Cover image: *Jurassic Park*, 1993, dir. Steven Spielberg © ArenaPAL

All rights reserved. No part of this publication may be: i) reproduced or transmitted
in any form, electronic or mechanical, including photocopying, recording or
by means of any information storage or retrieval system without prior permission
in writing from the publishers; or ii) used or reproduced in any way for the training,
development or operation of artificial intelligence (AI) technologies, including generative
AI technologies. The rights holders expressly reserve this publication from the text and
data mining exception as per Article 4(3) of the Digital Single Market Directive (EU) 2019/790.

Bloomsbury Publishing Inc does not have any control over, or responsibility for, any
third-party websites referred to or in this book. All internet addresses given in this
book were correct at the time of going to press. The author and publisher regret any
inconvenience caused if addresses have changed or sites have ceased to exist,
but can accept no responsibility for any such changes.

A catalog record for this book is available from the Library of Congress.

Library of Congress Cataloging-in-Publication Data

Names: Melia, Matthew, editor.
Title: The Jurassic Park book : new perspectives on the classic 1990s
blockbuster / edited by Matthew Melia.
Description: New York : Bloomsbury Academic, 2024. |
Includes bibliographical references and index.
Identifiers: LCCN 2023020676 (print) | LCCN 2023020677 (ebook) |
ISBN 9781501384868 (hardback) | ISBN 9781501384837 (paperback) |
ISBN 9781501384851 (epub) | ISBN 9781501384844 (pdf) |
ISBN 9781501384820 (ebook other)
Subjects: LCSH: Jurassic Park (Motion picture)
Classification: LCC PN1997.J833 J89 2024 (print) | LCC PN1997.J833 (ebook) |
DDC 791.43/72–dc23/eng/20230621
LC record available at https://lccn.loc.gov/2023020676
LC ebook record available at https://lccn.loc.gov/2023020677

ISBN: HB: 978-1-5013-8486-8
PB: 978-1-5013-8483-7
ePDF: 978-1-5013-8484-4
eBook: 978-1-5013-8485-1

Typeset by Newgen KnowledgeWorks Pvt. Ltd., Chennai, India

For product safety related questions contact productsafety@bloomsbury.com.

To find out more about our authors and books visit www.bloomsbury.com
and sign up for our newsletters.

This book is dedicated to Charlotte Melia who first saw Jurassic Park *with her old dinosaur.
And to my dad, Mike Melia—I would have loved to have seen it with you.*

CONTENTS

List of Illustrations x
Foreword by Linda Ruth Williams xi
Acknowledgments xiii

Introduction 1
  Matthew Melia

Part One Production, Adaptation, and Reception

1 Writing the Raptor: From Script to Screen 25
   Oliver Gruner

2 Rebellious Creations, Monstrous Animals, and (Un)Natural Disasters: The *Jurassic Park* Franchise and Box Office Hit Patterns 43
   Peter Krämer

3 Sounds of the Lost World: Musical World-Building in the *Jurassic Park* Franchise 59
   Daniel White

4 Beyond the Gift Shop: Onscreen Merchandise and Modeling the Consumer-Spectator 81
   Tom Livingstone

5 *Jurassic Park* and Dinosaur Fandom 97
   Ross Garner

6 *Jurassic Park*'s Smoothing Pass: The Dinosaur Input Device and Digital Materialism 113
   Julie Turnock

7 From "Six-Foot Turkey" to Marketing Monster: Marketing *Jurassic Park* and Its Sequels 131
Ed Vollans

Part Two Critical Perspectives and Interpretation

8 *Jew*-rassic Park 155
Nathan Abrams

9 Virility, Venality, and Victory: Three Faces of Masculinity in *Jurassic Park* 169
Katie Barnett

10 *Jurassic Park* and Spielberg's Scientists 185
James Kendrick

11 The Dinosaurs of *Jurassic Park* and the Portrayal of Prehistoric Life and Paleontology in Film 203
Ali Nabavizadeh

12 From Creatures to Companions: Representations of Dinosaur Violence in the *Jurassic Park* and *Jurassic World* Films 223
Jennifer Schell

13 *Jurassic Park*: Disaster, Chaos, and Existential Threat 239
Matthew Melia

Part Three Beyond *Jurassic Park*

14 Smoke and Mirrors: The 3D Reimaginings of *Jurassic Park* 263
Allison Whitney

15 The *Jurassic* Joke 277
Janet Staiger

16 "A Chance to Three-Dimensionally Live the Movie": *Jurassic Park* Attractions and Their Influence on Global Themed Experiences 295
Carissa Baker

17 Family, Nostalgia, and Dinosaurs on Stage:
   The Jurassic Parks 311
   Catherine Pugh

List of Contributors 327
Index 333

ILLUSTRATIONS

Figures

3.1 Composers involved in *Jurassic* films, TV series, trailers, and attractions 60
3.2 Composers involved in *Jurassic* videogames 60
3.3 Percentage musical underscoring in each *Jurassic* film 66
4.1 *Jurassic World* (2015): Innovation Centre Hologram 90
4.2 *Jurassic Park*'s *T-Rex* brings down the house (1993) 91
6.1 Ann Darrow (Fay Wray) is sacrificed to King Kong 114
6.2 Grant distracts the *T-Rex* 115
11.1 The sauropod dinosaur *Brachiosaurus* rearing up to feed from a tall tree 206
11.2 The ornithischian dinosaur *Triceratops* lying down sick 209
11.3 The theropod dinosaur *Tyrannosaurus* escaping its enclosure 213
11.4 A pair of the theropod dinosaurs *Velociraptor* in a kitchen 216
13.1 Arriving at *Jurassic Park* 243
13.2 Helicopter shot, *The Towering Inferno* 243
13.3 White House explosion in *Independence Day* 245
13.4 *T-Rex* in *Jurassic World: Dominion* 246
13.5 Dennis Nedry's Barbasol can 248

Table

3.1 Musical Tropes of the *Jurassic* Franchise 64

FOREWORD

Linda Ruth Williams
Professor of Film, University
of Exeter, UK

The single most powerful filmmaker in the history of the medium only began to attract serious academic attention some time into the twenty-first century. It took around thirty-five years after Steven Spielberg's cinematic career had launched (in the early to mid-1970s) for a gathering cluster of new work exploring the interest and complexity of his films to emerge (in the first decade of this century). This is—at the very least—an astonishing quirk of film studies, suggesting that this academic field has only replicated the screen industries' wider view of respect due—or not. Across the highs and lows of critical attention, and more highs than lows of box office profitability, Spielberg remained somehow too popular to merit serious analysis, functioning more as a New Hollywood symptom than as an auteur with a singular perspective. At the same time, he was also deemed too mainstream to reward the academic attention given to exploitation and B-cinemas, a burgeoning field of interest since at least the 1980s. My own work on the director identifies his association with the child and the pervasive charge that his films and influence function to infantilize culture as sticks regularly used to beat him with. It took until the year of *Jurassic Park* for the US Academy to seriously reward him, though the Oscars were not (predominantly) for this film, but for his other release in that career-high annus mirabilis, *Schindler's List* (both films were released in 1993 but rewarded in the Oscars ceremony in 1994, with the latter film garnering seven awards in the main categories, whilst *Jurassic Park* won three technical awards). This conflicted image of Spielberg the helmer of *Jurassic Park* rather than Spielberg the auteur of *Schindler's List* is interesting: he is at the same time too popular, too successful, too schlocky yet also not schlocky enough to be counterculturally challenging, and sometimes not above being a B-movie showman with an A-movie budget (as Roger Corman memorably characterized *Jaws*). Yet this filmmaker (the *Jurassic* Spielberg rather than the art house Spielberg of *Schindler's List* vintage) is also able to capture, explore, and exploit moments of great cultural significance while deploying the most popular of vehicles. Nowhere is this more the case than in *Jurassic Park*.

Many of these strands entwine in this fascinating book—the first to give dedicated and focused attention to this singular film, opening up serious questions around its cultural, historical, and textual complexities. The fresh perspectives brought together in this collection show *Jurassic Park* to be a singularly elastic film, resonant and culturally complex, able to speak to diverse audiences, and to speak of its specific 1990s moment, while calling loud and clear into this century as a stand-alone film and through its cinematic and paracinematic descendants. This legacy of sequels and franchises (and even a theatrical spin-off) is amply addressed here. But it is the distinctiveness of the first film itself that is the star of this volume, as it is scrutinized through a rich range of frameworks including paleontology, adaptation, musicology, histories of science and scientists, film industry studies, fans and audiences, the film's curious impact on language and humor, its transmedia tentacles and pathways (games, rides, merchandise), the genres it inhabits and reinvents, and of course textual representations including of masculinities, Jews, and the dinosaurs themselves. All of this manages to both reinforce something we now recognize about Spielberg—that his influences are not just industrial and corporate, but semiotically and culturally complex—and also something that we are coming to learn: that *Jurassic Park* crucially stands beyond Spielberg's career as well as squarely within it.

Despite the decades of change around screen and immersive technologies, *Jurassic Park* remains, then, a remarkably fresh take on event cinema and the disaster/creature feature genres. Key developments in screen technology drove its genesis through a combination of both practical and digital effects, and while this has of course been eclipsed many times over by SFX innovation, the film's look remains astonishingly convincing. This book reinvigorates our view of *Jurassic Park*, showing us around the film's engine room, the meanings and significations that drive it along, while also looking outward to its legacies and wider impact and implications. Through this, the figure of Spielberg emerges as both entirely and confidently in control of his monster, and as simultaneously left behind by its many lives and legacies. Thus the single-film focus of this book occupies a fascinating place in the meanings of both director and text, provoking and contesting auteur readings (Spielberg—after Crichton—originates but does not complete the film's story) at the same time as it resists canonizing the film itself (the *Jurassic* cultural phenomenon spills beyond its originary film). This book then both is and isn't a timely contribution to the growing field of Spielberg studies—but only because the film itself (in conjunction with its tenacious afterlives) is shown animated by so many resonances beyond this initial cinematic moment. It is a bravura and complicating chapter in this film's varied cultural history.

ACKNOWLEDGMENTS

I would like to thank Bloomsbury Academic for their support in putting this book together and especially Katie Gallof for being so accommodating and allowing the expansion of the Spielberg project from *Jaws* to *Jurassic Park* and for all her patience and help. I would like to extend my thanks to Ian Hunter with whom this project started and who kindly looked over the introduction for this book and made editorial suggestions. I would also like to extend my sincere thanks to Linda Ruth Williams for taking the time out of her busy schedule to write the foreword. Most of all I would like to thank all the contributors for their patience and their contributions to this project.

Introduction

Matthew Melia
Kingston University, UK

Opening Night: *Jurassic Park* as an Event Movie

Thirty years ago, in July 1993, I waited in line outside the Plaza Cinema in Waterloo (Liverpool, UK) for the opening night of the new and highly anticipated Steven Spielberg film, *Jurassic Park*. It had already been released on June 11th in the United States (with a preview on June 9 at the Uptown Theatre in Washington, DC), with an international campaign starting in Brazil and South America on June 25. On July 16, a month later, it was released in the UK and Japan and across the rest of the world.[1] Public anticipation had been growing since the previous year with a campaign of enticing, drip-fed, marketing whetting filmgoers' appetites while holding back the film's central attraction and surprise: the spectacular and revolutionary SFX of the dinosaurs themselves. Outside the Plaza, the queue for the film stretched from the front of the cinema, around the corner, and all the way down the neighboring street. This was, in a very real sense, an event movie on a scale not seen since *Jaws* (1975) and *Star Wars* (1977)—films that defined and shaped their respective cultural moments and historical markers on both a personal and wider cultural level. For those of us too young to have experienced either of those films the first time around, *Jurassic Park* became the defining event movie event of the 1990s. It was also a spectacular counterpoint to the smaller independent movies ("The Indies") that, with *Reservoir Dogs* (1992) and *Pulp Fiction* (1994), brought talents like Quentin Tarantino into the mainstream, and which had come to, in part, define the cinematic landscape of the decade. Furthermore, and as I note in a chapter later in this book, *Jurassic Park* also anticipated the large-scale spectacular disaster cinema (such as *Independence Day* [1997]) that would dominate commercial cinema from the middle of the decade.

In 2023, the term "event movie" may seem antiquated, a relic of a recent but bygone age of cinema. We have, perhaps, become inured to the thrill of expectation that awaiting a film like *Jurassic Park* gave expectant audiences, especially given the speed with which blockbuster films are now produced, released, and then transitioned to streaming services. The ubiquity of and continuous releasing from multibillion-dollar transmedial film franchises such as *The Marvel Cinematic Universe* (MCU) or the now-extended *Star Wars* universe have made the standalone event movie something of a rarity. These franchises, some of which have branched out into digitally streamed television, have come to dominate the landscape of popular cinema where others have failed. *Avatar* (2009), for instance, for all its box office success, immersive digital world-building (owing much to the then re-emergent vogue for 3D), and aspiration to "event cinema," failed to retain its place in the wider cultural consciousness.[2] We may also make an exception for Peter Jackson's *Lord of the Rings* trilogy (2001–03) and Christopher Nolan's *Batman* trilogy (2005–12) as the major "event" movies of the early to mid-2000s. However Jackson's attempt to expand the *Rings* franchise with another trilogy based on *The Hobbit* was met with a lukewarm critical and public response.[3]

Jurassic Park itself is now a franchise. In 2015 *Jurassic World* extracted the DNA from a series that had been considered extinct since *Jurassic Park III* (2001) and cloned it across another two films: *Jurassic World: Fallen Kingdom* (2018) and, latterly, *Jurassic World: Dominion* (2022).[4] The rejuvenated brand brought *Jurassic Park* roaring back onto the cultural landscape as part of a transmedia empire of blockbuster films, computer games (forty titles across different platforms—and counting), *Lego* toys and kits and animated Lego Netflix series': *Jurassic World: Legend of Isla Nublar* (2019); *Jurassic World: Secret Exhibit* [2019]), and the animated series, *Camp Cretaceous* (produced by Spielberg, *Jurassic World* director Colin Trevorrow, and director Frank Marshall). Despite its event movie status, *Jurassic Park* also occupies something of an intermedial position in 1990s cinema. It was certainly an event movie in the tradition of *Star Wars*—or *Jaws*, but it was also a big-budget Hollywood blockbuster in an era of low-budget, auteurist, independent cinema. The tension between independent and commercial cinema is highlighted by Justin Wyatt when he observes that Ang Lee's *The Wedding Banquet* (1993) "out earned *Jurassic Park* on a screen-by-screen basis" despite it taking a fraction of *Jurassic Park*'s box office.[5] *Jurassic Park*'s problematizing intermedial position between the blockbuster and the indie is re-enforced by the fact that its central cast of actors were not big-name film stars. Instead, they emerged from the world of television (Wayne Knight, whose corpulent and devious Dennis Nedry is a riff on his Seinfeld sitcom character "Newman," for instance), US Indie cinema (Laura Dern had a long-standing professional history with David Lynch for instance; while Jeff Goldblum had a long-standing indie career), and international independent art cinema (Sam Neill having previously worked on Andrzej Żuławski's 1981 art-horror film *Possession*).

1993 also saw the release of other competing big budget films such as Sydney Pollack's adaptation of John Grisham's best-selling novel *The Firm* starring Tom Cruise, and high-concept blockbuster *Last Action Hero*, starring Arnold Schwarzenegger—directed by John McTiernan. It was initially anticipated that this film would be the main rival to *Jurassic Park*'s success at the box office. *Last Action Hero* was released two days after Spielberg's film on June 13 but, as John Lyttle reported in the *Independent*, "Devastating reviews for Schwarzenegger's *The Last Action Hero* promise Spielberg's monster a clear summer sweep."[6] Simon Brew pointed out:

> *Jurassic Park* was surrounded by—and easily defeated—blockbuster movies headlined by big stars that summer season. There was Sylvester Stallone in *Cliffhanger*, Harrison Ford in *The Fugitive*, Tom Cruise in *The Firm*, Clint Eastwood in *In the Line of Fire*, Tom Hanks and Meg Ryan in *Sleepless in Seattle*, and Sean Connery and Wesley Snipes in *Rising Sun* ... Also, of course, Arnold Schwarzenegger was back in action cinema for the first time since *Terminator 2: Judgment Day*, headlining *Last Action Hero*. Every studio in town wanted to make the next Arnold Schwarzenegger film at the time. It was Columbia Pictures that won out, giving Arnie himself more influence than he'd ever had over any picture. So confident was Columbia about its big summer tentpole movie that—at a time when this wasn't common—the ads were running the Christmas before.[7]

In advance of both films, the press pitched their releases as a battle, with *The Times* running the headline "The Dinosaurs Take on Arnie in the Clash of the Film Giants."[8] Philip Robinson reported:

> Battle commences soon in the UK with the opening of Universal's *Jurassic Park*, a robotised, computerised epic by Mr Spielberg about genetically engineered dinosaurs that turn from fun to horror. Sony's leading summer contender is *Last Action Hero*, starring $15m a film tough guy Arnold Schwarzenegger.[9]

Universal threw its financial weight behind the marketing campaign for *Jurassic Park*, which mostly only teased the reveal of the dinosaurs. The film was released simultaneously in both London and Tokyo "for maximum impact," and as Robinson notes, there was a lot riding on it—not only the restoration of the Spielberg brand but also the "corporate pride" of investors—the Japanese electronics firm Matsushita.[10] Matsushita had "bought its way into Hollywood" in 1990 with a "$6.6 billion cheque for MCA and its Universal studios" and by 1993 had still not made back even £100m while Sony had "bought into Hollywood for only $5 billion had had topped the film charts with five films grossing more than $100m."[11]

Jurassic Park and *Jaws*

Jurassic Park was released with a PG-13 rating in the United States with a PG rating given by the UK's British Board of Film Classification (BBFC). The film's intense and frightening dinosaur scenes were embedded within and as part of the film's publicity. In the UK, the censors insisted on placing warnings about "Disturbing scenes" on the marketing material and even Spielberg himself got in on the act, publicly stating that he had banned his own young children from seeing it—so too, according to the *Evening Standard*, had author Michael Crichton.[12] Furthermore, comparisons in the press with *Jaws* abounded. Baz Bamigboye in the *Daily Mail* called it "*Jaws* with legs" and the *Evening Standard* drew comparisons with *Jaws* in terms of the attention drawn by the censors to the film's more frightening scenes. It noted that in 1975 similar warnings affixed to publicity material had been used ahead of the release of *Jaws* and

> Helped to make Steven Spielberg's previous essay in anthropophagy and fishy serial slaughter a hit ... The roaring, ravening, man-munching child-chasing dinosaurs of *Jurassic Park* cloned by an eccentric scientist from prehistoric DNA, are worthy descendants of Spielberg's great plastic shark. They are a reprise of that old theme of the monster on the rampage, which had been around since the first cave painting. The British film classifiers might have been cloned in Hollywood by the film's promotion men. Their classification plus warning of disturbance is the best publicity the film could have hoped for, on the crest of the monstrous wave of dinopublicity that is rolling across the Atlantic and Europe.[13]

Jaws exists in the DNA of *Jurassic Park* like the amphibian DNA that closes the gene sequence gaps in the genetic make-up of the film's dinosaurs giving them, ultimately, their identity. In both films out-of-place (and in *Jurassic Park*'s case out-of-time) monsters threaten a small island community; there are reluctant heroes who are called up to step up to the plate—*Jaws*' police chief Martin Brody (Roy Scheider) and paleontologist Alan Grant (Sam Neill); avaricious, hubristic, and naïve "community leaders" in the shape of lawyer Donald Gennaro (Martin Ferrero) and park owner John Hammond (Richard Attenborough); Jeff Goldblum's "expert," the chaotician Ian

Malcom, is this film's Matt Hooper (Richard Dreyfuss) and there is even a diluted Quint (Robert Shaw) character—the park ranger Muldoon (played by the late British actor Bob Peck).

In *Jaws*, however, female characters such as Ellen Brody (Lorraine Gary) and Mrs. Kintner (Lee Fiero) are pushed to the sidelines in favor of a heady male-dominated narrative that both reclaims and critiques romantic and heroic American (white) male myths (especially when the film relocates to The Orca, Quint's boat, in the film's third act).[14] *Jurassic Park* leavens this , however, with the presence of an active female lead character, paleobotanist Ellie Sattler (Laura Dern), who is NOT called upon to act as a surrogate mother figure to the film's two child leads—Tim (Joseph Mazzello) and Lex (Ariana Richards)—these surrogate parental duties fall to the reluctant Alan Grant (later in this book Katie Barnett considers Grant as one of the "three faces of masculinity" in the film).

It's hard to discuss *Jurassic Park* without discussing *Jaws,* and various authors across the course of this book necessarily draw on and refer to Spielberg's shark. *Jurassic Park*'s marketing and merchandising blitz are the direct legacy of *Jaws*' own pioneering merchandising strategies.[15] As with *Jaws, Jurassic Park* inspired a frenzy of monster mania and the *Independent on Sunday* (UK) observed, "Dino-Fever Grips Nation as Cultural Tyrant Is Born." Phil Reeves wrote:

> After months of furious hype, Americans headed to the cinemas yesterday on the opening weekend of Steven Spielberg's movie *Jurassic Park* which is already responsible for a national bout of dino-fever ... Record numbers of tickets were sold in advance as fans came to see the blockbuster, long billed as a milestone in popular culture and at the centre of a multimillion-dollar marketing blitz.[16]

Reeves notes how *Jurassic Park*, which cost $60 million (comparatively low by today's standards), was expected to break the earlier record set by *Batman Returns* (1992) in its opening weekend. *Jurassic Park* grossed $352 million in its domestic opening weekend alone—establishing itself as the highest grossing film of all time until *Titanic* (1997) by which point it had grossed $914 million worldwide.. It also earned enthusiastic reviews, outstripping *Jaws* at the box office (and a sequence in *Jurassic World*, twenty-three years later, depicts an enormous *Mosasaurus* being fed a comparatively tiny great white shark in front of an arena of thrilled spectators). Spielberg's shark took $7m in its opening weekend (adjusted for inflation in 1993 this is around $18m). Of course, in 1975, Spielberg was a young, relatively unknown director with one film behind him (*The Sugarland Express*, 1974) and a very effective TV film, *Duel* (1971), but by 1993 Spielberg was the most successful director in Hollywood, whose films had come to define American popular cinema. *Jaws* was key not only to the film's marketing but also in the build-up of public anticipation for *Jurassic Park*—here was Spielberg returning to the genre with which he had made his name: the monster movie. The opening gambit of *Jurassic Park*, in which a construction worker is devoured by an unseen monster, even recalls the opening scene of *Jaws* in which Chrissie (Susan Backlinie) is also violently devoured by an unseen threat on her midnight swim.

"The dinosaur film," as Reeves comments, "was considered to be of sufficient cultural importance by the editors of *Newsweek* and *USA Today* to merit cover stories. Suddenly Americans are experts on the *Tyrannosaurus Rex* and the *Dilophosaurus*, and PC has a new meaning: paleontologically correct."[17] Like *Jaws*, *Jurassic Park* was promoted with a massive merchandising campaign. As Louise Kehoe reported in the *Financial Times*,

> Even by Hollywood standards the hoo-ha surrounding *Jurassic Park* is mammoth. The new MCA/Universal dinosaur film directed by Steven Spielberg and based on Crichton's best-selling novel is at the centre of a publicity blitz fuelled by the entertainment industry's biggest licensing and merchandising programme to date ... In common with Crichton's fictional zoo in which cloned dinosaurs run amok, the film *Jurassic Park* has become the centrepiece of an enormous enterprise involving more than 100 companies licensed to sell over 1,000 products carrying the film's distinctive emblem: a dinosaur skull silhouetted against a blood red sky. Advertising for *Jurassic* products is expected to top $65m this year.[18]

She goes on to note:

> With *Jurassic Park* opening at thousands of US cinemas tomorrow stores are already loaded with everything from pyjamas and boxer shorts to video games, sweets and toys, training cards, stickers, board games and puzzles, baseball caps and, inevitably, cereal ... Ferrara Pan Candy expects to see $30m (£19.8m) to $40m of fruit gum dinosaurs, dinosaur snacks and jellies. Then there are stuffed animals from Dakin—a 30 inch *brachiosaurus*, smaller spitters, raptors and *triceratops* ... "We will take dinosaur mania to a new level" gushes Linda Berkely, senior vice president of development and head of merchandising at MCA/Universal.[19]

Furthermore, as Thomas Elsaesser argued:

> Set within a theme and adventure park, which exists only as a fiction, the film invites us to imitate the visitors in the fiction. Insofar as this fiction of a fiction will produce "real memorabilia," the film is itself an advertisement for the games, gadgets, and toys that one can buy after seeing the movie. It therefore does not come as a surprise to learn that six months before the release of the film, Amblin Films issued a *Jurassic Park*

style book for advertisers and merchandisers, which alone cost $500,000 to produce.[20]

Jurassic Park is also exemplary of the cultural shift in the 1990s toward the postmodern. Stuart Jeffries notes the close relationship between self-referential postmodern culture and neoliberal free-market economics.[21] *Jurassic Park* foregrounds the dangers of neoliberalism while at the same time advertising its own merchandising products as "in-text" items, part of the contextual and thematic mise-en-scène of the film itself. As Elsaesser argues:

> In today's media world—to paraphrase E. M. Forster—everything connects. A feature film, a theme park, a toy store, and a computer game have a lot in common: they feed off each other as they play off each other. When one considers that *The Lion King* (1994) took $80 million at the box office, but made $220 million as a videocassette, one can understand why commentators have argued that a film today is merely a billboard stretched out in time, designed to showcase tomorrow's classics in the video stores and the television reruns. *Jurassic Park* may make the intermedia connections more explicit than most, insofar as it mimics the links within its own fiction, but it also shows that if everything connects, this does not mean that anything goes.[22]

As with *Jaws*, *Jurassic Park* assimilated a range of genres and subgenres—some of which—such as the disaster film and "lost world" narratives are explored later in this book. Horror, however, is at the center of the Venn diagram binding both films, with both films featuring spectacular scenes of people being devoured by monstrous, atavistic creatures. *Jurassic Park*, however, looks not only to *Jaws* but also shares its DNA with various other creature feature "exploitation" horror films including *Alligator* (1980) and *Piranha* (1978). Interestingly both of these films were written by director John Sayles who would later collaborate with Spielberg on the unmade *Jurassic Park IV*—a film that would have taken the franchise in a very different direction.[23] Sayles also worked on the unmade sci-fi horror *Night Skies* with Spielberg (elements of which were recycled in *E.T.: The Extra Terrestrial* [1982] and *Poltergeist* [1982]). Furthermore, the final act of *Jurassic Park*, in which the raptors hunt Lex and Tim in the kitchen is a conscious homage to the climactic kitchen sequence in *The Shining* (1981). The presence and casting of Mazzello and Richards in *Jurassic Park*, however, leavens the film's horror dynamic, placing it more firmly within a category of "family friendly" horror (despite its director's own protestations).

Jaws paved the way for the summer blockbuster (although it was, technically, not "the first" as Sheldon Hall has pointed out),[24] and its legacy may be felt in the slasher movie (not least *Halloween* [1978]). The genetics of Spielberg's shark are also found in the Xenomorph of *Alien* (1979) while similarly, in *Jurassic* Park's presentation of the *Velociraptors* (as they hunt the park visitors), there are shades of James Cameron's sequel, *Aliens* (1986). Cameron's career had run parallel with Spielberg during the 1980s and he came to define the more adult-oriented big budget Hollywood blockbuster with films such as *The Terminator* (1984), *The Abyss* (1989), *Aliens*, and *Terminator 2* (1991). Cameron had also been one of the directors who had been keen to adapt Michael Crichton's novel and, in an interview, Cameron commented on both this and *Jurassic Park*'s more child-friendly orientation:

> I tried to buy the book rights and he beat me to it by a few hours ... When I saw the film, I realised that I was not the right person to make the film, he was. Because he made a dinosaur movie for kids, and mine would have been aliens with dinosaurs, and that wouldn't have been fair ... Dinosaurs are for 8-year-olds. We can all enjoy it, too, but kids get dinosaurs, and they should not have been excluded for that. His sensibility was right for that film, I'd have gone further, nastier, much nastier.[25]

Digital FX

The major contribution to *Jurassic Park*'s reception as an event movie was of course its dinosaurs, which the pioneering digital effects of Spielberg's Industrial Light and Magic (ILM) brought back from extinction. Unlike *Jaws*, which delayed the reveal of the shark till the final third of the film (a decision necessitated by the happy accident of the malfunctioning mechanical fish), the dinosaurs of *Jurassic Park* had to be front and center. They were spectacularly rendered through a combination of models and pioneering computer-generated effects, the work of renowned visual effects expert Stan Winston (*The Thing* [1982]; *Aliens*; *Predator* [1987]; *The Terminator*; *Terminator 2*) and the digital team headed up by ILM's Dennis Muren (who had previously worked on *Terminator 2: Judgement Day*, heading up the team responsible for its groundbreaking VFX).[26]

Although *Jurassic Park* is rightly celebrated for its CGI, there are considerably fewer digital effects shots than "old school" animatronic effects. As with *Jaws*, Spielberg efficiently maneuvered around the practical problems of making monsters look real, in this case, merging groundbreaking digital with established practical effects. If the delayed reveal of the shark in *Jaws* was in part down to the mechanical problems of the models, then in *Jurassic Park* (according to Ben Friedman in *Highbrow Magazine*), the *T-Rex* sequences posed their own set of production problems. The *T-Rex* had to be experienced as if it was a real creature (this is, of course a film that holds debates about the real and the simulated at its core). Ben Friedman notes,

To achieve realism, Winston created a full-size physical T-Rex model. He designed a 20-foot animatronic puppet. Yet, Spielberg understood that puppetry was not enough. Special effects were needed to make the dinosaur's movements feel lifelike. The director soon learned that a single frame of CGI required for the T-Rex would take hours, thus delaying the film's release, so he got creative with filming … The iconic scene of the T-Rex attacking the Jeep is designed to showcase the carnage and scale of the T-Rex, yet also limit the number of special effects needed in post-production. To achieve this, the scene was shot on a rainy night with only a damaged floodlight as a source of lighting. This allowed the dinosaur to be largely filmed in shadow or complete darkness. In doing so, the post-production visual effects team did not have to render substantial portions of the T-Rex, allowing the visuals to be kept to a minimum.[27]

There is an iconic moment early in the film in which Alan Grant and Ellie Sattler are confronted for the first time with the awesome spectacle of a *Brachiosaurus* as it munches away at leaves from the very top of a giant tree. Grant takes off his sunglasses and stares in disbelief, turning Ellie's head away from the prehistoric leaf she is inspecting. Her jaw drops in amazement as, in the cinema, our jaws drop too. Here, with sly self-reflexivity, the film emphasizes that we are witnessing a genuine cinematic "event"—the first truly convincing CGI dinosaurs onscreen. As several of the contributors to this book observe, this moment is a turning point in both the film and in cinema history. We gaze in wonder not only at the prehistoric beast before us but also at the scientific technology and digital cinematic apparatuses and techniques that John Hammond (Richard Attenborough) and Steven Spielberg, both purveyors of childlike wonder, have used in bringing the prehistoric back to life—a modern day "Cinema of Attractions."[28]

In September 1992, a year before the film was released, Christian Moerk, writing in *Variety*, reported that "Jurassic looks like an f/x classic." Comparing it with two recent effects extravaganzas, *The Abyss* and *Total Recall* (1990), Moerk cited Clay Gordon ("of New York based Rebo Research, a developer of high-definition technology"), stating:

> To my knowledge, this [*Jurassic Park*] promises to be the most complex undertaking of its nature. In order to convince us [their animators] will have to focus on things like, "Do the animals have scars? So, they kick up dust? Is there a sense of deliberateness about their motion? The hardest thing they will have to overcome is our concept of a real dinosaur, even though we have never seen one.[29]

Hence it was not only filmgoers who were eagerly awaiting this spectacular new film but also industry insiders, especially those working in the FX industry. As the article in *Variety* notes, the first few years of the 1990s saw a "digital compositing revolution"—marked by James Cameron's *Terminator 2*, which "showed you how you could do things." *Jurassic Park*, with its mixture of CGI animation and animatronics was at the very forefront of the "digital turn" in cinema that would start to fully take hold at the turn of the new millennium. As Julie Turnock draws attention to in her chapter, *Jurassic Park*'s (previously stated) intermedial position also applies to its pioneering and seamless mixing of analog effects (models) and cutting-edge digital technology. Turnock notes that the film refers intertextually to earlier dinosaur fiction from the early years of cinema—not least the animated *Gertie the Dinosaur* (1914) and the stop motion *The Lost World* (1924), based on the story by Sir Arthur Conan Doyle. However, it also provides a platform for the entirely digital rendering of the dinosaurs across the later franchise, such as the rendering of Blue the Raptor in the *Jurassic World* franchise. The tension between old and new ways of creature realization is embodied in the film's use of both models and digital effects and as Moerk points out (citing former ILM staffer and present visual FX consultant to Walt Disney studios, Tom Smith):

> Veteran designer Phil Tippett who ran the "creature shop" on George Lucas's *Return of the Jedi* set was stunned to get the news that he wasn't going to be needed for stop-motion animation. But he was hired because you still need designers, now he's working on a computer instead of manipulating a puppet.[30]

The work carried out by ILM effects experts such as VFX supervisor Muren also had a wider cultural reach providing the grounding needed for digital creature realization not only across the rest of the *Jurassic* franchise(s) but also in subsequent creature-based popular franchises including the transmedia *Star Wars* universe, *Harry Potter* (2001–11), and *The Lord of the Rings*.

However, if the popular media, audiences, and industry insiders waited eagerly for the film and reacted rapturously on its release, its reception in the scientific community was more muted. In an article in *The Times* Ben Macintyre reported on the feeling in the scientific community and in the scientific press that *Jurassic Park* compounded cinema's demonization of scientists (citing films like *Dr. Strangelove* or *How I Learned to Stop Worrying and Love the Bomb* [1964]). He notes:

> In a recent article in *The New York Times*, under the headline "Evil Science Runs Amok—Again!" Professor Carol Muske of the University of South California attacked the "predictable but no less disturbing anti science statement that runs through the novel and film … "[31]

In her article Muske wrote:

With this attitude on the part of the purveyors of popular culture, how can we expect to attract young students to science, a field they are snubbing in droves? We also might try a new take on the grinding cliches of scientists as test-tube nerds, corporate shills or genocidal killers.[32]

From Page to Screen: Adapting *Jurassic Park*

The process of adapting *Jurassic Park* to the screen was in some ways like the process of bringing *Jaws* to the screen. *Jaws* had been commissioned to be adapted as a film when Peter Benchley's novel was still in its galley stages.[33] Michael Crichton's novel was published in 1990 and Spielberg had first heard about it during the developmental stages of the TV hospital drama *ER* in 1989, which he was producing, during discussions with Crichton (who wrote the series). Crichton had already identified that the novel would attract the attention of Hollywood and had not only begun a screenplay of his own but had also asked for a non-negotiable fee of $1.5 million for the film rights and a percentage of the gross. Prior to Warner Bros. acquiring the rights for Spielberg, the novel had already attracted the interest of the directors Tim Burton, Joe Dante, and Richard Donner.[34]

By 1993, Crichton was already well established as writer and novelist of tech-based corporate thrillers and science fiction often with an interest in both the anthropocene and technocene. His first novel, the techno-thriller *The Andromeda Strain* (1969), was adapted into a film in 1971, directed by Robert Wise. Crichton also had a longstanding career as a Hollywood screenwriter and director with such films as *Coma* (1978), which he directed from his own screenplay and, most relevantly for *Jurassic Park*, *Westworld* (1973), which he both wrote and directed. *Westworld* centers around a leisure park, Delos, separated into various zones or "worlds" where guests can choose to stay (they include Western World, Medieval World, and Roman World) for a fully immersive and interactive animatronic (A.I) experience of the respective time periods. The animatronics/A.I, of course, break down, endangering the visitors with one persistent, murderous and seemingly unstoppable robot Gunslinger (Yul Brynner) targeting one of the guests (Richard Benjamin). *Westworld*, as much as *Jaws*, inserts its textual and narrative DNA into *Jurassic Park*—and it's easy to read both the raptors and the *T-Rex* as combining aspects of the Gunslinger. Westworld's influence can also be felt in the *Terminator* films, demonstrating just how the Crichtonesque narrative had become part of the language of popular science fiction cinema from the 1970s.

Jurassic Park rejuvenated both the Crichton and Spielberg brands. In their wake, Crichton's novels were increasingly came into demand in Hollywood.

The Japanese corporate thriller *Rising Sun* (1982) with Sean Connery and Wesley Snipes followed hard on the heels of *Jurassic Park* at the end of July 1993; this was followed by *Disclosure* in 1994 and *Congo* in 1995. In 1995 Crichton published a sequel to *Jurassic Park*, *The Lost World*—this was subsequently adapted by Spielberg as the first *Jurassic* sequel, *The Lost World: Jurassic Park*, in 1997. The experience of making the film was not a happy one for Spielberg and in an interview in the *New York Times*, he stated:

> My sequels aren't as good as my originals because I go onto every sequel I've made and I'm too confident. This movie made a ka-zillion dollars, which justifies the sequel, so I come in like it's going to be a slam dunk and I wind up making an inferior movie to the one before. I'm talking about *The Lost World* and *Jurassic Park*.[35]

Prior to *Jurassic Park*, Spielberg had not had a major hit since *Indiana Jones and the Last Crusade* (1989). *Always* (1989) and the saccharine Peter Pan film *Hook* (1991) had met with poor critical reviews and muted box office response. *Hook* had been particularly problematic. Spielberg suffered with both a difficult production and a poor working relationship with actress Julia Roberts (who played the fairy, Tinkerbell). He later reflected in an interview with UK film critics Mark Kermode and Simon Mayo on their BBC Radio film review show (when he was on the campaign trail for *Lincoln* [2021]) that in retrospect there was nothing he really liked about the film.

Jurassic Park, therefore, was a shot in the arm for Spielberg, who needed a hit and it reinvigorated his career. Its pioneering use of SFX, as Geoff King has pointed out positioned Spielberg at the epicenter of a historical moment in American cinema—the turn toward the digital and as responsible for the return of the "Spectacular Narrative."[36] It also stands as one half of a pair of films that demonstrated the director's propensity for combining childlike wonder with terror and trauma and as a director who was equally at home making films for adults as for children. *Jurassic Park* went into postproduction at the same time as Spielberg was shooting the Holocaust drama *Schindler's List* (1993). He found himself in the surreal and unenviable position of finishing work on *Schindler's List* for the day in Poland and then calling into Los Angeles via satellite link up to check upon the progress of postproduction for *Jurassic Park*:

> "When I finally started shooting ... in Poland, I had to go home about two or three times a week and get on a very crude satellite feed to Northern California ... to be able to approve T-Rex shots," he remembered. "And it built a tremendous amount of resentment and anger that I had to do this, that I had to actually go from [the emotional weight of *Schindler's*

List] to dinosaurs chasing jeeps, and all I could express was how angry that made me at the time. I was grateful later in June, though, but until then it was a burden."[37]

Later in this book, Nathan Abrams offers an analysis of the Jewish subtexts beneath the surface of *Jurassic Park* and draws a set of thematic links between it and *Schindler's List*, observing the encoded Holocaust imagery in *Jurassic Park*.

Crichton stated, in an interview in which he discusses adapting *Jurassic Park*, a task that would eventually fall to David Koepp, that his interest in dinosaur cloning dated back to 1983. The novel, Crichton claimed, was originally conceptualized as a screenplay, though initial attempts to develop the script were not being entirely successful:

> The script didn't work, and I just waited to see if I could ever figure out how to make it work. It took quite a few years ... It was a very different story ... It was about the person who did the cloning, operating alone and in secret. It just wasn't satisfactory. The real conclusion for me was that what you really wanted in a story like this was to have a sort of natural environment in which people and dinosaurs could be together. You wanted the thing that never happened in history: people in the forest and swamps at the same time as dinosaurs.[38]

It's worth noting here as well that *Jurassic Park* was not Crichton's first venture into dino-territory. The novel *Dragon Teeth* was posthumously published in 2017 but was written in 1974. It is set during "The Bone Wars" (1872–99) or "The Great Dinosaur Rush," which was a period of dangerously competitive fossil hunting in the American West. The novel focuses on the rivalry between two of the major paleontologists of the era, Edward Drinker Cope and Othniel Charles Marsh.

After Universal acquired the rights to *Jurassic Park* in 1990, Crichton was paid another $500,000 on top of the $1.5 million to write a draft of the script. This was later given an uncredited reworking by Malia Scotch Marmo, who had worked on *Hook*, and the final draft of the script was developed and written by Koepp. There are significant deviations from Crichton's novel in Koepp's final script. Similarities can also be drawn with *Jaws* and Carl Gottlieb's screenplay adaptation of Peter Benchley's novel. As Koepp reflected in a recent onstage "Script to Screen" Q&A with Matt Ryan, he shifted focus from the novel's emphasis on the dinosaurs escaping from the island (a storyline that would form part of the narrative for the *The Lost World: Jurassic Park*) to a more self-contained survival narrative (later in this book I discuss this in relation to *Jurassic Park*'s status as a "disaster movie").[39] There were several key character modifications. Koepp had felt that the Ian Malcolm character (Jeff Goldblum), a chaotician and the novel's moral compass, as well as the novel's discussion of chaos theory was too complex for a mainstream blockbuster. He had wanted to cut the character entirely, but Spielberg encouraged him to retain both Malcolm and the thematically important presence of chaos theory.

One of the most significant deviations was in the character of park owner John Hammond. In the novel Hammond is an avaricious, corporate monster who is finally devoured by his own creatures. Spielberg encouraged softening the character to an avuncular and well meaning (if naïve) PT Barnum-like showman and Koepp hints that Spielberg envisioned him as Walt Disney. Again, we can draw comparisons with similar character shifts from novel to screen in *Jaws*, in which Mayor Vaughn (Murray Hamilton) is presented more sympathetically in the film, as is the character of Quint the Ahab-like shark hunter who in Benchley's novel is much more sadistic, foulmouthed, and motiveless (there is, of course, no *USS Indianapolis* speech in Benchley's novel to explain Quint's monomaniac pursuit of the shark). Streamlining the novel's structure and editing out sections, such as the sequence in the aviary with the *Pterodactyl* attack and the sequence in which several of the raptors find their way on a boat to the mainland, ended up providing material for the film's sequels.

The *Jurassic Park* Book

Compared to *Jaws*, *Jurassic Park* has received comparatively little critical academic attention. It has, of course, been included in texts devoted to the wider canon of Spielberg's work. Nigel Morris, for instance, devoted a chapter to it in his career-spanning, *The Cinema of Steven Spielberg: Empire of Light*.[40] Critical discussions of *Jurassic Park* have been incorporated in books, articles, and collections covering subjects as varied as paleoethology, genetics, geology, ecology, monster theory, and the digital turn in cinema. In *Spectacular Narratives: Contemporary Hollywood in the Age of the Blockbuster*, Geoff King places *Jurassic Park*, historically, within the context of an early 1990s Hollywood in transition and as anticipatory of the spectacular digital SFX-laden films, such as *Independence Day*, which were to follow.[41] While there have been numerous critical articles dedicated to the film, it is somewhat surprising that there has been, to date, no extended critical study. This book aims to fill that gap as the first edited collection dedicated to the film and its attendant themes and histories.

This book is also a sequel of sorts to *The Jaws Book: New Perspectives on the Classic Summer Blockbuster*. That book was timed to commemorate the 45th anniversary of Spielberg's seminal film, while this book, published in 2023, celebrates thirty years of *Jurassic Park*. It presents an interdisciplinary collection comprised of seventeen chapters from a range of new, emerging, and established writers. *The Jurassic Park Book* offers a wide-ranging analysis of the film through the lens of fan and genre studies; paleontology, marketing, merchandising, and branding; adaptation studies; gender studies; and more. While the focus is on the 1993 film, the book (necessarily) also considers the wider franchise and the transmedial world of *Jurassic Park* that followed in its wake. Furthermore, this book is a companion piece to a special edition of the online journal *Cinergie—Il Cinema e le altre Arti*, "Franchising *Jurassic Park*," which looks specifically at the ways in which the franchise has extended itself (to be published in December 2023).

Part I: Production, Adaptation, and Reception

The first part of this book looks at the film's production, reception, and adaptive history. In Chapter 1, Oliver Gruner discusses *Jurassic Park*'s journey from page to screen. He begins with a discussion of the early attempts to bring Michael Crichton's novel to the screen and of the early characterizations of the characters John Hammond and Ian Malcolm. Gruner also offers a critical and comparative study of several screenplay treatments—including Michael Crichton's own treatment, production designer Rick Carter's development of Crichton's treatment, and the final treatments developed and written by screenwriters Malia Scotch Marmo and David Koepp.

In Chapter 2 Peter Krämer offers an analysis of *Jurassic Park*'s success at the box office. Through an experiential account of his own scholarly and personal engagement with the film and more broadly with Spielberg's cinema, Krämer offers a comparative study of the franchise's box office successes. He contextualizes all the *Jurassic Park* films by mapping the enormous success of the franchise and especially *Jurassic Park*, against trends in US, non-US, and global box office charts.

John Williams's stirring, dramatic, and evocative score is a defining element of *Jurassic Park* and it embedded the film firmly in the minds of a global audience. In Chapter 3, Daniel White offers discussion of Williams's score. White also examines the role of music in world-building across the extended franchise and illustrates how the sequels, the wider franchise, computer games, and Lego Netflix series (like *Camp Cretaceous*) are anchored to the original film through Williams's soundtrack.

In Chapter 4, Tom Livingstone turns to the self-referential and intertextual depiction of consumerism and merchandising in the *Jurassic Park* and the subsequent *Jurassic World* franchises and focuses on an area of the park(s) only briefly glimpsed in the first film—the gift shop. Livingstone offers several close readings of scenes in the films that feature real-world *Jurassic* merchandise and that model different ways of consuming both the film text and its associated branded products. He reflects on CGI's effect on consumer agency in the digital landscape and, drawing on Jonathan Beller's theorization of the "attention economy" and Leon Gurevitch's insight that all computer-generated assets are, in essence, "product placement," analyzing *Jurassic Park*'s representation of capitalism and consumerism.

Chapter 5 sees Ross Garner approach the film's reception through the prism of fan studies. The chapter asks how important the dinosaurs themselves are to *Jurassic Park*'s fan communities and to which subsections of the fan base are they most crucial? Garner also asks what other aspects of the franchise are afforded significance by areas of the fandom. He draws on a combination of qualitative survey results and ethnographic observation of fan-produced material (such as websites, podcasts, etc.) to better understand how, where, and for what types and groups of fans the dinosaurs form the core affective attachment to the property.

Turning to ILM's ground-breaking work, Julie Turnock discusses *Jurassic Park*'s digital effects and "digital realism." She addresses the "digital turn" from stop motion effects to digital effects in cinema and considers how ILM transitioned from one to the other, using stop motion techniques as a basis for their digital innovations. Turnock draws comparatively on a body of effects-driven cinema, from *King Kong* (1933) to *The Matrix* (1998) and *The Lord of the Rings* trilogy in assessing the digital legacy of *Jurassic Park*, and the "smoothing pass" between visible effects and digital realism.

Finally in this section, Ed Vollans discusses the marketing strategies for the film and its subsequent sequels. Vollans tracks and interrogates the marketing campaign for the first three movies. Blending investigation of newspaper and magazine archives with broader digital archaeology, he maps the campaigns for each movie and combines the structure, content, and reception of these into a framework for analysis. Doing so shows not only how these campaigns shifted with franchise success but also how they did so at a time of an emerging and new digital zeitgeist.

Part II: Critical Perspectives and Interpretation

This part offers a body of interpretive, critical readings of *Jurassic Park* and at times the wider franchise. Nathan Abrams, building on his exploration of the hidden Jewish subtexts in *Jaws* observes how Spielberg encodes Jewishness into Jurassic *Park*'s narrative, themes, and iconography. Observing the film's concurrent production schedule with *Schindler's List*, Abrams notes the thematic consistencies between the two and how the production of *Schindler's List* impacted on *Jurassic Park*. He excavates the film's Holocaust imagery, observing the dinosaurs as Golems and offers a close reading and analysis of Jeff Goldblum's *Menschlikayt* scientist, Ian Malcom.

Turning to a gendered reading of the film, Katie Barnett addresses the "three faces of masculinity" in *Jurassic Park*: "venality, virility, and victory." She offers a set of character analyses, focusing on four main male characters: Dennis Nedry, Donald Gennaro, Ian Malcolm, and Alan Grant. Barnett notes how the contours of American masculinity were increasingly under scrutiny during the 1990s, and how *Jurassic Park* presents images of flawed men in need of punishment, reform, or redemption.

The next two chapters offer a view of the film through a scientific lens. James Kendrick discusses the film's representation of scientists. Kendrick observes the multifaceted ways in which science and scientists are depicted in the film. He begins by offering a detailed critical overview of the representation of scientists across a range of Spielberg's films and how the representation of science in *Jurassic Park* was met with skepticism by the wider scientific community in the wake of the film's release. The chapter deals with the film's appropriation of the *Frankenstein* mythos examining *Jurassic Park*'s depiction of science, scientific hubris, and other ethical considerations, drawing comparatively on Spielberg's numerous other films that depict scientists as either heroes, villains, or something in-between.

In Chapter 11, paleontologist Ali Nabavizadeh scrutinizes the representation of the dinosaurs themselves. The chapter considers each of the dinosaurs featured across the franchise and draws on contemporary paleontological research to assess the accuracy of their representation on screen. Taking a franchise-wide perspective, he sets the representation of dinosaurs against historical film representations as well as observes the film's representation of paleontologists and the science of paleontology itself.

The next chapters offer genre studies of *Jurassic Park*. Jennifer Schell explores *Jurassic Park* within the context of "Lost World" cinematic narratives. In discussing the dino-violence in the film, Schell offers a critical overview of this history of Lost World texts in both literature and film and discusses the later *Jurassic World* films' relationship to "Boy-Dog" narratives. She argues that, insofar as their depictions of animal violence and violent animals are concerned, the *Jurassic Park* films draw on traditions established by Lost World novels, such as *Journey to the Centre of the Earth* (1864), *The Lost World* (1912), and *The Land that Time Forgot* (1924). Meanwhile, the *Jurassic World* films draw on traditions established by popular Boy-Dog stories, (e.g., *Big Red* [1945], *Old Yeller* [1956], and *Where the Red Fern Grows* [1961]) and depict some dinosaurs as companion animals, capable of sacrificing themselves to defend their humans from the violent onslaughts of other reptiles. Schell argues that these movies update this narrative paradigm for a twenty-first-century audience.

In my own chapter I show how *Jurassic Park* anticipates the reemergence of the spectacular disaster film that came to dominate popular cinema from the mid-1990s. The chapter considers *Jurassic Park* as a disaster film, also noting its absence from critical material surrounding the genre. I observe how it engages trends and generic tropes that typified the disaster genre in its 1970s heyday. I also examine how the film navigates a set of existential anxieties apposite to and present in the countdown to the new millennium. It considers the film's articulation of disaster, chaos, and unpredictability and how the character of Ian Malcolm is presented as the mouthpiece for impending apocalypse and existential crisis.

Part III: Beyond *Jurassic Park*

In this final part the book turns to a set of paratextual engagements with *Jurassic Park* including the film's reformatting as a 3D experience; the way the film was embedded within a wider media language; *Jurassic Park* theme park rides; and finally, a fringe theatrical stage production based around the film.

Allison Whitney turns to the 20th anniversary theatrical rerelease of the film in 3D. She explores how the 3D version of *Jurassic Park* capitalizes on the original's approach to depth, volume, and scale. *Jurassic Park 3D* was part of a trend in 3D conversions of "classic" films, such as *Titanic* (1997) and *Top Gun* (1986), intended to persuade audiences to venture to a theater with the promise of an expanded, more immersive experience of a well-known text. The chapter explores the technological and commercial impetus behind this trend and recognizes how this particular 3D transformation, and especially its giant-screen IMAX 3D iteration, both draw attention to and comment on the complex spatial logic of the original film and of its revolutionary visual effects.

Janet Staiger studies how the popularity of *Jurassic Park* ensured its embeddedness within wider media language; in particular, she highlights the ubiquity of *Jurassic Park* jokes in the media and discusses the power relations within thirty-two examples of comic uses of the term "Jurassic" within a month of the film's release. Drawing on Freud's theoretical conceptualization of the joke and the plurality of comic representations circulated within media culture, she shows how the presence of a joking network permits a fluidity of subject positions within it.

Carissa Baker's chapter turns to *Jurassic Park* attractions that opened at theme parks around the world exploiting the subsequent dinosaur craze in the film's wake. *Jurassic Park* was a spectacular, immersive thrill ride, a modern updating of what Tom Gunning termed the "Cinema of Attractions." In her chapter Baker notes how *Jurassic Park* theme park experiences predated and laid the groundwork for other immersive theme park experiences across the globe. The chapter examines these attractions as spatial narratives, metanarratives, in terms of transmedia storytelling, synergistic branding, and role-playing centers. Baker then observes how the attractions reflect the themes of the movie with an emphasis on illusion, and moving from, as creative director Neil Engel states, "beauty to horror."

In the final chapter, Catherine Pugh turns to a theatrical production, *The Jurassic Parks*, by the company Superbolt, which was performed at fringe theater festivals around the globe. Pugh considers how *The Jurassic Parks*, uses physical theater, comedy, music, puppetry, and audience interaction to engage with the nostalgia for the film while at the same time creating a new and absorbing narrative. As well as looking at some of the challenges of transferring such a visually rich and ambitious film onto a small stage, this chapter debates how this nostalgia is used to create a theatrical paratext that simultaneously honors and dissects Spielberg's films.

Notes

1 The UK premiere was a dual event taking place at the Lyric cinema in Carmarthen, South Wales. at the same time as its London showing. Elizabeth Evans, who ran the Lyric, which was under threat of closure, wrote to the film's London-based distribution company who went back on their word to send a copy of the film. In response the then Mayor of Carmarthen, Richard Goodridge, sent a fax to Steven Spielberg himself. The managing director of Universal International Pictures responded to Goodridge's plea by telling him Spielberg had received his missive and the town would be sent a print of the film, to be shown a day earlier than its general release alongside the London premiere.

   See Robert Harries, "The Day a Welsh Town Hosted the Jurassic Park Premiere after the Mayor Wrote to Steven Spielberg," *Wales Online*, November 16, 2019, https://www.walesonline.co.uk/news/wales-news/day-welsh-town-hosted-jurassic-17255327. Accessed July 29, 2023.

2 *Avatar* took $2,9233 billion at the box office—becoming the highest grossing film of all time. As a stand-alone film it was of course a roaring success, and while (despite the financial success of the film and the immersive 3D technology) it did not retain itself in the mind of the public, it has, however, been recuperated more recently in the cultural mindset by a belated sequel, *Avatar: The Way of Water* (2023), which at the time of writing, has also crossed the $2 billion threshold with several more films in the pipeline. In this respect we may argue that only now, fourteen years later, is it finding its success as a franchise.

3 At the time of writing, the Amazon series *The Rings of Power* (2022), the most expensive television show ever made, has not long completed its first series run and was greeted with a muted response.

4 At the time of writing, the third and final film in the rebooted *Jurassic* franchise, *Jurassic World: Dominion,* has not long been released to very poor critical reviews despite it taking just over $1 billion at the box office and on streaming.

5. Justin Wyatt, "Marketing Marginalised Cultures: *The Wedding Banquet*, Cultural Identities, and Independent Cinema of the 1990s," in Jon Lewis (ed.) *The End of Cinema as We Know It: American Cinema in the 1990s* (New York: New York University Press, 2001), 66.
6. John Lyttle, "FILM/Rushes," *Independent*, June 17, 1993. https://www.independent.co.uk/arts-entertainment/film-rushes-1492331.html. Accessed July 11, 2023.
7. Simon Brew, "*Jurassic Park vs. Last Action Hero*: The Marketing Battle," *Den of Geek*, June 18, 2019. https://www.denofgeek.com/movies/jurassic-park-vs-last-action-hero-the-marketing-battle/. Accessed November 22, 2022.
8. Philip Robinson, "The Dinosaurs Take on Arnie in Clash of the Film Giants," *The Times*, June 25, 1993, 27.
9. Ibid.
10. Ibid.
11. Ibid.
12. Author name not available. "Spielberg Bans Family from Dinosaur Thriller," *Evening Standard*, June 11, 1993.
13. Baz Bamigboye, "Jaws With Legs," *Daily Mail*, June 7, 1993.
14. Matthew Melia, "Relocating the Western in *Jaws*," in I. Q. Hunter and Matthew Melia (eds.), *The Jaws Book: New Perspectives on the Classic Summer Blockbuster* (London: Bloomsbury, 2020), 185–99.
15. IQ Hunter and Matthew Melia, 'Introduction' in Hunter and Melia (eds.), 4.
16. Phil Reeves, "Dino-Fever Grips Nation as Cultural Tyrant is Born," *Independent on Sunday*, June 13, 1993, 13.
17. Ibid.
18. Louise Kehoe, "Merchandising Monster on the Rampage," *Financial Times*, June 10, 1993, 11.
19. Ibid.
20. Thomas Elsaesser, "The Blockbuster: Everything Connects but not Everything Goes," in Jon Lewis (ed.), *The End of Cinema as We Know It: American Film of the 1990s* (New York: New York University Press) 11.
21. Stuart Jeffries, *Everything, All the Time, Everywhere: How We Became Postmodern* (London: Verso, 2021).
22. Elsaesser, "The Blockbuster," 11.
23. The script for *Jurassic Park IV* emerged online on the website *Jurassic Outpost* several years ago. The story details the hybridization of humans and dinosaurs and it contains several elements that anticipate *Jurassic World*. Matthew Melia explores the unproduction history of *Jurassic Park IV* in his article "John Sayles and the Unmade *Jurassic Park IV*" for a special edition of the online film journal *Cinergie—Il Cinema e le altre Arte*, "Franchising *Jurassic Park*" (forthcoming at the time of writing).

24 Sheldon Hall, "Not the First: Myths of *Jaws*," in I. Q. Hunter and Matthew Melia (eds.), *The Jaws Book: New Perspectives on the Classic Summer Blockbuster* (London: Bloomsbury, 2020), 33–49.

25 Caroline Frost, "Titanic Director James Cameron Reveals He Wanted Jurassic Park but Steven Spielberg Beat Him to It," *Huffington Post*, September 11, 2012. https://www.huffingtonpost.co.uk/2012/09/07/titanic-director-james-cameron-jurassic-park-steven-spielberg_n_1864996.html?utm_hp_ref=uk-entertainment. Accessed November 27, 2022.

26 Winston created visual effects for both *Jurassic Park: The Lost World* and *Jurassic Park III*, which was the last film he worked on prior to his death in 2008. In 2003 he gave an interview stating he was brainstorming for the unmade *Jurassic Park IV* with Spielberg. When asked in the interview how the film would *improve* on previous instalments he responded:

> All I can say at this stage is that it's extremely exciting. Expect to see many new dinosaurs, as well as some old favorites from the last three movies. There are also several previously unfilmed scenes from Michael Crichton's novels which Steven is looking to adapt, plus a whole bunch of really creative new stuff. It's all coming together to create what should be a remarkable cinematic experience. If you thought we sent the world into dino-mania back in 1993, hah! You ain't seen nothin' yet. If dinosaurs are big now, they're going to be huge come 2005.

27 Ben Friedman, "Why '*Jurassic Park*'s' Special Effects Look Much Better Than '*Jurassic World*'s," *Highbrow Magazine*, November 20, 2022. https://www.highbrowmagazine.com/20027-why-jurassic-park-s-special-effects-look-much-better-jurassic-world-s. Accessed February 20, 2022.

28 Tom Gunning, "The Cinema of Attractions: Early Cinema, Its Spectator, and the Avant-Garde." *Wide Angle* 8 (1986): 3–4.

29 Christian Moerk, "Jurassic Looks Like an F/X Classic," *Variety*, September 7, 1992, 5.

30 Ibid.

31 Ben Macintyre, "Mad Scientists on the Loose," *The Times*, June 25, 1993, 14.

32 Carol Muske Dukes, "Evil Science Runs Amok..Again," *New York Times*, June 10, 1993. https://www.nytimes.com/1993/06/10/opinion/evil-science-runs-amok-again.html. Accessed July 11, 2023.

33 I. Q. Hunter and Matthew Melia, "Introduction," in I. Q. Hunter and Matthew Melia (eds.) *The Jaws Book: New Perspectives on the Classic Summer Blockbuster* (London: Bloomsbury, 2020), 2.

34 Drew Taylor, "Five Versions of *Jurassic Park* You Never Saw," *Indiewire. Com* June 11, 2015. https://www.indiewire.com/2013/06/5-versions-of-jurassic-park-you-never-saw-97110/. Accessed December 13, 2022

35 Manohla Dargis, "A Word with Stephen Spielberg," *The New York Times*, May 15, 2016. https://www.nytimes.com/2016/05/17/movies/a-word-with-steven-spielberg.html. Accessed March 12, 2023.

36 Geoff King, *Spectacular Narratives Hollywood in the Age of the Blockbuster* (London: I. B. Tauris, 2008), 41–69.

37 Joey Nolfi, "Steven Spielberg Felt Resentment and Anger Making *Schindler's List* and *Jurassic Park* Simultaneously," *Entertainment Weekly*, April 27, 2018. https://ew.com/oscars/2018/04/27/steven-spielberg-schindlers-list-jurassic-park-tribeca-film-festival/. Accessed November 20, 2022.

38 Steve Biodrwoski, "*Jurassic Park:* Michael Crichton on Adapting His Novel to the Screen," *Cinefantastique* Blog, August 1, 1993.

39 Matt Ryan, Interview with David Koepp, "Script to Screen: *Jurassic Park* with David Koepp." https://www.youtube.com/watch?v=CnfopGCe27A&ab_channel=MattRyan. Accessed November 20, 2022.

40 Nigel Morris, *The Cinema of Steven Spielberg: Empire of Light* (London: Wallflower, 2007), 239–51.

41 Geoff King, *Spectacular Narratives Hollywood in the Age of the Blockbuster* (London: I.B. Tauris, 2008), 41–69.

PART ONE

Production, Adaptation, and Reception

1

Writing the Raptor: From Script to Screen

Oliver Gruner
University of Portsmouth, UK

Introduction

In March 1993, *Variety* magazine paid tribute to a man it declared to be the "King of High Concept." This glowing profile of a "towering, cerebral, marvelously eccentric ... doctor-turned-director-turned-novelist," reminded its readers that Michael Crichton novels were the basis of two forthcoming, big-budget movie extravaganzas, *Jurassic Park* and *Rising Sun* (both 1993). Crichton was "at the center of Hollywood power, yet utterly removed from it. He is the king of 'high concept,' yet has never pitched an idea or asked a studio exec, 'what's selling today?'" And, to illustrate his independent spirit, the article explained Crichton's modus operandi in the following terms: "He writes the novel ... will do a first draft screenplay, structuring the story as a film. But when a director starts whining about character nuance or story polishes, Crichton ambles off into the night." Interviewed for the piece, the writer-filmmaker rebuffed familiar complaints that his "characters lacked empathy" with a quip that may have raised some eyebrows amongst the movie intelligentsia. "*Citizen Kane* didn't have particularly sympathetic characters," relayed Crichton. "Somehow the film seemed to work okay."[1]

They might not perch atop many artistic pantheons, but, without a doubt, Michael Crichton's novels, films, and television series have *worked okay*; publishing twenty-seven novels during his lifetime, and writing and directing for film and television, Crichton enjoyed literary megahits, movie blockbusters, and small screen rating successes.[2] As the author of the 1991 novel *Jurassic Park*, he was also the first of three screenwriters to attempt its adaptation into film, his creative efforts serving as a starting point for this chapter's analysis.

Tracing *Jurassic Park*'s script development through a series of drafts produced between September 1990 and November 1992, I explore the reshaping of the novel's original narrative, themes, and, importantly, characters, as it travelled from script to screen. Certainly, much popular and academic discourse surrounding *Jurassic Park*'s scripting has emphasized changes made to protagonists and emotional relationships.[3] But, while many accounts mention the screenplays—and especially the impact director Steven Spielberg had on influencing character design, narrative structure, and thematic content—there are few detailed examinations of specific drafts and the *writers* that produced them. Furthermore, an examination of *Jurassic Park*'s script development sheds new light on the collaborative relationships, dramatic imperatives, and commercial forces that underpinned this spectacular production and, more generally, blockbuster filmmaking of the early 1990s. Providing a close textual analysis, I reflect on the screenplay as "a commercial and aesthetic product," as a multiply authored entity, and as a canvas upon which various creative practitioners left their mark.[4]

The three screenwriters involved in *Jurassic Park* were Michael Crichton, who worked on the screenplay until January 1991; Malia Scotch Marmo, who had collaborated with Spielberg on his previous directorial effort *Hook* (1991) and joined *Jurassic Park* from October 1991 to March 1992; and David Koepp, who had cowritten the dark comedy *Death Becomes Her* (1992) and was introduced to Spielberg by that film's director Robert Zemeckis. Koepp delivered several drafts from April 1992 until the end of that year.[5] All three worked closely with Spielberg, as well as other creatives involved in the project. Notably, thanks to the research of Derrick Davis, creator of the *Jurassic Time* website, we have clear evidence that production designer Rick Carter was also involved in shaping ideas that made it into the finished film (discussed further below).[6] While only Crichton and Koepp received a screenplay credit, I argue that all played a part in influencing the film's formal and thematic content.

The chapter begins with early efforts to adapt Crichton's novel for the big screen. After providing some background to *Jurassic Park*'s origins, I focus on the development of two key characters: the showman-impresario John Hammond (Richard Attenborough) with whom, it has been widely reported, Spielberg felt a certain affinity; and the mordant chaotician Ian Malcolm (Jeff Goldblum) who, at least in the novel, serves as the vessel through which Crichton channels his critique of commercialized science. I am interested here in how the characters were rewritten over the years, becoming sites of creative and thematic tension.

Section Two explores the scripting of *Jurassic Park*'s spectacular set pieces, familial relationships, and self-conscious allusions—elements that Peter Krämer has identified as central to what he terms the "family adventure movie," the "most successful production trend in American cinema since the late 1970s."[7] This section also considers the dramatic conventions, characterizations, and narrative arcs that turned this from a "Michael Crichton novel" to a "Steven Spielberg film."

First Iteration: Crichton, Spielberg, and Adapting *Jurassic Park*

"Technology goes wherever there's a use for it," a thirty-year-old Michael Crichton informed *Vogue* magazine in 1973, "wherever there's a financial reservoir to support it." And, in a comment that could have been a prophecy of his dinosaur theme-park created a decade later, he noted that "technology is going more and more into leisure."[8] Of course, Crichton was not referring to *Jurassic Park*; he was discussing his first effort as a feature film writer-director on *Westworld* (1973). As many critics have observed, this dystopic vision of techno-entertainment run amuck—a futuristic holiday park where the robots turn on human guests—provided some basic elements upon which Crichton would draw when writing *Jurassic Park*.[9] *Westworld* is set on an isolated island, Delos, where guests can choose to live out their fantasies in one of three historical eras: the Western World, the Medieval World, and the Roman World. "Our teams have engineered and *spared no expense* in this recreation," announces a promo spiel early in the film, a line that anticipates John Hammond's iconic "spared no expense" catchphrase of the *Jurassic Park* film twenty years later. In a broader sense, *Westworld* was one of several creative outputs that, throughout the 1970s, helped establish Crichton's reputation and build a prominent public persona.

The doctor-turned-novelist arrived in Hollywood in 1970, visiting the film set where his successful novel *The Andromeda Strain* (1969) was being adapted for the big screen. With its ominous tale of a deadly virus arrived from outer space, the book was the first of Crichton's trademark technothrillers (a "mix of hard and speculative science" woven into procedural, action-packed narratives) and served as his gateway into the literary and cinema elite.[10] Serendipitously, a young and at that stage underemployed director by the name of Steven Spielberg was charged with showing Crichton around the Universal lot. By all accounts, this early meeting established a friendship and mutual respect that in later years would turn into a highly successful professional collaboration.[11] From greenhorn filmmakers beginning to learn their trade to the seasoned screenwriters and directors behind hits such as *Westworld*, *Jaws* (1975), *Close Encounters of the Third Kind* (1977), and *Coma* (1978), both would enjoy meteoric career ascents as the decade progressed.

Without wishing to stretch an analogy too far, Spielberg and Crichton's public personae, as developed through the 1970s and 1980s, evoke touches of *Jurassic Park*'s John Hammond and Ian Malcolm: one, a filmmaker associated with spectacular narratives (and equally spectacular financial returns), often celebrated, or criticized, for his ability to capture a sense of awe and wonder associated with childhood; the other, presented in interviews as cerebral, acerbic, and known for his biting, if not always critically admired, arraignments of the modern world. Of course, such simple definitions fail to capture the diverse bodies of work produced by both.[12] But as film scholars such as Patricia Pace and Nigel Morris note, media discussions of Spielberg were throughout the 1980s referring to him as the "perennial Peter Pan," "locked in Neverland" and "cinema's *ur*-child who will not grow up."[13] Even after helming "prestige" pictures and "serious" literary adaptations such as *The Color Purple* (1986) and *Empire of the Sun* (1987), the filmmaker found himself continually linked with child-friendly or, to use the criticism so often levelled, "juvenile" entertainment.[14]

Crichton, on the other hand, had—since *The Andromeda Strain*—built a reputation as the purveyor of scientifically "credible" fiction. Countless profiles and articles through the 1970s and 1980s reminded readers that he had started out as a doctor at Harvard Medical School, before turning to writing, while also touting the extensive research undertaken in advance of each novel.[15] Such a background invested Crichton with a certain authority when it came to technological dystopias (however far-fetched they may be).[16] By all accounts, Spielberg was attracted to Crichton's *Jurassic Park* novel for the very reason it did offer a "believable" concept, one around which a gripping adventure narrative was woven. It was furthermore an opportunity to revisit the "revenge of nature" theme, found in his previous productions, most notably *Jaws*. As the director put it: "I have no embarrassment in saying that with *Jurassic* I was really just trying to make a good sequel to *Jaws*. On land."[17] They began working together in the late 1980s, when Spielberg purchased Crichton's screenplay *Code Blue*, which ultimately become an immensely successful primetime drama, *ER* (1994–2009). It was during a discussion of this script that Crichton revealed he had just finished a novel about dinosaurs running rampant at a prehistoric theme-park. Spielberg was "slipped" a copy of the galleys and expressed an interest in directing.

Spielberg recalls that Crichton "promised me the book privately" but the author's agents, Creative Artists Agency (CAA) nonetheless put *Jurassic Park*'s film rights out for tender (apparently instructed by Crichton to set a nonnegotiable fee of $1.5 million.[18] Even if Crichton had promised the book to Spielberg, there was much publicity to be generated by encouraging a bidding war—hardly a bad thing for a novel not yet published—and, at a time when the power and impact of talent agencies were being felt across

Hollywood, it was certainly in Crichton's interest to involve CAA.[19] Indeed, not only were the rights sold to Universal for $1.5 million, which ensured Spielberg's participation, but Crichton was also paid another $500,000 to write a first draft screenplay, was guaranteed a share of the film's profits, and a portion of the merchandising royalties, which were expected to be substantial.[20]

Already, in 1990, Crichton was informing Spielberg that the film would need "somebody else to polish the characters. I think that sort of surprised him, because writers never say, 'Get somebody else.' "[21] As the following analysis makes clear, the "polishing" of characters remained a concern throughout *Jurassic Park*'s script development. One of the most frequently cited changes as *Jurassic Park* moved from novel to screen is how the character of John Hammond is turned from "Crichton's raging megalomaniac into a gentler and more charming character."[22] The novel introduces readers to a "flamboyant … born showman" whose life's purpose appears to have been to get rich off technologically advanced entertainments. We read early on that, when fund-raising for his prehistoric theme-park, Hammond would take with him a "dwarf elephant," which he would show off to impress investors while asking them for contributions to his scheme. This is just the first instance of him exploiting animals in aid of a project whose purpose he will declare later was to "make money. A lot of money."[23]

There is, however, another side to John Hammond. Spielberg was attracted to a man with a "childlike quality," alive to the idea of bringing entertainment to the masses, to seeing "children delight" in his creations.[24] Through several draft scripts, we witness the shifting of a money-obsessed, uncompromising Hammond toward the more avuncular character that reached cinemas. In the finished *Jurassic Park* film, we first meet him at the site of a fossil dig in Montana, being led by paleontologist Alan Grant (Sam Neill) and paleobotanist Ellie Sattler (Laura Dern). Hammond appears unannounced in Grant's trailer, helping himself to an unopened bottle of champagne. There is an impish charm to Hammond, in this scene and throughout the film. Whether expressing his enchantment with the dinosaurs or holding forth on his past experiences as a showman, Hammond casts an alluring, if flawed, character throughout. It would, however, take some significant rewriting—not to mention careful additions and omissions—to bring this loveable Hammond to the big screen.

Crichton's first draft of September 1990 begins immediately at the dinosaur dig where we meet scientists Grant and Sattler. Within four pages, they are on a private jet, about to arrive at the prehistoric theme park on the secluded Isla Nublar. Hammond himself is introduced as "a compact man with an enormous, handsome head. He has a crusty, vaguely British speech, and wears a banker's suit." The script concludes this introduction with the punchy description: "Exudes old, corrupt money."[25] From the clothes he wears to the dialogue he uses, there is an affectedness, a falseness even, to

Hammond at this stage. The very fact that, in Crichton's first draft (September 1990) and revised first draft (January 1991), he sends his lawyer rather than coming himself to fetch Grant and Sattler from their dig, presents a more aloof figure than the man who eventually made it to cinema screens.[26] More generally, it is notable that Hammond is a less significant presence than in later drafts (and the finished film). He appears as quasi-peripheral, someone to embody the spectacles (and dangers) of commercialized science at the start of the film and encapsulate its implosion at its end.

There is, however, some effort in the revised draft to present Hammond in more sympathetic terms. Crichton recalled that this draft was completed in forty-page chunks, in collaboration with Spielberg, and with the help of sketches and storyboards that were already being drawn up throughout 1990.[27] As Steven Price and Chris Pallant note, *Jurassic Park*'s screenplay and storyboard development "took place in parallel," whereby the latter served as a "key production document" for so many of the film's scenes.[28] Some of these images are available in Don Shay and Jody Duncan's book-length account, *The Making of Jurassic Park*, including an early sketch of John Hammond by art director John Bell.[29] In white shirt and trousers, with a soft smile, arms gently akimbo as if welcoming (or presenting) his park to visitors, Hammond cuts a markedly different appearance to that alluded to at the start of Crichton's first draft. Whether the author was inspired by this sketch or not, the revised draft introduces Hammond as "gracious, flamboyant, persuasive, in constant motion, he has charm to burn."[30] Given to hyperbolic outbursts—"a fabulous, fabulous resort," "Fantastic ... those beautiful animals"—he speaks of his creation with an exuberance and vivacity.[31] This is the beginnings of the John Hammond familiar to viewers of the film, the energetic purveyor of spectacular inventions. And, yet, midway through the script his participation becomes little more than the occasional one-line outburst—a barked order or show of concern about his grandchildren.

In both of Crichton's drafts, Hammond is killed; in the first, as is the case in the novel, he is dispatched by diminutive but deadly "Compy" dinosaurs as he lays injured and prostrate, crushed by the collapsed scaffolding of his unfinished theme-park. In the revised draft he is dispatched by raptors. "His screams fill the deserted rotunda," writes Crichton in the first draft, "as we pull back over dead dinosaurs, shattered bones, and complete destruction." Fleeing the island as the Costa Rican army sets it ablaze, Hammond's lawyer Don Gennaro and colleagues search for their boss in vain. "We haven't found Hammond," says one as they make final preparations to escape via a helicopter. "Justice is served," retorts Gennaro—a grimly fitting end for the progenitor of so much destruction.[32] On this apocalyptic note, it is worth remembering that in Crichton's novel the dinosaurs of Jurassic Park have already escaped Isla Nublar (in the film they remain confined to the island).[33] Crichton's revised draft begins with a scene in which the daughter of a vacationing family is bitten by dinosaurs on a beach (a scene cut from *Jurassic Park* but recycled in a different form at the opening of the film's sequel *The Lost World: Jurassic Park* [1997]).[34] Fears of global devastation pervade the novel throughout. In Crichton's screenplay—again, much as in the novel—these fears are given most prominent airing in the doomsaying pronouncements of chaotician Ian Malcolm.

At the end of Crichton's first draft, Malcolm offers a characteristically grandiloquent speech about humanity "in jeopardy." Sweeping through a potted history of the Earth's origins and the threats facing humanity, he concludes: "We haven't got the power to destroy the planet—but we might have the power to save ourselves."[35] Authoritative and arrogant, Ian Malcolm has been described as the novel's "educating voice," an "iconoclast mathematician," and the character with whose opinions of corporatized scientific endeavor Crichton most identifies.[36] Throughout these early screenplays, Malcolm can be read pontificating on the theme-park's dismal future and, more generally, celebrating his own intelligence. He is introduced in the revised draft as dressed "all in black with buzz cut hair" and quickly corrals Grant and Sattler into a discussion of "Chaos Theory." With a "depreciating smile" he declares Jurassic Park "a disaster." His outbursts are not yet tinged with the humor that defines Goldblum's rendition (as discussed below, this would be developed by Koepp). Rather, Malcolm comes across as rather somber and plaintive in his assessments of the park, of the dinosaurs, and of humanity: "The greatest animals in history. Maybe someday human beings will earn the right to be called that."[37]

After completing a final draft in January 1991, Crichton left the project. His scripts had established the basic narrative, shown the way forward in terms of the action-packed set pieces to be included, and suggested ways in which characters could be developed for the big screen. But much would be altered, added, and omitted as the film moved toward its second year of preproduction. On this note, it is worth considering evidence available in the Illustrated Audio Drama *Rick Carter's Jurassic Park* (2022), which offers new insight into script changes and story development at this time. The video, produced by the writer and researcher Derrick Davis, draws on interviews with production design Rick Carter and a script "collage," produced in March 1991.[38] Carter had been involved in story conferences throughout the writing of Crichton's drafts, suggesting ideas, especially on the film's spectacular set pieces and the representation of dinosaurs. When Crichton left the project in January 1991, Spielberg also took a break from *Jurassic Park*, devoting his energies to his current project, *Hook* (1991). Carter, on the other hand, continued his work on the production. Having been present in many meetings, where new ideas had been discussed, he felt that "the only way for me to see how these ideas might actually play out in the story was to 'collage' them into Michael's latest script" (Crichton's revised draft of January 1991).

While many scenes are familiar to readers of Crichton's script, there are some quite significant innovations. For the first time, it is Hammond, the "powerful financial benefactor" that arrives personally in Montana to recruit Grant and Sattler. While short on description and dialogue, there is a jovial touch to Hammond as he "parades around and laughs."[39] Equally notable, there is an (underdeveloped) sequence at the Jurassic Park visitor center featuring Hammond delivering a lively introduction to the biological wonders on display. Crichton gave the intro to PR representative Ed Regis, a character ultimately expunged from the film, and this change is an opportunity to emphasize Hammond's showman-like qualities. "On a giant screen, the video begins with an introduction by Hammond, much like Walt Disney used to do on television," we read.[40] While this sequence would be developed and expanded by Marmo (and Koepp) in later drafts, its presence here suggests that the idea had been floated in story conferences prior to their arrival on the project. Similarly, there are early efforts to expand upon Hammond's character arc, whereby he comes to understand, just before he dies, that his theme-park was doomed from its inception.[41] From a lively bon vivant to an introspective and chastened old man, the Hammond of his draft begins to undergo the transformation seen in the finished film.

Carter made clear that his "draft" was never intended to usurp those of subsequent writers involved in the project. The dialogue, and many of the scenes and sequences, would be completely rewritten, or erased, in the coming year. Nonetheless, the work provides some insight into the discussions taking place at the time. If Marmo and Koepp claimed not to have read this, or any previous draft before embarking on their own versions, Spielberg himself would certainly have absorbed and taken the ideas to the table during his close collaborations with both. An analysis of this next stage in the screenwriting process provide some insight into the thinking behind new drafts and the creative relationships between the screenwriters and director.

"Spared No Expense": *Jurassic Park* from Script to Screen

"Here I was," recalled the screenwriter David Koepp, "writing about these greedy people who are creating a fabulous theme park just so they can exploit all these dinosaurs and make silly little films and sell stupid plates and things." Koepp was discussing his contributions to the *Jurassic Park* screenplay and, like so many other commentators *c.* 1993 (and beyond), drew inevitable parallels between the film's fictional plot and the "reality" of Hollywood's business operations. He continued: "And I was also writing for a company [presumably a reference to his employers at Universal] that's eventually going to put this in their theme parks and ... sell stupid plastic plates and things."⁴² As Koepp informed the *Los Angeles Times*, "I had to laugh as I typed out the dialogue. Who are the good guys and who are the bad guys here."⁴³ If Koepp offered his thoughts in the form of sardonic self-critique, they were nonetheless part of a wider popular (and, in later years, scholarly) discourse on *Jurassic Park* as a self-conscious blockbuster, a film that alludes to its own status as spectacular entertainment and marketing phenomenon. For good or ill, much writing touts referentiality (or what Thomas Elsaesser calls "doubling") as central to *Jurassic Park*'s narrative thrust, cultural significance, and commercial success.⁴⁴

Developing this self-conscious element was something Koepp and Marmo devoted themselves to throughout late 1991 and 1992. Moreover, their screenplays evince a careful focus on everything, from character portrayal, narrative (in particular, the incorporation of effects-laden scenes), and the very idea of *Jurassic Park* as a "Spielberg" film. As numerous interviews make clear, so many of the ideas were either requested by the director or emerged from a (very) close working relationship. Of course, both writers were also aware of Spielberg's filmic back catalog and constructed scenes, sequences, and characters that aligned with his previous work. This section, therefore, also reflects on Spielberg as a key driver of continuity and change during script development—the one person who *had* read previous drafts and could draw on these when making suggestions—and, by way of his imposing oeuvre, a powerful influence on the formal and thematic strategies adopted by Marmo and Koepp.

While Marmo did not receive a screenplay credit for the film, her work is interesting for its efforts to develop the film's protagonists Ellie Sattler and Alan Grant. As an up-and-coming screenwriter and collaborator with Spielberg on his revisioning of the Peter Pan story, *Hook*, one can see why the director might have believed she could flesh out the character relationships and familial dramas present, but underdeveloped, in *Jurassic Park*.⁴⁵ On the one hand, *Hook* was an exploration of absent, irresponsible father figures and familial relations. The film also reveled in spectacular worlds and contained moments of self-reflexivity—making connections between the pleasures associated with J. M. Barrie's tale of a boy who never grew up and the power of cinema (or the power of Spielberg!) to elicit childlike awe and wonder.⁴⁶ It was therefore very much a continuation of ideas so central to Spielberg's work and anticipated *Jurassic Park*'s own formal and thematic content.

Marmo began work on *Jurassic Park* in October 1991. She has emphasized the close collaboration with Spielberg, to the extent that she was apparently sending him fifteen-page sections, discussing them with him and then rewriting.⁴⁷ In retrospect, she claimed that her primary contribution was ensuring paleobotanist Ellie Sattler and *Jurassic Park*'s children, Lex and Tim (Ariana Richards and Joseph Mazzello), were "more assertive."⁴⁸

Certainly, we can see some evidence of Marmo augmenting the dialogue and presence of Sattler and the children. Marmo's Sattler is more dynamic, described as "tough if she wants to be … exuberant, she leaves a trail of dust behind her," cerebral when solving scientific questions, and sharp-tongued "you created dinosaurs? Who gave you the right to do that?"[49] Importantly, however, Sattler's character is developed alongside that of Alan Grant. On the one hand, there are brief flashes of a close relationship between the two, and their taking on the role of symbolic protectors (or "parents") of Lex and Tim.[50] On the other hand, both characters are bequeathed more dialogue and appearances at the expense of Ian Malcolm. The most noticeable aspect of Marmo's draft is her removal altogether of Malcolm. She places much of the scientific jibber-jabber (the province of Malcolm in Crichton's screenplays) into their mouths. "You interrupted natural law … Mr. Hammond, you've disrupted the pattern and look what it's done," says Grant, one of several instances where this scientist adopts the posture—and antipathy to Hammond—of the Ian Malcolm presented in earlier drafts. "The audacity of man to get here at the last second and think he runs the show," observes Sattler, in a speech that almost feels a rehashing of Malcolm's concluding lines in Crichton's revised draft (discussed earlier).[51]

If Malcolm's removal only lasted for a few months (Koepp would reinstate him in May 1992), it does provide a sense of the difficulties the screenwriters and Spielberg were encountering when it came to enriching characters and developing character arcs. As her draft progresses, Marmo seeks to juxtapose stories of emotional and philosophical revelation (for Sattler and Grant) with a narrative that emphasizes Hammond's dangerous obsessions and state of denial. This is the first script to have Hammond deliver the introduction to Jurassic Park in a screening room while interacting with the film running in the background, making self-consciously apparent the Hammond-Spielberg connection, the theme-park impresario taking on a "directorial" role of sorts.[52] We have an early incarnation of the cafeteria scene, where Hammond eats ice-cream, reflects on his ambitions, and discusses the park's merchandising. "Take a look at these, Donald," he says to his lawyer, Gennaro. A script direction reads: "Hammond dumps things out of the bag. They are souvenirs of the park." Hammond talks about "Wind-up toys" and "T-shirts" and "Dinosaur bingo."[53]

Brimming with vitality, Hammond is also presented as acquisitive and obsessive to the point of self-destruction. By the screenplay's end, he is raging at Grant for being one more "negative voice in a universe of negativity." He refuses to join the other characters fleeing the island, choosing instead to breathe his last on Isla Nublar. Collapsed in a pool of water, a screen direction informs that "a mosquito lands on his hand."[54] An obvious reference to his theme-park's origins—the discovery that dinosaur DNA could be extracted from mosquitos fossilized in amber—the implications here are surely that Hammond too, will now become "extinct." Grant and

Sattler, on the other hand, spend the final pages enlightening themselves on why Jurassic Park could *never have worked*: the inability to accurately clone dinosaur DNA meant that, as Sattler puts it in the screenplay's final line: "The very process was flawed."[55] It is also Sattler who undertakes the screenplay's final act of heroism, firing a "fire-extinguisher" into the face of the *T-Rex*, which is trying to prevent their helicopter's escape. Grant and Sattler hug—a suggestion that their relationship has become closer as a result of all that has transpired—and the helicopter flies into the distance.

Marmo's screenplay was ultimately rejected by Spielberg, and Koepp claims not to have read the draft, but it does provide insight into the issues bedeviling the filmmakers involved in *Jurassic Park* in late 1991 and early 1992. Evidently, there were concerns around characterization—the need to enrich and make more resonant the narratives associated with Grant, Sattler, Tim, Lex, and Hammond. Marmo begins to develop the relationship between Grant and Sattler and there was also an increased effort to invest the screenplay with a self-conscious quality, whereby *Jurassic Park* does start to continually refer to its "own status as cinematic entertainment for a captive audience."[56] Koepp would continue a number of these ideas, while greatly enhancing the paternal narrative associated with Grant, as well as injecting some much-needed humor into proceedings. From April 1992, early scenes have Grant observing that he is "afraid" of children and balking at the idea of Tim and Lex joining them in the park. Sattler needles him about his response, implying they have been discussing Grant's problem with children for some time.[57] By the end of May 1992, there are extended jokes and skits based around Grant's aversion to children (including the scene where Tim and Lex follow the hapless paleontologist in and out of jeeps at the start of the tour, desperate to sit next to the man who will ultimately become a surrogate father figure).[58] And later drafts introduce a "kid" at the fossil dig in Montana, who receives a terrifying lecture from Grant on the proclivities (and appetites) of raptors.[59] Thus is the groundwork laid for Grant's transformation, in very Spielbergian terms, from an antipathetic, irresponsible loner to the symbolic "family man" he becomes by the film's conclusion.

Koepp also reinstates Ian Malcolm as cynical foil to John Hammond. Now, his familiar pomposity is offset by self-deprecation and mockery. "See? Here I am now, by myself, talking to myself ..." This snippet of dialogue, added in May 1992, appears during a guided tour of Jurassic Park and is familiar to film viewers as the point at which Malcolm's ramble about "chaos theory" comedically fizzles out.[60] As both a prediction of the park's demise and a bumbling attempt to woo Sattler, Malcolm's impromptu lecture ends with his colleagues abandoning him, dashing from their jeep in search of dinosaurs. It becomes emblematic of his identity throughout the film as the authoritative, but much-ridiculed, voice of scientific reason: "Here I am now, by myself, talking to myself—that's chaos theory." Malcolm's critiques of the theme park are now couched in a gentler, more sympathetic, rhetoric. Koepp reintroduces the lunch scene where Malcolm and Hammond argue over the ethics of the theme park, the former speaking lines (present in a similar form in the novel): "Your scientists were so preoccupied with whether or not they *could* that they didn't stop to think if they *should*."[61] He even expresses a soft spot for his adversary, again, couching his comments in quirky humor: "You're all right, John. You just don't have intelligence ... You're very good at solving problems, at getting answers—but you just don't know the right questions."[62] Much of this remains in the finished film, producing a far more endearing, if humorously irritating, character.

The Hammond of Koepp's screenplays is far less avaricious than in Crichton and Marmo's screenplays, actively speaking out against the very idea of profiting from his creations. At one point in the script, he declares: "Oh, I'll make money, sure, but that doesn't mean much to me. Not anymore. I did it for the kids. To watch their faces shine with the joy of seeing the animals they so love."[63] Revisions through July and August would see Hammond's final creation. During the aforementioned lunch scene, Gennaro announces that "we can charge anything we want! ... And then there's the merchandising." Hammond's reply is immediate: "Donald, this park was not built to cater only to the super rich. Everyone in the world's got a right to enjoy these animals."[64] Koepp emphasizes the clash between the dreamer Hammond and the money-grabbing lawyer Gennaro, adding the latter's grisly, and comic, demise in a restroom, a victim of the *T-Rex*.[65] Also added is a scene of Hammond talking about his past life as a showman, exhibiting "flea circus" in London: "Had a wee trapeze, a roundabout—what do you call it—a carousel, a seesaw." It's certainly a far cuddlier version of Hammond's past than the "dwarf elephant" episode of the novel (discussed above). He concludes: "With this place, I just—I just wanted to give them something real, something that wasn't an illusion, something they could see and touch—an idea that's not devoid of merit."[66] Here was overwhelming evidence, if any more was needed, of a man less interested in economic advantage than in entertaining his beloved, child-like, audience, and, perhaps, another knowing reference to the power of cinema—a defense of Spielberg's own creative endeavors.

In many ways, this softening of Hammond runs hand-in-hand with an extra emphasis on the "wonder" of the world he has created. As all the screenwriters produced their drafts, *Jurassic Park*'s art department and special effects team were developing some of the most sophisticated CGI (and non-CGI) action set pieces to grace the big screen. The film has long been at the center of a debate about "whether the spectacularity of the digital image subverts the narrative function of movies."[67] Episodes prominently featuring the dinosaurs are given especial treatment in Koepp's drafts. The much-analyzed scene where Grant and Sattler see brachiosaurs for the first time is couched in superlatives: "Grant's reaches over and grabs Ellie's head, turning it to face the animal ... Her face is lit up in abject wonder."[68] Geoff King has discussed the ways in which this scene functions within *Jurassic Park*'s as both a dramatic revelation and also a way of offering, in Grant and Sattler, a point of identification for the film's viewers.[69] To an extent, this effect is invited in screen directions, which gradually and dramatically reveal in increments the gigantic brachiosaurs. Grant "starts to raise his head, looking up the length of the trunk. He looks higher ... and higher ... that's no tree trunk. That's a leg ... Grant's jaw drops ... as he watches, several of the top branches are ripped away ... a dinosaur."[70]

It is notable that Koepp adds a new opening scene, one that is both action-packed and very much in keeping with Spielberg's previous adventure films. From April 1992, the screenplay begins with a sequence familiar to viewers of the finished production. We are immediately taken to Isla Nublar, where the raptor holding pen is in transit. Something goes wrong with its delivery and all hell breaks loose—"a claw flashes out from inside the crate" and a workman is killed.[71] As with films such as *Jaws* and *Raiders of the Lost Ark* (1981), *Jurassic Park* now begins with a moment of mayhem, a taster of the excitement and danger to come. From this opening through the indomitable *T-Rex* attack, the raptor hunts and, of course, the final showdown in Jurassic Park's visitor center, the screenplay was shaped into the sort of frenetic "theme-park ride" so often associated with Spielberg films. On this count, one of Koepp's significant script changes is to reintroduce the *T-Rex* in the final scene. Previous drafts featured Grant, Sattler, and the children struggling against raptors in the visitor center, with the last dinosaur killed by a falling *T-Rex* skeleton. But the July 1992 script brings back *T-Rex* herself to kill off the remaining raptor.[72] It's both a fitting summation of Malcolm's oft-made comment that "life finds a way"—balance is restored not by any human heroics but by an animal acting out its natural inclinations—and another chance to show off the *Jurassic Park*'s much-feted special effects.

Jurassic Park started shooting in August 1992, and it is clear from revisions and alterations in the scripts that Koepp was redrafting, adding, removing, and changing scenes and characters throughout the process, at least up until November. The new ending, developed throughout the summer and fall of that year, attempts to tie up loose ends: fleeing the island on a helicopter, Grant sits with his arms around Tim and Lex, having presumably discovered his innate paternal instincts; Hammond, who now ends the film alive, has realized the park—and by extension, his dreams of biological engineering—is fatally flawed; Malcolm's prophesies have come to pass, but he does not speak (a first for him!) and is seemingly chastened by the enormity of events.[73] Sattler's character arc is perhaps the least developed of all. While Koepp had added some of her most iconic lines—the "woman inherits the Earth" speech and rebuke to Hammond about "sexism in survival situations"—she ends the film gazing rapturously at Grant, as if *his* transformation has been her reason for being. Sattler may constitute a rare, if not unproblematic, portrayal of a heroic female scientist in 1990s Hollywood and an active participant in the film's action and scientific debate.[74] But, at the same time, the film's (the screenplay's) inability to suggest any change, realization, or transformation means she remains underdeveloped as an emotional player in the narrative. The final shots of the helicopter and birds flying across the sea and into the sun were first introduced in Koepp's April draft. Notes on this script suggest the birds to be a symbol of life's onward march: "Maybe dinosaurs didn't die out. Maybe they evolved into birds."[75] Interlinked with the helicopter's flight into the distance we have the metaphorical suggestion that life—human and animal—will "find a way."

Conclusion

Interviewed in August 1993, Koepp ultimately downplayed his contributions to that summer's biggest blockbuster. "There are," he declared, "some movies that are produced, some that are directed, and some that are written." And, addressing his most recent credit, he concluded that "*Jurassic Park* was primarily directed. It's Spielberg's movie."[76] Blunt and ambiguous—what does "*primarily* directed" even mean?—Koepp's comments were, nonetheless, in keeping with so much debate on *Jurassic Park*. The endless articles announcing "Spielberg's" latest monster movie found their echo in the words of a screenwriter ready and willing to couch their endeavors within the rhetoric of auteurism. Of course, as the driving force behind the film, the link between screenwriters (who all claim not to have read each others' drafts!), a significant voice in story conferences, and more generally an imposing presence for any screenwriter looking to succeed in the film industry, Spielberg's indomitable mark is unmissable—it pervades so many moments throughout the film. However, to read *Jurassic Park* as a single-authored text is to elide the lengthy collaborative processes that brought it to fruition.

The screenplay, as Adam Ganz and Stephen Price argue in another context, is a "constantly changeable site of negotiation between different participants with different specialisms."[77] As canvases upon which ideas were explored, developed, and worked through, the scripts of Crichton, Marmo, and Koepp offer some insight into the complex back-and-forth that underpinned the film's lengthy gestation. In broad terms, we can say that Crichton's drafts established the basic narrative, Marmo's sought to develop the characters of Grant, Sattler, and Hammond, while expanding on ideas for scenes that would make it into the finished film (references to merchandising, Hammond's showman-like performances), and Koepp's reinserted Ian Malcolm, added humor, developed the spectacular set-pieces, and elaborated Grant's relationship to children. But more than the sum of their parts, these scripts are a record of endless discussion, negotiation, writing, and rewriting. Each scribe brought their own sensibility to the project; each appears to have been selected by Spielberg with certain tasks in mind; and each, through the adding of new scenes, dialogue, and narrative twists, provided fuel for *Jurassic Park*'s imperious march toward the big screen. Without a doubt, Michael Crichton's novel was reduced to its basic elements—background information lost, characters cut, scientific extrapolation pruned. Certainly, in its evocation of themes and character types familiar to his oeuvre, *Jurassic Park* became a "Steven Spielberg film." And yet, it was also the product of creative collaboration, a multiply-authored text—an adventure several years (and several writers) in the making.

Notes

1. Peter Bart, "King of 'High Concept,'" *Variety*, March 1, 1993: 3.
2. For annual sales figures on Crichton's novels up to and including *Disclosure* (1994), see Daisy Maryles, "Crichton on the Bestseller Runway," *Publisher's Weekly*, November 1, 1999.
3. Don Shay and Jody Duncan, *The Making of Jurassic Park: An Adventure 65 Million Years in the Making* (London: Boxtree, 1993), 9–10, 39–42, 53–7; Tom Stempel, *Understanding Screenwriting: Learning from Good, Not-Quite-So-Good, and Bad Screenplays* (London: Bloomsbury, 2008); Joseph McBride, *Steven Spielberg: A Biography* 2nd edn. (London: Faber and Faber, 2010), 369–70.
4. Claudia Sternberg, *Written for the Screen: The American Motion-Picture Screenplay as Text* (Tübingen: Stauffenburg Verlag, 1997), 1, 11–21.
5. There are an unusually large number of *Jurassic Park* draft screenplays available freely online. Full dates and referencing details below.
6. Derrick Davis, "See an Early Version of *Jurassic Park* with Concept Art and Storyboards in an Epic Audio Drama," *Jurassic Outpost*, March 12, 2021, https://jurassicoutpost.com/see-an-early-version-of-jurassic-park-with-concept-art-storyboards-in-an-epic-audio-drama/.
7. Peter Krämer, "Would You Take Your Child to See This Film: The Cultural and Social Work of the Family-Adventure Movie," in Steve Neale and Murray Smith (eds.) *Contemporary Hollywood Cinema* (London: Routledge, 1998), 295, 294–311.
8. Barbara Rose, "Hollywood Gets a New Man," *Vogue*, September 1, 1973, 224.
9. McBride, *Steven Spielberg*, 369.
10. Jeff Zaleski, "The High Concept of Michael Crichton," *Publishers Weekly*, November 1, 1999, 54.
11. Patrick McGilligan, "Ready When You Are, Dr. Crichton," *American Film*, March 1, 1979, 51.

12 For a riposte to the idea of Spielberg's 1970s and 1980s output being strictly family-oriented, see Peter Krämer, "'He's Very Good at work not Involving Little Creatures, You Know': *Schindler's List*, *E.T.*, and the Shape of Steven Spielberg's Career," *New Review of Film and Television Studies* 7:1 (2009): 23–32.

13 Patricia Pace, "Robert Bly Does Peter Pan: The Inner Child as Father to the Man in Steven Spielberg's *Hook*," in Charles L. P. Silet (ed.) *The Films of Steven Spielberg: Critical Essays* (Lanham: Scarecrow Press, 2002), 159; Nigel Morris, *The Cinema of Steven Spielberg: Empire of Light* (New York: Columbia University Press, 2007), 178–9.

14 Thomas Schatz, "Spielberg as Director, Producer and Movie Mogul," in Nigel Morris (ed.) *A Companion to Steven Spielberg* (London: John Wiley, 2017), 56–7.

15 Michael Owen, "Director Michael Crichton Films a Favorite Novelist," *New York Times*, January 28, 1979,: D17; McGilligan, "Ready ...."

16 Garry Abrams, "Alien Dreams and Atomic Bombs," *Los Angeles Times*, July 12, 1987, 13.

17 McBride, *Steven Spielberg*, 418.

18 Shay and Duncan, *Making of*, 6–7.

19 Stephen Prince, *A New Pot of Gold: Hollywood under the Electronic Rainbow, 1980–1989* (Berkeley: University of California Press, 2000), 160–1.

20 "U to Pay $2-mil for Sci-Fi Novel," *Variety*, June 6, 1990, 20; Alan Citron, "Agency Adds Twist to Movie Deal," *Los Angeles Times*, May 25, 1990, D5

21 Shay and Duncan, *Making of*, 9.

22 Lester D. Friedman, *Citizen Spielberg* (Chicago: University of Illinois Press, 2006), 137.

23 Michael Crichton, *Jurassic Park* (London: Arrow Books, [1991] 2015), 68, 230–1.

24 Ibid., 230, 392.

25 Michael Crichton, *Jurassic Park*, September 7, 1990, 4. Excerpts of this script have been sourced from: https://jurassictime.wixsite.com/memoirs/script-resources. Accessed June 6, 2023.

26 Michael Crichton, *Jurassic Park*, Revised First Draft, January 19, 1991, 10. Available at: https://jurassicoutpost.com/downloads. Accessed June 6, 2023.

27 Shay and Duncan, *Making of*, 9.

28 Steven Price and Chris Pallant, *Storyboarding: A Critical History* (London: Palgrave Macmillan, 2015), 148.

29 Shay and Duncan, *Making of*, 5.

30 Crichton, Revised First Draft, 12.

31 Ibid., 13, 15, 34.

32 Crichton, September 7, 1990, 125–7.

33 Crichton, *Jurassic Park* (Novel), 28.

34 Crichton, Revised First Draft, 1–3.
35 Crichton, September 7, 1990, 129.
36 Gary Hoppenstand, *Perilous Escapades: Dimensions of Popular Adventure Fiction* (Jefferson: McFarland, 2018), 163–5; Dustin R. Iler, "From Split Atoms to Spliced Genes: The Evolution of Cold War Fear in Michael Crichton's *Jurassic Park* and Richard Powers's *The Gold Bug Variations*," *Critique: Studies in Contemporary Fiction* 57:2 (2016): 140–1.
37 Crichton, Revised First Draft, 17–18, 110.
38 Derrick Davis, *Rick Carter's Jurassic Park (An Illustrated Audio Drama)*, May 7, 2022, https://jurassictime.wixsite.com/memoirs/rcjp-illustrated-audio-drama.
39 Rick Carter, *Rick Carter's Jurassic Park*, March 7, 1991, 5. Available at: https://jurassictime.wixsite.com/memoirs/script-resources.
40 Ibid., 16.
41 Ibid., 96.
42 Quoted in Shay and Duncan, *Making of*, 56.
43 Elaine Dutka, "With This Player, You Get a Brain," *Los Angeles Times*, May 16, 1993, 76.
44 Thomas Elasaesser, "The Blockbuster: Everything Connects, but not Everything Goes," in Jon Lewis (ed.) *The End of Cinema as We Know It: American Film in the Nineties* (London: Pluto Press, 2002), 20; Krämer, "Would You…," 304.
45 Carrie Rickey, "Philafilm '80: A Roster of High-Quality Movies," *Philadelphia Inquirer*, July 29, 1989, 1E, 4E.
46 Morris, *Steven Spielberg*, 178–85.
47 Shay and Duncan, *Making of*, 41.
48 McBride, *Steven Spielberg*, 418.
49 Malia S. Marmo, *Jurassic Park*, March 14, 1992, 2, 21, 30, 36–40. Available at: https://jurassictime.wixsite.com/memoirs/script-resources.
50 Ibid., 4, 82, 92, 95, 100, 121.
51 Ibid., 14, 121.
52 Randy Laist, *Cinema of Simulation: Hyperreal Hollywood in the Long 1990s* (London: Bloomsbury, 2015), 160.
53 Marmo, *Jurassic Park*, 84.
54 Ibid., 122–4.
55 Ibid., 123.
56 Krämer, "Would You…," 304.
57 David Koepp, *Jurassic Park*, Working Draft, April 23–May 1, 1992, 13, 42–3. Available at: https://davidkoepp.com/script-archive/jurassic-park/.
58 David Koepp, *Jurassic Park*, May 26, 1992, 13, 43–4. Available at: https://jurassictime.wixsite.com/memoirs/script-resources.

59 David Koepp, *Jurassic Park*, July 30, 1992 (with revisions through November 1992): 7A–9. Available at: https://davidkoepp.com/script-archive/jurassic-park/.
60 Koepp, May 26, 54.
61 Ibid., 40.
62 Ibid., 106.
63 Ibid., 97.
64 Koepp, July 30, 36A.
65 Ibid., 71.
66 Ibid., 94.
67 Fredrick Wasser, *Steven Spielberg's America* (Cambridge: Polity, 2010), 152.
68 Koepp, Working Draft, 25–6.
69 Geoff King, *Spectacular Narratives: Hollywood in the Age of the Blockbuster* (London: I.B. Tauris, 2000), 43–4.
70 Koepp, Working Draft, 25.
71 Ibid., 1–2.
72 Koepp, July 30, 124A.
73 Ibid., 126.
74 Rachel L. Carazo, "Through Heroism and Science 'Woman Inherits the Earth': Female Scientists and Dramatic Acts in the *Jurassic Park* Film Franchise," in Rebecca Janicker (ed.) *The Scientist in Popular Culture: Playing God and Working Wonders* (Lanham: Lexington Books, 2022), 97–9.
75 Koepp, Working Draft, 126.
76 Jerry Roberts, "Write On: One Man's View of the Screen Trade," *San Pedro News-Pilot*, August 9, 1993, A9.
77 Adam Ganz and Steven Price, *Robert De Niro at Work: From Screenplay to Screen Performance* (Cham: Palgrave Macmillan, 2020), 21.

2

Rebellious Creations, Monstrous Animals, and (Un)Natural Disasters: The *Jurassic Park* Franchise and Box Office Hit Patterns

Peter Krämer

De Montfort University, UK

Introduction

At the time of this writing (summer 2022), I can look back on thirty years of engaging, one way or another, with *Jurassic Park*. I first came across the teaser poster for the movie back in the summer of 1992: the black-and-white/yellow-and-red *Jurassic Park* logo set against a black background, at the bottom "Summer 1993," next to it, very small, the Amblin and Universal logos.[1] There was so little information that one could not even be sure that the poster concerned a movie. Perhaps the summer of 1993 would see the opening of a new theme park at the Universal Studios complex in Orlando. The logo featured a *Tyrannosaurus Rex* skeleton, which in itself was not so special, this kind of attraction being familiar from museums. But if *Jurassic Park* really was a Universal theme park, then perhaps the use of animatronics at market leaders Disneyland and Walt Disney World suggested that this new park would, mechanically, bring dinosaurs to life.

When I first encountered the *Jurassic Park* poster, I had just embarked on the study of annual and all-time box office charts in the United States. For this purpose I went through film industry trade papers, notably *Variety*, which made me realize that the *Jurassic Park* poster was for the next Steven Spielberg movie. According to my preliminary analysis of the all-time domestic rentals chart (at that time most charts still used figures for rentals, i.e., the share—usually 40–60 per cent—of the box office gross going to the distributor), Spielberg, together with George Lucas, had dominated Hollywood's output of truly big hit movies since the mid-1970s.

As of the beginning of 1992, the ten all-time top grossers in the United States included four films directed by Spielberg (two of them produced by George Lucas who was also responsible for three *Star Wars* films in the top ten): *E.T. The Extra-Terrestrial* (1982, at no. 1), *Jaws* (1975, no. 8), *Raiders of the Lost Ark* (1981, no. 9) and *Indiana Jones and the Last Crusade* (1989, no. 10).[2] Outside the top ten there were several more films directed by Spielberg—notably *Indiana Jones and the Temple of Doom* (1984, no. 12) and *Close Encounters of the Third Kind* (1977, no. 23; Spielberg also wrote this film)—plus many films he (co-)produced, mostly for his own production company Amblin Entertainment, including *Back to the Future* (1985, no. 14) and *Who Framed Roger Rabbit* (1988, no. 27).

While Spielberg had directed some films which had not been so successful, his hit rate was very high indeed. The fact that *Jurassic Park* was an adaptation of a bestselling Michael Crichton novel from 1990, which told the story of a somewhat futuristic island adventure about dinosaurs having been cloned as attractions for an amusement park, Spielberg's next film thus following in the footsteps of his major hits in the science fiction and adventure genres, suggested that another major box office hit might be forthcoming.

Jurassic Park was indeed an almost unprecedented success at the US box office. In *Variety*'s all-time rentals chart from May 1994, with earnings of $205 million, the film was second only to *E.T.* ($228 million).[3] And in a 1995 all-time *grosses* chart, *Jurassic Park*'s $357 million box office gross was second only to *E.T.*'s $400 million.[4] Also in 1995, video sales of 16 million units placed *Jurassic Park* fifth in the all-time video sales chart in the United States, an extraordinary achievement in light of the fact that this chart was dominated by Disney animations (the only other non-animated film in the top ten was *E.T.* at number 10 with 12 million units).[5] Even more extraordinary were the film's foreign earnings, which put *Jurassic Park* far ahead of the competition in a 1996 all-time worldwide (that is domestic plus foreign) box office chart, with a total gross of $913 million, followed by *The Lion King* (1994, $772 million) and *E.T.* ($701 million).[6] *Jurassic Park*'s global record would stand until the release of *Titanic* (1997).[7]

Like most of the other all-time top grossers since 1977, *Jurassic Park* is what I have called a "family-adventure movie."[8] Family-adventure movies are characterized by sources or subject matter associated with childhood (in this case dinosaurs and amusement parks), a focus on familial relations (here John Hammond [Richard Attenborough] and his grandchildren [Ariana Richards and Joseph Mazzello], with Alan Grant [Sam Neill] reluctantly stepping into the paternal role), a child-friendly rating (*Jurassic Park*'s PG-13 rating most likely increasing its appeal to younger children), association with child-oriented merchandise and a release in the run up to, or during, school holidays (so that families can go to the cinema together).

But the film also belongs to a long tradition of stories about humanity's (intentional or accidental) creations turning against their creators, whereby such creations can be biological, mechanical, and/or digital; and, relatedly, stories about humans encountering monstrous animals, whereby "monstrous" here signals that the animals are unusually, perhaps unnaturally, large or vicious, also perhaps that they are displaced in space or time.[9] Classic examples from the nineteenth and early twentieth centuries include Mary Shelley's 1818 novel *Frankenstein; or, The Modern Prometheus*, Herman Melville's *Moby-Dick; or, The Whale* (1851), H. G. Wells's *The Island of Doctor Moreau* (1896), Arthur Conan Doyle's *The Lost World* (1912), Czech writer Karel Capek's 1921 play *R.U.R. (Rossum's Universal Robots)*, and the 1933 movie *King Kong*.

After first outlining the overall success and impact of the whole *Jurassic Park* franchise, with a focus on the United States, in the second section I locate the *Jurassic Park* films within long-term trends by examining US box office charts with regard to stories about humanity's creations turning against it and about humans encountering monstrous animals. In the third section I focus on the success of the *Jurassic Park* films, and on box office hit patterns, *outside* the United States and *globally*, whereby I pay particular attention to those films that, since the 1970s, have dramatically exceeded existing records for non-United States and global box office earnings: *Jaws*, *E.T.*, *Jurassic Park*, *Titanic*, and *Avatar* (2009). I discuss thematic similarities between these five films, mainly to do with human hubris and humanity's interaction with the natural environment, in the fourth and final section.

The *Jurassic Park* Franchise and US Box Office Charts

Looking around and also back in time from the vantage point of the summer of 2022, it is striking how expansive the *Jurassic Park* franchise launched by Crichton's novel and Spielberg's film has become.[10] Remarkably, there *is* a real Jurassic Park in the form of a themed section, which opened in 1999, at the Universal Orlando Resort.[11] Starting in 1996, there have also been "Jurassic Park" and, later, "Jurassic World" rides in Universal theme parks in Los Angeles, Osaka, and Singapore.[12] Following the exhibition "The Dinosaurs of *Jurassic Park*" which opened at the American Museum of Natural History in 1993, there have been several full-scale exhibitions and smaller-scale exhibits travelling around the United States and indeed the world ever since.[13] In recent years, a live "Jurassic World" show has been on tour in several countries.[14]

In addition to stepping into, or looking at, physical replicas of key locations and attractions in the franchise's fiction, there is also the possibility to inhabit its story-world imaginatively through, among other things, toys, games, an animated series, and books.[15] Apart from Crichton's two bestsellers (the second of which, *The Lost World*, was at number two in the US sales chart for 1995),[16] there are novels as well as comic books retelling the stories of the films or telling new stories, guides to the fictional world of the franchise, coloring, activity and pop-up books, plus volumes about the making of the films and the real science underpinning them.[17] Outside the commercial sector, there is a huge amount of fan fiction.[18]

As a search for "Jurassic Park" on Nexis (a database containing countless, largely English language newspapers, magazines, and other publications) reveals, among the thousands of items that have referenced the book or the film, there are many that do not actually focus on the franchise, but rather deal with other topics to do with science, history, and much else. Sometimes "Jurassic Park" is used in such articles without any explanation of what it originally referred to. This is particularly obvious in scholarly publications. Searching for "Jurassic Park" on Google Scholar leads one to articles and books not only about dinosaurs, paleontology, de-extinction, ecology, genetics, cloning, and chaos theory, but also, for example, on microbes, jurisprudence, the history of human violence, psychopharmacology, unpredictability in medicine, historical culture, management consulting, law firms, innovation in Canada, and Tunisian democracy. With or without explicit reference to the entertainment franchise, the phrase "Jurassic Park" is everywhere in scholarly writing, press reporting, and public debate.

The main reference point continues to be the movies that have been extraordinarily successful at the box office.[19] Here are the grosses of all six films and their rankings in the annual US charts:

Jurassic Park ($404 million, no. 1 in 1993),[20]
The Lost World: Jurassic Park ($229 million, no. 3 in 1997),
Jurassic Park III ($181 million, no. 9 in 2001),
Jurassic World ($652 million, no. 2 in 2015),
Jurassic World: Fallen Kingdom ($418 million, no. 4 in 2018),
Jurassic World Dominion ($366 million, no. 4 in 2022; as of 25 July 2022).

The films' rankings in Box Office Mojo's adjusted all-time chart, which takes into account ticket price inflation and all of a film's re-releases and includes films up to and including 2019, are (from top to bottom): *Jurassic Park* at no. 18, *Jurassic World* at no. 30, *The Lost World* at no. 113, *Jurassic World: Fallen Kingdom* at no. 136, *Jurassic Park III* at no. 295; *Jurassic World Dominion* will end up just within the top 200.[21] To put this in perspective, ten of the eleven *Star Wars* movies are in the top 100 (the outlier is *Solo: A Star Wars Story* at no. 534), which surpasses the success of the *Jurassic Park* franchise by a wide margin. Something similar can be said about the *Indiana Jones* films and the films set in the Marvel Cinematic Universe. On the other hand, as compared to five out of six *Jurassic Park* movies, only three of the five *Pirates of the Caribbean* movies are in the top 200 (at nos. 94, 133, and 150); only three out of six *Transformers* movies (nos. 94, 133, and 150); seven out of the eight *Harry Potter* movies (the highest at no. 80) but none from the *Fantastic Beasts* series; all three *Lord of the Rings* films (the highest at no. 59) but none of the Hobbit movies; and only two of the twenty-five Bond films. While certainly not the best performing franchise at the US box office, the *Jurassic Park* series does beat most of the competition in terms of the scale and consistency of its commercial success.

The *Jurassic Park* Films and Generic Trends

None of the other franchises mentioned above deals centrally, like the *Jurassic Park* series does, with humanity's creations turning against it or with humans encountering monstrous animals, but quite a few films among the 1,000 titles in the inflation-adjusted all-time US chart do. Many of them concern robots/computers turning against humans.[22] They include (in chronological order): *2001: A Space Odyssey* (1968, no. 154), *Terminator 2: Judgement Day* (1991, no. 119), *The Matrix* (1999, no. 269), *The Matrix Reloaded* (2003, no. 132), *The Matrix Revolutions* (2003, no. 518), *I, Robot* (2004, no. 513), *Terminator Salvation* (2009, no. 862), and *Avengers: Age of Ultron* (2015, no. 101). In *Star Trek: The Motion Picture* (1979, at no. 283) the Voyager 6 space probe has been upgraded by alien machines and threatens to destroy the Earth. Of all the films in which humans intentionally create new *biological* entities, apart from the *Jurassic Park* series, only the comedy *Young Frankenstein* (1974) made it into the top 1,000 (at no. 139), but there are two films featuring Godzilla, a creature that has come into existence as an unintended consequence of nuclear weapons tests: *Godzilla* (1998, no. 363) and *Godzilla* (2014, no. 488).

When it comes to human encounters with monstrous animals, in addition to the *Godzilla* and *Jurassic Park* titles, the all-time adjusted US chart includes films dealing with various animals that actually exist (*Jaws*, 1975, no. 7; *Jaws 2*, 1978, no. 253; *Congo*, 1995, no. 748) or with enlarged versions of real animals, notably *King Kong* (1976, no. 464), *King Kong* (2005, no. 268), and *Kong: Skull Island* (2017, no. 728). There also are films in which dangerous animals, some but not all of which decidedly monstrous, are present but less central to the story such as *Jumanji* (1995, no. 531), *Jumanji: Welcome to the Jungle* (2017, no. 153), and *Jumanji: The Next Level* (2019, no. 260). Films like *Tarzan* (1999, no. 271), *How to Train Your Dragon* (2010, no. 393), *Life of Pi* (2012, no. 946), *The Legend of Tarzan* (2016, no. 987), and *The Jungle Book* (2016, no. 178) feature deadly animals but are mainly concerned with peaceful coexistence, even friendship and love between humans and animals, a theme that comes to the fore in the latest sequels to *Jurassic Park*.

One could also consider films prominently featuring supernatural or alien life forms that appear to be animals (in some cases possibly genetically engineered), such as *Alien* (1979, no. 297), *Gremlins* (1984, no. 141), *Aliens* (1986, no. 546), and *Avatar* (2009, no. 15). Another interesting borderline case are the *Planet of the Apes* films in which animals have become monstrous (in the eyes of humans) by acquiring dramatically increased intelligence, whereby it is suggested that this evolutionary leap was partly, even largely, the consequence of human interference. The original *Planet of the Apes* (1968) is at no. 459 in the all-time adjusted US chart, and the 2001 remake at no. 298. Then there is the later film series: *Rise of the Planet of the Apes* (2011, no. 553), *Dawn of the Planet of the Apes* (2014, no. 431), and *War for the Planet of the Apes* (2017, no. 892).

The chart I have used includes only a few films from before 1950 (and most of these only made it into the chart because of several re-releases) but the decades after 1950 are all represented with numerous titles. And yet none of the films discussed above was released before 1968. Starting in that year there are titles in the all-time chart about humanity's creations turning against their creators and about human encounters with monstrous animals. To be clear, it is not the case that there were no such hits at the US box office before 1968. *The Lost World* was at no. 6 in the *annual* chart for 1925, and later examples include *King Kong* (no. 1 in 1933), *Moby-Dick* (no. 13 in 1956), *The Seventh Voyage of Sinbad* (no. 6 in 1958), *Journey to the Center of the Earth* (no. 17 in 1959), and *The Birds* (no. 15 in 1963).[23] But compared to the films in the all-time adjusted top 1,000, these were hits of a lesser magnitude.

Should we attach any significance to the fact that from 1968 onward both types of stories (creations against creators, monstrous animals) generated major hits in the United States and that the success of the *Jurassic Park* series may therefore be only one aspect of a broader cultural transformation? The case for such significance is supported by a parallel shift in hit patterns to do with catastrophes. The all-time adjusted US chart includes many highly ranked pre-1970s films featuring destruction and devastation on a grand scale, brought on by war, civil war, or divine intervention, notably *The Four*

Horsemen of the Apocalypse (1921, no. 137), *Gone With the Wind* (1939, no. 1), *Sergeant York* (1941, no. 123), *The Ten Commandments* (1956, no. 6), *Ben-Hur* (1959, no. 14), *The Bridge on the River Kwai* (1957, no. 93), *Lawrence of Arabia* (1962, no. 84), and *Doctor Zhivago* (1965, no. 8).

But there are few, if any, pre-1970s films in the top 1,000 revolving around natural disasters, that is, those not caused by humans or by divine intervention.[24] Such films become quite prominent from the 1970s onward (complementing the ongoing success of films dealing with war, civil war, and other human-created or supernaturally caused catastrophes): *Airport* (1970, no. 70; a weather-related disaster is narrowly avoided), *The Poseidon Adventure* (1972, no. 89; a tidal wave caused by an earthquake upends an ocean liner), *The Towering Inferno* (1974, no. 61; the elemental force of fire is unleased in a skyscraper), *Earthquake* (1974, no. 173; the titular force devastates Los Angeles), *Superman* (1978, no. 75; the protagonist's home planet Krypton is destroyed by its exploding sun), *Outbreak* (1995, no. 949; death and destruction is caused by a disease), *Twister* (1996, no. 91; tornadoes), *Titanic* (1997, no. 5; iceberg), *Deep Impact* (1997, no. 339; comet), *Armageddon* (1998, no. 164; asteroid), *The Perfect Storm* (2000, no. 267; hurricane), *2012* (2009, no. 570; solar flare), *World War Z* (2013, no. 452; disease), *The Croods* (2013, no. 536; earthquake and volcano eruption), *Interstellar* (2014, no. 542; plant disease), *San Andreas* (2015, no. 772; earthquake), and *Moana* (2016, no. 37; plant disease). There is also a group of films in which what appear to be "natural" disasters have actually been caused by humans: *Waterworld* (1995, no. 646; flooding of the globe, presumably due to anthropogenic climate change), *The Day After Tomorrow* (2004, no. 332; climate change), and *I Am Legend* (2007, no. 231; to fight the destructive force of cancer a virus is developed, which then kills most of humanity).[25]

The emphasis in most of these films is not so much on the elemental forces that bring about disaster but on the vulnerability of humans, the fragility of the technological and social systems they have set up, their lack of preparedness, and their carelessness—and also of course their resilience, ingenuity, courage, and skill. The majority of these major hits since the 1970s are set in the present or the near future in the United States (perhaps standing in for highly developed societies everywhere) and focus on disasters that are all too familiar from the news or from discussions about future risks. These films demonstrate that modern cities, buildings, and vehicles can quickly become deathtraps, that humans cannot control natural forces on Earth, and that there are lethal dangers for life on Earth from beyond its boundaries. Even if there is no war or civil war or terrorism or divine punishment, disaster can strike at any moment.

This does seem to link up to the two types of film discussed earlier—humanity's creations turning against their creators and human encounters with monstrous animals—insofar as, just like the films about natural disasters, such films (including the *Jurassic Park* series) reveal the lethal potential of what humanity has created and the threat posed by elemental forces beyond its control. This in turn suggests that it is no coincidence that films of these types first achieved major success in the late 1960s and 1970s, because, as the analysis of public opinion polls has shown, large segments of the American population became deeply concerned about environmental issues and were critical of established institutions and ways of life and also more pessimistic about the future across the 1960s and 1970s—and by and large such concern, criticism, and pessimism have been maintained ever since.[26]

We have to be cautious about making connections between public opinion and shifts in hit patterns in the United States because most of the biggest hits in the United States were also extremely successful outside the country.[27] Therefore, to pursue this line of argument would require studying box office charts in all the countries in which such films were particularly successful (whereby in many countries non-Hollywood films, especially domestic productions, have successfully competed with Hollywood imports), to check whether shifts in hit patterns similar to those in the US charts can be found and, if so, whether shifts in public opinion similar to those in the United States have taken place as well. While this goes far beyond the scope of this essay, it is worth taking a closer look at Hollywood's export charts and at global box office charts, starting with the success of the *Jurassic Park* series.

The *Jurassic Park* Films and Global Box Office Charts

As the following rankings in annual charts show, the *Jurassic Park* series was just as successful outside the United States as it was in the United States:[28]

Jurassic Park (1993): at no. 1 worldwide for the year with a box office gross of $1,046 (1,100) million, made up of $643 (696) million from outside the US (no. 1 in the foreign chart) and $403 (404) million from the US (no. 1 in the domestic chart);

The Lost World: Jurassic Park (1997): no. 2 worldwide with $619 million, no. 2 outside the US with $390 million, no. 3 in the US with $229 million;

Jurassic Park III (2001), no. 8 worldwide with $369 million, no. 8 outside the US with $188 million, no. 9 in the US with $181 million;

Jurassic World (2015), no. 2 worldwide with $1,670 million, no. 3 outside the US with $1,018 million, no. 2 in the US with $652 million;

Jurassic World: Fallen Kingdom (2018), no. 3 worldwide with $1,308 million, no. 2 outside the US with $891 million, no. 4 in the US with $418 million;

Jurassic World Dominion (2022), no. 3 worldwide with $921 million, no. 3 outside the US with $555 million, no. 4 in the US with $366 million (as of 25 July 2022).

Since the late 1980s, most of Hollywood's biggest global hits have generated more, in many cases much more, than half of their total box office revenues outside the United States.[29] Hence the *Jurassic Park* series is not unusual in this respect. But there is something unusual about the global success of the first film. While it is not possible to adjust the all-time global chart for ticket price inflation (because such an adjustment would have to take into account changes in ticket prices in many countries and also fluctuating exchange rates between their currencies and the American dollar), there are other ways to process the information in this chart so as to identify important trends of which the enormous global success of *Jurassic Park* is a part.

The 1,000 titles in Box Office Mojo's all-time worldwide box office chart include very few films from before the 1970s, and only a few from that decade, because of incomplete data sets and of much lower ticket prices around the world.[30] When looking at the highest grossing films of the 1970s, it would seem that both *The Exorcist* (1973) and *Jaws* (1975) dramatically exceeded previous records, but a closer look at the former reveals that its overall figures ($441 million globally of which $208 million came from outside the United States) include a substantial amount from a re-release in 2000. During its original release *The Exorcist*'s performance—$329 million worldwide/$136 million outside the United States—was closer to that of *The Godfather* (1972; $250 million/$114 million) than to that of *Jaws* ($471 million/$211 million).[31] Indeed *Jaws*' non-US revenues are over 50 percent more than those of *The Exorcist* during its original release. *Jaws* can therefore be considered a true game changer with regard to the amount of money a film could generate outside the United States and globally (also, of course, in the United States but here I am only interested in export and global income).

It would appear that *Star Wars* was another game changer with worldwide revenues of $775 million, of which $314 million came from abroad. But the *Star Wars* figures once again include income from successful re-releases. While the re-releases in the late 1970s and early 1980s could be considered to be merely an extension of the original release, the income from the 1997 "Special Edition" re-release should be deducted to arrive at the following figures for what we might call the extended original release of *Star Wars* from 1977 to 1982: $520 million worldwide of which $207 million came from outside the United States.[32] Thus, by 1982 *Star Wars* had still not topped *Jaws*' record foreign revenues, and it only exceeded the film's global revenues on the basis of being brought back into theaters several times from 1978 to 1982; ticket-price inflation between 1975, on the one hand, and the period 1977 to 1982 on the other has not been taken into account either. Having long argued for the importance of the release of *Star Wars* as a film historical turning point,[33] I now have to admit that outside the United States *Jaws* was in commercial terms (and also perhaps in other respects) the more important film.

The next dramatic leap in foreign and global earnings came with *E.T. The Extra-Terrestrial* (1982): $793 million worldwide, $358 million internationally. Once revenues from the re-releases in 1985 and 2002 are deducted, the result is still a record: $683 million worldwide, $324 million outside the United States.[34] The latter figure represents an increase of more than 50 percent over the figures for *Jaws* and *Star Wars*.

Jurassic Park brought another drastic increase. From the overall figures—$1,100 million worldwide and $696 million outside the United States— we have to deduct the revenues from the 2013 re-release to arrive at the following for the original release: $978 million worldwide and $621 million outside the United States.[35] The latter is a 90 percent increase on the previous record. Next comes *Titanic*: $2,202 million worldwide and $1,542 million outside the United States; after deduction of re-release earnings we get: $1,843 million worldwide and $1,243 million outside, the latter a 100 percent increase on *Jurassic Park*'s record.[36] Finally, there is *Avatar*: $2,847 million worldwide and $2,087 million outside the United States; after deducting re-releases we get: $2,744 million worldwide and $1,994 million outside the United States.[37] However, we would be justified, I think, to include the 2010 re-release as part of an extended original release, which gives us: $2,788 million worldwide and $2,028 million outside the United States. In either case, the non-US figure is over 60 percent more than *Titanic*'s record.

With regard to the exceptional status of the game-changing films—*Jaws*, *E.T.*, *Jurassic Park*, *Titanic*, and *Avatar*—it is important to note that before a new record breaker comes along, few films even get close to the previous record. For example, in the years from 1975 to 1981, apart from *Star Wars*, no other titles challenged the worldwide and non-US earnings of *Jaws* during their original releases, and from 1997 to 2008 the closest any film came to *Titanic*'s record was *The Lord of the Rings: The Return of the King* (2003; $1,146 million worldwide/$768 million outside the United States). The only film released since 2009 that could claim to have matched *Avatar*'s record is *Avengers: Endgame* (2019), which did ever so slightly go beyond the figures for the former film's original release, but only because it was helped by a general rise in ticket prices and also the explosive growth of the Chinese market since 2009 (where it earned $629 million as compared to *Avatar*'s $262 million).[38]

Male Hubris and Mother Nature

So in 1975, 1982, 1993, 1997, and 2009 existing records for foreign (and in most cases also global) box office revenues generated by individual

Hollywood films were shattered, and, very intriguingly, the five films that did so form clear patterns. The first three—*Jaws*, *E.T.*, and *Jurassic Park*—were directed by Steven Spielberg, the last two—*Titanic* and *Avatar*—by James Cameron. This not only confirms Spielberg's exceptional status but also highlights Cameron's importance, in particular when considering the fact that he also *wrote* the two movies in question and did so without basing his screenplays on already published, popular material. Since the late 1990s, the vast majority of Hollywood's biggest box office hits have been adaptations (of novels, comic books, television shows, etc.), remakes, sequels, prequels, spin-offs, and reboots. With *Titanic* and *Avatar* Cameron really stands out. While Spielberg rarely writes his own scripts and bases many of his films (including both *Jaws* and *Jurassic Park*) on books, it is important to note that *E.T.* had an original script (based on an idea by Spielberg for which he did, however, not receive a credit).

All of the five game-changing export/global hits have American protagonists (who are teamed up with aliens in numbers two and five), but only the first two are set in the United States. At first sight, the scope of these films may appear limited, especially when compared with the galaxy-, even universe-spanning *Star Wars* and Marvel sagas. *Jaws* and *Jurassic Park* only concern small island communities, *Titanic* a single, albeit very large ship, and *E.T.* primarily a suburban mother and her three children (as well as a stranded extra-terrestrial). *Avatar* first and foremost concerns a human outpost on a distant moon and one particular tribe of natives. But in all of these films there is clearly much more at stake.

After all, *E.T.* depicts what appears to be the first extended and intimate contact between humans and extra-terrestrials. The sinking of the Titanic is offered as an allegory for the destruction of one form of society (strictly hierarchical in terms of class and gender) and the emergence of another (more egalitarian) one. In *Avatar*, humans, having already destroyed their own planet's biosphere, embark on the gradual destruction of Pandora's tribal cultures and ecosystems. Quint's Indianapolis speech in *Jaws* suggests a link between the appearance of the great white shark near Amity Island and the naval transport of the first nuclear bomb that was to destroy Hiroshima. And, of course, *Jurassic Park* shows that "life finds a way" and suggests that the nonhuman world cannot be controlled by humans.

In different ways all five films explore the relationship between humans and their nonhuman natural surroundings, between science and technology on the one hand and nonhuman forces on the other, between human ambitions and the limits imposed upon them by the world around them. This is rather obvious in *Jaws* (note, e.g., the commercial dependence of Amity on the exploitation of its beautiful beaches, the scientist's ultimate failure in confronting the shark, sharks killing the people who "delivered the bomb"), *Jurassic Park* (the above themes are explicitly and extensively discussed in dialogue), *Titanic* (note, e.g., dialogue lines such as "God himself could not sink this ship," or the superior power of the iceberg when it collides with the ship) and *Avatar* (again, the above themes are the subject of much dialogue). Like the other four films, *E.T.* is about a confrontation between humanity and that which is not human, and also—mainly through the figure of Keys—concerns the impact of science and technology as well as human ambitions to reach out into the nonhuman world, but, unlike the other films, this one does not focus on violent and destructive clashes, and limitations are freely chosen by, rather than forced upon, the human protagonists: both Elliott and Keys are willing to let E.T. return to the mothership and fly away with it.

Importantly, in all five films there appear to be mysterious nonhuman forces at work in the world: the technologically superior and parapsychologically empowered aliens in *E.T.*; sharks that seem to be guided, or motivated, in some way to do damage to transgressive humans; the life-force itself in *Jurassic Park*; an iceberg that serves to punish human arrogance in *Titanic*; the nature goddess Eywa, described as a global neural network of tree roots, who wins the final battle in *Avatar*. In fact, in all films, these forces are more or less explicitly associated with the female: Eywa is a goddess; the extra-terrestrials in *E.T.* are dependent on their mothership (and there is also Gertie's question about E.T.: "Is it a boy or a girl?"); the shark in *Jaws* is phallic but also a vagina dentata (killing only males after the initial attack on a young woman, culminating in the death of Quint the lower half of whose body is bitten off); the ocean in both *Jaws* and *Titanic* is a grave but also perhaps a kind of womb; all the dinosaurs in *Jurassic Park* are female (except for some that spontaneously change sex so as to be able to impregnate the rest). While nemesis is thus female (like the goddess of that name in Greek mythology), human hubris is very much a male affair in these films (except for *E.T.*). It is males against Mother Nature, and the latter always wins in the end.

One might also say that several of these films specifically explore the damage that Americans have done. *Jaws* refers back to the American attack on Hiroshima, and *Avatar* shows an American-identified company ravaging foreign lands. *Jurassic Park* concerns the work of American scientists and a Scottish entrepreneur (who is, however, reminiscent of Walt Disney) turning an exotic island into an amusement park. *Titanic* works much more indirectly (among other things, it is the UK, America's predecessor as global superpower, which is the origin of the ship), as does *E.T.* (American scientists and government agents are initially perceived as a threat to E.T. but then turn out to be well-meaning, if ineffective).

In any case, I wonder whether there might be a connection between the films' emphasis on particular themes (to do with ecology, gender, and the role of the United States in the world) and their record-breaking success outside the United States. Indeed, on the basis of the five game-changing films discussed above, we might more generally observe that many of Hollywood's biggest export hits since the 1970s (which in most cases have also been its biggest hits in the domestic market) have addressed fundamental questions about the place of humans (their societies and technologies, especially as manifested in the United States) in the nonhuman, wider world, not by celebrating conquest and domination, but by suggesting limitations and even inferiority and, implicitly, recommending caution and humility.

Conclusion

While the present essay does not have much to say textually about *Jurassic Park* and virtually nothing about the stories, style, and themes of its sequels, it does attempt to contextualize all of these films by mapping the enormous success of the franchise and by situating the films, especially the first one, within trends, across many decades, in US, non-US, and global box office charts.

I have been cautious about offering substantial, let alone definitive, answers to the question of how we might explain these general trends or what significance they might have for our understanding of the world we live in. But I hope that I have been able to demonstrate that Hollywood's biggest blockbusters quite persistently address fundamental questions about humanity's place in that wider world, about our collective deployment of science and technology, and the limits to the control that can be exerted through them; about unavoidable "natural" and human-made disasters; about monsters of our own, or someone else's, creation; about mysterious forces seemingly at work in the world to thwart our collective ambitions and even to carry out punishment for misdeeds and arrogance. All of this is presented in a way that offers maximal sensual and emotional (as well as some intellectual and moral) stimulation because these films, and none more so than *Jurassic Park*—a film named after an amusement park—are first and foremost about our need to be entertained.

Notes

1 See http://www.impawards.com/1993/jurassic_park_ver1_xlg.html. This and all other websites were last accessed on July 25, 2022.

2 Lawrence Cohen, "Top 100 All-Time Film Rental Champs'," *Variety*, January 6, 1992, 86. The American trade press includes Canada in the domestic market. For simplicity's sake I use "American market" synonymously with "domestic market" and thus include Canada in it. Similarly I later refer to the non-US or export or international market, meaning the world market without the United States and Canada.

3 Leonard Klady, "All-Time Film Rental Champs," *Variety*, May 15, 1994, 40–52.

4 "Top 100 Domestic Grossers," *Variety*, February 20, 1995, A84. From now on I refer to box office grosses rather than rentals. Different sources can give slightly different figures, and the same source may, in the course of time, adjust figures due to corrections of errors or due to re-releases.

5 "Kid Vids Top the Chart," *Variety*, April 24, 1995, 7.

6 See chart in *Variety*, June 3, 1996, 70.

7 "Top 20 Global Grossers of '98," *Variety*, January 4, 1999, 9.

8 Peter Krämer, "Would You Take Your Child To See This Film? The Cultural and Social Work of the Family-Adventure Movie," in Steve Neale and Murray Smith (eds.) *Contemporary Hollywood Cinema* (London: Routledge, 1998), 294–311. On *Jurassic Park*, see 302–4.

9 *Cf.* https://www.merriam-webster.com/dictionary/monstrous.

10 A useful overview is provided on https://en.wikipedia.org/wiki/Jurassic_Park.

11 See https://en.wikipedia.org/wiki/Universal's_Islands_of_Adventure#Jurassic_Park and https://www.universalorlando.com/web/en/us/theme-parks/islands-of-adventure/jurassic.

12 See https://en.wikipedia.org/wiki/Jurassic_Park:_The_Ride and https://en.wikipedia.org/wiki/Jurassic_World:_The_Ride.

13 See https://en.wikipedia.org/wiki/Jurassic_Park#Exhibitions.

14 See https://jurassicworldlivetour.com/choose-country.

15 The wide range of commercially available items is on display when searching for "Jurassic Park merchandise" or "Jurassic World merchandise" on Amazon.com.

16 See https://en.wikipedia.org/wiki/Publishers_Weekly_list_of_bestselling_novels_in_the_United_States_in_the_1990s#1995.

17 These can be found by searching "Jurassic Park" or "Jurassic World" on, for example, Amazon.com or Google Books.

18 See the thousands of stories on, for example, https://www.fanfiction.net/movie/Jurassic-Park/, https://www.wattpad.com/stories/jurassicworld, and https://archiveofourown.org/tags/Jurassic%20Park%20-%20All%20Media%20Types/works.

19 In addition, a chart of the most successful films in the United States on VHS, DVD and Blu-ray has *Jurassic Park* at no. 9 with sales of 26 million units; the only two non-animated films selling more units are *Avatar* at no. 8 and *Titanic* at no. 6. *Jurassic Park* is the fifth biggest selling VHS tape of all time, the only higher ranked non-animated film being *Titanic* at no. 4. *Jurassic World* is at no. 8 in the all-time Blu-ray sales chart for the United States. See https://en.wikipedia.org/wiki/List_of_best-selling_films_in_the_United_States.

20 See https://www.boxofficemojo.com/year/1993/?grossesOption=totalGrosses. In the top left corner there is a tab with which to select other years. The annual charts include revenues generated in later years, due to a film having a long run into the year after its original release and due to re-releases. Thus, when I refer to the number one film of a particular year, it is the film with the

highest life-time gross released that year. The domestic gross figure for *Jurassic Park* is not given correctly in the 1993 chart, and I therefore take it from https://www.boxofficemojo.com/title/tt0107290/.

21 See https://www.boxofficemojo.com/chart/top_lifetime_gross_adjusted/?adjust_gross_to=2019.

22 Note that in this context the *Transformers* movies do not qualify because the robots in question were not created by humans.

23 My main source is an unpublished set of annual charts that Sheldon Hall compiled from a 1993 list of all films with rentals of at least $3 million in the United States: Lawrence Cohen, "All-Time Film Rental Champs," *Variety*, May 10, 1993, C76–C108. Perhaps surprisingly, *Frankenstein* (1931) was not a substantial hit.

24 Once again, this is not to say that such films were not at all successful before the 1970s but their success was of a lesser magnitude. Examples include *San Francisco* (no. 1 in 1936), *The Hurricane* (no. 3 in 1937), and *The Wizard of Oz* (no. 2 in 1939).

25 Both old and new films about natural disasters or about human encounters with monstrous animals were huge ratings hits on American television in the late 1960s and the 1970s. For example, in a 1979 list of the top-rated movies of all time (including both theatrical releases and made-for-TV movies), the 1973 broadcast of *Airport* is at no. 3 with a rating of 42.3 (which means that the film was watched in 42.3 percent of all US households). Other examples include *The Birds* (1963, broadcast in 1968, at no. 7 with a 38.9 rating), *Planet of the Apes* (broadcast in 1973, no. 19, 35.2) and *The Poseidon Adventure* (broadcast in 1974, no. 6, 39). After its first broadcast late in 1979, *Jaws* would be added to this list at joint no. 6 with a 39 rating. *The Wizard of Oz*, with its devastating but strangely benevolent tornado, is an important transitional film with top ratings for its many television broadcasts from the late 1950s to the 1970s. See Cobbett Steinberg, *Film Facts* (New York: Facts on file, 1980), 31–6. *Jurassic Park*'s relationship to the disaster movie is also discussed elsewhere in this book by Matthew Melia.

26 I discuss these developments, with reference to a range of primary and secondary sources, in Peter Krämer, *The New Hollywood: From Bonnie and Clyde to Star Wars* (London: Wallflower Press, 2005), 68–79, and in the "Coda" of Peter Krämer, *American Graffiti: George Lucas, the New Hollywood and the Baby Boom Generation* (London: Routledge, 2023), 103–6.

27 Peter Krämer, "Hollywood and Its Global Audiences: A Comparative Study of the Biggest Box Office Hits in the United States and Outside the United States Since the 1970s," in Richard Maltby, Daniel Biltereyst, and Philippe Meers (eds.) *Explorations in New Cinema History: Approaches and Case Studies* (Oxford: Wiley-Blackwell, 2011), 171–84.

28 The information in this paragraph is taken from https://www.boxofficemojo.com/year/world/. Years other than 2022 can be accessed via the tab on the top left. Rankings for US and non-US charts can be accessed through the tabs "domestic" and "foreign" on the top right. Box Office Mojo's worldwide

charts are incomplete before 1998, which is why I use figures from The Numbers for 1997 and 1993. See https://www.the-numbers.com/box-office-records/worldwide/all-movies/cumulative/released-in-1993 (one can move on to later years via the tab at the top right). Some figures given by The Numbers differ from the ones given by Box Office Mojo; as I mostly use Box Office Mojo in the rest of this essay, I have given its gross figures for *Jurassic Park* (from https://www.boxofficemojo.com/title/tt0107290/) in brackets.

29 Krämer, "Hollywood and Its Global Audiences," 175–6. *Cf.* https://www.the-numbers.com/box-office-records/worldwide/all-movies/cumulative/released-in-1988 (click on to subsequent years) and https://www.boxofficemojo.com/year/world/?ref_=bo_nb_hm_tab (click on to previous years).

30 See https://www.boxofficemojo.com/chart/ww_top_lifetime_gross/?area=XWW.

31 See the individual entries for the three films on Box Office Mojo (so as not to complicate matters too much I ignore minor re-releases): https://www.boxofficemojo.com/title/tt0068646/?ref_=bo_se_r_1, https://www.boxofficemojo.com/title/tt0070047/?ref_=bo_se_r_1 and https://www.boxofficemojo.com/title/tt0073195/?ref_=bo_se_r_1.

32 See https://www.boxofficemojo.com/title/tt0076759/?ref_=bo_se_r_1 and https://en.wikipedia.org/wiki/Star_Wars_(film)#Box_office.

33 See, for example, Peter Krämer, ""She Was the First": The Place of *Jaws* in American Film History," in Ian Hunter and Matthew Melia (eds.) *The Jaws Book: New Perspectives on the Classic Summer Blockbuster* (New York: Bloomsbury Academic, 2020), 19–32.

34 See https://www.boxofficemojo.com/title/tt0083866/?ref_=bo_se_r_1 and https://en.wikipedia.org/wiki/E.T._the_Extra-Terrestrial#Release_and_sales.

35 See https://www.boxofficemojo.com/title/tt0107290/?ref_=bo_se_r_1.

36 See https://www.boxofficemojo.com/title/tt0120338/?ref_=bo_se_r_1.

37 See https://www.boxofficemojo.com/title/tt0499549/?ref_=bo_se_r_1.

38 See https://www.boxofficemojo.com/title/tt4154796/.

3

Sounds of the Lost World: Musical World-Building in the *Jurassic Park* Franchise

Daniel White
The University of Huddersfield, UK

Introduction

A distant choir crescendos over a soaring symphony orchestra, joining with a heroic violin melody full of promise and expectation. John Hammond (Richard Attenborough) delivers the now-infamous line "Welcome to *Jurassic Park*" and the camera cuts to Alan Grant (Sam Neill), closing in to frame the look of distant wonder and astonishment on his face. The music swells and with a majestic roll of the timpani the objects of Dr. Grant's bewilderment—several enormous *Brachiosauruses* grazing and emerging from a lake—are triumphantly revealed. This time, however, the orchestra and choir are suddenly replaced with a comedically terrible rendition of John Williams's *Jurassic Park* theme on melodica.

This internet meme created by Patrick Lo parodies one of the most iconic and memorable moments within the first *Jurassic Park* film (1993), confounding our expectation of a grand musical climax with a significantly weaker imitation done for humorous effect.[1] This effect is amplified by the disparity between the sight of some of the most impressively realistic CGI (computer-generated imagery) dinosaurs of the era and the utter failure of Lo to land any of the right notes in anything resembling the right order. In the nineteen years between the film's release and the uploading of this

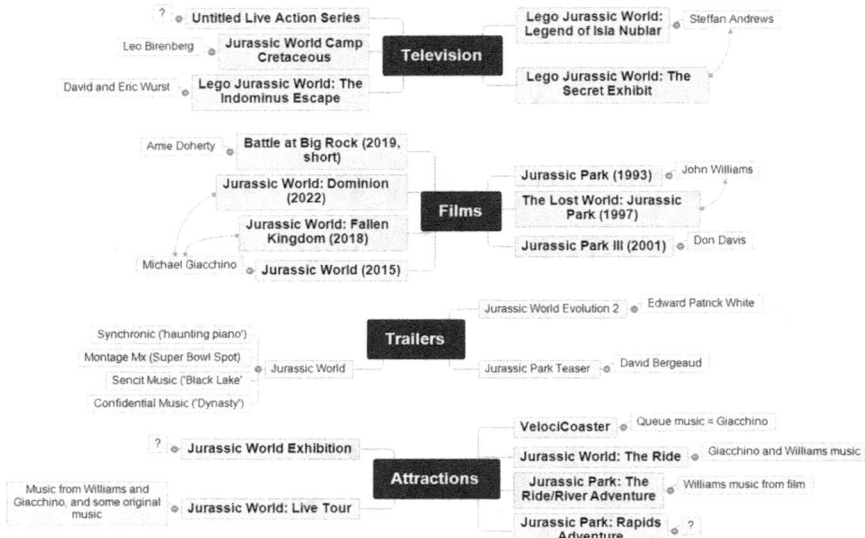

FIGURE 3.1 Composers involved in Jurassic *films, TV series, trailers, and attractions*

FIGURE 3.2 Composers involved in Jurassic *videogames*

video, John Williams's Main Theme for *Jurassic Park* and its pairing with these dinosaurs in their (un)natural habitat has implanted itself into public consciousness, and it is this shared awareness of the motif that gives the meme its comedic power.

When we think of *Jurassic Park*, or when we remember some of those iconic scenes, such memories are likely accompanied by a recollection of the musical scores and their most prominent themes.[2] Just as the world of the *Jurassic Park* franchise has grown into a transmedial universe of films, games, shows, rides, toys, and exhibits, so the musical world of the franchise has also grown and been added to by numerous composers and music supervisors. As the first of these composers, John Williams provided an entryway to this fantasy universe by establishing its sound and thereby setting a number of musical parameters and listener expectations. Since then, the power to add music to the canonical world of the franchise has been passed not only to subsequent film composers such as Don Davis, Michael Giacchino, and Amie Doherty but also to numerous others working on videogames, television series, promotional trailers, and theme park rides. Figures 3.1 and 3.2 show just some of the composers who have contributed in these ways, and although not exhaustive, they show an extensive and multifaceted musical world. This chapter does not aim to provide analytical detail on every one of these musical contributions, nor does it examine the central role of sound design as a complementary agent of world-building within these canonical entry points to the series, a key facet of which is the creation of dinosaur vocalizations.[3] Instead, it explores the musical world of the *Jurassic* franchise, starting with its creation by Williams and its evolution by other film composers, before picking up on representative moments here and there in the wider *Jurassic* world, to survey the ways in music has built and continues to build this world around those who dare to go adventuring within it.

The Films: Williams, Davis, Giacchino, Doherty

Ask someone to sing the theme tune to *Jurassic Park* and you will likely be met with one of two melodies: the slower, more majestic "Main Theme" (also known as "Theme from *Jurassic Park*" that accompanies the aforementioned *Brachiosaurus* reveal, or the more energetic, trumpet-led "Island Fanfare," otherwise referred to by the track name "Journey to the Island."[4] Together these themes form the central part of John Williams's score for *Jurassic Park*, each appearing on at least five different occasions within the first film. The first appearances of the themes and the moments they accompany are also noteworthy in that these combinations become reference points or musical calling cards later in the franchise, and thus these first hearings can be thought of as, to use a semiotic concept borrowed from Saul Kripke by James Buhler, the "primal baptisms" of the themes—that is, the linkages of the signifiers with the signifieds, or of the themes with the filmic or narrative elements they come to stand for.[5] The "Island Fanfare" is heard sixteen minutes into the film on first sight of Isla Nublar as the helicopter containing John Hammond and his guests makes its approach, and the "Main Theme" follows three or four minutes later at the abovementioned reveal of herbivores moving in herds. Although the themes return at different moments, for example, the fanfare accompanying a shot of the jeeps heading through the park gates or coinciding with the *Tyrannosaurus* saving the day by attacking the raptors (deus Rex machina?), these first associations are reused and recycled in subsequent films and other media, strengthening the linkage of the "Island Fanfare" with helicopter rides or aerial shots of the island, and of the "Main Theme" with the majesty and grandeur of the island and the gentler herbivores that inhabit it.

Aside from these two Williams themes, the music includes a range of other cues and motifs in a score that has consistently been heralded as one of the composer's best.[6] The most prominent of these subsidiary motifs is the raptor/carnivore theme (labeled differently by different analysts and fans) that is first heard in the opening moments of the film.[7] Here its rendition on the shakuhachi (a bamboo flute of Japanese and ancient Chinese origin) accompanies the *Jurassic Park* title card amid swelling strings and dissonant choir, but the motif is not heard again until the second half of the film. Depending on whether the theme signifies carnivorous dinosaurs or raptors more specifically, the theme's "primal baptism" could be its next iteration in the *T-Rex* chase scene around seventy-seven minutes into the film, or its later use from ninety-three minutes onward to accompany the broken raptor fence, raptor footsteps, and the ensuing raptor chases and attacks where it becomes the main, repeated melodic material. Here the effect of the motif's chromaticism and internal dissonance is maximized by Williams to heighten the sense of distress and danger through the film's third act. There are a number of other motivic figures employed by Williams such as the ominous "Hunted" motif (a frantic string of notes moving stepwise and harmonized in compound minor thirds) and the "Military March," an orchestral march figure that first appears in the emergency bunker as the characters weapon up and hatch a plan.[8]

The film's poignant ending, though, sees the characters safely and reflectively departing the island by helicopter, though the sound of the chopper is barely heard; instead we hear a full rendition of the "Main Theme," here in a much softer form beginning on sentimental solo piano before being taken up by a gentler and more restrained orchestra as the image fades and the credits begin to roll. The mystery and tension of the film's opening cue is resolved by the safety and comfort of these closing musical moments, leading to a subtler and more reflective filmic ending.

The opening and closing sequences of the Jurassic films do much to establish and build the fantasy world of the franchise, and music plays a key role in this world-building process.[9] In the first few moments of *Jurassic Park* the world is built of sound—a thick array of jungle noises and distant animal calls accompany the Universal vanity card, and the aforementioned shakuhachi theme follows the last of three synth bass thuds and dissonant choral swells to align with the *Jurassic Park* logo. It is noteworthy, perhaps with the hindsight of the "Main Theme's" eventual prominence, that the world of *Jurassic Park* is not established motivically first and foremost but sonically and timbrally. Furthermore, although the themes already identified form a prominent part of the musical world of the film, the majority of the soundtrack comprises more textural or atmospheric musical underscoring that provides color and detail to the world and the action without overt motivic references. Williams's now recognizable approach to orchestration and texture (features such as fluttering winds, aleatoric string writing, and prominent horn melodies) becomes a key part of the sound of the *Jurassic* world, and some of these features and styles become tropes that are referenced in later films and by other composers.

Table 3.1 lists six of these tropes, all of which are established in *Jurassic Park* and then employed in later films, games, and television series.

The Lost World: Jurassic Park (1997) takes us back to the Muertes Archipelago, this time to neighboring Isla Sorna to study more genetically engineered dinosaurs (and barely escape them once again). Musically, Williams employs his two main themes, though sparingly, and adds two further ones: a *Lost World* theme and an Isla Sorna theme, the former a pounding figure in strings and brass with heavy drums and an answering arabesque on woodwinds, and the latter a slow and simple rising gesture on the first three notes and octave of a minor scale.[10] The feel of the *Lost World* score differs from that of *Jurassic Park* through its much more prominent use of hand drums and other percussion, aligning the music with the deeper and wilder jungle feel of the film in a nod to Max Steiner's influential and pioneering score for *King Kong* (1933). Preexisting themes are used skilfully, such as the two subtle horn iterations of the "Island Fanfare" that drift through the highly discordant violin underscore as Nick (Vince Vaughn) discovers the old *Jurassic Park* facilities—an echo of the former glory of a park now fallen into disrepair. In terms of world-building, the ominous Isla Sorna theme is the first music heard, emerging from the wind and rain to coincide with our first view of the island and a caption clarifying the location ("Isla Sorna—87 Miles Southwest of Isla Nublar")—the motif's primal baptism. The theme reappears on at least ten different occasions in the rest of the film, and the *Lost World* theme is similarly pervasive. The film's ending, though, reverts to the more established and familiar themes, using

TABLE 3.1 *Musical Tropes of the* Jurassic *Franchise*

Trope	Signification or Use	Musical Elements
March or martial music.	Soldiers, guns, military intervention, rescue missions, human defense.	Snares and other drums, march patterns, repeated short motifs, bass pedals, minor tonality.
Sentimental music or theme settings.	Family relations, history, or reunion.	Soft piano, harp, lush string chords, simple functional harmony, major tonality.
Heroic or triumphant music (i.e., "Island Fanfare").	Heroes, adventure, "deus ex machina" moments.	Trumpets and other brass, fanfare, functional harmony.
Majestic or hymnal music (i.e., Main Theme).	Herbivores and "gentle giants," aerial shots of the island or park.	Broad string lines, slow tempo, full orchestra, choir, generally major tonality.
Attack, fight, or tension music.	Dinosaur attacks and chases, running and hiding.	Quick and busy, often aleatoric, no clear functional harmony, rhythmic and repetitive, highly dissonant stabs and flurries.
Unnerving or unearthly music	Laboratories, science, dinosaur eggs, incubation and hatching.	Soft, chromatic, dissonant string chords, twinkly percussion, choral/child choir "aah's."

a sentimental setting of the "Main Theme" to underscore John Hammond's closing television interview, which segues into the "Island Fanfare" as he utters the closing line "life will find a way," heralding the dominion of the dinosaurs as the credits begin to roll. Here once again a familiar theme smooths over the beginning of the credits and thus the ending of the film.

It is here that John Williams hands over the musical reigns to his successor Don Davis who provides the soundtrack for *Jurassic Park III* (2001). Davis's approach is one of pastiche, creating a score with some significant new thematic material but with a profound sense of respect in the way he handles and uses preexisting motifs. This imitation of style is self-confessed; in one interview he said, "The idea, going in, was that it was going to be an expansion of John Williams' concepts, and I would use his themes. I suppose if I hadn't written it in a John Williams style, no one would have noticed it, really."[11] Elsewhere Davis identifies that the intricacy of his music is what helps to align it with the style of Williams's scores.[12] He makes clear reference to some of the abovementioned tropes, including the use of Williams's majestic "Main Theme" for a moment (at 1:07:47) when the characters come round a river bend to be met with a grazing herd of "gentle giant" *Brachiosauruses*, or the use of dissonant choral "ahh's" for the discovery of several nests of raptor eggs (at 35:08). Davis introduces his own theme for the reunification of the Kirby family (at 52:18), and this gently emotive major theme lines up closely with the "sentimental" musical trope for moments of family or reunion.[13] He also introduced a further theme for the *Spinosaurus*, and cleverly places this theme in a sort of "battle" with Williams's carnivore theme to score the *Spinosaurus*' fight with the *T-Rex*, and though this material can be heard on the rip-roaring "Clash of Extinction" cue on the soundtrack it was ultimately cut from the film as the fight was deemed not to require music.[14]

The point Davis makes about musical intricacy reflecting that of the preceding Williams scores can clearly be heard through his approach to orchestration as well as texture. Fight or chase scenes feature frenetic string and brass writing with prominent percussion and very thick textures, and the score also includes significant use of solo horn, heavy brass chords, flurrying woodwinds—all of which imitate Williams's style. Describing his own approach, Davis stated that "as the audience becomes more and more attuned to what's going on in the movies I think the function of music gets more and more clear, and I think the audience are starting to expect the score to function in a way that brings them into the movie."[15] This highlights Davis's awareness of the significant role music plays in building the world of the film, and indeed the importance of referencing existing musical material in the right moments to satisfy audience expectation. It is also noteworthy that as the film series goes on, the films start to have more and more musical underscoring. If we consider the amount of music within each of the films as a percentage of the film's duration, the gradual increase in musical presence is depicted in Figure 3.3.[16] This trend points to an increasing emphasis on music as a narrative and world-building agent, suggesting that not only the type and style of music but indeed the increasingly pervasive presence of music itself is vital in making the film *sound* and *feel* like a *Jurassic* film. This musical saturation reaches its peak in the *Jurassic World* films that both feature over 85 percent musical underscoring.

As Michael Giacchino takes the compositional helm for the *Jurassic World* films (2015, 2018, and 2022), we hear a slight shift in musical style. He maintains the same reverent and respectful treatment of the most prominent Williams themes, and the soundtracks remain largely orchestral, making use of the same instrumental colors and textures that have become part of the musical fabric of the world but also introducing some prominent

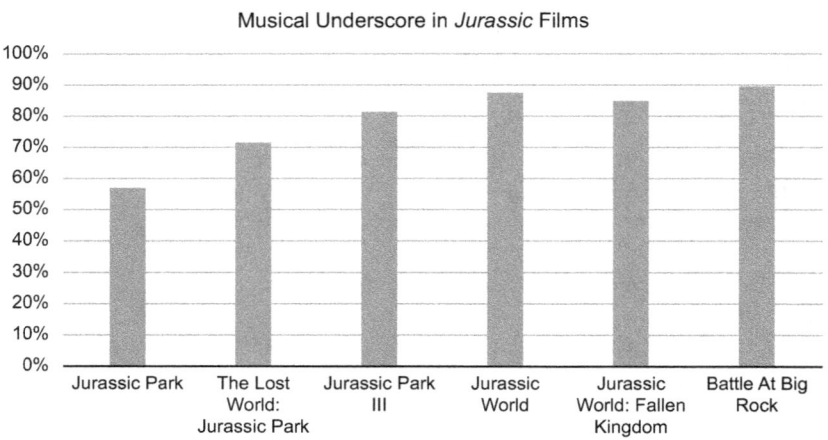

FIGURE 3.3 *Percentage musical underscoring in each* Jurassic *film*

new themes and a little more of his own voice. Again, as in *The Lost World* and *Jurassic Park III*, *Jurassic World* includes sequences that directly reference moments of the first film both visually and musically. For example, Giacchino and director Colin Trevorrow take the opportunity of Simon Masrani's (Irrfan Khan) precarious helicopter ride with Claire Dearing (Bryce Dallas Howard) to reference the preceding examples of chopper rides and aerial shots of an island, by using a full brassy statement of Williams's "Island Fanfare" and even coinciding the triumphant final cadence of the theme with the chopper's bumpy landing.[17] Similarly, the boys' arrival on Isla Nublar uses a full iteration of William's Main Theme in such a reverent way that the cuts are made to follow the music rather than vice versa. The chromatic opening horn motif returns to coincide with the first sight of the island, but this note of disquiet quickly gives way to optimism with high woodwinds and gentle harp, before the Main Theme proper begins in low violins, coinciding with a cut to the monorail in such a way that makes the music sound potentially diegetic—as if the music is being piped into the park as part of the attraction. The theme then continues as the boys hurry (or not) to their hotel room, climaxing as the younger brother Gray (Ty Simpkins) throws open the blinds to reveal the new park in all its glory, the brass and choir heralding the splendor of the park as the camera flies over the glistening lake toward the central compound. The Main Theme also appears later in the film (at 1:05:27) on solo high piano amid dissonant string pedals to echo the former glory of the first park as the boys explore its ruins. Giacchino shows a keen awareness not only of the power of employing Williams's now nostalgic themes at the most effective moments, but also of drawing on some of the non-thematic tropes identified in Table 3.1. For example, in direct reference to the trope of unnerving music for the hatching of dinosaur eggs, the opening of *Jurassic World* (after the Universal vanity card) features fifty-eight seconds of horror music tropes to accompany shots of unknown dinosaurs hatching in a laboratory environment. Sounds and musical elements here include a constant, quickening pulse or heartbeat, a chromatic solo flute arabesque, gamelan or singing bowls, bowed cymbals and waterphone, taiko drums and shaker percussion, diminished harmony and chromatic mediant progressions, and most notably here a female voice choir on open and closed vowel sounds.[18]

Besides referencing and reusing the existing musical language of the *Jurassic* films, Giacchino also extends this language with his own thematic contributions, taking on the style of the world while using it to express new elements or characters within it. Among these contributions are a theme for the film's new antagonist the Indominus Rex (indeed two themes or a theme in two parts), a family theme, a theme for Owen or the raptors (or both) and a main *Jurassic World* theme.[19] These themes align with and in a sense replace many of the existing Williams or Davis ones; the Family theme is first heard under a phone call between sisters Claire (Howard) and Karen (Judy Greer) and features long violin and cello pedals and a wistful piano melody with some chromatic movement, perfectly fulfilling the "sentimental family theme" trope. The two sides to the Indominus theme appear throughout the film, both highly chromatic in nature and in a sense replacing the Carnivore theme with added nuance—one element seems to represent the Indominus' violent and aggressive nature (first heard alongside the Universal vanity card at the film's opening) while the other seems to stand for its genetic manipulation or perhaps its intelligence (though appearing in the egg-hatching sequence, its true primal baptism is at Claire's first mention of the Indominus in discussion with investors at 0:07:48).[20] Giacchino's main *Jurassic World* theme is first heard on the boat ride to the island, though it is quickly interrupted by Williams's evocative Opening Horn Motif as the island comes into view—its first full iteration accompanies the closer aerial shot of the park and further shots of the boys exploring the exhibits (0:08:26).[21] The theme is comparable to Williams's Main Theme in a number of ways: majestic arrangement for full orchestra and choir, legato string lines and a long upward trajectory, and it even features a direct melodic reference to the former motif at the final perfect cadence (three trumpet notes from the tonic to the leading note and back again). The use of the motif also directly mirrors that of Williams's Main Theme, as it appears in a later scene (0:59:45) where Owen and Clare nurse a dying *Brachiosaurus*, this time much slower on solo piano joined by lush string pads.

Jurassic World: Fallen Kingdom (2018) continues in the same vein, although with a more prominent "action" sound, and employs all of Giacchino's established themes. These are implemented logically throughout, alongside some clever uses of the long-standing Williams themes at specific moments: the ominous and now well-established Opening Horn Motif (here first on harp) precedes Claire's sight of a portrait of John Hammond; another sentimental piano rendition of the Main Theme accompanies Claire's nostalgic recollection of her first ever dinosaur encounter; the "Island Fanfare" heralds the start of the closing credits. There is also continued reference to tropes outlined in Table 3.1 through the new material introduced by Giacchino: a new sentimental motif and some more militaristic action music, named the Compassion theme and the Mercenary theme, respectively, by Jonathan Broxton, and a unifying *Fallen Kingdom* theme that appears at the title card and throughout.[22] This theme with full orchestra and choir is much more ominous and dramatic than its predecessors, largely through its dissonant harmony. Shifting from E minor to B♭ minor and back again before cadencing on B♭ major, these harmonic progressions can be thought of as very distant—indeed, in his typology of "tonal triadic progression classes" Scott Murphy classifies these particular shifts (named "m6m") as "[accompanying] mortal threats and dangers issued less from adversarial characters, and more from situations, objects, or natural phenomena," and this description is fitting for a film that features an erupting volcano, leaking hydrogen cyanide, and a range of new genetically modified dinosaurs.[23]

Although only ten minutes in duration, the short film *Battle at Big Rock* (2019) still packs in a number of musical punches, building its own corner of the musical world of the *Jurassic* franchise while drawing on the preexisting tropes and devices. Amie Doherty pulls on a range of material such as a gentle flute-led iteration of Giacchino's *Jurassic World* theme that gives the entrance of a baby *Nasutoceratops* an air of beauty and innocence. The short contains a lot of action music, being predominantly focused on a holidaying family barely escaping the attacks of numerous dinosaurs roaming the wilds of northern California, but the opening and closing moments feature particularly noteworthy uses of music. The Universal title card directly references the openings of the rest of the film series, recreating the shakuhachi rendition of Williams's carnivore theme from the *Jurassic Park* opening and following it with Williams's Opening Horn Motif, mimicking the openings of *Jurassic Park III* and *Jurassic World* whose title cards also feature solo horn melodies. Mirroring this, at the very end of the action as the camera pulls away to reveal the destruction left by the rampaging *Allosaurus*, Doherty combines the opening horn and carnivore themes, overlapping their first/last notes to create one bombastic and overly dramatic ending. She then references the now highly tropified solo piano rendition of the Main Theme (which has also featured on numerous trailers including that for *Jurassic World*), though here the piano seems to have been detuned and destroyed to match the carnage on screen, with the final piano note reduced to a thumping hammer and rattling string.[24] The world-building continues right to the end of the credits, with the first half (home-videos of dinosaurs infiltrating everyday life) continuing the dramatic underscoring and referencing other parts of the musical world including Williams's *Lost World* theme, and the second half (rolling credits) featuring a fireside rendition of the Main Theme on solo acoustic guitar by Brian Winslow, complete with campfire crackle and distant cicadas. This merging of the physical setting of the film with this usually non-diegetic musical theme (though it has also featured diegetically in *Jurassic World*'s park/monorail scenes) reflects the mixing of these two previously separate worlds and the invasion of dinosaurs into the primary world as we know it.

Battle at Big Rock provides not only a peek into a world learning to coexist with dinosaurs—which is the world of *Jurassic World: Dominion* (2022) —but musically it also paves the way for Giacchino's final score, which draws significantly on preexisting musical themes and uses them much more prominently than any of his new material. With the longest runtime of two hours and twenty-seven minutes, the film draws just as much on John Williams's material (including the "Main Theme," "Island Fanfare," "opening horn" motif, and "carnivore" theme) as it does on Giacchino's themes (including the main "Jurassic World" theme, the sentimental "family" theme, Owen's theme, and the main theme from *Fallen Kingdom*), presenting a nostalgic conflation of these two musical worlds and taking every opportunity to recall specific *Jurassic* moments and tropes. Some of the musical writing presents themes *slightly* less overtly, such as the semi-disguised "Island Fanfare" that is buried in tense and dissonant scoring as Dr. Malcolm sets off on a rescue mission in a 4 × 4, in a way similar to many of the visual "Easter eggs" that abound.[25] Copious use of sentimental piano settings of the main themes also exploits one of the main franchise tropes, occurring at least seven times including predictably at the final helicopter escape. Besides the significant reuse of existing franchise themes, Giacchino also makes a clearer effort to pastiche some of Williams's orchestrational styles with figures such as light-hearted, scurrying winds, low bassoon interjections for impending dinosaur attacks, hand drums for the more exoticized scene in Malta, and percussive martial cues and wind or brass playing in wide parallel harmony, both of which hark directly to Williams's music for *The Lost World: Jurassic Park* whose themes are notably absent. In summation, Giacchino's final score is an effective and highly nostalgic tying-up of the musical world of the franchise.

What we find by listening closely to these various filmic entry points to the world of the *Jurassic* franchise is that John Williams is responsible for the vast majority of the world-building that takes place, by establishing the distinct sound of the world and setting the tone both thematically and timbrally. The sound of the lost world evolves throughout the franchise but remains largely orchestral and indeed stays within the thick and detailed orchestrational style of John Williams, and all new material aligns closely with the specific musical tropes that are established in the first film. Preexisting material (particularly Williams's two most prominent themes) is continually referenced and recycled for specific effect, often to (re)create certain *Jurassic* moments, such as majestic helicopter rides, aerial shots of the island, high-octane dinosaur chases or the climactic moments that show the ferocity and autonomy of the main predators. Having identified these commonalities in the filmic part of the *Jurassic* world, the following section looks at examples from television, videogame and other media, to track how far these tropes go and how they are used to extend the musical world of the franchise.

Television, Games, and Other Media

The full extent of the *Jurassic* franchise's multimedia expansion is detailed in Figures 3.1 and 3.2, and a quick glance shows that although serial televisual formats are becoming more popular with several series currently in development, the ludic side of the franchise has been an important revenue stream for Universal Pictures/Amblin Partners and a significant way for fans to engage in, interact with, and imaginatively inhabit the lost world.[26] The above figures also detail the vast number of composers involved in the extension of the musical world of the franchise, and it is perhaps unsurprising that the legacy and themes of John Williams continue to loom large in these scores and soundtracks. It would be impractical here to provide analytical detail on all these musical contributions (though the author hopes that Figures 3.1 and 3.2 will prove useful for future researchers), but a few examples will serve to show some of the ways composers have added their own voices to these access points while still drawing on the established thematic language and musical tropes to satisfy user expectation, either through the general sound of the world or through the referencing of specifically "*Jurassic*" moments.

One contributor who draws on the preexisting musical world in both these ways is Leo Birenberg, composer for the Netflix series *Jurassic World Camp Cretaceous* that comprises fifty episodes across five seasons (including an interactive special episode). The series follows a group of teenagers brought to Isla Nublar for a once-in-a-lifetime dinosaur experience, who end up being stranded on the island to fight for survival when the dinosaurs predictably escape. Birenberg approaches scoring the series by maintaining the orchestral palette, contributing his own themes but drawing on preexisting themes at significant moments. The first episode of season one features prominent use of both the Williams themes that have become the hallmark of the franchise. The "Island Fanfare" accompanies the first aerial shots of Isla Nublar (6:57) as well as the group's first sight of and entry through the oversized wooden gates of the camp (12:40, both repeated tropes from the films), and the Main Theme also appears twice in episode one, first at the moment when the characters (and us) lay eyes on the dinosaurs for the first time. This two-minute scene (15:40–17:30), where the group encounter a variety of large and small herbivores being herded to their enclosures and enjoy a zip-wire ride above them, is accompanied by an extended orchestral and choral setting of the Main Theme where the climaxes synchronize with cuts to the gentle giants, referencing established cutting practices from the films and creating a nostalgic "*Jurassic*" moment. Reflecting on his employment of existing themes, Birenberg notes,

> In the first episode we do it a little more than we do any other time just because you really want to set up that sonic world. If you're sitting down to watch Camp Cretaceous you want it to feel like Jurassic Park and you want to get jacked when they're going through the gate so you got to give them a taste of the Island theme.[27]

The second iteration of the Main Theme appears with the rolling of the end credits of episode one, and this is a combination that continues without fail at the end of every episode. The opening titles of every episode are also the same each time, drawing again on established *Jurassic* opening tropes: distant dinosaur/jungle sounds, booming footsteps rippling in watery puddles, and an adaptation of Williams's Opening Horn Motif all draw viewers into the world via the same recognizable and now well-worn paths.[28]

The adaptation of the most prominent Williams and Giacchino themes (original themes by Davis and Doherty perhaps not having gained the same prominence or memorability) continues in a similarly sensitive fashion through the rest of the series. As the first episode closes on a cliff-hanger with two protagonists trapped in an enclosure with four angry raptors, Birenberg invokes Williams's raptor theme. Elsewhere in episodes four (1:20) and seven (13:56) of season one Birenberg references more sentimental piano settings of Williams's Main Theme, both moments of either family recollection or post-escape reflection, aligning closely with similar instances in the films. He also makes continued allusions to existing material, including Giacchino's theme for the Indominus Rex, which he references in episode three of season one (10:50). Besides this, though, Birenberg's own themes fit nicely alongside these quotations. He creates his own "main" theme for the series that he calls the Camp Theme, and with its strings and horns, its major tonality and an opening ascending perfect fifth it sits somewhere between the two Williams themes, in a sense drawing on both.[29] The theme is also established at the first mention of Camp Cretaceous (6:37 into the first episode) when protagonist Darius learns he has won a ticket to the camp, and the theme grows to include more pensive or energetic settings.

The LEGO extensions of the *Jurassic* world include three short filmic specials and a miniseries comprising thirteen episodes, as well as a *LEGO Jurassic World* (2015) videogame for a wide range of platforms. With the exception of *The Indominus Escape* (2016), all subsequent shorts and the

Legend of Isla Nublar (2019) miniseries have been scored by Canadian composer Steffan Andrews, and once again the music pays faithful homage to the musical world of the franchise through both the intentional employment of existing motifs, and the less overt imitation of orchestrational styles or scoring techniques. There are specifically "Jurassic" moments that are nostalgically rescored such as the moment antagonist Larson Mitchell (Kirby Morrow) first lays eyes on the dinosaurs on a jeep ride with Claire Dearing (here Britt Mckillip), which coincides with a spritely Main Theme (10:40 in episode one). Other moments in the score relate specifically to Williams or Giacchino's use of instrumentation, as detailed by Andrews:

> To keep the sound consistent and evocative of the franchise, I drew on melodic and orchestrational devices that were established in the films. One example might be a piercing, threatening solo muted trombone for the sinister threat of a *Velociraptor*, or lower register woodwind glisses for larger sneaky dinosaur threats.[30]

All in all, the majority of these scores feature original material with the occasional preexisting theme (intellectual property licensing having been highly complex in this and indeed most other scenarios), and it is clear that Andrews sought to "keep the sound evocative of the franchise and make it feel like it was another chapter in the same anthology musically."[31] What is perhaps different in LEGO adaptations is the combination of faithfulness to original media texts and an often comedic and parodic sense of humor and self-awareness. Jessica Aldred states that "rather than expanding the franchise story world established in the films they are based on …, LEGO games tend to revel in the repetition and even parody of their source material's most famous scenes and set pieces."[32] Thus, some of the more comedic moments are scored light-heartedly by Andrews, with ample "mickey-mousing" and an instrumentational approach to match, such as the moment in "The Secret Exhibit" (2018) where pizzicato strings and woodwind flourishes help to take some of the bite out of the newly hatched *Velociraptors*, making them more playful than their threatening filmic counterparts.[33] Similarly, Chad Seiter's music for the *LEGO Jurassic World* game contains themes that are clearly influenced by Giacchino's "Jurassic World" theme, and also resettings of this theme, some of which reharmonize it for an even weightier feel (in the cue "LEGO Jurassic World Main Theme") or indeed riff on it for comedic effect (such as the oboe setting in "Welcome to Jurassic World").[34]

Looking elsewhere in the ludic world of the *Jurassic* franchise, many other composers have contributed their own extensions through game scores, including Jeremiah Pena who has scored the two most recent additions, *Jurassic World: Evolution* (2020) and *Jurassic World: Evolution 2* (2021). Here, as in each franchise extension, licensing rights to the original music presented unique restrictions in that the number of uses was limited, and

Pena was unable to present licensed Williams or Giacchino themes alongside his own, leading to a significant amount of original material, and the use of preexisting themes in specific cutscenes, particularly in the game's opening cutscene to draw the player in and align the game with the film world.[35] Pena's musical world in each game is vast and varied, and in a similar vein to previous composers he establishes his own themes in the style of Williams, such as the Evolution theme that he describes as "a more slow-paced, passive grandeur" and that acts as a stand-in for the Main Theme.[36] Harmonically this music moves a little further from the simple functional harmony of the Williams themes, incorporating more filmic harmonic language such as chromatic mediants that give the world a more unique yet still highly cinematic feel. For the second game Pena felt freer to move further away from the world established by Williams and Giacchino, often incorporating a denser orchestration with more repetitive influences and a wider range of colors.[37]

What is particularly noteworthy among the composers I have spoken to and the interviews given by numerous others is the sense of indebtedness toward John Williams that is keenly felt by all. Stephan Schütze, composer for the 2003 game *Jurassic Park: Operation Genesis*, speaks of the significant role that the music of John Williams played in his life growing up, and the ways in which this influenced his approach to scoring the game.[38] He also confirms his view of the famous *Brachiosaurus* scene and Williams's Main Theme as central to the world and sound of the franchise:

> The main thing for me in Jurassic Park is the scene in the movie where they're all sitting in the Jeep and they see the *Brachiosaurus* for the first time, I still to this day, even having worked on that project, can't watch that scene without basically shedding a tear, because that is one of the most beautiful scenes in any movie ever ... It was a gob-smacking cinematic moment, and I still think that that particular bit of music is probably one of the best things John Williams has ever written. So, to be asked to emulate that was terrifying and also wonderful, but what it allowed me to do is really listen to how he constructs his music and bring that style into my process.[39]

With this in mind, and listening to the music of this particular game, his approach is representative of all other game composers in the franchise— creating additional music for an existing world by sensitively pastiching Williams or Giacchino, mimicking their broader styles in order to link the original music with the carefully employed or reorchestrated existing themes. For Schütze this means often referencing a few notes of either the "Island Fanfare" or the Main Theme before developing them into something new. In his words, "it's essentially a little bit like a game of hide and seek— where I play the first few notes to get your attention—then I run away and go somewhere else that you weren't expecting—but you know it sounds JUST like Jurassic Park."[40]

An Ever-Expanding Musical World

Besides the films, television series, and games, only a few of which have been analyzed here, there are numerous other entry points to the world of *Jurassic Park*, many of which use music to create more immersive experiences and smooth a visitor's transition into the world while further enabling its imaginative inhabitation. One example of this is the range of *Jurassic World* rides that can be found at five Universal Studios sites around the world (Orlando, Hollywood, Beijing, Osaka, and Singapore) and all of which feature music. Unsurprisingly, John Williams motifs abound in the *Jurassic*-themed areas of these parks (including the main themes as well as some more percussive cues from the *Lost World* score), but Giacchino's music is also featured frequently, including in queue areas such as those for the new "Velocicoaster" at Universal Islands of Adventure, Orlando, and on parts of some of the other rides.[41] "Jurassic World: The Ride" is an updated version of the preexisting "River Adventure" ride at Universal Studios Hollywood, and the slower pace of parts of this water coaster mean that music becomes a more prominent narrative agent. For example, when the boat enters the first underwater enclosure as the gates slowly open and riders lay eyes on the *Mosasaurus* behind the "glass" (screens) they hear a full orchestral and choral setting of Giacchino's *Jurassic World* theme, creating a majestic moment and linking the ride to the riders' cinematic memory. One other canonical entry point to the franchise is via "Jurassic World: The Exhibition," a touring showcase of life-size animatronic dinosaurs alongside educational information. This also features prominent use of John Williams's "Island Fanfare," notably on first entry to the exhibit when exiting the "ferry" and on first sight of a giant *Brachiosaurus*, again echoing a key cinematic and perhaps nostalgic moment.

There is not room here to detail the wide range of noncanonical or "unofficial" routes to the imaginative inhabitation of the lost world. This includes a significant amount of fan-labor, such as fan films created using stop motion animation or adapting game mechanics from *Jurassic World: Evolution*, most of which include fan-composed scores.[42] Other ways of sonically accessing the world of *Jurassic Park* include a range of YouTube videos featuring several hours of "Jurassic Park Music and Ambience," mixing soundtrack cues with rainstorms and jungle sounds to enable someone to (imaginatively) work, study, or even sleep in their favorite dinosaur habitat. Enthusiasts can enjoy live-to-screen orchestral performances of the films through touring productions, thanks to "Film Concerts Live!"[43] A musical *Jurassic Park* fan might also choose to play the most famous themes from the franchise through commercially available piano transcriptions or orchestral arrangements, and could even buy or exchange a range of tailor-made gifts including music boxes that play twinkly versions of the motifs when wound up. There is also "Jurassic Park the Musical," a parody of the original film said to have been performed multiple times by "college students."[44] The main theme has even been lyricized several times, including notably by Jeff Goldblum and also by comedian Nick Mohammed in a viral clip from an episode of British program *8 Out of 10 Cats Does Countdown*.[45]

What has become clear through this survey of the musical world of *Jurassic Park* is that the legacy of John Williams' very first score for the franchise is strongly and firmly embedded in the cultural memory of the series. Emilio Audissino has written extensively on the cultural importance and afterlife of many of Williams' works, noting the importance of melody and orchestration in what he calls Williams' "neo-classical" style, and he outlines Williams's "innate sense of drama and knack for penning melodies that are instantly recognizable and uncannily fitting for the characters and situations they depict."[46] It is the strength of his two primary themes and of their connection to the excitement and grandeur of the islands and their dinosaur inhabitants that makes them such powerful musical emblems for the franchise, and indeed so impossible for subsequent composers to move away from. That said, Michael Giacchino makes a strong canonic contribution with his *Jurassic World* scores and the fact that these newer additions stand up to the primary themes is evidenced by their continual referencing in subsequent media texts. What is perhaps clearest is that none of the composers involved in the extension and evolution of the *Jurassic* universe seem troubled by the presence of Williams and his legacy themes. Indeed, the reverence and sensitivity with which these themes are appropriated, stylized, and reimagined, paired with the deep and heartfelt connection to Williams expressed by so many, is indicative of a sense of privilege and gratitude for the opportunity to produce scores and soundtracks which echo and amplify music that holds such a prominent position within the hearts, minds, and childhoods of so many. Although many of the games, television programs, and other texts analyzed here move in different directions and make room for new voices, it seems that the legacy of John Williams and his music for the first *Jurassic Park* film will remain a central touchstone for as long as the franchise continues to grow.

Notes

1 Patrick Lo, "Jurassic Park Theme Song (Melodica Cover)," *YouTube*, January 31, 2012. https://youtu.be/-w-58hQ9dLk. Accessed November 23, 2021.

2 Ben Winters has written extensively on music as part of filmic memory in his discussion on music and diegesis. See Ben Winters, "The Non-Diegetic

Fallacy: Film, Music, and Narrative Space," *Music & Letters* 91:2 (2010): 224–44.

3   For more on this, see Heidi Wilkins, "Steven Spielberg's *Jurassic Park*: Sounding Dinosaurs," *New Soundtrack* 4:1 (2014): 73–87.

4   Theme names here are the ones widely used by fans and other internet-based commenters and analysts. For reference, the "main theme" appears in numerous iterations after a solo horn introduction on the track "Theme from Jurassic Park" on the *Jurassic Park* soundtrack, and the "Island Fanfare" appears at 1:20 on "Journey to the Island."

5   James Buhler, "*Star Wars*, Music and Myth," in James Buhler, Caryl Flinn, and David Neumeyer (eds.) *Music and Cinema* (London: Wesleyan University Press, 2000), 33–57.

6   Adam Chitwood, "The Top 10 John Williams Scores of All Time," *Collider*, February 8, 2021. https://collider.com/best-john-williams-scores/. Accessed December 2, 2021; and Joe Lynch, "John Williams' 10 Best Movie Scores, Ranked," *Billboard*, December 6, 2015. https://www.billboard.com/music/music-news/john-williams-best-movie-scores-ranked-6598025/. Accessed December 2, 2021.

7   This shakuhachi version is heard at 0:17 on the "Opening Titles" track of the soundtrack.

8   These theme names come from an analysis by Redditor Joe Mama (u/MoMoXp) in "Film Score Analysis II—*Jurassic Park*," *Reddit*, April 11, 2018. https://www.reddit.com/r/soundtracks/comments/8bebxa/film_score_analysis_ii_jurassic_park/. Accessed December 7, 2021. The "Hunted" motif can be heard at 3:22 in the track "Incident at Isla Nublar" and the "Military March" is heard at 3:02 in the track "Eye to Eye."

9   I have written in greater detail about the world-building role of music in opening sequences elsewhere—for a more in-depth discussion, see Daniel White, "One Does Not Simply Walk into Mordor: Sound and Music as Suture in the Opening Sequences of Peter Jackson's Middle-earth Films," *Music, Sound, and the Moving Image* 14:2 (2020): 93–117.

10 The Lost World theme appears at the start of the very first track "The Lost World" from the film's soundtrack, though here it is heard in 6/4 time where it more often appears in 5/4 time in the film, and the Isla Sorna motif can be heard from 0:16 of "The Island Prologue".

11 Kenneth Plume, "Composer Don Davis Talks *Jurassic Park III* and the *Matrix* Sequels", *IGN*, May 20, 2012. https://www.ign.com/articles/2001/07/25/composer-don-davis-talks-jurassic-park-iii-and-the-matrix-sequels. Accessed December 16, 2021.

12 Rudy Koppl, "Don Davis On Scoring *Jurassic Park III*," *Soundtrack* 20 (78), 2001. https://cnmsarchive.wordpress.com/2013/07/20/don-davis-on-jurassic-park-iii/. Accessed December 16, 2021.

13 This Reunification theme can be heard on the track "The Hat Returns/End Credits" from the *Jurassic Park III* soundtrack at 1:25.

14 Plume, 2012.
15 Laurent Bouzereau, "The Sound and Music of *Jurassic Park III*" documentary, as featured on Laurent Bouzereau "Beyond *Jurassic Park*", DVD, 2001.
16 All data collected from the *PRS for Music* cue sheets database at https://apps.prsformusic.com/wacs/ProductionSearch.aspx. Accessed December 16, 2021.
17 This moment is at 0:14:32 in the film.
18 This can be heard from 0:50 in the track "Bury the Hatchling" on the *Jurassic World* soundtrack.
19 A fascinating example of intertextual scoring is found in some of Giacchino's music for the raptors, heard in the track "Raptor Your Heart Out," where he directly references the raptor theme from his own music for the 1997 videogame *The Lost World: Jurassic Park* (Sony PlayStation and Sega Saturn). Scoring this game was Giacchino's first step into game/film composition, so this reference is not only one that would only be noticed by the most extreme fan, but also one that symbolizes Giacchino's return to a familiar fantasy world. See Michael Giacchino, Interview in *PlayStation Official Magazine-UK*, https://archive.ph/20150124151002/http://www.michaelgiacchinomusic.com/features/interviews/playstation-magazine.html. Accessed January 28, 2022.
20 On the soundtrack the first part of the Indominus Rex theme is heard on solo horn six seconds into the track "Bury the Hatchling", and the second part at 1:00 of the same track. Melodically the Indominus Rex themes share similar properties with Williams's Carnivore theme as well—both feature stepwise movement by semitone, and the Carnivore theme and the first part of the Indominus theme both end in a downward tritone.
21 This can be heard from 0:58 in the track "As the *Jurassic World* Turns" on the soundtrack.
22 Jonathan Broxton, "*Jurassic World: Fallen Kingdom*—Michael Giacchino," *Movie Music UK*, July 20, 2018. https://moviemusicuk.us/2018/07/20/jurassic-world-fallen-kingdom-michael-giacchino/. Accessed January 28, 2022.
23 Scott Murphy, "Transformational Theory and the Analysis of Film Music," in David Neumeyer (ed.) *The Oxford Handbook to Film Music Studies* (Oxford: Oxford University Press, 2013), 488.
24 This particular moment can be heard at 7:33 in *Battle At Big Rock*, which in turn can be viewed at https://youtu.be/C7kbVvpOGdQ. Accessed January 28, 2022.
25 See Rita Dorsch, "Easter Eggs Only True Fans Noticed in Jurassic World Dominion," *Looper*, June 12, 2022. https://www.looper.com/892583/easter-eggs-only-true-fans-noticed-in-jurassic-world-dominion/. Accessed August 5, 2022.
26 Michael Saler explores the concept of the imaginative inhabitation of a fantasy world through his concept of the "ironic imagination" in great detail in his book *As If* (Oxford: Oxford University Press, 2012).
27 Charlie Brigden, "Interview: Behind the Music of *Jurassic World: Camp Cretaceous* with Composer Leo Birenberg," *Vodzilla.co*, January 23,

2021. https://vodzilla.co/interviews/interview-behind-the-music-of-jurassic-world-camp-cretaceous/. Accessed February 22, 2022.

28   It should be noted that the mechanics of Netflix inhibit viewers from hearing any more than the first seven seconds of the Main Theme (unless they opt in to watching the credits), instead preferring to cut straight to the action of the next episode, thereby also skipping the opening fifty seconds of the next instalment and with it the tropes identified here. It is arguable that if a viewer is already "within" the world then the intrusion of end credits and opening titles might only serve to take them out of it, but although this narrative breathing space or moment of reflection might serve to enhance the viewing experience, it sits at odds with rapidly changing viewing habits and Netflix's more consumerist goals in the age of binge-watching.

29   See Brigden, "Interview," *Vodzilla.co*, January 23, 2021.

30   Steffan Andrews, personal communication (March 7, 2022).

31   Ibid.

32   Jessica Aldred, "(Un)blocking the Transmedia Character: Digital Abstraction as Franchise Strategy in Traveller's Tales' LEGO Games" in Mark J.P. Wolf (ed.) *LEGO Studies: Examining the Building Blocks of a Transmedial Phenomenon* (New York: Routledge, 2014), 105–17, 108.

33   This clip can be found at https://www.youtube.com/watch?v=V02C8aWvV2c. Accessed March 9, 2022.

34   Seiter's cues for the game can be heard at https://app.reelcrafter.com/reel/chadseiter/homepage. Accessed March 9, 2022.

35   Jeremiah Pena, personal communication (November 17, 2021).

36   Ibid.

37   Ibid.

38   Tim Cianfano, "Stephan Schütze Interview," *Jurassic Outpost*, May 20, 2020. https://jurassicoutpost.com/interviews/stephanschutze/. Accessed March 10, 2022.

39   Ibid.

40   Ibid., original emphasis.

41   There is an impressive twenty-minute documentary detailing the "Making of …" the Velocicoaster, and this along with several official "POV" videos features significant and indeed constant use of *Jurassic World* music, pointing to the studio's keenness to create a highly cinematic experience. One commenter on YouTube with the handle HowToParkour said, "I love this ride, but the only thing it's missing is music. A little music goes a long way," "Official Jurassic World Velocicoaster 360 HD POV." https://www.youtube.com/watch?v=mftrUnUiZT0. Accessed March 10, 2022.

42   Some examples of these fan-scores, often clearly Williams-inspired, include those by Jack Mills at https://www.youtube.com/watch?v=T5OnR3GPN84 and https://www.youtube.com/watch?v=prbkmBDgUyI or one created entirely

of LEGO, which features music by Voodoo Highway: https://www.youtube.com/watch?v=5KNMYi5MDhE. Accessed March 10, 2022.

43 See https://filmconcertslive.com/movies/jurassic-park/. Accessed March 16, 2022.

44 Peter Pinne, "Jurassic Park the Musical," *Stage Whispers*. https://www.stagewhispers.com.au/reviews/jurassic-park-musical. Accessed March 10, 2022.

45 Full lyrics and video can be found at https://www.classicfm.com/composers/williams/comedy-jurassic-park-lyrics-nick-mohammed/. Accessed March 16, 2022.

46 Emilio Audissino, "John Williams and Contemporary Film Music," in L. Coleman and J. Tillman (eds.) *Contemporary Film Music: Investigating Cinema Narratives and Composition*, (London: Palgrave Macmillan, 2017), 221–37, 225. See also Audissino, E., *John Williams's Film Music: Jaws, Star Wars, Raiders of the Lost Ark, and the Return of the Classical Hollywood Music Style* (Madison: University of Wisconsin Press, 2014).

4

Beyond the Gift Shop: Onscreen Merchandise and Modeling the Consumer-Spectator

Tom Livingstone
University of the West of England, Bristol (UWE), UK

Introduction: Gift Shops

In the climactic final scenes of *Jurassic World* (2015), Zach (Nick Robinson) and Gray (Ty Simpkins) take shelter in a little gift shop with Owen Grady (Chris Pratt) while Claire (Bryce Dallas Howard) unleashes the *T-Rex* so that it can take on the *Indominus Rex*. As the dinosaur rampages outside, dino-merch tumbles off the shelves and the characters take shelter in a cascade of branded T-shirts. Moments later, in what is perhaps the signature shot of the film, the *Velociraptor*, "Blue," appears to help the *T-Rex* battle with the *Indominus Rex*. The human characters race through another, larger gift shop but their escape is almost ruined when "Blue" smashes through the front window of the store forcing them to skid to a halt in between the children's pyjamas and a table full of plywood dino-skeletons; "Blue" scrambles to her feet and bounds back out of the store, the characters run out the main entrance that is strewn with merchandise; the camera pans as the dinosaurs smash into, of all places, a Jimmy Buffet's Margaritaville (a chain restaurant and story themed around the 1977 chart hit); the wounded *Indominus Rex* is eaten by a *Mosasaurus*, all in an unbroken single take.

This sequence echoes a small moment from *Jurassic Park* (Steven Spielberg, 1993) where the never-to-be used gift shop of John Hammond's original theme park is briefly put into the foreground. The scene consists of two comparatively simple shots. The first is shot from a low angle looking up at a soft-toy version of a *Brontosaurus*, the focus pulls as the camera pans left and tilts down, bringing several shelves of soft-toys, branded lunch boxes, and pyjama sets into view. In the second shot the camera travels along a shelf that is stacked with stamp sets, a branded cup, and a book called *The Making of Jurassic Park* by Don Shay and Jody Duncan.[1] The camera pulls focus to John Hammond eating ice cream, and the brief tour of the gift shop is over.

On first glance, beyond the glimpse of a gift shop in a theme park context, there is very little to bring the two scenes into closer comparison. The 1993 film lingers for merely two shots in the *Jurassic Park* gift shop, whereas the later film relays the action taking place in the gift shop from a variety of angles. In the first film, the gift shop shots are disconnected from the narrative, suspended between key portions of the story. In the later film, the characters' escape through the gift shop represents the pinnacle of the action. In 1993, the gift shop sequence features no visual effects or digital manipulation at all. The 2015 sequence is substantially composed of digital effects.

That said, there are deeper commonalities that are worth noting. For example, in both scenes, the merchandising on display in the gift shop is real-world merchandise that is available to buy. The toys that shower down on Zach and Gray are from the Hasbro line of *Jurassic World* dino-figures. Don Shay and Jody Duncan's book remains readily available across a range of online book sellers. This doubling of diegetic and real-world merchandising allows us to place these two scenes into a more interesting relationship. In both instances, these shots provide a glimpse onto the merchandising and consumer economies that surround the film.

Writing in reference to the first film Constance Balides describes this overlapping of diegetic and real-world merchandise as a strategy of "commercial intertextuality."[2] Balides argues that the profound commercial success of the film, in combination with its foregrounding of the commercial and retail economies that surround it, necessitate a way of reading the film as more than simply a cultural object. "The specific circumstances of *Jurassic Park* militate against securing a textual boundary around the film or locating the spectator in a non-commercial text or treating the economy as a textual presence in overly generalized terms," Balides writes. "*Jurassic Park* suggests the necessity of a more precise attention to its extra-textual and textual economies."[3]

"Commercial intertextuality" and the textual presence of commercial economies characterizes both sequences in a way that transcends their obvious differences at a technical and aesthetic level. They are both scenes that literalize and put on clear display the processes of commodification taking place inside and outside of the film: cultural phenomena give rise to economic phenomena, where there are dinosaurs, there must also be gift-shops. More than just being comparable instances of product placement, however, this chapter will argue that the relationship between these two scenes is indicative of an intensification of this strategy of "commercial intertextuality," and an intensification of the way in which, in Balides's words "*Jurassic Park* addresses its spectators as economic subjects ... as literal (not only semiotic) consumers."[4] Across the course of this chapter I'll explore the impact of these parallel intensifications on the on-screen content of the films as well as the subjective experience of the films' spectators, and explore the degree to which the film's cultural, textual, and aesthetic features can be considered economically operative, cogs in the larger machine of franchise film-making and digital capitalism.

Formally speaking, this process of intensification is self-evident. To begin with, the first film features two shots of some merchandising lines, the later film has two shops, each explored in detail, with other brands, such as Warren Buffett's Margaritaville, also featuring throughout the film. This intensification from product placement to product pervasion is indicative of the way in which each film operates with respect to its economic context, and what Andrew Wernick names "promotional culture."[5] The 1993 film gestures to the consumer economies that surround it, the 2015 film is a fully instrumentalized element within a mature franchise, and the broader economic operation that implies. The additional self-evident intensification occurs in the use of digital techniques to produce hybrid images, combining live-action elements with CGI. It is the contention of this chapter that these aesthetics that undergo a process of intensification between the two films, through the proliferating use of CGI, can also be seen as instrumental within a wider economic pattern. Ultimately, I will suggest that the technical and aesthetic differences between the two gift shop scenes, more than just comparable exercises in "commercial intertextuality" are symptomatic of a wider evolution of consumer economies as they operate within and as visual culture.

The implications of this perspective are relevant to both the study of the *Jurassic Park* franchise and also to the study of mainstream cinema more broadly. Balides writes: "My argument is that the specific case of *Jurassic Park* involves various imbricated relations between economics and the film as a cultural text, one of which is the representation of economics in the film."[6] I will confirm and extend this assertion, suggesting that *Jurassic Park* initiates a trend wherein this imbrication of economics and film text intensifies until the aesthetic procedures of capital-intensive mainstream film emerge as economic operations in and of themselves. I will pursue my argument by suggesting that the particular aesthetics of *Jurassic Park* and its sequels, characterized by innovations in the hybridization of live-action cinematography with CGI elements, contribute to (or are instrumental within) an ongoing process of epistemological reshaping, the horizon of which is the embedding of the subject within a social and economic field increasingly defined by digital media.

Spectator/Consumer: Cinema/Post-Cinema

To make this argument I'll first outline the theoretical criteria underlying the presumption that cinematic media and capitalism are interlinked, before focusing specifically on writing within the field of "post-cinema" that thinks through the coextension of visual media and capitalism within the context of the digital turn. There are several perspectives that interrogate the sociopolitical modeling taking place in and around concepts of the cinematic spectator. Of particular relevance to my argument is the writing of Mary Ann Doane[7] and Jonathan Beller,[8] both of whom argue that, from its very inception, cinema operated as a function of capitalism. For Doane, in her book *The Emergence of Cinematic Time*, the new medium responded to a need for "new conceptualizations of space and time and the *situatedness* of the subject" brought about by the massive changes to socioeconomic life under twentieth-century industrial capitalism. Cinema emerged as an answer to the question, posed by capitalism: "How does the subject inhabit this new space and time?"[9] For Doane, cinema articulates a new relation to time and contingency, that makes the spectator amenable to the new conditions of Modernity, thus molding a subject who can tolerate the pressures of capitalism.

Beller takes this argument a step further, in his book *The Cinematic Mode of Production*, by suggesting that over the course of the twentieth-century, cinematic spectatorship emerged not just as a practice amenable to the operations of capitalism but as a central site of the production of value. Beller's thesis describes a process that he calls the "industrialisation of the visual,"[10] out of which emerges not only the metrics of the attention economy ("to look is to labour" in Beller's phrase)[11] but also a visual culture that operates on behalf of capital. The reorganization of the epistemological parameters of experience brought about by cinematic media, in Doane's account, continue beyond the framework of spectatorship and into the structures of subjectivity. Thus, cinema, in Beller's model, comes to mean not merely a limited exhibition practice but a defining phenomenological mode, a way of being in the world. In Beller's phrase "'Cinema' means a fully mediated mise-en-scène that provides humans with the context and options for response that are productive for capital."[12] Within these theoretical paradigms the cinematic spectator and the subject under capital are more or less analogous forms.

Both Beller and Doane have a strong focus on cinema as an emergent medium in lockstep with industrial capitalism, and therefore pay less attention to the entwined phenomena of digital media and consumer capitalism. If cinematic spectatorship, in Doane's term, "situates" the subject in the wider operations of capital, and, with Beller, transforms the act of looking into a site of production, it follows that the emergence of the digital image with its propensity to micromanipulation will accentuate and optimize this trend. Extending these models of spectatorship to the late twentieth century and beyond, "post-cinematic" writing, such as the work of Steven Shaviro[13] and Roger F. Cook,[14] considers the way in which the continued reorganization of space and time brought about by digital media, deepens the imbrications between visual media and capitalism. For Shaviro, the novel effects of digital media create "affective maps, which do not passively trace or represent, but actively construct and perform, the social relation, flows and feeling that they are ostensibly 'about.' "[15] Cook iterates the epistemological ramifications of digital media even further, pointing out that "digital technology has inserted itself so pervasively between the body and the external physical world."[16] Within this context film and digital media serve a specific function that is "to promote adaptation to our altered interface with the environment."[17]

Taking the theoretical framework of post-cinema into account, I can begin to justify the hyphenation "consumer-spectator." *Jurassic Park*'s strategy of commercial intertextuality and the dissolution of the boundaries between the representation and enaction of economic activity is built on a fundamental affordance of cinematic media and its inculcation of an attention economy. As Balides's argument suggests, there is no such thing as a neutral spectator of the *Jurassic Park* film text, the audience is always being addressed "as economic subjects ... as literal (not only semiotic) consumers."[18] The question is, to what extent does this address follow the trajectory of intensification and micromanagement brought about by the emergence of digital media?

In the following section I look at the ways in which the two films (and the respective gift shops) establish, after Jonathan Beller, a capitalist mise-en-scène, shaping human experience on behalf of capital. In doing so, I will begin to situate *Jurassic Park* as a text that highlights (and perhaps catalyzes) the incursion of digital technologies into the coextensive operations of visual media and capitalism.

Consumerism and Digital Visual Media

The gift shop scene of the original film endeavors to reproduce and valorize both the standard atmospherics of the gift shop (the soft lighting, the hushed ambience) and the upward reverential gaze of the child beholding the array of soft toys and pyjamas. What is more, in the context of the film's narrative these shots come as a respite, coming after the viscerally demanding scene in which the *T-Rex* chases down the jeep. As such, the two shots of the gift shop not only promote the visibility of certain items of merchandise but also entrench a fine-tuned structure of feeling surrounding the gift shop itself, as a place of refuge and respite. In this simple reading, the mise-en-scène of the gift shop contributes to a generalized mise-en-scène of escapist consumption. The sequence participates in an ideological framing of retail and, given the overlap between diegetic and real-world merchandising, establishes affective patterns associated with merchandise in the real world.

The capitalist mise-en-scène has grown increasingly complex since 1993, which is reflected in the complexity of the franchise's depictions of consumption. This is the case, in both the representation of the economic activity within the park (cf. the two gift shops and the range of restaurant franchises and ancillary industries populating the park), in the later *Jurassic World* and in its representation of looking at dinosaurs as a form of consumption. By way of example, actually looking at the dinosaurs is framed as an intensively mediatized and digitized event. When the boys, Zach and Grey, visit the aquarium and the *Mosasaurus* makes its first spectacular appearance, the crowd all lift their phones to film it. A reverse shot shows the boys's POV of the *Mosasaurus* and an array of phone screens filming the same scene. Just as the low-angle framing of the soft toys places the spectator in the mise-en-scène of early 1990s consumer economy, the plethora of screens puts the spectator firmly within the mise-en-scène of a contemporary attention economy.

The films don't just reflect dominant commercial structures, they are active participants in the ongoing articulation of consumer experience and new media products. This can be demonstrated through an examination of how the aesthetics of each film feeds into the capitalist mise-en-scène and surrounding extratextual economies. This occurs most acutely in the use of digital special effects. In this vein, Balides categorizes *Jurassic Park*'s action set pieces as "movie-ride scenes"[19] in which "the visceral sense of an amusement park ride becomes part of the attraction for the spectator."[20] Her essay (and subsequent discussions of VFX found in her essay "Virtual Spaces and Incorporative Logics: Contemporary Films as 'Mass Ornaments'")[21] devotes substantial time to drawing a homology between the "immersion effects" of turn-of-the-millennium VFX and the experience of theme park rides.[22] This homology suggests a feedback loop between the film's aesthetics and phenomena within the experiential economy of theme parks, the movie-ride scenes evoke rollercoaster rides and vice versa. Today there are several premium exhibition models, such as D3D, IMAX, 4DX, and ScreenX screening facilities, that transform the act of watching a film into an immersive experience. These special exhibition modes, with their inflated ticket prices, wouldn't function without the whiplash kinesthetics of the action sequences and that have become increasingly prevalent in tandem with the VFX-intensive blockbuster. Here, unlike Balides's example where the film aesthetically evokes the rollercoaster experience, big action films anticipate various forms of kinesthetic re-mediation, meaning that their specific aesthetics are a meaningful part of the economy of premium exhibition.

The specific technical and aesthetic connection between film aesthetics and extratextual economies that I'd like to explore involves the gyrosphere sequences of both *Jurassic World* and *Jurassic World: Fallen Kingdom* (Trevorrow, 2018) and the augmented- and virtual reality (AR and VR) offerings that accompanied both films at the time of their release.[23] In the first *Jurassic World* the two boys, Zach and Gray, ride in a gyrosphere as part of their safe and successful experience of the park. These gyrosphere sequences evoke and model a mode of VR spectatorship that is fully exploited in the range of VR products associated with the film. This is evident in the basic design of the vehicles themselves. They require the boys to be strapped into their seats, the movement of the gyrosphere is controlled by a single joystick and the boys must crane their necks and move their heads in order to look around. It could be argued that, in the context of all the speculative technologies that make up the world of Jurassic World (like the holograms in the Innovation Centre, of which more later), the gyrospheres are largely redundant. Surely, the (limited) embodied experience offered by the gyrosphere could easily be simulated by a VR headset. But ultimately, that's part of the point. This overlapping of the gyrosphere experience and the affordances of real-world VR technologies is accentuated by the smooth cinematography. The tilts and pans of the camera, supposedly motivated by the appearance of a dinosaur overhead, strongly evoke the experience of moving through a VR environment. For example, the mechanics and visuals of VR game *Jurassic World: Aftermath* (2019) bears a striking resemblance to the flow of the gryosphere sequences. In the game, our perspective is kept low to the ground in order to justify a plethora of visual lures up and away from our horizontal visual axis, and movement through space is smooth, as if the character is rolling rather than walking. Here, then, the commercial intertextuality of the film is not limited to the doubling of diegetic and real-world merchandise, or even the construction of a mise-en-scène harmonious with the complexities of the attention economy. The gyrosphere sequences operate within the aesthetic affordances of adjacent media economies and, in so doing, presuppose the spectator as a consumer of VR and AR digital media. In the words of Roger F. Cook, this cross-platform, trans-media dialectic of technical and aesthetic characteristics serves to "promote adaptation" to the capitalist mise-en-scène in which VR and AR digital media represents a significant emergent market. This is continued elsewhere in the franchise, the opening sequence of animated series *Jurassic World: Camp Cretaceous* (2020) consists of the protagonist's POV as he plays a VR *Jurassic World* game, confirming the franchise's investment in VR exhibition modes and further articulating what a VR dinosaur experience might look like within the real digital media economy.

Having established that the visual language of the films anticipate certain phenomenological characteristics prevalent outside of the cinema, in the consumer economy of gift shops, theme parks, and VR, it remains to confirm how this imbrication of film text and economic function intensifies in line with the escalation of VFX and digital media. There are two angles to employ at this point. The first concerns the way in which digital media and VFX in mainstream cinema are part of a broader digital media industry, operating principally in the visual field. Leon Gurevitch's work focuses on the increasing financialization of the cinematic image in the era of CGI and can help illuminate the way in which the use of VFX and computer-animation in cinema operates outside the narrative, in a manner akin to product placement.[24]

Gurevitch's work points to the shared digital technologies that underpin a range of industries, from automobile and architectural design and manufacture, to computer-animation pipelines and VFX postproduction.[25] For example, Gurevitch notes that the toys we see on screen in the *Toy Story* films (1995–2019) "are not simply images, they are industrial simulations" given that the digital models built in computer-animation production can serve as digital prototypes within the manufacturing process. Thus, what we see on screen are not just characters in a story, they are manufacturing blueprints in which "size, structural integrity, aerodynamics and material construction are all worked out and dependent upon each other in a myriad of complexly interrelated computer algorithms."[26] This is a form of product placement. Only here, the image precedes the product.

The same goes for the software that generates the image, which is a product in and of itself. Gurevitch argues that within the digital media regime "the distinction between the object, the image and the advertising image through which imaged and actual objects gain meaning is considerably reduced if not removed completely."[27] Given the cross-industry applicability of software this implies that every appearance of a digital asset within the film is, in essence, an advertisement for the software that produced it. This is an interlinking of aesthetics and economics that has precedents in, for example, Technicolor's policing of its aesthetic uses, through Natalie Kalmus and her Technicolor Color Advisory Service, which consulted on color design on more than 400 films throughout the middle of the century, in order to optimize Technicolor's dominance within the film industry and (profitably) shape the popular conception of what color on film should look like.[28.] This interlinking of aesthetics and the economies of filmmaking is of particular relevance to the emergence of digital visual media in *Jurassic Park*. Very literally, the computers and the software that runs on them, both of which feature prominently throughout the film, can be viewed as pieces of merchandise that the film is advertising through its aesthetic strategies. When Lex locks the doors against an angry *Velociraptor*, the computers she uses are branded Silicon Graphics, Inc. machines. This is the same hardware on which the digital imaging software used by Industrial Light and Magic was run in order to build, rig, animate, and render the digital effects that are the hallmark of the film. Not only that, but according to Jacob Gaboury, an employee handbook from Silicon Graphics, Inc. boasted that all the software seen running on those machines throughout the film belonged to real-world applications.[29] The line between image and advertising image disappears, and the image of a dinosaur becomes an advert for computing hardware and software that, in turn, is prominently advertised in the film. Thus, the digital asset of the *T-Rex* operates not just as a narrative element but opens up a new vector of commercial intertextuality, demonstrating the affordances of Silicon Graphics machines and guaranteeing the centrality of that company to mainstream visual culture. Gaboury illustrates this point in an aside that notes "from 1995 to 2002, all films nominated for an Academy Award for Distinguished Achievement in Visual Effects were created on SGI computer systems."[30]

Post-Cinematic Consumer-Spectators

Embracing the full media-epistemological scope outlined earlier in this chapter the question for this final section is: how are digital effects involved in the articulation of a form of consumer-spectatorship commensurate to the new demands brought about by digital capitalism? Do the effects of 1993 and 2015 answer the question "how does the subject inhabit this new space and time?" posed by more recent iterations of capitalism?

Eric Jenkins's book *Special Affect* deals directly with the relationship between new media and modes of consumption starting from the premise that "a consumer boom seems to accompany the emergence of every new communication medium, as the alterations of perceptual capacities transform into habits that subsequently become the source of economic value."[31] Jenkins charts this transformation from new communication medium to new consumer boom in the following way:

> By making new modes available, media create the potential for new affections, affections that, when habituated result in newly perceivable consumers, newly articulable commodities, and new translations of consumerist ideology. In short, there is a fundamental connection between media and consumerism because media enable new modes of affection, and affection underwrites both the desire to consume and the translation of those desires into consumerist ideology.[32]

Using this framework allows us to trace a path from the novel use of hybrid images in *Jurassic Park*, to their ubiquity in *Jurassic World* as an evolution in the new media of digital visual technology and connect this

FIGURE 4.1 Jurassic World *(2015): Innovation Centre Hologram (DVD, Screengrab)*

path to a similar evolution in modes of consumerism. The intensification of the films' "commercial intertextuality" is connected to the intensification of certain aesthetic strategies within the film that "alter perceptual capacities" and generate new epistemological habits that are then translated into consumer ideologies. The task of this final piece of analysis, then, is to connect the nascent techniques of *Jurassic Park* to their mature iterations in *Jurassic World* and suggest the ways in which this aesthetic evolution is intertwined with the variegated evolutions that have taken place in the socioeconomic field, with the emergence of digital media, digital capitalism, and their impact on modes of spectatorship and subjectivity.

One detail that encapsulates the emergence of digital media and digital capitalism both within and beyond the world of the franchise is the hologram that dominates the atrium of the Innovation Centre in *Jurassic World* (Figure 4.1). This image is emblematic of several things, first it demonstrates the degree to which the aesthetic affordances of compositing a CGI dinosaur within a cinematographic environment have evolved since 1993 (Figure 4.2). Second, the hologram exemplifies the relation of intensification between the two films making my analysis of the 2015 film, by necessity, an analysis of elements and dynamics germane to the original. Last, in its ostentatious, yet narratively marginal, deployment of compositing, it demonstrates the degree to which hybrid procedures such as digital compositing are becoming invisible within visual culture by merit of sheer ubiquity.

The first encounter with the hologram occurs when the boys meet up with Claire. The establishing shot sketches a busy multimedia environment: kids dig up an enormous fossil, there are video presentations and interactive

FIGURE 4.2 Jurassic Park's T-Rex *brings down the house (1993) (DVD, Screengrab)*

displays. In the middle of this space is a vast hologram of a dinosaur that circles around as the characters talk. This combination of the ostentatious presence of the effect and its supposed neutrality within the environment, the indifference with which it is treated by the characters within the story, is telling. It denotes many things about the ubiquity of hybrid images and the growing instrumentality of the aesthetics brought about by hybridity within a range of economic operations. The effects that were so pioneering in 1993 are now so naturalized as to be boring, just as in the *Jurassic World* narrative the park needs to keep on creating bigger, scarier dinosaurs in order to drive profits.

Tackling first the dual issue of the character's seeming indifference to the huge hologram, and the audience's own indifference to the ubiquitous phenomena of digital compositing, what is striking (and comic) in this scene is the way the enormous hologram is largely ignored. Holographic depictions of enormous dinosaurs are presented, within the diegesis, as if they were totally naturalized and neutral elements within a multimedia environment. Claire's line from an earlier scene, that "no one is impressed by dinosaurs anymore," is equally applicable to the huge holograms. This happy tolerance of the massive holograms within the diegesis models a consumer experience where the principal commodities (dinosaurs) are mediated in such a vast array of competing ways that a hovering, shimmering, giant hologram is barely worthy of attention. This reflects the success of the films' strategies of commercial intertextuality as it envisions the saturation of the environment with dino-related *Jurassic World* branded content. As such, the

Jurassic World hologram is of a piece with the ever-present holograms in, for example, *Ghost in the Shell* (Rupert Sanders, 2017) and *Blade Runner 2048* (Denis Villeneuve, 2017), but without a hint of their dystopian bite. The Innovation Centre is a microcosm of the wider commercial environment in which we, the audience live: like visitors to *Jurassic World* we must become experts at studiously ignoring the constant rush of branded content that floods our field of vision.

On a more technical level, the reason why the characters don't pay any attention to the hologram of the dinosaur is because it was never there in the first place and has been composited into the footage of actors delivering lines for the camera. It is a quintessential example of what Lev Manovich, in his early discussion of compositing, describes as "ontological montage."[33] It follows that any interplay of the effect and profilmic performance, or in this case the pointed lack of interaction between the two elements, foregrounds the technical operation that brought the two ontologically distinct elements within the image into a coherent diegetic space. In this light, the hologram effect is a reflexive illusion celebrating itself as a technical achievement. As such, it is automatically a piece of commercial intertextuality as it foregrounds the affordances of compositing software and demonstrates the fungibility of digital assets.

Indeed, the simulation of a hologram of a simulated dinosaur confirms Gurevitch's core contention that the "the CG attraction is a single currency that acts as legal tender in multiple audiovisual economies."[34] The hologram represents the apotheosis of practices of unlimited remediation of digital dinosaurs that is at the core of the franchises' strategy of commercial intertextuality. It dissolves any meaningful parameters on the remediation of dinosaurs as a digital commodity. This is operative both within the diegesis, where dinosaurs occur as living creatures, holograms, and branding, and in the visual culture that surrounds the film, where digital dinosaurs proliferate. To demonstrate this, in the run-up to 2021 COP 26 meeting in Glasgow, the United Nations Development Programme released a video in which a digitally animated dinosaur addressed the UN, exhorting the world "Don't Choose Extinction." In 2015 an advert featuring a depressed *T-Rex* discovering Pilot Driving in an Audi was used to sell cars. The hologram, the UN dinosaur, and Audi's *T-Rex* are the visual and cultural manifestation of a common technological and economic culture in which digital assets of computer-animation can be instrumentalized in the service of often conflicting agendas. Looking past the dinosaurs, however, it is important to note that within visual media the pervasiveness of digital dinosaurs is greatly exceeded by the pervasiveness of the hybrid techniques and procedures that underpin the effect. And it is these procedures, and not the appearance of dinosaurs, that have the greatest impact on our sense of "situatedness" in digital capitalism.

The representation of the holographic dinosaur manifests the degree to which hybrid image procedures have become normalized and—after Eric

Jenkins—are making visible a new set of consumer desires. The hologram, its naturalization within the diegesis, and its legibility to audiences well-used to digital compositing, makes explicit the way in which digital manipulation of live-action cinematography is bringing about "alterations of perceptual capacities [that] transform into habits that subsequently become the source of economic value."[35] To speculate, the habits of spatial perception engendered by digital compositing are transforming into sources of economic value in, for example, the field of AR where ocular spatial experience is supplemented with an informational overlay, composited into the visual field in real time. At the very least, the *Jurassic World* hologram, and by implication the basic compositing of *Jurassic Park*, is operating as what David Kirby termed a "diegetic prototype,"[36] in that it is imagining a form of supersaturated space, where the advertising image has migrated away from screens and has become fully integrated into the 3D physical space. This is why the Innovation Centre, despite a few sci-fi details, strongly resembles the hybrid physical-digital commercial environments we experience today. While holograms remain firmly in the realm of science fiction, what is being diegetically prototyped is the way in which spectator-consumers occupy supersaturated and mediatized spaces. Our neutral acceptance of the presence of the hologram evidences our ongoing adaptation to the augmentation of our physical environments by digital technologies. This naturalization of compositing effects, the ubiquity of digitally interpellated spaces, is symptomatic of a new relation to physical space brought about by increasingly incursive digital media. Compositing is everywhere, not just big budget film, it is a core part of social media photography and AR and VR, a central operation within today's experience of physical-digital situatedness. In directly reflecting on the legacy of *Jurassic Park*, the compositing that enabled the appearance of CGI dinosaurs in the original film lies deep within the genealogy of many characteristic features not only of contemporary visual culture but of contemporary digital capitalism as it operates within and through the visual field.

This chapter has argued that a productive way of analyzing the strategies of "commercial intertextuality" that occur in both *Jurassic Park* and *Jurassic World* is as a process of intensification. This is an intensification of the aesthetics of the films, as well as their economic operativity. Onscreen, this intensification is instantly visible in the density and integration of merchandising lines within the diegesis, the range of commercial tie-ins and integration within promotional culture both inside and outside of the narrative. This intensification is also present in the density of VFX and hybrid image techniques. The task of this chapter has been to demonstrate the ways in which these processes of intensification are interrelated. Beyond product placement, I have examined the ways in which the visibility of digital assets played into the explosion of digital visual media industries in which the digital asset, and its fungibility across narratives and platforms, inflected the operations of the consumer economy. I also showed how the affordances of digital media fine-tune the way in which the films address the audience as consumer-spectators embedded in a larger socioeconomic field. However, the lasting and most significant legacy of *Jurassic Park*, to my mind, is the way in which it inaugurated an era in which digital capitalism and visual media became increasingly and inextricably cooperative, especially in the way in which visual culture exerts an epistemic pressure on spectators on behalf of capitalism. As such, any examination of capital-intensive visual culture today, wherein the aesthetics of mainstream cinema can be perceived as economically operative, must gain coherence from a perspective incorporating the original innovations of *Jurassic Park*.

Notes

1. Don Shay and Jody Duncan, *The Making of Jurassic Park* (London: Boxtree, 1993).
2. Constance Balides, "Jurassic Post-Fordism: Tall Tales of Economics in the Theme Park," *Screen* 41:2 (2000): 142.
3. Ibid., 142.
4. Ibid., 154.
5. Andrew Wernick, *Promotional Culture: Advertising, Ideology and Symbolic Expression* (London: Sage, 1991).
6. Balides, "Jurassic Post-Fordism," 141.
7. Mary Ann Doane, *The Emergence of Cinematic Time: Modernity, Contingency, the Archive* (London: Harvard University Press, 2002).
8. Jonathan Beller, *The Cinematic Mode of Production: Attention Economy and the Society of the Spectacle* (Lebanon, NH: Dartmouth University Press, 2006).
9. Doane, *The Emergence of Cinematic Time*, 23.
10. Beller, *Cinematic Mode of Production*, 3.
11. Jonathon Beller, "Wagers within the Image: Rise of Visuality, Transfomation of Labour, Aesthetic Regimes," *Culture Machines* 13 (2012): 5.
12. Beller, *Cinematic Mode of Production*, 27.
13. Steven Shaviro, *Post-Cinematic Affect* (London: Zero Books, 2010).
14. Roger F. Cook, *Post-Cinematic Vision: The Coevolution of Moving-Image Media and the Spectator* (Minneapolis: University of Minnesota Press, 2020).
15. Shaviro, *Post-Cinematic Affect*, 7.
16. Cook, *Post-Cinematic Vision*, 204.
17. Ibid.
18. Balides, "Jurassic Post-Fordism," 154.
19. Ibid., 152.

20 Ibid., 144.
21 Constance Balides, "Virtual Spaces and Incorporative Logics: Contemporary Film as 'Mass Ornaments'" *MIT Communications Forum*. http://web.mit.edu/comm-forum/legacy/papers/balides.html. 2000.
22 Balides, "Jurassic Post-Fordism," 147.
23 Cf. *Jurassic World Alive* (Universal: Ludia Inc., 2018), *Jurassic World: Aftermath* (Oculus Studios; Coatsink Software, 2020).
24 Cf. Leon Gurevitch, "From Edison to Pixar: The Spectacular Screen and the Attention Economy from Celluloid to CG," *Continuum: Journal of Media & Cultural Studies* 29:3 (2015): 445–65; Leon Gurevitch, "The Cinemas of Transactions: The Exchangeable Currency of the Digital Attraction," *Television & New Media* 11:5 (2010): 357–86.
25 Leon Gurevitch, "Cinema Designed: Visual Effects Software and the Emergence of the Engineered Spectacle," in Denson and Leyda (eds.) *Post-Cinema: Theorizing 21st-Century Film* (Falmer, Brighton: Reframe Books, 2016).
26 Leon Gurevitch, "Computer Generated Animation as Product Design Engineered Culture or Buzz Lightyear to the Sales Floor, to the Checkout and Beyond!," *Animation* 7, no. 2: (2012) 131–49, 40.
27 Ibid., 144–5.
28 Scott Higgins, *Harnessing the Technicolor Rainbow: Color Design in the 1930s* (Austin: University of Texas Press).
29 Jacob Gaboury, *Image Objects: An Archaeology of Computer Graphics* (Cambridge, MA: MIT Press, 2021), 253, fn 69.
30 Ibid., 184.
31 Eric Jenkins, *Special Affect: Cimema, Animation and the Translation of Consumer Culture* (Edinburgh: EUP, 2014), 1.
32 Ibid., 13.
33 Lev Manovich, *The Language of New Media* (Cambridge, MA: MIT Press, 2001), 159.
34 Leon Gurevitch, "The Cinemas of Transactions," 359.
35 Jenkins, *Special Affect*, 13.
36 David Kirby, "The Future Is Now: Diegetic Prototypes and the Role of Popular Films in Generating Real-World Technological Development," *Social Studies of Science* 40:1 (2010): 41–70.

5

Jurassic Park and Dinosaur Fandom

Ross Garner
Cardiff University, UK

Introduction

The contributions that *Jurassic Park* fans can make to exploring debates within fan and audience studies is a topic that has received little critical attention. This is surprising given that *Box Office Mojo* lists the franchise as the twelfth most profitable of all time, with the films across the series cumulatively grossing US$1.9 billion in North America alone.[1] Whereas other high-revenue and high-profile IPs such as *Star Wars* and *Harry Potter* have had myriad articles, book chapters, and collections dedicated to examining the contours of their fan communities and practices, *Jurassic Park* fandom has instead been overlooked. In the place of empirical research into *Jurassic Park* fans there only exists speculation about the interests and identities of these communities. For example, José Luis Sanz has argued that "*Jurassic Park* (1993) and its sequels, *The Lost World: Jurassic Park* (1997) and *Jurassic Park III* (2001) have generated a great deal of dinosaur mania, or "dinomania," in recent years."[2] Despite lacking evidence to support these claims, Sanz nevertheless raises another question about *Jurassic Park* fans by implying that the franchise's primary appeal concerns its prehistoric inhabitants.

This assumption has certainly been reinforced at the paratextual level of marketing. The franchise's iconic logo depicting the silhouette of a *T-Rex* skeleton against a bloodred backdrop showcases the continual importance of dinosaurs in providing brand distinction. These strategies—evident of what Justin Wyatt named high concept cinema—have also extended to licensing and merchandising contexts—both historically and at present—as imagery of rampaging *Tyrannosauruses* and *Velociraptors* has dominated product lines from action figures, to apparel, posters, and beyond.[3] How important, though, are *Jurassic Park*'s dinosaurs to its fans? In what ways are the franchise's dinosaurian representations rendered significant to the franchise's appeal? This chapter addresses these questions by presenting the results of an online survey into *Jurassic Park* fandom and so highlights both the demographic and affective contours of this community pertaining to dinosaurian representations. By doing so, arguments are made in favor of the continuing use of Laurence Grossberg's approach to fan affect as a platform from which theories of fan attachments and identities can be constructed.

Methodology

This chapter analyzes fan responses to an online survey into the meanings afforded to the dinosaurs as part of the *Jurassic Park* franchise and how the creatures' significance compares to and intersects with other aspects of the property. The questionnaire consisted of sixteen questions and included both closed-ended quantitative and open-ended qualitative requests; the former focused on obtaining data concerning the profile of survey respondents, whereas the latter invited detailed discussions of *Jurassic Park*–related preferences and consumption habits. In line with best practice, ethical clearance for the questionnaire was obtained from the Ethics Committee of Cardiff University's School of Journalism, Media and Culture.[4] The survey was hosted by Google Forms and available for a four-week period from mid-November to mid-December 2021.

The form was primarily distributed through Twitter under the hashtags #JurassicPark, #JurassicWorld, #dinosaurs, #paleontology, #naturalhistory, and, on the relevant day of the week, #FossilFriday. These popular hashtags were selected to attract respondents and encourage retweets. Additionally, prominent fan accounts including Jurassic Outpost (@JurassicOutpost—48.5k followers), *Jurassic Park* Podcast (@JurassicParkPod—approx. 9.5k followers), Collect Jurassic (@CollectJurassic—approx. 8.5k followers), and Jurassic Cast Podcast (@JurassicCast—approx. 6.8k followers) were directly asked to retweet the survey link. Only *Jurassic Park* Podcast obliged, but this led to the survey gaining attention from another fan-produced podcast, Jurassic Unicast (@JurassicUnicast—approx. 1.5k followers), which subsequently retweeted the link to their followers. The survey was also posted on my personal Facebook account as well as in academic groups run by the UK Fan Studies Network and the US-based Society for Cinema and

Media Studies (SCMS) Fan and Audience Studies Scholarly Interest Group to boost circulation. Consent was also obtained from the administrators of the closed *Jurassic Park* fan group on Facebook (which has 42.4k members) to post the survey link, with the request garnering positive reactions and responses from members.

In total, the survey generated 117 valid responses. This sample size might seem small given *Jurassic Park*'s popularity; the official *Jurassic World* page on Facebook, for example, has 8.7 million "likes." However, as Mario Cardano argues, within qualitative research, "the aim of representativeness is replaced by that of eloquence," where "eloquent means a sample composed of information-rich cases."[5] The survey's respondents thus represent what Janice Morse names "'excellent' participants."[6] These are fans who are "enunciatively active" and so prepared to act as representatives of the wider community's interests by actively sharing both knowledge of and enthusiasm for *Jurassic Park* (albeit within the distribution constraints outlined above and additional factors inhibiting participation addressed in the next section).[7] All responses were analyzed using the qualitative coding software NVivo, where responses to individual questions were scrutinized thematically to identify recurring clusters of meaning.

Jurassic Park Demographics: Profiling Survey Respondents

The age of survey respondents was primarily split between those aged 25–34 (41 percent) and 35–49 (38.5 percent). The remainder of participants fell in the 18–24 bracket (14.5 percent) with only 6 percent occupying the 50–69 group. This demographic information is significant when correlated with data concerning how respondents first encountered the franchise. Of the respondents, 97.4 percent identified the original *Jurassic Park* film as the first of the movies that they'd seen, with 46.2 percent having first seen it through home media and 42.7 percent within the cinema (this category included anniversary rereleases and special one-off screenings). An image of the respondents subsequently emerges where the dominant profile is either of growing up, reaching maturity, or being born during the 1990s. This is when the original movie was released in theaters, achieved popular culture ubiquity, and became available in the home for (re-)consumption through platforms including television broadcasts, VHS, and, latterly, DVD. In combination, the data alludes to the commercial, historical, and technological factors enabling *Jurassic Park* to remain visible throughout respondents' lives, and so become a locus for experiencing affect. As returned to shortly, such affective responses are important to how both the franchise itself and its dinosaurian representations have remained meaningful for fans.

Delving further into the identity of survey respondents, most identified as white (73 percent), cisgender-heterosexuals (63 percent), and were living in the Global North (36 percent were based in the United States, 27 percent in countries that make up the UK, and 19 percent in countries that are part of the European Union). Highlighting these markers is important. As Rukmini Pande argues, the "normative fan identity" that is constructed by fan studies scholars is almost always characterized by an unquestioned assumption that that identity is "US or UK-centric ... white, [and] cisgender."[8] Failure to either reflect upon or disclose these biases reinforces fan studies' "glaring whiteness" and so reasserts hegemonic power structures including Western-centrism, heteronormativity, and white privilege.[9] Recognizing these concerns, it must be noted that this chapter's arguments concerning *Jurassic Park* fans are limited to "excellent individuals" who overwhelmingly occupy intersecting hegemonic identity positions—especially in terms of race and geographical location—and so are primarily the perspectives of white, Western fans.

The survey's embedding within preexisting networks of hegemony is also reflected at a linguistic level. That is, the survey was only available in English, meaning that responses from non-Anglophone *Jurassic Park* fans were not able to be collected. These limitations further point to the need for additional research into the meanings and significance of the *Jurassic Park* franchise among non-Western, and non-hegemonically positioned, fans. This need is especially prominent in the case of studying popular meanings of dinosaurs for two reasons. First, preceding scholars have suggested that an interest in the Mesozoic period and its inhabitants is tied to Western and/or Americanized identities.[10] This is largely due to the enduring tradition of colonial adventure narratives and ideologies of frontier exploration initiated by novels like *The Lost World* (Conan-Doyle, 1998 [1912]), and then popularized further by films including *King Kong* (1933) within these territories (also Noble, 2016).[11] Second, given the upsurge in dinosaur fossils found in China and Mongolia in recent years, addressing non-Western attitudes toward *Jurassic Park* and its prehistoric inhabitants would make an interesting counterpoint to this chapter's arguments.[12]

One noteworthy trend among survey respondents concerned the sample's gendered make-up. Although most participants identified as men (52 percent of respondents), 42 percent of respondents identified as women, with the remaining 6 percent of respondents identifying as either non-binary or preferring not to comment. That women made up over one-third of the sample size challenges existing assumptions concerning gendered interests in dinosaurs. W. J. T. Mitchell glibly speculated that the profile of adult dinosaur fans is "romantic boys who never outgrew their dinomania."[13] While recent popular publications on adult dinosaur fandom do little to dislodge these gendered suppositions,[14] the tone of his discourse nevertheless aligns an interest in dinosaurs beyond childhood with the infantilized and stunted masculinities associated with long-standing stereotypes of white, male adult fans.[15]

Contrasting with Mitchell's assumption, thirty-four of the forty-nine women respondents explicitly named dinosaurs—whether generally or by naming specific species—among their favorite franchise elements. The correlation of dinosaurs as significant to how and why *Jurassic Park* appeals to women is especially interesting in that a total of 66 of the survey's 117 respondents explicitly named dinosaurs as part of what interests them in the franchise, suggesting that the franchise's dinosaurian representations are of *greatest* significance to female-identifying adult fans. A high percentage of interest in *Jurassic Park* among women is not surprising in and of itself as texts with science fiction underpinnings have long attracted significant numbers of female fans.[16] Additionally, fan communities centered around contemporary commercial media IPs often demonstrate high levels of women participants: as Suzanne Scott has demonstrated, it is often the case that these fans are either subculturally and/or industrially marginalized in comparison with their male counterparts.[17] Nevertheless, the data collected indicate that more feminist-oriented inquiries into *Jurassic Park* and "dinosaur fandom" are also required.

Jurassic Park Investments: Dinosaurs, Mattering Maps and Fan Preferences

As previously discussed, when respondents were asked about their favorite elements of the *Jurassic Park* franchise, the term "dinosaurs" featured in 66 of the 117 answers, meaning that these were the most frequently mentioned aspect. Some stated that "Dinosaurs" (Respondents 17, 45, and 94), "The dinosaurs" (Respondents 33 and 70), "Definitely the dinosaurs" (Respondent 56) or "Simply the dinosaurs" (Respondent 87) were their sole favorite franchise elements. However, others listed the creatures alongside additional characters and themes and so provided lists of their various interests:

Velociraptors, Ellie Sattler, and Ian Malcolm
(Respondent 112)

> The dinosaurs
> The themes of science & nature v. Capitalism

Stylistic choices (e.g. how Spielberg evokes Hitchcock in the *T. rex* paddock breakout scene)

> The original film's dedication to portraying up-to-date palaeontology

> They're generally good action films
> Park and vehicle designs
> Iconic characters
>
> How the original film essentially ushered in this current era of filmmaking (for all its good and bad)
>
> Watch-ability: I could sit down and watch any of them start to finish and enjoy myself
>
> JP and TLW's dedication to portraying dinosaurs as animals rather than monsters (Respondent 63)
>
> Dinosaurs!
> Animatronics,
> Story,
> Owen,
> Music,
>
> Dinosaurs! (Respondent 97)

The use of exclamation marks, as well as the repetition of "dinosaurs!" in the final list, connotes a playful-yet-strong desire to communicate enthusiasm for *Jurassic Park*'s prehistoric inhabitants. Yet, these lists are also significant as they exemplify Laurence Grossberg's concept of "Mattering Maps."[18] For Grossberg, "mattering maps are like investment portfolios" in that by listing either favorite media properties, or identifying specific elements of these, individual fans demonstrate the aspects to which they have formed affective attachments to from the range of available cultural resources at specific points in time.[19] As Grossberg offers, "affect plays a crucial role in organizing social life because affect is constantly constructing, not only the possibility of difference, but the ways specific differences come to matter."[20] Beyond choosing to affectively "invest" in *Jurassic Park* per se, the lists' recurrent positioning of dinosaurs as reasons why *Jurassic Park* matters to respondents suggests a correlation between interest in the films and in representations of dinosaurs and, albeit tentatively, intersections between *Jurassic Park* fandom and dinosaur fandom.

What is useful about Grossberg's concept, though, is that it recognizes that the elements of media properties that resonate with fans are structured within processes of commercial culture:

> For the fan, popular culture becomes a crucial ground on which he or she can construct mattering maps. Within these mattering maps, investments are enabled which empower individuals in a variety of ways. They may construct relatively stable moments of identity, or they may identify places which, because they matter, take on an authority of their own ...

By making certain things or practices matter, the fan "authorizes" them to speak for him or her, not only as a spokesperson but also as surrogate voices (as when we sing along to popular songs).[21]

Some respondents demonstrated Grossberg's position on commercial structures when discussing *Jurassic Park*'s dinosaurs by mentioning the *T-Rex* as their favorite species due to its continued use in high-concept branding strategies. Respondent 30 stated that "the T-rex has a special place within the franchise being the mascot of the series" while Respondent 2 identified that they favored *Tyrannosaurus* "as it is an emblem of the series and appears in all of the films, it has been my favorite since I was young." In these instances, the surveyed fans demonstrated their embedding in processes of commodification by using *Jurassic Park* and its dinosaurs as important parts of commercial media culture that they invest for constructing and communicating their identity. More than this, the franchise's extra-diegetic marketing and branding practices have extended into broader expressions of dinosaur fandom in terms of selecting a favorite species because of its recurrent use in the franchise's public image. Although these fans are demonstrating agency by selecting first from the range of commercial IPs offered by the culture industries, and then prioritizing certain (dinosaurian) elements of the *Jurassic Park* franchise over others, they also demonstrate how *Jurassic Park*'s corporate and brand identity comes to impact upon their preferences for prehistoric content.

Although Grossberg's concept of "mattering maps" can account for why individual fans identify *Jurassic Park*'s dinosaurs *as* significant, these positions cannot tell us *how* these depictions matter. Addressing this issue requires shifting register to instead focus on theories of emotions. Whereas Grossberg argues that affect "is what gives 'color,' 'tone' or 'texture' to our experiences," emotions have been contrastingly understood as operating at an alternative, less internalized, level.[22] Stefanie Armbruster argues that whereas affect constitutes generalized bodily experiences, emotional responses are shared, social, and "characterised by high affect intensity, shorter duration, and a higher directedness towards an object or a certain circumstance."[23] Among survey respondents, a large part of how *Jurassic Park*'s dinosaurs mattered to fans concerned their ability to evoke emotion-infused memories concerning childhood:

> As a child it was awesome to see these dinosaurs come to life on the big screen. I was already very fascinated by dinosaurs that [sic] & 9 years old at the time when JP came into theatres. I remember having to convince my mother to see it. (Respondent 107)
>
> The dinosaurs in the original film really caught my imagination as a child, the raptors in particular. I also enjoyed the sense of fun and the amusing moments. (Respondent 42)

The emotions articulated here are multilayered. Nevertheless, since each is partly characterized by "a bittersweet longing for former times and spaces" directed toward seeing both the movie and its dinosaurian representations for the first time, they suggest that nostalgia forms a key part of why *Jurassic Park*'s dinosaurs were, and continue to be, important.[24] In each response, what Annette Kuhn names a "past/present register" in relation to cinematic memory, where "informants ... shift or 'shuttle' back and forth between past and present standpoints," is employed toward how representations of the dinosaurian in *Jurassic Park* are assigned significance.[25] The way that this register is used can be analyzed further to demonstrate the level at which dinosaurs matter to respondents and how this coding of nostalgic remembrance occurs. For example, in both above responses, a past/present register is used to remember not only the emotions that were stirred by seeing prehistoric creatures on screen, but also the familial and generational contexts within which the film was consumed.[26] These expressions of nostalgia therefore represent what Ed S. Tan names "artefact emotions" as memories of seeing dinosaurs onscreen provoke nostalgia for the creatures alongside the feelings cued by remembering seeing *Jurassic Park* for the first time.[27]

In contrast, an alternative inflection of the "past/present register," which demonstrates greater complexity in terms of how "past" and "present" are shuttled between, is evident in the following response:

> When I was a child, it was the dinosaurs. I lived in New York City, I already loved the dinosaur exhibits at the Museum of Natural History, and ... that moment of wonder, when the dinosaurs in Jurassic Park first come into Dr. Grant and Dr. Sattler's view, and their awe is palpable? That's how I felt about dinosaurs, even before the movie. And I think I loved Jurassic Park for making other people feel that, even for a moment. (Respondent 4)

In this instance, contextual memories of a "past" fan identity are identifiable, but these exist alongside nostalgia being directed toward *Jurassic Park*'s dinosaurs at a diegetic level. The respondent's nostalgic memory of seeing dinosaurs onscreen thus represents a "fiction emotion" as the feelings remembered are "rooted in the fictional world and the concerns addressed by that world."[28] In other words, it is processes of identifying with and mirroring the emotions that are expressed by the characters onscreen and directed toward the dinosaurs that provoke greater nostalgia for this respondent. Dinosaurian representations and nostalgia are intertwined with both memories of the self *and* with their status as creatures resurrected into the "present" in this instance, suggesting that links between dinosaur fandom and nostalgia among *Jurassic Park* fans can intertwine textual and extratextual levels.

Alongside being loci for nostalgia, respondents discussed the significance of *Jurassic Park*'s dinosaurs through employing what I would call a "zoological disposition." This involved adopting a detached, observational, and arguably scientifically indebted discourse through which to express the importance of dinosaurs. For example, one respondent afforded significance to "the dinosaurs and seeing them move naturally in their environment" (Respondent 68) while another stated that "the parts where you see the dinosaurs living peacefully when they are free" (Respondent 5) were their favorite scenes from the movies. Elsewhere, other respondents expressed preferences for seeing "the little intricacies of the dinosaurs' behaviour" (Respondent 62) or enjoying "the depiction of some of the dinosaurs in the wilderness, which allows us to imagine how they might have lived" (Respondent 59). Preferences for these sequences recall arguments concerning the aesthetics of natural history programming where viewers are invited to "'take in' the spectacle of the beauty of the natural world without becoming so overwhelmed or absorbed in it that we lose our senses."[29] In the case of the *Jurassic Park* films, moments where audiences adopt a zoological disposition temporarily take audiences out of the movie's dominant action codings to instead consider the dinosaurs as objects of scientific interest and inquiry.

The preferences expressed by fans for these calmer, more reflective sequences is interesting as they are never more than momentary pauses within *Jurassic Park* films. Scenes such as Drs. Grant and Sattler (Sam Neill and Laura Dern, respectively) observing the *Brachiosaurus* "moving in herds," or the short sequence in *Jurassic World* where patrons are seen undertaking leisure activities such as kayaking alongside species such as *Stegosaurus* and *Apatosaurus* are by no means normative narrative beats of a *Jurassic Park* movie. These moments instead stand in contrast to dominant and widely established perceptions of the movies as loud, expensive, and special effects–dependent set piece-driven blockbusters.[30] These preferences nevertheless dovetail with others offered by another survey respondent, which did not explicitly mention dinosaurs but implied their significance by expressing a preference for moments exploring the "hyperdiegesis," or "vast and detailed narrative space, only a fraction of which is ever directly seen or encountered within the text,"[31] of the park's spaces while operational:

> I've seen all the movies, but if I were to pinpoint one moment or aspect of "why": my level of excitement and anticipation of Jurassic World. I was beyond excited before Jurassic World was released. I saw it at the cinema three times, even though, when I rewatched it this year, I see so many flaws. I love the energy of, especially, Jurassic Park and Jurassic World. I love the idea of the park and the way the fiction of it has been brought to life. I love the scene in Jurassic World when the doors to the park open for the first time and you can finally see what it was "supposed" to look

like, only to later see why it never should have actually become reality and how people playing God and not learning from past events will result in disaster. There is also an element of nostalgia for, I reckon, a lot of people in the audience who saw Jurassic Park when it first came out or who, like me, grew up with it. (Respondent 72)

To date, moments of showcasing the park have not been provided in any *Jurassic Park* or *Jurassic World* films. Instead, the films have been driven by action-oriented scenarios of escaped dinosaurs that characterize the prehistoric creatures as antagonists and so outside of the zoological disposition that some respondents prefer. These readings of *Jurassic Park*'s dinosaurian representations occurred alongside those of other fans who aligned themselves more with the film's popular and marketing discourses and so afforded dinosaurs significance through discourses of action and antagonism. Fans adopting this position stated that "there's also simply enjoying watching dinosaur battles and morbid as it sounds, people getting eaten" (Respondent 30) or otherwise identified "dinosaurs, special effects (practical and digital), characters, themes (science gone wrong)—and when it is there (not often), blood and gore!" (Respondent 19) as the characteristics of their mattering map. Although the second respondent's list does locate their preference for monstrous representations of dinosaurs alongside other sci-fi and horror fan preferences, such as an interest in narrative thematics and production contexts concerning special effects, these fans reject the zoological disposition of others in favour of the franchise's dominant blockbuster codes.[32] Other respondents expressed these preferences as "artefact emotions" via using the "past/present" register to nostalgically associate meanings of dinosaurs-as-monsters with enduring childhood memories of being scared:

> The first movie came out when I was 6 months old. It has been a part of my life for all [sic] my life and I have always loved it. The velociraptors as shown in the franchise are my favorite. I remember having a nightmare as a small child about them that I thought of as a memory for years after. (Respondent 78)

How to account for these divergent fan attitudes toward *Jurassic Park*'s dinosaurs, then? Brian Noble's concept of "the *specimen-spectacle complex*" arguably offers useful insights for tackling such questions as it invites us to consider conflicting meanings concerning dinosaurs as mutually informing rather than oppositional.[33] Regarding the meanings of dinosaurs across both "scientific" and "popular" interpretive communities, Noble argues for addressing "the more specific and yet broader relation of specimens with spectacles, and the actions of the trading between them" rather than seeing either (or both) has wholly disconnected from each other.[34] Subsequently, Noble argues from a historical perspective:

Dinosaurs were an entity both constituted as specimen [within scientific communities—RPG] and, in turn, reconstitutable in public form as spectacle, and indeed as characters in science fiction literature and film. ... Incorporating dinosaurs and other ancient creatures into a stabilized natural order and natural world picture, a time and a space, made them to some extent, more normal—that is, natural rather than monstrous or preternatural beings.[35]

Similar practices are arguably identifiable among the range of fan responses documented here. On the one hand, some fans adopt a more "specimen-oriented" or, as I have named it, zoological disposition toward *Jurassic Park*'s dinosaurian representations. For these fans, the property is to be celebrated for the fleeting glimpses it offers in to observing the (speculative) behavior of dinosaurs as they might have lived (albeit through the "whistles and bells" of visual effects wizardry).[36] Additional survey responses identifying "the original film's dedication to portraying up-to-date palaeontology" (Respondent 63) or expressing preference for "the way the dinosaurs look and move onscreen and the behind the scenes info on the research that went into figuring out these details" (Respondent 116) further demonstrate these preferences. However, these exist alongside—and often intermingle with—discourses of dinosaurs as spectacle. In the case of *Jurassic Park*, this latter set of associations might range from a love of how dinosaurs are used within the franchise's logo design through to the nostalgia-infused feelings of awe that intertwines with the zoological disposition, through to love of the set piece moments where dinosaurs such as *T-Rex* and *Velociraptor* are used as antagonists. The key point is that the playing out of this specimen-spectacle complex across *Jurassic Park* fans' attitudes toward dinosaurian representations should be embraced as paradoxical, rather than positioning one disposition as superior. That is, it is better to embrace and examine the contradictions arising within fan attitudes to the franchise's dinosaurian representations and consider how *Jurassic Park* attracts, sustains, and courts dinosaur fandom.

Conclusions

By using Grossberg's theory of mattering maps, and so arguing for its ongoing use as a foundation from which the analysis of fans' affective responses can begin, the data discussed in this chapter indicated that *Jurassic Park*'s representations of dinosaurs are a highly important component that generates and sustains individual investments in the franchise. *Jurassic Park*'s dinosaurian representations can generate a number of overlapping and simultaneous emotions among fans. These include nostalgia, awe, and fear, and so add credence to existing assertions made in relation to text-based readings of popular dinosaurian imagery that their meanings are overdetermined.[37] Consequently, instead of dismissing the affect that audiences direct toward *Jurassic Park*'s dinosaurian representations as inferior to other, typically more scientifically grounded readings, this chapter has argued in favor of taking such emotion-based readings on their own terms. What's more, continuing to do so could help further existing debates in fan studies. For example, the differences between fan readings of dinosaurs that adopt what I have named here as the "zoological gaze" and those that instead intersect with discourses of "the blockbuster" and spectacle could be analyzed through a Bourdieusian perspective and so used to hypothesize about formations of fan taste and subcultural hierarchies within dinosaur fandom.[38]

Nevertheless, and as Cornell Sandvoss argues, "The affective attachments of fans to their fan object ... appear as key motivational factors facilitating participation."[39] The respondents surveyed in this chapter demonstrate Sandvoss's argument, both within *Jurassic Park* fandom and then beyond by suggesting a wider interest in dinosaurs and the Mesozoic more generally. This point is significant for three reasons. First, it highlights the ongoing need to address the concept of affect in fan studies and how this assists our knowledge of attachments and identity construction within heavily mediated societies. Second, it must be noted that, when articulated in relation to a commercial media franchise like *Jurassic Park*, fan affect is always underpinned by commercial imperatives that shape preferences for and meanings of the prehistoric era. Mitchell has argued that "the major 'types' of dinosaurs in folk or vernacular taxonomy (the 'cookie cutter' stereotypes of *T-Rex*, *Brontosaurus*, *Triceratops*, *Stegosaurus*, and *Pterodactyl*) provide a ready-made bestiary for the differentiation of individuals and groups."[40] *Jurassic Park*'s relationship to dinosaur fandom therefore reinforces preexisting dino-preferences by encouraging affect toward species like *T-Rex* and *Velociraptor*, and so reinforcing the commercial viability of certain dinosaurian representations. Finally, and building on Nick Couldry's calls regarding the continual need to better understand fans' "textual environments" at the expense of discussing fans of individual franchises, the responses gathered from the survey indicate that further investigation is needed in to how and whether *Jurassic Park* fans' interest in dinosaurs translates to other practices such as attendance at natural history events, museums, and attractions or a broader interest in earth sciences, climate science, extinction, and the like.[41]

These are not the only criteria concerning *Jurassic Park* fans that require further examination, however. As highlighted above, the status of dinosaurs as loci for fannish affect among *Jurassic Park* fans was found to be indicative of female fans and so greater insight is needed into the cultural meanings of dinosaurs across gendered lines. What's more, sensitivity toward the interrelationship between *Jurassic Park* fandom, affect, and dinosaurs is required in non-Western, non-White, and other non-hegemonic audience groups so that a fuller picture of dinosaur fandom as a set of cultural identities can be obtained.

Notes

1 "Franchises (US and Canada)—Box Office Mojo," Box Office Mojo. https://www.boxofficemojo.com/franchise/?ref_=bo_lnav_hm_shrt. Accessed December 31, 2021.
2 Jose Luiz Sanz, *Staring T.Rex!: Dinosaur Mythology and Popular Culture* (Bloomington: Indiana University Press, 2002), 46.
3 See Justin Wyatt, *High-Concept: Movies and Marketing in Hollywood* (Austin: University of Texas Press, 1994).
4 See Lucy Bennett, "Surveying Fandom: The Ethics, Design, and Use of Surveys in Fan Studies," in Melissa A. Click and Suzanne Scott (eds.) *The Routledge Companion to Media Fandom* (London: Routledge, 2017), 37.
5 Mario Cardano, *Defending Qualitative Research: Design, Analysis, and Textualization* (London: Routledge, 2020), 71.
6 Janice Morse, "Sampling in Grounded Theory," in Antony Bryant & Kathy Charmaz (eds.) *The SAGE Handbook of Grounded Theory* (London: SAGE, 2007), 231.
7 Cornel Sandvoss, "Toward an Understanding of Political Enthusiasm as Media Fandom: Blogging, Fan Productivity and Affect in American Politics," *Participations: Journal of Audience and Reception Studies* 10:1 (2013): 261.
8 Rukmini Pande, "Who Do You Mean by 'Fan'?: Decolonizing Media Fandom Identity," in Paul Booth (ed.) *A Companion to Media Fandom and Fan Studies* (Oxford: Wiley-Blackwell), 418.
9 Ibid.
10 See Svetlana Boym, *The Future of Nostalgia* (New York: Basic Books, 2001), 33–4. Also, Sanz, *Starring T.Rex!*, 20–9.
11 Brian Noble, *Articulating Dinosaurs: A Political Anthropology* (Toronto: University of Toronto Press, 2016), 50–69.
12 See both Felix J. Augustin, Andreas T. Matzke, Michael W. Maisch, and Hans-Ulrich Pfretzschner, "A Theropod Dinosaur Feeding Site from the Upper Jurassic of the Junggar Basin, NW China," *Palaeogeography, Palaeoclimatology, Palaeoecology* 560 (2020): 1–12 and Lida Xing, Martin G. Lockley, Hendrik Klein, W. Scott Persons IV, Mengyuan Wei, Li Chen, and Miaoyan Wang, "The First Record of Cretaceous Non-Avian Dinosaur Tracks from the Qinghai-Tibet Plateau, China," *Cretaceous Research* 115 (2020): 1–12.
13 W. J. T. Mitchell, *The Last Dinosaur Book: The Life and Times of a Cultural Icon* (Chicago: University of Chicago Press, 1998), 253.

14 See journalistic publications including Sam Chiarelli, *Dig: A Personal Prehistoric Journey* (Lancaster, PA: Hippocampus, 2018) and Paige Williams, *The Dinosaur Artist: Obsession, Betrayal, and the Quest for Earth's Ultimate Trophy* (London: Scribe Publications, 2018).

15 Henry Jenkins, *Textual Poachers: Television Fans and Participatory Culture, Updated Twentieth Anniversary Edition* (London: Routledge, 2012 [1992]), 10–11.

16 Camile Bacon-Smith, *Science Fiction Culture* (Philadelphia: University of Pennsylvania Press, 2000), 96–108.

17 See Suzanne Scott, *Fake Geek Girls: Fandom, Gender, and the Convergence Culture Industry* (New York: New York University Press, 2019).

18 See Laurence Grossberg, "Is There a Fan in the House?: The Affective Sensibility of Fandom," in Lisa Lewis (ed.) *The Adoring Audience: Fan Culture and Popular Media* (London: Routledge, 1992), 50–65.

19 Ibid., 57–8.

20 Ibid., 58.

21 Ibid., 59.

22 Ibid., 56–7.

23 Stefane Armbruster, *Watching Nostalgia: An Analysis of Nostalgic Television Fiction and its Reception* (Verlag, Biefeld: Transcript, 2016), 58.

24 Katharina Niemeyer, "Introduction: Media and Nostalgia," in Katharina Niemeyer (ed.) *Media and Nostalgia: Yearning for the Past, Present and Future* (Basingstoke: Palgrave Macmillan, 2014), 1.

25 Annette Kuhn, *An Everyday Magic: Cinema and Cultural Memory* (London: IB Tauris, 2002), 10.

26 See Amy Holdsworth, *Television, Memory and Nostalgia* (Basingstoke: Palgrave Macmillan, 2011).

27 Ed S. Tan, *Emotion and the Structure of Narrative Film: Film as an Emotion Machine* (London: Routledge, 1996), 65.

28 Ibid.

29 Helen Wheatley, *Spectacular Television: Exploring Televisual Pleasure* (London: IB Tauris, 2016), 110.

30 See Steve Neale, "Hollywood Blockbusters: Historical Dimensions," in Julian Stringer (ed.) *Movie Blockbusters* (London: Routledge, 2003), 47–60.

31 Matt Hills, *Fan Cultures* (London: Routledge, 2002), 104.

32 Bob Rehak, *More Than Meets the Eye: Special Effects and the Fantastic Transmedia Franchise* (New York: New York University Press, 2018), 42–9.

33 Noble, *Articulating Dinosaurs*, 13; original emphasis.

34 Ibid., 16.

35 Ibid.

36 Wheatley, *Spectacular Television*, 103.

37 See Ross Garner, "Doctor Who and the Dinosaurs: Spectacle, Monstrosity, Melodrama and Ideology in Dinosaur Mediations," in Marcus K. Harmes and Lindy A. Orthia (eds.) *Doctor Who and Science: Essays on Ideas, Identities and Ideologies in the Series* (Jefferson, NC: McFarland, 2021), 173–89.
38 See Hills, *Fan Cultures*, 20–36.
39 Sandvoss, "Toward an Understanding of Political Enthusiasm as Media Fandom," 287.
40 Mitchell, *The Last Dinosaur Book*, 78.
41 Nick Couldry, *Inside Culture: Re-imagining the Method of Cultural Studies* (London: Sage, 2000), 67.

6

Jurassic Park's Smoothing Pass: The Dinosaur Input Device and Digital Materialism

Julie Turnock
University of Illinois, USA

Introduction: *King Kong* and *Jurassic Park*

In a well circulated story about the production of *Jurassic Park* (1993), when animator Phil Tippett, whose company, The Tippett Studio, had been hired to produce traditionally animated stop-motion dinosaurs for the film was told his contracted footage would instead be digitally animated, he proclaimed, "well, I'm extinct."[1] However, instead of Tippett's services being no longer necessary, his experience in traditional stop motion proved to be more important than ever in creating the film's photoreal digital dinosaurs. Tippett and his stop-motion team operated the animation rig that was known as the "Dinosaur Input Device," or DID. With that apparatus, digital sensors were applied to dinosaur stop-motion puppets made up of a posable metal armature. The team's traditional operating of the frame-by-frame stop-motion animation formed the basis for how the Industrial Light & Magic (ILM) artists animated the movement of several of the digital dinosaurs, most notably the *T-Rex*. Tippett's decades-long experience with how to animate artificially generated characters and objects to move naturalistically and plausibly was knowledge his hands knew, and no computer algorithm, especially at that time, could reproduce.[2]

When the *Jurassic Park* production went digital, Tippet as well as the other effects artists had to rethink everything they had ever known about making effects—from tactile manual handwork to his animation being abstracted into motion data and used as the basis for movement, manipulated by others tapping on computer keys. In order to understand the human/technology interaction that *Jurassic Park* and other films of the time of the "digital turn" began to reconfigure, let us consider a traditional example, a shot from the original *King Kong* (1933) where Kong first appears, emerging from the forest to find Ann Darrow (Fay Wray) tied to a platform (Figure 6.1) Pared to its simplest description, to realize this sequence, a crew builds a scaled environment using foam, metal, and other parts. Another crew builds a physical posable Kong armature covered in foam and rabbit fur. Eventually camera operators point a physical camera at the puppet on the miniature set and animate Kong's movement frame by frame. A different crew shoots the live-action Fay Wray element for separate photographed elements. Once committed to film, the discrete pieces of film become 2D elements. They are now the realm of the compositor, who arranges the various elements with an optical printer so that they (ideally) appear in the final version as if shot by a single live-action camera on a live-action set.[3]

The sequence in *Jurassic Park*, in which we first fully encounter the *T-Rex* as she emerges past the electrified gates to menace Sam Neill's Dr. Grant, who

FIGURE 6.1 *Ann Darrow (Fay Wray) is sacrificed to King Kong*

is trying to wave her away with a flare from the children's overturned jeep, begins with a similar conceptual understanding but is produced by different means (and with a revised final aesthetic goal [Figure 6.2]). Similarly to Fay Wray, the actors and the jeep are 2D elements shot by a live-action film camera that will be composited with the animation later on. To create the *T-Rex*, instead of foam, rubber, and fur the stop motion puppeteers manipulate the DID—a bare metal armature. Effects artists never pointed a physical camera at the *T-Rex* armature, instead, a series of sensors and wires were attached, collecting a series of motion data points. Although it would become state of the art about ten years later, motion capture was an uncommon technique at the time. However other, non-ILM productions had experimented with it, most notably the work completed by PDI (Pacific Data Images) and DQI (DreamQuest Images) for Barry Levinson's *Toys* in 1992. While ILM would return to motion capture in the late 1990s, another company, Weta Digital would be the primary driver of innovation in the technology through the Peter Jackson-directed *Lord of the Rings* films (2001–3) as well as Jackson's version of *King Kong* in 2005.[4] On *Jurassic Park*, the stop-motion animators animated the armature traditionally, and then sent the data to the digital animators. The digital animators then recreated the armature in the computer, "dressed" it with skin and muscles through software texture mapping and used the animator's motion data as a basis to keyframe animate the *T-Rex*'s naturalistic movement. The compositing takes place not on an optical printer, frame-by-frame, but on a computer screen, via (new to the time) digital software. As in *King Kong*, the illusion of physical presence of the stop-motion creature was solidified by intercutting the animation footage with large-scale animatronics when the full body of the creature was not needed.

FIGURE 6.2 *Grant distracts the* T-Rex

In the *King Kong* example, the way the final image is achieved is evidently and visibly physical, manipulated by human hands, although perhaps the evidence of the artists' handwork (famously, the thumbprints in Kong's fur) means it reads as less "realistic" by contemporary standards. It is also captured by an onset camera. The *Jurassic Park* example shifts the relation between the human and the technological, first of all by losing the onset camera. Moreover, in the name of "smoothening" and thereby achieving "greater realism," the highly material stage of production must be transcoded into numerical representation. Most importantly, perhaps, the goal of smoothening of the digital motion is to erase its effects process, rather than flaunting it with *King Kong's* "jerky" irregularity.

I bring up these examples and the familiar story about *Jurassic Park*'s production in order to rethink the film's relationship to the film industry's so-called "digital turn." Although the digitization of various sectors (such as sound and editing) of the film industry occurred at different rates, the special/ visual effects of *Jurassic Park*, along with those of James Cameron-directed *Terminator 2: Judgment Day* in 1991, are widely cited as the synecdoche for the beginning of digital cinema, both popularly and academically[5] *Jurassic Park* digital cinema's "big bang."[6]

However, the material process of "going digital" was hardly as straightforward, rapid, or inevitable as the success of *Jurassic Park* made it seem, not least of all for the companies that produced the effects. Most credit for cinema's digital turn is given to the impressive effects work produced under the aegis of effects company Industrial Light & Magic (ILM). As I have argued elsewhere, a great deal of misinformation has circulated about ILM's digital work on the film itself and how the company continued to digitize over the next decade.[7] At the time of *Jurassic Park*'s production, ILM had a very limited team dedicated to CGI as well as surprisingly meager hardware and software capabilities.[8] The actual dinosaur effects were created as a team effort among ILM, stop-motion specialists (and long-time ILM collaborator) The Tippett Studio, and the animatronics of the Stan Winston Studio (as well as careful editing).

This chapter will consider how artists at the Tippett Studio and their associates at ILM (alongside the other effects artists at the Stan Winston Studio) had to begin to rethink their relation to their profession, their artistry, and their processes to make the film come off; and by extension, how these adjustments, small at first, eventually meant a shift in conceiving how images are made, and to a certain degree, experienced.

These changes were characterized at the time as a progressive step forward toward greater realism. Although the Tippett team were wary of the new digital approach, even they had to admit, the hybrid technique generated a powerful new kind of reality effect even to its hardened stop-motion loyalists. Tippett stop-motion animator Randal Dutra recalls the thrill of seeing the parts put together for the first time:

> It was a rare treat indeed to view our animation fully rendered, lit, and integrated so beautifully and expertly by Dennis Muren and his team after being run through the ILM pipeline. To "see" the effect of those blurs of action, muscle/skin tweaks, added unsteady camera, and environmental interactions ... it truly was magic.[9]

Tippett team member Craig Hayes likewise exclaimed on seeing the final render, "OK, here is the spark of life that we had been trying to get across the whole time."[10] Rather than a simple account of the triumph toward a greater ideal notion of "total cinema" realism that is common in effects stories, the digital/traditional hybrid technique points to a frequently less noticed aspect of cinematic realism: that performing innovation and novelty is essential in refreshing a reality effect. The DID stop-motion/digital animation hybrid technique was the link between the familiar techniques and the "march to smoothness" that would characterize the aesthetics' early digital period. Simply put, because it looked a little digital, the digitally smoothed dinosaur motion just felt excitingly new.[11] For the dinosaurs of *Jurassic Park*, incorporating the fluid aesthetic of "digitalness" grounded them first of all in the stop motion of *The Lost World* (1925) and Harryhausen while at the same time launching into the digital future.

It is tempting to assume that digital effects work is the opposite of analog; that is, non-physical and generated entirely with computer software, or exclusively in the "digital domain" as James Cameron put it in the early 1990s.[12] This study argues that effects work remains intensely physical and material—including its digital components. *Jurassic Park* instead materially reconfigured the human/technology interface first in effects work, and then later in film and moving image production as a whole. *Jurassic Park*'s spectacular digital display is frequently pointed to as the moment when cinema decidedly decorrelated from traditional profilmic camera reality. However, focusing on the index is a misunderstanding regarding effects work. Effects artists have always approached its filmed material as plastic elements to reconfigure at will. That being said, *Jurassic Park* does in fact mark an historical and technological turning point where artists realized their approach had to change, and precisely demonstrates the artists in real time rethink their relation to effects technology. They had to change because the producers of *Jurassic Park*—once they were convinced by digital tests undertaken by a faction at ILM—believed the coming digital era required a new digital realism, and counted on the effects artists to figure out what that meant. Their result, the hybridization of traditional approaches tweaked with digital smoothness, refreshed older forms with a bracingly new performance of technological realism. Finally, although the results of *Jurassic Park* were immediately hailed as a "step forward" in cinematic realism, I argue that there is nothing inherently "more realistic" about digital technology, or traditional analog technology for that matter.

The final result of *Jurassic Park* attests that realism is always a performance and one that must be renewed.

Attention to the production of realist aesthetics in *Jurassic Park* shows clearly the material substrate in digital imagery, one that becomes even more important to recover as artists try harder and harder to erase the visible trace of the digital in an illusory notion of what the industry calls "grounded photorealism"—that is, digitally generated imagery grounded in pre-digital aesthetics. Instead of severing cinema's connection to the analog, what *Jurassic Park* started tipping effects production toward was erasing the technological trace, and the materiality of that process that the *King Kong* example flaunts. Recent productions look back to 1980s and early 1990s productions as models for how to recreate the look of analog photography and revive some select analog techniques, but through established digital pipelines. So that today, is not important for blockbuster directors that the final image is intensively digitally animated, only that it looks like live-action.

Re-Correlating Images

In Lev Manovich's 2002 *The Language of New Media*, one of the most cited lines of his study is "Cinema can no longer be clearly distinguished from animation. It is no longer an indexical media technology but, rather, a subgenre of painting."[13] This statement understands animation's importance (what he also calls "the logic of animation") to how digital technology has shifted our rhetorical relation to the index. He also prophetically writes, "When a future historian will write about the computerization of cinema in the 1990s, she will highlight such movies as *Terminator 2* [James Cameron, 1990] and *Jurassic Park*."[14] I am surprised to discover that I am that historian. Manovich is correct, the example of *Terminator 2* and *Jurassic Park* are vital to accounts of "the computerization of cinema," but not exactly in the way he was imagining. *The Language of New Media* remains an incisive exploration of digital technology's impact on our conception of the ontology of cinema.

While Manovich got a surprising amount right about what digital technology eventually would wrought, a historical perspective of twenty years helps us reconsider the status of the index as well as the relationship between live-action and animation. Certainly the "problem" of the index was much more central to the turn of the millennium than twenty years later. While crucial to Manovich whether or not an event happened profilmically (or "actually" in front of the camera) seems today to be rather a quaint anxiety. Instead, it is the status of the index as definitive of live-action that is more in question. According to Manovich's definition, "[live action films] largely consist of unmodified photographic recordings of real events which took place in real physical space."[15] In the time when a categorically live-action film like *Gravity* (Alfonso Cuarón, 2013) or a Marvel film has many sequences in which the only live-action element is the actors' heads, this definition now feels like one of Manovich's most outmoded.[16] To be considered live-action thirty years after *Jurassic Park*, as I have argued elsewhere, the film need only *look* like live-action.[17]

Certainly, Manovichs's detailed descriptions of emerging digital aesthetics is its strength. What Manovich identifies as the "principals of new media"—numerical representation, modularity, automation, variability, and transcoding—all insist upon traits that are the opposite from those associated with indexicality (materiality, particularity, handwork, immutability) through an increasing sense of abstraction. That brings us back to the issue of animation. I agree that cinema today is more akin to the logic of animation than ever. However, instead of abstracting into complete arbitrariness, the "real" (always a representation) is represented through a different set of technology coordinates manipulated by human agency, that are nevertheless material in their substrate.[18] Instead of "discorrelated" images, much of contemporary cinema is made of images that are correlated differently, through different material processes, different aesthetics, and different logics.

Most discussions of cinematic CGI center around imagery that is most evidently digital. Namely, those from the late 1990s and early 2000s, perhaps most famously the gravity defying "Bullet Time" Kung Fu of *The Matrix* (Wachowskis, 1998) or impossible camera shots such as those in *Fight Club* (Fincher, 1999) that extend through the protagonist's gullet. Shane Denson has discussed recent cinema in terms of what he calls the "discorrelated image," "a transformation of subjectivity itself" that reorders our sensory ratios and reforms them "in accordance with the new speeds and scales of imaging processes."[19] Denson discusses discorrelated images as shots that "subtly dismantle the rational orderings of time and space that served, conventionally, to correlate spectatorial subjectivity with cinematic images."[20]

Specifically, he describes this phenomenological process as accomplished through imagery produced by post-cinematic virtual "crazy cameras" that "fail to situate viewers in a consistently and coherently designated spectating-position."[21] The mainstream examples Denson uses, such as those from action directors Neveldine and Taylor as well as the *Paranormal Activity* series (2007–21), are illustrative for being highly exaggerated and therefore clear examples of evidently "impossible" digital cinematography. Lisa Purse likewise superbly describes the *c.* 1993–2008 style and thematics of digital foregrounding in her work *Digital Imaging in Popular Cinema*.[22] However, though excellent examples illustrating their theses, this exaggerated, evidently digital style is only one particularly visible aesthetic form digital images have taken. Moreover, though common to digital cinema's novelty era, I argue elsewhere it is a style that has not been prevalent in mainstream filmmaking since the one-two punch of *The Dark Knight* (Nolan, 2008) and *Iron Man* (Jon Favreau, 2008) and effects mark a turn toward grounded photorealism (and made even stronger through the total dominance of Marvel Cinematic Universe [MCU] properties in the meantime).[23]

What I am more interested here is much the more common and less obvious, often unnoticed moments that take the theoretically digitally "discorrelated" image and attempt to "re-correlate" them into an aesthetic of grounded realism. I imagine that Denson would argue that re-correlation, at best, is never complete, and I do not dispute that. The phenomenologically based discorrelated image requires the viewer not just knowing but also seeing that the image is digital, and furthermore, that the viewer knows on some level the digitally generated images to be categorically "ungrounded" from reality. However, the power of a film like *Jurassic Park* (as well as many more recent films) comes from the illusion of re-correlation. What is under examination here is the dominant tendency to use digital tools to erase the signs of the kinds of digital aesthetics Denson calls attention to.[24] Manovich describes early digital aesthetics as the "cyborg eye" that reproduce a "too perfect" machine vision. Elsewhere, I have called the more recent iteration of digital aesthetics the optical cyborg eye, or the desire to use the most up to date digital tools to make images that look like no digital tools were used.[25] This is indeed a discorrelated image in that it has abstracted the object from its referent—what Denson refers to as the disruption of the spatial-phenomenological relations between the viewer and the camera—that, I argue, has been "virtually re-correlated" phenomenologically.

Nevertheless, my argument is largely not phenomenological about the viewer's experience of these images but understanding them more as a historical material aesthetic process concerning how artists make images. Jacob Gaboury describes the "image object," as "digital images ... materially structured by those historical objects that produce them—objects that have been rendered out of the visible image, but that fundamentally shaped the function and appearance of computer graphics as a distinctly computational technology."[26] The digital dinosaurs of *Jurassic Park* retain a material substrate, material that includes its hardware, software, artistic approach, and creative decisions. As Gaboury claims, "computer graphics exist simultaneously as both an assemblage of technical objects and an image that has been rendered out from them".[27] Further he claims,

> Unlike those media that claim an indexical relationship to the world they represent, the thing reproduced by computer graphics is not the world but another medium in simulation. Computer graphics are thus always already mediated, and the goal of nearly all graphical research is the accurate reproduction of the effects of this prior mediation.[28]

Effects work both before and after computer graphics likewise reproduce another media in simulation rather than "the world." I work with the assumption that the "image object" of the digital cinematic image is constructed, and is neither about an indexical relation to the world nor how the world gets digitalized, nor how computers abstract and operationalize the phenomenological world. To the effects artists, as in the *King Kong* and *Jurassic* examples, the world viewed here is an already imaginary cinematic world. I want to explore this specific moment where effects, via computer graphics, took a decisive step toward transcoding this particular human-machine interface, with the introduction of new tools.

Effects, Animation, and Digital Smoothness

If Manovich suggests that digitally generated images are more driven by the "logic of animation" than by the logic of live-action cinema, that is certainly even more so now.[29] The optical cyborg eye aesthetic means there is little to distinguish live-action and animation footage in digital filmmaking on the basis of the techniques and software used to produce them (even if the personnel are often quite different). Indeed, the term "live-action" has become in effect a reference aesthetic produced by processes more akin to animation than intrinsically linked to camera technology.[30] In fact, effects artists have worked within the logic of animation all along. While indexicality arguments make a great deal out of the actual physical presence of the object and its tracing in light onto the light sensitive emulsion, historically filmmakers realized very quickly that profilmic reality and the screen image need not line up. Early on, people, objects, and locations either looked different when photographed or needed various manipulations to look like they were "supposed to," whether that be forced perspective sets or special filters for blue eyes in the silent period. In effects work, within a few years of cinema's invention, matte shots, miniatures, and other kinds of composites, though not easy to accomplish, were able to be done by those with the time, skill, and need to do so. From early on, as Christian Metz has asserted, what we might call the "final image" projected on the screen was a highly manipulated version of camera reality, with varying intentions toward "convincingness" as profilmic reality, both on the set and in postproduction.[31]

As much as *Jurassic Park* required a new way of thinking about live-action photography, it likewise required a new way of thinking about effects animation. If *Jurassic Park*'s production was a "digital turn," the producers themselves did not know the extent to which they were involved in it.[32] Instead, as the production progressed, they found themselves forging a hybrid production, where traditional practitioners re-made themselves and their skill set as the movie was being made, and in doing so began to rethink cinema's human-machine interaction. To be clear, I'm not suggesting *Jurassic Park* is the first time this happened. I'm using its well-documented production as an especially influential example, because due to ILM's outsized influence on the industry as well as the huge worldwide success of the film, the film stands in for this process in cinema history.[33]

Once director Steven Spielberg and the production made the decision to incorporate digital technology instead of traditional stop-motion techniques and their variants, not surprisingly, the animators at the Tippett Studio were unhappy they would have to adapt their long-honed traditional techniques for the production. However, as Tippett realized, adaptation would be the only way his team would continue to be involved with the project. Randal Dutra, senior animator at the Tippett Studio, described the advent of CGI as "a huge upheaval for all of us," since they had no prior, or practical, computer background to speak of.[34]

ILM was also undergoing uncomfortable upheaval. ILM's self-promotion touts *Jurassic Park* as the moment when the company stepped definitively into digital realm. However, and as I have argued elsewhere, only a very small handful of effects artists at ILM in 1992–3 could be described as "digital animators" or otherwise CGI artists. Reportedly, the few CGI-enthusiasts on the ILM side had to produce "secret dinosaur tests" to convince Dennis Muren, the only ILM effects supervisor strongly interested in CGI, who still was doubtful they could pull it off. And once the tests won over Muren and Spielberg, there was reportedly grumbling at ILM that the Tippett Studio was to be brought in to "help" the ILM team.[35] It is worth stressing here that due in large part to rendering and storage capabilities in the early 1990s, there are only about fifty computer-generated shots in finished film. Those few shots were split between ILM and the Tippett Studio.[36]

Accounts of the process of making the film's dinosaurs frequently acknowledge the impressive large-scale animatronics completed by the Stan Winston Studio but perhaps do not give enough credit for the conception of the dinosaurs themselves. With their previous extensive work on such films as *Star Wars* (1977), *The Empire Strikes Back* (1980), *Dragonslayer* (1981), and *Robocop* (1987) Tippett and his team at Tippett Studios were the acknowledged masters of creature motion, but the Winston Studio designed and built the 3D physical models upon which the digital dinosaurs were based. Led by famed creature designer Crash McCreery, *Cinefex* reports the Stan Winston Studio was responsible for designing all of the dinosaur characters, "even those that would be created at other facilities and through other means."[37] In other words, McCreery and his team at the Winston Studio designed the dinosaurs and also built maquettes that served as the basis for both the Tippett Studio's skeletal stop-motion armatures and the digital dinosaurs that ILM would build in the computer.

While the Winston team's physical maquettes got everyone on the same page, the physical dinosaurs went through their first process of abstraction when used as the basis for the Tippett Studio's stop-motion work. As well as converting the dinosaur models into skeletal metallic armatures, another level of abstraction was introduced regarding the camera. As the conference paper resulting from their team's combined efforts described,

> the DID is ... easy to use. Animators with stop-motion experience are able to start animating immediately, and usually prefer the setup over the traditional setup because they don't have to work around cameras, lights, and props, and because they can see how the motion looks in the shot right-away, instead of having to wait for film to return from a lab.[38]

In the DID, we see how stop-motion animators were among the first to realize that with digital technology the physical camera became contingent to the filmmaking process. Again, they were working within the logic of (2D) animation. ILM software developer Brian Knep recalled: "When Tippett's team first started doing the dinosaur input device ..., they would move it and then they would run out of the frame, like they used to with a real camera. They didn't realize that they wouldn't be in frame anymore! I loved that."[39] That did not mean they were now unconstrained by the physical world. Randal Dutra noted, "I still had to animate exactly to the intended camera angle for each shot."[40] Cameras still had to be present, if only to be translated into one of many data points.[41]

The Tippett team was tasked with the considerable job of conceiving and generating the dinosaurs' motion data that the ILM team would apply to computer models. Although that process seems abstract and immaterial (animators animating into a digital void), their actual working method of abstracting motion into the digital realm was intensely physical. Hayes describes the team's focus on the right metals, wires, sensors, optical encoders, and even machine grease that he himself and armature builder Tom St. Amand needed to make it happen. As Hayes put it, "What we were doing in a way was effectively reproducing a nervous system, a very crude nervous system on this mechanical armature."[42]

The Tippett team also had to think about how the results of this animation "nervous system" would read to the ILM team they were sending it to since it would be their job to transcode the data they were given into photorealistic dinosaurs. The ILM team took the digitized traditional stop-motion and then built onto it with digital motion blur, proprietary software Softimage texture mapping, and other software adjustments that gave texture to the dinosaur data derived from the motion data. But the major aesthetic shift the ILM team brought to the Tippett material (the transcoding of the stop-motion data) was digital smoothness.

Manipulating the Tippett team's inputted motion from the DID was a way to "improve" the earlier Tippett-derived technique of Go-Motion, which relied on servo motors to move the puppets between shots to create motion blur. The original plan was to use Go-Motion on *Jurassic Park*, but it was deemed by the Spielberg production "too jumpy," for what the production wanted.[43] As the paper describing their work (written after the fact for an industry conference presentation) attests, the team saw their work as an offshoot off motion capture, the then-uncommon technique of attaching sensors to a person or other moving object and using that as the basis for a CGI person or creature.[44] Motion capture itself was derived from rotoscope animation, a Fleischer brother's technique patented in 1917. The paper describes the aesthetic of combining stop-motion and computer animation as a fusing of the advantages of both systems: "The resulting animation lacks the artifacts of stop-motion animation, the pops and jerkiness," but "retains the intentional subtleties and hard stops that computer animation often lacks."[45]

However, the *Jurassic Park* production had to think about how animation renders motion in a live-action context, and one of those sites was in thinking about the relationship between stop-motion and keyframe animation. The DID conceptualized the notion of motion capture as similar to the Fleischer's rotoscope animation, but as a more refined and abstracted way to separate motion data from a specific object. In this way, we might think of the motion data as a "motion object" with a material substrate much like Gaboury's image object.

Stop-motion animates every frame by taking a still image of every movement of the 3D puppet armature. Keyframe animation is more akin to traditional 2D cell animation. The artist determines the starting and ending points of a given animated motion, and the technology interpolates the parts in between. *Jurassic Park*'s production would combine the two predominant traditional animation approaches, in order to get, as the conference paper suggested, the handmade "intentional subtleties and hard stops" but also smooth out the "pops and jerkiness." As Tippett's Craig Hayes put it, from his perspective as a computer animator, keyframing would be sufficient and the stop-motion process was not strictly necessary. "But it turns out that, psychologically, or just due to human nature, the animator still needed this motion control basis as part of their workflow. It was not realistic to expect them to be able to just completely abandon certain parts of their craft."[46] In order to reconfigure the traditional animation process to the new digital context, it required, as Hayes put it, a "crutch" as much as it required the actual technique.

Dutra thought the advantage of the hybrid process was that it already looked more realistically smooth than the stop-motion. However, to Dutra's stop-motion taste, the resulting motion was *too* smooth. "The two Raptors entering the kitchen, ... remains an effective shot," he said, " but my accents, timings and extremes were somewhat dampened in this smoothing process. But again, we were all learning."[47]

In fact, the tension between the smoothness of digital keyframing and the greater manual finesse of stop-motion was the primary conflict between

Tippett team and the ILM team. For Dutra at Tippett, ILM's digital keyframing was about privileging the performance of innovation over refined human artistry:

> Our DID shots also underwent what was called a *smoothing pass*: a procedure that "remedies" any anomalies of the key frames shaping the animation function curves that do not fall within perfect alignment. But in so doing, I feel we lost portions of the more positive, inherent *organic* aspects of the original, hand-wrought DID animation. At the time, with CG being such a new visual, production at large wanted to keep things "smooth," avoiding at all costs any artifacts resembling the "older," traditional stop-motion. After all, this was the *future*.[48]

In other words, the "smooth stop-motion" hybrid effect they had produced looked "more real" in part because it combined digital and traditional to look novel, but familiar.

The march to keyframed smoothness meant that the DID technique, despite its hugely successful outing in *Jurassic Park*, was not a long-lived technique. Even the sequel *The Lost World: Jurassic Park* (1997) just a few years later did not use the DID, nor did the production use the Tippett Studio.[49] According to Tippett Studio animation supervisor Trey Stokes, the technique as such did not even last very long at Tippett, but only was used again for the *Starship Troopers* (Paul Verhoeven, 1997) production.[50] As he explained, "the DID's had to be very specifically machined and calibrated for *Jurassic Park* and *Troopers*, and even on *Troopers* we only had warrior bug DID's—all the other bug types were keyframed."[51] In other words, the DID was too artisanal (not easily automatable) to convert to digital production, where digital keyframe animation became much more efficient.

Conclusion

The *Jurassic Park* effects production was highly collaborative across several studios (ILM, Tippett and Winston) and included many varied skill sets: an "innovative traditional" approach combining new technologies with legacy techniques. It was also exceedingly physical, involving the creative input of artists' hands from start to finish, from sketches to maquettes to armatures to hands-on animation to keyframing to software development. The artists who contributed to *Jurassic Park* to a person all had to think about how to translate their long-held skills into another medium, to much ambivalence at best.

These details demonstrate three major points. First, that *Jurassic Park*'s "digital dinosaurs" were not the result of an abstracted immaterial process but a hybridized highly material set of processes. Second, the production demonstrates a new human/technological conception in effects work that reorganizes the material processes into reference aesthetics data points designed to smoothen and ideally erase the digital trace. And third, that there is nothing inherently "more realistic" (or less realistic) about digital technology, but realism is always a performance of newness combined with familiarity. Instead, *Jurassic Park* started tipping effects production away from a craft mentality of handwork and materiality as what produces "live-action," (mixed-media though it has always been) toward live-action as a performance performed with an animation mentality. This is the contradiction of contemporary digital realism for many prominent filmmakers of blockbuster franchises: it must deploy thousands of digital effects shots but take care to look like only analog technology was used.

In the early 1990s the future was where digital technology's smoothness would remove not just the "stops and barriers" of traditional animation but also the snags and impediments to special/visual effects pipelines. It looked like the future because it performed the fantasies associated with the digital. The transitional dinosaurs of *Jurassic Park* made those dreams seem real.

Notes

1. Repeated in Chris McGowan, "Phil Tippett: Following His Imagination to the Stars and Beyond." *VFXVoice.com*, December 13, 2018; and Angela Watercutter "Jurassic Park Turns 21," *Wired.com*, June 10, 2014.
2. A note about animation: the kind of animation I will be discussing here is special/visual effects animation, which is designed to blend with a live-action, or live-action-looking diegesis, what I refer elsewhere as "optical animation." Turnock, *Plastic Reality* (Columbia University Press, 2015): 23.
3. This intense interaction between human manipulation and the camera's mechanism is one of the reasons stop-motion has had a passionate practitioner and also fan base.
4. ILM itself did not especially take up motion capture until into the early 2000s (*The Phantom Menace's* Jar Binks was not motion captured. ILM referenced the actor Ahmed Best's on-set motion largely through a kind of rotoscoped keyframe animation. The actor was not equipped with motion capture sensors). Turnock, *Plastic Reality*, 320 n.26.
5. Elsaesser, Prince, Buckland.
6. Manovich, Sito, Norman Klein.
7. Julie Turnock, *Empire of Effects* (University of Texas Press, 2022): 136.
8. Ibid.
9. Ian Failes, "The Oral History of the Dinosaur Input Device," *BeforesAndAfters.com*, March 15, 2020. https://beforesandafters.

com/2020/03/15/the-oral-history-of-the-dinosaur-input-device-or-how-to-survive-the-near-death-of-stop-motion (2020).

10 Ibid.
11 Previously, non-digital Go-Motion was considered an "improvement" on the realism effect of traditional stop-motion due to its addition of motion blur that moved the movement closer to the look of live-action.
12 At the press conference announcing Digital Domain, his new effects company, Cameron proclaimed, "It will all be done at a workstation. Your film will now be in the digital domain." Matt Rothman, "H'wood Enters Digital Domain," *Variety*, February 26, 1993.
13 Lev Manovich, *The Language of New Media* (Cambridge, MA: MIT Press, 2002), 250.
14 Manovich, 180; Alexander R. Galloway, "What Is New Media? Ten Years after 'The Language of New Media'," *Criticism* 53:3 (2011): 377–84.
15 Manovich, *The Language of New Media*, 249.
16 Those categories being primarily award and marketing categories. According to the Academy's rules defining the Animation award category,

> if the picture is created in a cinematic style that could be mistaken for live action, the filmmaker(s) must also submit information supporting how and why the picture is substantially a work of animation rather than live action. "Animated Feature Film Award—Additional Resources," Rules & Eligibility, Oscars. https://www.oscars.org/oscars/rules-eligibility.

17 Turnock, *Empire of Effects*.
18 Tom Gunning. "Moving Away from the Index: Cinema and the Impression of Reality," *Differences* 18:1 (2007): 29–52.
19 Shane Denson, *Discorrelated Images* (Durham, NC: Duke University Press, 2020), 16, 1.
20 Denson, *Discorrelated Images*, 8–9.
21 Ibid., 26.
22 Purse is especially brilliant describing the *Resident Evil* franchise. Lisa Purse, *Digital Imaging in Popular Cinema* (Edinburgh: Edinburgh University Press, 2013).
23 A term the producers themselves use, as I present in *Empire of Effects*.
24 ILM effects artists were referring to the evident look of digitally derived effects as the "digital curse" at least as far back as the *Star Wars* prequel production in the late 1990s. See *Empire of Effects*.
25 Turnock, *Empire of Effects*.
26 Jacob Gaboury, *Image Objects: An Archaeology of Computer Graphics* (Cambridge, MA: MIT Press, 2021), 7
27 Gaboury, *Image Objects*, 11.
28 Ibid., 4.

29 To Manovich, the logic of animation is, "the logic of an animation stand where the stack of images is arranged parallel to each other, rather than of live action cinema where the camera typically moves through 3D space." Manovich, *The Language of New Media*, 149.

30 Of course, it is the visual effects industry that materially produces this "live action" effect, and *The Empire of Effects* argues why and how effects company ILM conceived of and produced the style of effects realism that we accept fairly readily as cinematic realism, despite the rather extreme stylization and even deformation of notions of perceptual reality and camera reality that comprises that industry dominant style.

31 Christian Metz and Françoise Meltzer. "'Trucage' and the Film," *Critical Inquiry* 3:4 (1977): 657–75.

32 This is despite what they say in hindsight. See for example Mark Cotta Vaz and Patricia Rose Duignan, *Industrial Light and Magic: Into the Digital Realm* (New York: Del Rey, 1996); a Lucasfilm-authorized publication that casts ILM's digital transition as smooth, orderly, and inevitable, which was far from the truth.

33 See my essay "The Auteurist Special Effects Film: Kubrick's *2001: A Space Odyssey* and the 'Single-Generation Look,'" in Peter Krämer and Yannis Tzioumakis (eds.) *The Hollywood Renaissance: Revisiting American Cinema's Most Celebrated Era* (London: Bloomsbury Academic, 2018), 71–90, for a discussion of the effects work on Kubrick's film as a complex re-working of cinema's human-machine interaction before digital effects.

34 Failes (2020).

35 It was announced to the shop in April of 1992 that *Jurassic Park* was going CG, according to Dutra. Failes (2020).

36 According to *Cinefex*, the computer graphics assignment was divided between Tippettt and ILM. Tippettt Studio animated fifteen shots for two major sequences, the *T-Rex* attack on road and the stalking *Velociraptors* in the kitchen. ILM did thirty-seven shots reveling the browsing brachiosaurs, the *Gallimimus* herd stampede with the *T-Rex*, and climactic battle between *T-Rex* and raptors. Jody Duncan, "The Beauty in the Beasts," *Cinefex* 55 (August 1993): 60.

37 Duncan, "The Beauty in the Beasts,", 49–50.

38 Brian Knep, Craig Hayes, Rick Sayre, and Tom Williams. "Dinosaur Input Device," in *Proceedings of the SIGCHI Conference on Human Factors in Computing* Systems (1995), 304–9.

39 Failes (2020).

40 Ibid.

41 This "loss of the camera" had a number of wide-ranging implications, not least of which were dire labor consequences. While since the late 1910s, most effects workers were covered by union and guild (usually ASC) representation due to their use of and intensive training in physical camerawork, the move away from cameras toward screens and software meant that those entering the

business after *Jurassic Park* largely were not trained on cameras, and therefore did not have traditional unions to join.

42 According to Hayes,

> [Tom St. Amand] had it worked down to a science. He knew which type of materials to use. He knew that he you could mix the aluminum, and the phosphor bronze washers and the steel shoulder screws, et cetera. He had a grease that came from an army surplus store. He had this olive drab can of grease that was his special grease, and it was the perfect grease …. We were really lucky at the time in that Phil knew Stuart Ziff, who … is kind of an electromechanical artistic genius. And he came in to help out and brought another world of experience in terms of things like the wires that we would use. So one of the things he introduced us to was this wire made by a company called, Cooner, which had literally hundreds of strands. Each strand in the wire was so fine that the wire was incredibly supple and incredibly resilient and flexible and it was not going to break. (Failes 2020)

43 ILM artists had initially experimented with using the proprietary MORF software they had originally developed for *Willow* in 1988 as a way to render motion blur digitally. But, according to Brian Knep, "We got some good results but it was very slow and a pain in the ass" (Failes 2020).

44 Although it would become state of the art about ten years later, motion capture was an uncommon technique at the time. However other, non-ILM productions had experimented with it, most notably Barry Levinson's *Toys* in 1992. PDI (Pacific Data Images) and DQI (DreamQuest Images) completed the work on *Toys*' effects. Brian Knep, Craig Hayes, Rick Sayre, and Tom Williams. "Dinosaur Input Device," in *Proceedings of the SIGCHI Conference on Human factors in Computing Systems*, pp. 304–309. 1995:1.

45 Again, digitally derived motion capture would not be a common practice in the effects work until the 2000s, especially after the success of Weta's work on Gollum in the second *The Lord of the Rings*.

46 Failes (2020).

47 Ibid.

48 Ibid. Emphasis original.

49 According to Dutra in Failes (2020).

50 As Stokes elaborated,

> We often talked about developing a more modular system that could adapt quickly to new projects but never had the time or money for it. Also, when *Troopers* began Tippett Studio was a stop-motion company that dabbled in CG. By the end of *Troopers*, it was a fully-functioning CG production house—we basically built the facility around ourselves along the way. The DID's helped make that transition, but to my knowledge Tippett hasn't used them since. (Failes 2020)

51 Failes (2020).

7

From "Six-Foot Turkey" to Marketing Monster: Marketing *Jurassic Park* and Its Sequels

Ed Vollans
University of Leicester, UK

Introduction: "Park" or "World"? Establishing the Franchise

Jurassic Park, released on June 9, 1993, moved into the public consciousness at speed. The combined weight of both Steven Spielberg and the underpinning authority of Michael Crichton's novel provided a sturdy platform from which to launch a mainstream film loaded with marketing potential. Crichton subsequently published a sequel—*The Lost World* and in 1997 this in turn also became a Spielberg-directed film adaptation: *The Lost World: Jurassic Park*. The first two instalments of the franchise are adaptations of existing work and provide the basis for authorial acclaim during promotion. The third instalment, however, *Jurassic Park III* (2001), was written solely for the screen by Alexander Payne, Jim Buchanan, and Jim Taylor, and as such it represents the first deviation away from existent source material into a written-for-screen franchise. *Jurassic Park III*'s campaign thus necessitated a shift in promotional address. Analysis of this promotional shift not only offers unique insight into how the first three films were promoted, but the wider promotional landscape before the series also became a clear franchise.

As if foregrounding a franchise, Crichton subsequently republished both books into one under the title *Jurassic World*.[1] This branding has been adopted for the subsequent *Jurassic* trilogy from 2015 onward: *Jurassic World* (2017) *Jurassic World: Fallen Kingdom* (2018), and *Jurassic World: Dominion* (2022). The public presence of this intellectual property is so large it currently spans six feature-length movies, a short movie (*Battle at Big Rock* [2018]), a Netflix spin-off (*Camp Cretaceous* [2020–present]), an augmented reality game (*Jurassic World: Alive* [2018]), and has more properties too numerous to list here.

Such is the success of this world-framing that, although a film in its own right, "Jurassic World" appears on current franchise-licensed Lego sets and promotion, including those depicting iconic sequences from the 1993 *Jurassic Park*. This titular transfer refers to the 2015 film and the franchise more broadly in an act of retrospective brand-building, while offering commentary on the marketing and licensing concerns of Lego, and to the complex nature of franchise marketing generally. To talk about any of these is inherently to invoke a wider cultural network of interrelated texts and all serving to reinforce "*Jurassic Park*-ness" in the public eye.

Yet the status of the franchise is not solely a result of popular acclaim, nor of simply saturating the market with content, but rather of a curated promotional rhetoric manifesting in toys, interviews, merchandise, and more. The franchise itself did not, could not have emerged "ready-made" ultimately changing promotional stances with *Jurassic Park III*, including the introduction of new dinosaurs aiding new merchandising opportunities. Breaking from the established source text of Crichton's novels and Spielberg's directorial acclaim of the prior movies, the third, *Jurassic Park III*, was the worst financially performing movie (grossing $368.78m worldwide[2]) and rated the lowest of the first three movies.[3] As it was neither a Spielberg film nor based on a Crichton novel, it represents a key moment of departure from both the directorial and authorial acclaim that surrounded the first two movies' promotion, and is the last contribution to the franchise before *Jurassic World* and the franchise signifiers that are now associated therein. Thus, it is a moment of promotional transition from the authorial adaptation and sequel logic previously established as it moves to the rhetoric of a stand-alone or unified product.

In terms of industrial logic, a franchise may be retroactively signaled, and/or constructed through successive films and their associated marketing adding to, reinforcing, and thus perpetuating key elements of the diegetic world as an identifiable whole. Promotion in this manner sets the existent material and any future instalments in a kind of duality of (re)presentation and promotion. This double articulation of promotional intertextuality manifests a tension between the overall franchise and the film as an individual contribution with a range of different agents; journalists, actors, film critics, fans, and merchandising mechanisms all mediating the public presence and competing for attention within their own spheres of influence. While specific paratexts may be more or less closely connected with an individual film within the franchise, collectively they all point to and reinforce the core ideals of the franchise world itself, constituting a platform for the "consumable identity" of the product.[4]

Considering *Jurassic Park*, *The Lost World: Jurassic Park*, and *Jurassic Park III* as a formative period incorporating the transition from "films" to "franchise" offers a way of bracketing the movies into broadly pre-franchise marketing logic, and thus can expect to see a pivot in terms of promotional logic. There are of course significant challenges in exploring the marketing and positioning of a film in retrospect, not least because the late 1990s saw nascent development of promotional digital ephemera now at risk of loss:[5] neither subject to systematic archiving, nor always readily available thanks to link-rot, software and hardware compatibility. As Johnston has pointed out, there is a significant dearth in standardized practices of promotional material methodologies.[6] In terms of the scale of promotion, work by Marich points to the mammoth task of exploring this, as *Jurassic Park* had "more than one hundred companies making more than a thousand types of [interconnected] products."[7] Attempting to follow the merchandising for example, would be difficult enough even if a list of licensed holders could be found, echoing the kinds of challenges Barker and Mathjis's *Lord of the Rings* project encountered.[8] As the work of Bacon-Smith and Yarborough show,[9] everything from press release, to trailer to fan responses toward merchandise form part of multilayered macrotext, blending and negotiating various authorial, directorial, and critical-acclamatory rhetoric all shaping the promotional surround and informing the public discussion.

Mapping exactly how a single product is positioned is a problematic task and proposes a set of challenges, as Wright illustrates.[10] Few specialist promotional material archives exist, though existing archives of press discourse do, and these form a repository for discourse noting what promotion was happening, and when. The archivable qualities of newspapers provide both temporal organization, and accessibility, while analysis of discourse indicates the kind of approaches used by the primary promotional team. As Maat and De Jong note, there is often a causation between journalistic tone and press release.[11] Within press discourse of course, we can expect to find references to the kinds of promotional content, while conversely excluding that which is not seen as noteworthy. Articles may actively discuss promotional events otherwise lost or excluded from a priori corpus: such as fast-food tie ins, book signings, television scheduling. Certainly, some promotional materials garner more press attention than others; trailers and opening night information will likely feature higher than say, cereal-box toys. But as a broad benchmark for understanding a campaign retrospectively, they serve to provide a clear starting point for further study. Blending newspaper and magazine archives, with broader digital archaeology where relevant, this chapter first uses press archives within the "Nexis" database to map the campaigns for each movie, then combines the structure, content, and reception of these into a framework for analysis of the campaign's promotion overall.

Jurassic Park

In many ways the promotion for the film mirrors that of its narrative. In the film we see different forms of dinosaur before the cinematic "reveal": first fossils, then dinosaurs on screens, then reincarnated beasts themselves. This is similar to the marketing campaign, in which dinosaurs were often visually absent and foregrounded with an emphasis on known representations: notably archaeology. Within the film a volunteer scoffs: "That doesn't look very scary. More like a six-foot turkey." Almost as if in anticipation of this response, the marketing logic did everything it could to convince potential viewer that the forthcoming monsters were serious, authentic and a scientific event in their own right, birthed by a visionary (Spielberg) who would spare no expense.

Initial promotion of *Jurassic Park* (prior to January 1992) focused on three core elements: budget, source material, and above-the-line production team. Understandably, preproduction announcements are likely to be (working) title, lead production team, location, and stars. *Jurassic Park*'s budget was initially reported at 70m USD, with subsequent variations between $60m and $75m.[12] Box Office Mojo puts the budget retrospectively at $63m.[13] Far beyond industry posturing, the announcement of a budget offers the suggestion of faith on the part of the studio, it suggests an anticipatory correlation between cost and quality. In a similar vein, in 1993 MCA/Universal Merchandising placed the estimated budget for marketing and advertising alone at "at least $60m,"[14] around the same amount as the total cost of the film's production suggesting the sheer volume of promotional materials and content available, with around $100m in merchandise sales and a further $65m in wider promotional support.[15] This latter announcement in effect speaks to potential stakeholders ("our film *will* be successful") but also can be read as a warning to competitors: "our film will be everywhere, don't compete with us." Thus, initial press discussion focuses on the proprietary value of the forthcoming film, typically through promoting the narrative:

> In preproduction: Steven Spielberg's "Jurassic Park," based on the Michael Crichton novel about a resort that offers guests a chance to mingle with dinosaurs cloned from DNA. The $70 million movie—the highest tab for a film yet—is due in 1993.[16]

While discussing preproduction on *Jurassic Park* references are regularly made to Spielberg's prior and contemporaneous work, such as *Jaws* (1975) and *E.T.* (1982), as well as *Hook*, which was released shortly before *Jurassic Park* in December 1991. This kind of authorial emphasis dominates the early press reports and beyond being core origin story for the film's existence it can be traced back to a 1991 press release.[17] Within this release we see relatively little information beyond "Spielberg is adapting Crichton's work," yet it frames the work through Crichton's source material and Spielberg's ability to deliver it on screen. In both cases, referencing prior work and thus borrowing the established capital therein from both creatives, "I doubt that there is any filmmaker other than Steven Spielberg with whom we would make 'Jurassic Park,'" said Pollock. "Michael Crichton's terrific story, in Steven's hands, will be transformed into a spectacular motion picture."[18]

The press release itself concludes by emphasizing both Crichton and Spielberg equally. The penultimate paragraph emphasizing Crichton's prior work ("Four of Crichton's novels have been made into films") and the final paragraph emphasizing Spielberg's production of "Universal's three biggest hits: 'E.T., the Extra Terrestrial,' 'Jaws,' both directed by Spielberg, and 'Back to the Future,' directed by Robert Zemeckis, presented by Spielberg and produced by Amblin."[19]

Notably this early release doesn't include any mention of finances suggesting that cultural capital gave way to financial capital. Such financial discussions, typically of the proposed budget, and of the $2m paid for the film rights, move rapidly to speculation surrounding the application of the budget. As Ryan writes in the *Toronto Star*, "Much of the expense of the project lies in building full-size robotic dinosaurs of various species from the Mesozoic Era, which include the fearsome *Tyrannosaurus Rex*."[20] This phrase, almost verbatim appears in a November 1991 work by Ford,[21] suggesting heavy reliance on a press release for the reporting, though none so far has been found.

Creative prowess becomes woven into commentary and later into discussions of speculative authenticity, implicitly equating a Spielberg experience as "authentic." Many early discussions situate *Jurassic Park* within the context of wider public consciousness, likely brought about based on knowledge of the book. Discussions, often of scientific findings, allude to *Jurassic Park* in passing: for example, of DNA developments in dinosaur analysis ("Does it sound like the scary best-seller Jurassic Park?").[22] Similarly, Frankensteinian parallels are often drawn, usually between scientific developments and popular culture, albeit often tongue-in-cheek.[23] This suggests the permeation of the film's sci-fi premise into wider culture and popular scientific discourse. Moving chronologically through the dataset this emerges as a key theme perhaps unsurprising considering earlier reports of academic research being the basis for Crichton's novel.[24] This secondary discourse is likely due to journalistic or academic contextualization, trying to ensure the topic is understood within a specific context rather than a deliberate attempt to promote the film or to solicit the capital of authenticity. Yet authenticity is actively solicited elsewhere, emphasis falls on the ways in which this unknown, forthcoming, experience was created. This tends to run parallel with discussions of the science of dinosaur resurrection and the act of creating pseudo-indexical replicas on screen:

> For example, a palaeontologist [sic] has been hired to consult on the authenticity of the dinosaur toys which will be sold when Jurassic Park is released next year. Brad Globe, Spielberg's marketing man, says the toy dinosaurs will be "more real than anyone has ever seen."[25]

Globe's "more real" quote informs speculative discussions of merchandise despite those discussions often alluding somewhat cynically to the future merchandise saturation. That the dinosaurs are "real" implicitly justifies much of the merchandise. This notion of "the real" becomes the frame for discussing the creation of dinosaurs, despite cinematic representations being deliberately downplayed in early promotion.

In short, we see the idea of authentic dinosaurs before we see any cinematic incarnations, suggesting that this authenticity becomes a frame of consumption on which merchandise and marketing is offered. Authenticity becomes useful in unpacking Spielberg as creative power, discussions of authentic dinosaurs, rain, and effects abound.[26] Indeed, Universal went so far as to found the "Jurassic Foundation," a charitable nonprofit dedicated to furthering paleontologic research.[27] As Wright notes, such discussions of authenticity form a "legitimation exercise"[28] reinforcing Barker's suggestion of promotional materials "trying to ensure that something occurs by dint of announcing it."[29] This legitimation of the spectacle becomes interconnected with authorial creativity and the spectacle of cinema as an indexical form, not uncommon elsewhere, as Hadas summarizes: "The study of authorship in promotion is also the study of deeply embedded cultural ideas and narratives about genius and expression, the authentic and the fake, and power relations in the construction of meaning around the texts of popular culture."[30]

It is unsurprising that having established the Spielberg–Crichton basis, the promotional rhetoric speculates upon how the film might manifest and thus affects the space in which merchandising is released and discussed. As Groves attests, the marketing strategy was drawn up two years prior to the release, and sought to succeed where *E.T.* had failed: "After creating the logo, marketing programs were drawn up in every territory. Initially only one photo of a dinosaur, showing the head of T-rex tipping over a park vehicle, was released. That was Spielberg's strategy."[31]

In the UK the *Jurassic Park* campaign teased information first with ambiguous "next summer" teasers in December '92; this was followed by the release of publicity shots of the actors looking at a dinosaur egg in February and finally a second trailer showing moving dinosaurs in April.[32] Despite the general reluctance to "give away a lot of the movie early on in trailers or publicity"[33] the dinosaurs-as-authentic discourse led to significant tertiary promotion, potentially without any formal licensing arrangement but adding to the wider spirit of consumption—such as Kokoro Dinosaurs:

> Kokoro Dinosaurs in the Los Angeles area of Tarzana said its traveling automated dinosaur exhibit is booked until early next year. "We're doing lots of exhibits for museums because of the movie," said company president Jun Shimizu. "It's going to be a big dinosaur year."[34]

While Kokoro Dinosaurs appear to be unsolicited, it is not isolated, with reports of another peripheral film "*Jurassic Park: the Science Behind the Story*" being produced by the Academy of Natural Sciences (though it's unclear if this was before or after mainstream release of the film and if this was approved, or used film footage).[35] There's little doubt that many instances of edutainment were solicited, however. Keith Issac, MCA/Universal merchandising vice president, claimed: "Part of the plan has been to use the dinosaur theme to do tie-ins with natural history museums all over Europe."[36]

In the UK, as the marketing campaign followed this same route: study packs on DNA and the novel-to-screen adaptation work were sent out to schools.[37] The film's premiere was followed by an after-party at the Natural History Museum, complete with *Jurassic Park* branded buses for celebrities.[38] The *Daily Mirror* hosted a children's essay competition: "What's the best extinct creature to bring back?"[39] As the marketing campaign had started two years prior, it suggests a clear attempt to legitimize adult elements of the film through the lens of education—perhaps suggesting the MPAA's PG-13 rating was in-keeping with a desired school-age demographic.

Early behind-the-scenes previews of *Jurassic Park* released over the holiday period in the United States suggest the solicitation of family audiences—pointing to the somewhat paradoxical image of dinosaurs as both educational topic and object of terror. Free-floating signification of dinosaurs thus passively contributed to the wider consumption of dinosaurs in the public consciousness. Concurrent with *Jurassic Park*'s campaign we see properties actively cross-promoting. *The Dinosaurs!* (PBS, 1992) being a four-episode series run by *PBS*, using a collection of existing documentary materials, and Jim Henson's *Dinosaurs* (1991–4)[40] an animatronic anthropomorphic dinosaur family sitcom. Both had Thanksgiving holiday releases and were centered on prehistoric themes. While the exact content of the behind-the-scenes footage is unclear, the context of *Jurassic Park*'s holiday preview maintains Spielberg's star-status:

> MCA/Universal and Sears, Roebuck & Co. are sponsoring a seven-minute behind-the-scenes preview of Steven Spielberg's summer release "Jurassic Park," which will follow one of the best lead-ins of the season: the rebroadcast of "E.T. The Extra-Terrestrial" Thanksgiving night on CBS.[41]

A year prior, the TV broadcast of *E.T.* had ratings indicating a viewership of approximately 17.1 million homes,[42] and the draw of family-friendly holiday viewing suggests an attempt to capitalize on similar audience figures, demographic, and the careful reiteration of Spielberg's prior success. That the slot of 7 minutes and 14 seconds is a "behind-the-scenes" rather than a trailer or teaser suggests an emphasis on creativity and artistic challenge as promotional draw, while simultaneously capitalizing on a series of associated "making of" books.[43] "Making of" featurettes recur within the campaign, with Spielberg while on location in Poland for *Schindler's List* (1993): "Amblin shot an hour-long interview between the director and British film journalist Iain Johnstone."[44] This resulted in a newspaper feature, a 45-minute documentary on Spielberg's career and a 30-minute documentary with some scenes from *Jurassic Park*.[45] Creative control is carefully interwoven with modes of production, which were in turn aligned with suggestions and claims about the film's "educational" potential.

Beyond the educational lens of the campaign, it also formed a vehicle for exhibition technology. Here again issues of budget and resultant industry assurances resurface. The trailer itself was previewed to a select audience at ShoWest in March '93, amid accusations of elitism, shown to 130 top exhibitors with "thousands" excluded.[46] According to Block, the screening itself was surrounded by ballyhoo typical of spectacle promotion:

> The private presentation was held in a two-room suite. Guests were ushered down a long hall with posters detailing each prehistoric era, with smoke blowing around them, under black lights as eerie music from the film played. ... After about 20 minutes, the sound of giant dinosaurs marching was heard. Suddenly, a green military style jeep crashed through the wall (actually the front end of a jeep on a catapult). Guides in jungle uniforms, with black berets and black automatic weapons, shook flashlights as they directed the guests into a theater in the back room.[47]

This kind of experiential event promotion, echoing early film industry "ballyhoo," is typical of Hollywood blockbuster event marketing, tying in with what we now know to be "event movies."[48]

Upon the UK announcement of a PG certification "*The Sun* [Newspaper] hooked up kids to heart monitors to see how their tickers reacted to the scary beasts."[49] But the ShoWest spectacle sits in contrast to reports of the content of the trailer having neither dinosaurs nor special effects.[50] Yet it did offer *Jurassic Park* as a vehicle for Universal's new digital sound system: Digital Theater Systems; the ShoWest screening being the first demonstration of the technology aimed at selected exhibitors.[51] Indeed, technology-as-experience and creative control reappears as a theme within this campaign. By April 26, the three-minute trailer was on 1,000 laser discs and distributed across America's consumer electronic stores to be played on a loop, presumably taking advantage of both claims surrounding cinematic aesthetic on laser discs and the additional consumer exposure—setting up the possibility for secondary home entertainment sales,[52] a tactic we see later for the *Lost World*'s promotion of *Jurassic Park III* on DVD.[53]

Ultimately, in *Jurassic Park*'s promotional surround, Spielberg's prior creative reputation was mobilized alongside finance and frames of scientific authenticity to legitimate the broader experience. On the one hand Jurassic Park is clearly framed as a blockbuster, from emphasis on budgets and creative aesthetics, but within it is also framed as an "authentic" experience. This set the tone for future work; indeed, it seems that *Lost World* largely replicated these processes, with an added emphasis on merchandise.

The Lost World: Jurassic Park (1997)

Published in September 1995, Crichton's *The Lost World* was immediately identified as both sequel and soon-to-be-a-major-motion-picture project, with reports of the movie rights being sold before the book was released.[54] Before its publication, Spielberg claimed that the novel would be released soon and that preproduction planning was already underway, and that "no cast has been chosen. We're just trying to decide which new dinosaurs will be introduced in the sequel."[55] This comment suggests a practice of promoting the dinosaur as star, but it also suggests an element of foresight into the marketing and merchandising opportunities.

It is difficult to believe that merchandising did not influence this key production decision. Early reports suggest Spielberg was reluctant to direct the work,[56] and it seems that both Crichton and Spielberg were involved in negotiations that saw them trade up-front fees for "extremely lucrative backends," likely a percentage of merchandise and ticket sales and rights to an animated spin-off.[57] The film's ontological conditions though differ significantly from those of *Jurassic Park*. While both are adaptations of Crichton works, the proximity of the film's promotional discussion with the source materials' initial release suggests some collaboration between publishing and cinema; certainly, this was intimated in reviews of the book.[58]

As a sequel, the film and book needed to find a clear sense of product differentiation. Indeed, as Crichton put it "the demand of the sequel is, it's got to be the same, but different."[59] In terms of the promotional surround, this mantra echoes the wider understandings of genre promotion, as Neale notes, the discursive process of genre is one of "repetition and difference."[60] As Gong et al. note, sequels often have a reduced risk as they represent a familiar concept.[61] We might expect, in the spirit of this paradox, that the promotional campaign for *The Lost World* might continue where *Jurassic Park* left off. Indeed, the core elements remain: early promotion focused on the proprietary values, making connections that establish the *Lost World* as a sequel. Early announcements firmly framed the project as Spielberg's, rather than Crichton's, or even Crichton-and-Spielberg project. Even in early discussions of the book, Spielberg's authority is often emphasized.[62] As Whitehead put it, "Unavoidably, Michael Crichton is now an entertainment broker on the level of Steven Spielberg, the man who anointed him; inevitably, 'The Lost World' can't be 'The Lost World' so much as it is 'Jurassic Park 2.'"[63]

Indeed, though a sequel, this is quickly erased from the film's promotional discourse through the authorial prowess of Spielberg, with United Pictures President Casey Silver supporting this framing:

> There is no other filmmaker who can provide the level of creative brilliance and unprecedented vision necessary to bring "The Lost World" to the screen. "We can now be assured that this film will not only be a follow-up to 'Jurassic Park,' but a unique and tremendously exciting motion picture event in its own right."[64]

Around the same time in November 1995, a *Jurassic Park* theme park ride was announced. Again, Spielberg's authorial prowess was retained with reports that he was "closely associated" with the experience.[65] Discourse surrounding the ride was similar to that of the film, an emphasis on cost—"billed as the most expensive ($110 million) and most elaborate theme park ride of all time"—and the ride having the "most realistic animatronics."[66] Thus, investment and authenticity remained central to the wider promotional discourse of the brand, echoing the earlier faux syllogism that suggest a quality experience. By June of 1996, though, discussions emerged surrounding merchandising:

> Retail revenues for "The Lost World: Jurassic Park" will exceed the $1 billion for "Jurassic Park" merchandise by 25 percent. Film licensing deals for the sequel with partners such as Hasbro, DreamWorks Interactive, Fruit of the Loom and Sega of America have been nailed down and others with Burger King and Mercedes-Benz are reportedly being finalized. About 500 licensees and international agents were given a fashion show at Universal Studios last week featuring conceptual designs for eight different upscale lines of "Lost World" apparel.[67]

Almost immediately after this release Mercedes Benz confirmed the M-Class All-Activity Vehicle was to be included in the film, presumably seeking to replicate the same placement success of the "Z3 roadster" in *Goldeneye* (1995).[68] While reports suggested that the majority of the merchandise licenses would be aimed at the mass market, some point to a "specific program for department stores."[69] The VP of merchandising for Universal claimed that "We are absolutely tailoring our programs toward the department stores ... It's a priority, because it's a good channel to capture the nostalgia market."[70] The specifics of what this "nostalgia market" might equate to are unclear—perhaps for the first *Jurassic Park* film—but given the proximity to *Jurassic Park*'s release it's more likely soliciting adults buying goods evocative of their own childhood for their own children.

Later, in February 1997, an unusual press release circulated: a list of the merchandising license categories.[71] It denotes categories clearly aimed at children (stationary, super soakers, bandages, sweets, figurines), though there were items listed as adult—mostly clothing and apparel alongside demographically ambiguous products: prepaid phone cards, videogames, pinball, and playing cards. This merchandising could (and perhaps, should) form the subject of a separate inquiry, but it's worth noting that the inclusion of a press release list serves the same kind of industrial performance of faith in the product and competition warning seen with claims of *Jurassic Park*'s budget. A cynical reading may suggest such merchandising is a calculated move given Spielberg and Crichton's contract, particularly given the comparative lack of attention for *Jurassic Park*. Yet it also speaks to market economics: if the new dinosaurs represented a mode of product differentiation, it makes sense to prepare the market through introducing these new characters. If, as with *Jurassic Park*, dinosaurs are essentially "hidden" from the promotional material, it makes sense to let non-cinematic incarnations of dinosaurs introduce them as the film's principal antagonists. Indeed, the tag line "something has survived" is usefully ambiguous, while the trailer itself largely shows complete herbivores, with carnivorous dinosaurs being shown largely through close-ups of teeth and claws.

In August 1996, to support the release of entertainment software "Directors Chair"—in which players master Hollywood basics such as budget, editing, and so on—a competition was launched with a prize of a day on the *Lost World* set. Placing this in context, in an interview that same month, Pendreigh notes that Goldblum has yet to start filming *Lost World*, suggesting that marketing and merchandising had been lined up (conceptually at least) far in advance of production.[72] As principal photography commenced, the usual discourse from casting news, to discussions of specific locations appears. At this time, Burger King announced it would promote both *A Land Before Time*[73] and *Lost World*, indicating the kind of synergy of dinosaur products seen with *Jurassic Park*, and offering the opportunity to implicitly market dinosaurs to children. This appears a calculated move designed to compete with McDonalds after the company won a lucrative Disney contract previously held by Burger King.[74] In the UK, Tetley Tea issued "Lost World" collectible coins,[75] combining themes of both adventure and discovery (perhaps echoing Spielberg's previous association with *Indiana Jones*), collectible lenticular "holographic" cards and colorful lenticular medal toys.[76] Such a focus on the dinosaurs and the visualizations therein implicitly emphasized the dinosaur as celebrity alongside an inseparable nod to education—the very inclusion of the dinosaur's name in a collectible context offers a form of dinosaur taxonomy. In this context the collectible is known to appeal to children, with variations on a theme acting in partnership with Kellogg's, KP Foods Skips, Mini Cheddars, and Hula Hoops.[77]

By early January '97, a single reference in the UK press to "advanced publicity materials" noted the tagline "something has survived"[78] and this was followed by wider discussions of the trailer itself made by Universal's in-house team.[79] Kirk Honeycutt of *The Hollywood Reporter* noted that signs appeared reading "This Trailer Is Intense. ... [if] you are sensitive to strong flashing light or sound effects or if you are attending this theatre with children who may be sensitive to these effects, we strongly recommend that you leave the auditorium when this trailer is being shown."[80]

Despite this warning, however, the trailer was given a "green band" rating—suitable for all—suggesting that the theatricality here is itself part of the publicity campaign, similar to *Jurassic Park*'s launch. It was released in the United States in forty sites on December 13.[81] By March of 1997 several press articles referenced a website, suggesting that merchandise preceded the website.[82] Comprising a landing page resembling John Hammond's (Richard Attenborough) office, visitors were encouraged to open the notebooks, searching for passwords and usernames that unlocked short sequences.[83] They were also encouraged to unlock dinosaur files, both emphasising the "monster-as-star" rhetoric and potentially setting the tone for this material's consumption. Here the users are literally positioned in Hammond's chair as director of InGen, entering passwords to unlock project files and unlock dinosaur content. The site also hosted a competition for a day on the set.[84] The focus on dinosaur *content* seems a clear marketing strategy. Broadcast on *CBS This Morning* film roundup gave a guided discussion alongside six *Lost World* excerpts. While the exact sequences are unclear, the context suggests depiction of central characters and dinosaurs—in effect replicating and reinforcing existing information.[85]

Despite the variations, an increased focus on merchandise to an established market and fanbase, *Lost World* follows established lines of promotion designed to promote the film's authenticity, with a clear emphasis on the existing formula: dinosaurs as mobile signifier, stars in their own right, combined with Spielberg's auteur reputation, and claimed educational potential. The dual market of implied horror, coupled with a clear solicitation of the child demographic follows that of *Jurassic Park*. However, the legitimation activity as reported in the press is less extensive with *Lost World*. While Museums did cross-promote,[86] this seems more opportunistic than orchestrated suggesting a reliance on the experience of *Jurassic Park*. Thus, while *Lost World* was a sequel, it offers the same process of event marketing.

Jurassic Park III (2001)

Building on the prior success of the first two movies, *Jurassic Park III* represents something of a gamble for Universal. Spielberg claimed to have "hatched' the story line, despite it being written by Peter Buchman. Spielberg also instead acted as executive producer, handing directorial control to Joe Johnston.[87] As such, it represented a significant departure from the prior films, removed from both Crichton's source material and Spielberg's creative authority. It represented the moment at which the franchise was considered as a possibility. Spielberg's long-time production partner Kathleen Kennedy noted:

> We knew there had to be a *Jurassic Park III* when we did *The Lost World*, Believe me, once everybody gets wind of the fact that there's a franchise possibility, there's so much pressure to keep it going. It's twofold: it's not just the studio (Universal) putting on the pressure. It's the audience as well because we wouldn't do this if the people didn't come.[88]

Except the audience came, and went, and at the time it was unclear if this was a franchise, or a trilogy. *Jurassic Park III* had the trappings of another high-concept film, a clearly sold premise and an established audience, yet is the poorest performing film in the IP to date. The film was critiqued upon release, and no further cinematic development was had over a decade. The reasons for poor financial performance are varied, and complex, but the attempts to position the film as a franchise (rather than Spielberg movie or Crichton adaptation) show the difficulties in separating the concept and launching a franchise. In comparison to *Jurassic Park* and *Lost World*, *Jurassic Park III* had a significantly reduced marketing campaign.[89] In an interview prior to the film's release Johnston noted, "I'm not a huge fan of sequels, but I'm a fan of this franchise."[90] While not the sole attempt to claim *the Lost World* as part of the franchise, this awareness from someone party to above-the-line decisions supports the suggestion that this film was actively trying to position itself as a wider cultural event, breaking away from the dual pillars of established creative control and authenticity.

Unlike *Jurassic Park*, and *Lost World*, there were stark references in the press to merchandise and promotion. In part, due to wider financial concerns, *Jurassic Park III* was reported as having a "limited roster of partners," noting only that Coca-Cola was running an in-cinema cup promotion, and was Walmart promoting merchandise in store.[91] It was further reported that the campaign was "under the radar" amid the suggestion that awareness of the movie was so high it risked negative backlash if it promoted too early.[92] Lacking the same kind of media blitz, and without the clear supporting network of creative authority, the film cannot be positioned as a Spielberg film. Compounding this, Spielberg released *A.I. Artificial Intelligence* in June of 2001. To emphasize Spielberg's production credit for *Jurassic Park III* would risk competing with *A.I.* directly, and on the same terms. When Crichton and Spielberg were mentioned in the press it was in passing reference to the preceding films. So, with limited promotional cooperation, the film drew on previously established trends: dinosaurs-as-cast-members, and timidly, "dinosaurs-as-education."

Within the educational promotional pathway, we see a reliance on the legacy of the previous films, with a CD-ROM "Dinosaur Encyclopaedia" providing background on the new creatures,[93] the inclusion of an "easy-to-read storybook" for young readers, and "Dinosaur Field guide"[94] all of which feed into established promotional themes.[95] Indeed, a week prior to the film's release, Johnston as director drew attention to this symbiosis somewhat baldly: "I love dinosaurs and the scientific side of it."[96] This doesn't seem manifest in *Jurassic Park III*'s promotion; however, it suggests awareness of the interconnected themes that underpin prior promotional strategy. Notably within the same interview, almost nothing is made of artistic authority or association with creative "genius" as appeared with *Jurassic Park* and *Lost World* vis-à-vis Spielberg.

Alongside the limited educational elements, we see an emphasis on technology as forming promotional rhetoric, such as animatronic dinosaurs being an outright technological feat. *Jurassic Park III* lacked the extensive legitimation exercises that the previous films deployed, but instead embraced technology to disseminate the promotional message. Partly resulting from wider socio-technical developments, in context we see the entertainment industry using a range of new media technology for promotion. Contemporary uses being the word-of-mouth success of *The Blair Witch Project*,[97] and Spielberg's *A.I.*[98] and wider cultural shift in digital promotion generally. There is clear attempt to capitalize on increased technology in the home, we see this work in effect building on the early website and wider online culture.[99] As with *Jurassic Park* and *Lost World*, there is a videogame tie-in; however, *Jurassic Park III* saw the development of a desktop-based "marketing application":

> "Runaway Spino," a marketing application for the launch of Jurassic Park III. The intention is for the product to be distributed over the Internet by e-mail. With Runaway Spino, an interactive Spinosaurus will live on the computer desktop. Users have the opportunity to stun, x-ray or capture the dinosaur in a net—a fun atmosphere designed to generate excitement about the movie release.[100]

Unlikely the first instance of such "promotional software," this application serves to reinforce the notion of the dinosaur as star, articulating the single rhetorical stance of the film's promotional identity. As Johnston noted in an interview the week of the film's release, "you design the story and the production around the dinosaurs. That's the history of these movies."[101] Without a clear conceptual development, the promotional concept can be reduced to a single theme of capture/escape the dinosaur. The interconnected themes of dinosaurs as product of technology (both within the diegesis, and broadly within the act of filming) forms an implicitly key promotional pillar of the first two films and is continued implicitly within the third. Similar to *Jurassic Park* and *Lost World* we see reports of animatronic dinosaurs being out of control, but there is little beyond this.

The previous emphasis on technology allows for the symbiotic promotion of *Jurassic Park III* and the DVD release of the two preceding movies. October 2000 saw the DVD release of so-called System seller DVDs of *Jurassic Park* and *Lost World*. Designed as vehicles for DVD player purchases, and thus ensuring a secondary market, box set DVD releases of the first two films were sold with certificates of authenticity, and included storyboards, models, and production stills, alongside making-of documentaries.[102] The DVD-Rom in the special issue offered the public a "direct hotlink to the set of *Jurassic Park III*" through the use of online chat rooms,[103] and webcasts from key creative personnel.[104] It's likely that through emphasizing the creative process of *Jurassic Park* and *Lost World*, these featurettes frame *Jurassic Park III* in a similar manner, but the differentiation between the films is unclear.

In November 2000, eight months prior to the film's release, the announcement of the central featured dinosaur, the Spinosaurus, drew quips about the human actors being the supporting cast.[105] Just as with *Jurassic Park* and *Lost World* this follows a pattern, emphasizing the dinosaur and then announcing cast members. This preceded the announcement of Téa Leonie as a co-star, by several weeks.[106] It becomes clear, as with previous films, that this is a film about dinosaurs.[107] In February 2001, the first film stills were released showing characters being attacked by dinosaurs,[108] and in May the main trailer was released,[109] with a follow up in June. Here, in a similar manner to *Lost World*, we see technology being embraced to encourage discovery with multiple trailers hosted on apple trailers:

> But if you're looking forward to "Jurassic Park III" which opens July 18, here's a Web site that offers two slightly different versions of the movie's trailer. You can choose from four sizes, smallest to largest—or, as the site has them, "velociraptor," "pteranodon," "tyrannosaurus rex" or "spinosaurus" (reportedly the newest, biggest coldblooded villain in the sequel).[110]

In contrast then, *Jurassic Park III* offers a significantly muted campaign, lacking the same event feel of previous movies. Despite this it follows the same promotional pathways seen clearly and consistently established within *Jurassic Park*. The concept across the three films doesn't change much, and we see clearly established patterns emerging, changing slightly with each respective campaign.

Conclusion

This discussion has provided an account of some of the key ways in which *Jurassic Park*, *Lost World*, and *Jurassic Park III* courted publicity. We can see that *Jurassic Park* did significant amounts of promotional thematic framing, while *Lost World* continued this and built upon the marketing efforts actively soliciting a child audience through ancillary materials. In both cases the interconnected themes of authenticity in various manifestations appear either through star persona or through the educational framing at work. Across each campaign we see a number of supporting cross-promotion, ranging from the coincidental to the planned all of which form an incredibly complex macrotext of wider consumption. We may never know exactly how effective the various promotional lenses were; similarly we may never know the complete rationale behind each key promotional decision made. However, we can see clearly that *Jurassic Park*, *Lost World*, and *Jurassic Park III* clearly built on established themes, and *Lost World* and *Jurassic Park III* could not have held the marketing campaigns they did without the existence of *Jurassic Park*. While *Jurassic Park III* perhaps sought to capitalize on the existing success, it acted as a clear platform for the IP to break away from the legacy of Spielberg and Crichton and set the stage for the possibility of the franchise existing. If we consider *Jurassic World* as a reboot that enabled the retrospective franchise as we know it, then we have to allow for the fact that *Jurassic Park III* had to halt demand in order to be rebooted later. In many ways the promotional campaign for *Jurassic Park III* existed as a litmus test. Turning a profit with a minimal campaign allows for significant return on investment, while demonstrating that the franchise could exist without its original supporting figures. Indeed, for the film to generate a significant financial return without a clearly established marketing campaign demonstrates the success of the film's core concept. In reviewing what is in effect the first mapping of *Jurassic Park*'s promotional campaign we can see that despite the critical panning, the concept survives.

Notes

1 Michael Crichton, *Michael Crichton's Jurassic World* (New York: Alfred A. Knopf, 1997).
2 Box Office Mojo.com. https://www.boxofficemojo.com/title/tt0163025/. Accessed June 13, 2022.

3   Based on Metacritic (a score of 42, compared with 68 and 59 for the preceding movies, respectively).
4   Barbara Klinger, "Digressions at the Cinema," *Cinema Journal* 28:4 (1989): 3–19.
5   See, for example, the now incomplete website for *The Lost World: Jurassic Park*. For a discussion of this, see John McNab, "'The Lost World: Jurassic Park' website from 1997 is somehow still online," 2015. https://web.archive.org/web/20220613184755/https://ca.movies.yahoo.com/blogs/wide-screen/-the-lost-world--jurassic-park--website-from-1997-is-somehow-still-online---162319066.html?guccounter=1&guce_referrer=aHR0cHM6Ly93d3cuZ29vZ2xlLmNvbS8&guce_referrer_sig=AQAAALAaLbkpepjthHc7_l7aOZewbSqFxvs-QOgtCpYq6BalUbi6xGcCEknuOpUoXPY91YGDJBHIpx4KTcdEpq5uFU66mylpKVrR9hILLowRL_FynygjvH7W-_U8045lRgmbZnHvKv-sFLRX9kDuoYPLjmJhtMGlMTq6IoOGyH4_un8. Accessed June 13, 2022.
6   Keith M. Johnston, "Researching Historical Promotional Materials: Towards a New Methodology," *Historical Journal of Film, Radio and Television*, 39:4 (2019): 643–62.
7   Robert Marich, *Marketing to Moviegoers: A Handbook of Strategies Used by Major Studios and Independents* (Oxford: Focal Press, 2009), 132–3.
8   Martin Barker M. and Ernest Mathjis, *Watching* The Lord of the Rings: *Tolkien's World Audiences* (New York: Peter Lan, 2008), 11.
9   Camille Bacon-Smith and Tyrone Yarborough, "Batman: The Ethnography," in Roberta Pearson and William Uricchio (eds.) *The Many Lives of Batman* (London: Routledge, 1991): 90–16.
10 Esther Wright, "Marketing Authenticity: Rockstar Games and the Use of Cinema in Video Game Promotion," *Kinephanos* 7, no. 1 (November 2017): 131–64; and Esther Wright, *Rockstar Games and American History: Promotional Materials and the Construction of Authenticity* (Oldenbourg: DeGruyter, 2022).
11 Henk Pander Maat and Caro De Jong, "How Newspaper Journalists Reframe Product Press Release Information," *Journalism* 14:3 (2013): 348–71.
12 J. Dineen, [No Headline in Original Document] *The Toronto Star*, "Life," October 31, 1991; and C. Ford "Steven Has It Down to a T-rex," *Herald Sun* (NY), November 8, 1991.
13 Box office Mojo.com *Jurassic Park* [Online]. https://www.boxofficemojo.com/release/rl2354939393/. Accessed March 2, 2021.
14 D. Yu, "From Film to Burgers to Backpacks, MCA Brings Dinosaurs Back from Extinction," *Ottawa Citizen*, March 2, 1993.
15 A. B Block, "U.S. Films Get New Promos for the 'MTV World,'" *'Hollywood Reporter*, March 9, 1993.
16 [No Author] "Giants Galore: Where to Find Facts and Fiction on the Creatures; Films," *Atlanta Journal-Constitution*, July 27, 1991, 20.

17 [No Author] "Universal Amblin Begin Pre-Production of Steven Spielberg's 'Jurassic Park,'" *PR Newswire*, August 29, 1991.
18 Ibid.
19 Ibid.
20 D. Ryan, "Dinosaurs versus Batman," *Toronto Star*, Entertainment, April 3, 1991.
21 C. Ford, "Steven Has It Down to a T-rex," *Herald Sun* (NY), November 8, 1991.
22 G. Boyd, "Bities' Hold the Clue to Dinosaurs' Demise," *Sunday Mail* (Queensland), October 11, 1992.
23 See, for example, M. Locke, "Report: Prehistoric Insects May Hold Secrets of the Dinosaurs," *Associated Press*, September 4, 1992.
24 R. Heller, "Will Dinosaurs Ever Live Again?: How a Midge That Bit the Monster May Hold the Key to Its Recreation the Search for a Clue That Could Turn Blockbusting Fiction in to Fact," *Mail on Sunday* (London), March 14, 1993, 48; and M. Toner, "New Genetic Technology Bringing Evolution to Life: DNA of Extinct Species Helps Map Out the Past," *Atlanta Journal and Constitution*, National News, September 15, 1991.
25 C. Ford, "Pesci the Patcher. Joe Meds [sic] Sinead's Mess," *Herald Sun*, October 16, 1992. See also [no Author] "Sidelights," *St Louis Post-Dispatch: Everyday Magazine* (Missouri), October 18, 1992; and J. Galbraith, "Jurassic Park Movie Mania Imminent," *Toronto Star*, October 13, 1992.
26 Such as C. Johnson, "P.D., call Home! Spielberg's People Like Your 3-D Weather," *Star Tribune*, Minneapolis, MN, August 8, 1992.
27 D. Vergano, "Jurassic Roadshow," *USA TODAY*, December 21, 2000.
28 Esther Wright, *Rockstar Games and American History: Promotional Materials and the Construction of Authenticity* (Oldenbourg: DeGruyter, 2022) and correspondence with author, 2022.
29 Martin Barker, "News Reviews, Clues, Interviews and Other Ancillary Materials—A Critique and Research Proposal," *Scope* no. 18 (October 2010).
30 Leora Hadas, *Authorship as Promotional Discourse in the Screen Industries: Selling Genius* (London: Routledge , 2020), 24.
31 D. Groves, "Long Lead Time Eased Marketing Efforts," *Variety*, December 27, 1992–January 2, 1993, 62.
32 M. Brady, "Steering Dinomania in U.K . Special Report: The Business of Jurassic Park," *Variety*, December 27, 1992–January 2, 1993, 64.
33 Amblin's Marketing Consultant Gerry Lewis in D. Groves, "Long Lead Time Eased Marketing Efforts," 62.
34 D. Yu, "From Film to Burgers to Backpacks, MCA Brings Dinosaurs Back from Extinction," *Ottawa Citizen*, March 26, 1993.
35 J. M. Klein, "Dino Dominion They're Back, by Popular Demand, Our Very Old Friends the Dinosaurs," *Philadelphia Inquirer*, October 31, 1995.

36 Block, "U.S. Films Get New Promos for the 'MTV World.'"
37 Brady, "Steering Dinomania in U.K.," 64.
38 Ibid.
39 Ibid.
40 Jim Henson Productions, Walt Disney Productions (1991–4).
41 A. Busch, "'Jurassic' Gets 7-Minute Spot on 'E.T.' Airing," *Hollywood Reporter*, November 10, 1992.
42 Ibid.
43 [No Author] "Sidelights," *St. Louis Post-Dispatch* (Missouri), Late Five Star Edition, October 18, 1992.
44 D. Groves, "Long Lead Time Eased Marketing Efforts," 62.
45 Ibid.
46 A. M. Block, "Exhibs elated by sneak peek at 'Jurassic'," *Hollywood Reporter*, March 10, 1993.
47 Ibid.
48 R. Maltby, "Nobody Knows Everything. Post-classical Historiographies and Consolidated Entertainment," in S. Neale and M. Smith (eds.) *Contemporary Hollywood Cinema* (London: Routledge, 1998) 21–44. See also S. Jockel and T. Dobler, "The Event Movie: Marketing Filmed Entertainment for Transnational Media Corporations," *International Journal on Media Management* 8:2 (2006): 84–91; and J. Wyatt, *High Concept. Movies and Marketing in Hollywood* (Austin: Texas University Press, 1994).
49 Brady, "Steering Dinomania in U.K.," 64.
50 S. Spillman, "Picking Summer Flicks/ Theater Operators Bet on Spielberg Schwarzenegger," *USA Today*, March 15, 1993.
51 A. M. Busch and J. Daniels, "Biggest Convention in the History of ShoWest," *Hollywood Reporter*, March 15, 1993.
52 T. Lefton and L. M. Petersen, "Panasonic Boom Aimed at Sony," *Ad Day*, April 26, 1993, 4.
53 R. Salas, "DVD Notebook: 'Jurassic Park' and Sequel: Dino-Might Releases," Variety section, *Star Tribune* (Minneapolis), October 10. 2000, 4.
54 D. O'Briant, "'Jurassic' Sequel Is Expected to Show Its Dino-Might in Sales," *Atlanta Journal and Constitution*, September 20, 1995.
55 CNN Transcripts, Larry King Live, CNN, 9:00 p.m. ET August 2, 1995.
56 [No Author] "Spielberg Agrees to Direct Sequel to Jurassic Park," *Wall Street Journal*, November 10. 1995, 9.
57 A. M. Busch, "Spielberg U get 'Lost,'" *Variety*, November 13–November 19, 1995; and E Schmuckler, "Spielberg Plans 'Jurassic' 'Toon,'" *Media Week* 16:32 (1996): 6.
58 M. Jones Jr. "Publishers' Sweepstakes," *Newsweek*, September 18, 1995, 78.
59 C. Vinzant. "Jurassic Revisited," *Daily Telegraph Mirror*, September 30, 1995.

60 Stephen Neale, *Genre* (London: BFI Publishing, 1980), 48.
61 S.M Young Gong and W. A Van der Stede, "Real Options in the Motion Picture Industry: Evidence from Film Marketing and Sequels," *Contemporary Accounting Research* 28:5 (2010):1438–66.
62 P. Millar, "Laugh? I Nearly Screamed," *The Times* (London), September 30, 1995.
63 Whitehead. "Jurassic Park Redux," *The Tampa Tribune (Florida) Metro Edition* September 24, 1995.
64 [No Author] "Spielberg to direct 'Jurassic' Sequel," *United Press International*, November 9, 1995.
65 J. Watson, "Spielberg to Direct New Jurassic Park," *Evening Standard* (London), November 10, 1995, 15.
66 J. Graham. "A Wild, Wet Jaunt to Jurassic Park Technology Gives Prehistoric Ride Life," *USA Today*, June 21, 1996. [No Author], "Blockbuster Movie Becomes Thrill Ride," *United Press International*, January 26, 1996.
67 [No Author], [No Headline in Original] *Hollywood Reporter*, June 24, 1996.
68 M. Gleason, "Mercedes Is Going Jurassic," *Advertising Age*, June 17, 1996.
69 J. C. Erlick, "Licences Seen Crossing Channel," *Home Furnishing Network* 70:28 (1996): 8.
70 Ibid.
71 [No Author], "Universal Studios Consumer Products Group & Amblin Entertainment Announce Licensing and Promotional Program for Universal Pictures"; "The Lost World: Jurassic Park"; "Dinosaurs Come to Life in Many Exciting Ways Games, Toys, Books, Home Furnishings, and Apparel," *PR Newswire*, February 10, 1997.
72 B. Pendreigh, "The Flying Sorcerer," *The Scotsman*, August 10, 1996, 16.
73 It is unclear which specific instalment of the *Land Before Time* franchise. Separate content was released in 1997 *The Mysterious Island*, Dir. Grosvenor, and a Singalong Album, *The Land Before Time: Sing-Along Songs* (1997), and *The Songs from The Land Before Time* (1997) all owned by Universal.
74 L. Kramer, "Burger King: There's Life after Disney as chain Posts 'Whopper' $9B in Sales," *Nation's Restaurant News* 30:50 (December 23, 1996): 3.
75 These can be found on many online auction sites. Tyronweb, "RARE!! Tetley Jurassic Park Full Set of 8 Solid Bronze Coins. Very Rare to Find!," *Ebay.co.uk* 2022 .Online]. https://web.archive.org/web/20220414183809/https://www.ebay.co.uk/itm/154059819665?var=0&mkevt=1&mkcid=1&mkrid=710-53481-19255-0&campid=5338268676&toolid=10044&_trkparms=ispr%3D1&amdata=enc%3A1JVNy1DMtS6OUIJhamuObzA14&customid=Cj0KCQjwjN-SBhCkARIsACsrBz4tTMH_koMms2DBnCwAvJFRDpdHx0QW4PJk-ilGtKJSn6HHnVIxQwIaAssMEALw_wcB. Accessed April 14, 2022.
76 Keltonkeyhole, "5 x Jurassic Park The Lost World Kellogg's Holographic Lenticular Medal Toy 1997," *Ebay.co.uk*, 2022. https://web.archive.org/

web/20220414184041/https://www.ebay.co.uk/itm/154636498861?hash=ite m24010db7ad%3Ag%3A98kAAOSw6pZhWaSB. Accessed April 14, 2022.

77 pauuk.35za36 *Ebay.co.uk,* 2022. https://web.archive.org/web/2022041 4184744/https://www.ebay.co.uk/itm/115293569844?hash=item1ad8084 334%3Ag%3ANS8AAOSwSRNg3z6F. Accessed April 14, 2022.

For work on collectibles and children, see Page R., Montgomery K., Ponder A., and Richard A., "Targeting Children in the Cereal Aisle," *American Journal of Health Education* 39:5 (2008): 272–82.

78 Pendreigh B, "Dinosaurs Set for Epic Battle with Space Invaders," *The Scotsman,* January 2, 1997, 16.

79 K. Honeycutt, "Scare Tactic Warning with 'Lost' Trailer," *Hollywood Reporter,* January 3, 1997.

80 Ibid.

81 Ibid.

82 J. Beveridge, "Spielberg Is Back behind the Lens," *Hobart Mercury* (Australia), March 21, 1997.

83 During the course of researching the site http://www.lost-world.com/Lost_ World02/indexText.html became unavailable. Initial viewings were unable to access the unlocked content, with only the menu pages being available. An Archive of this can now be found via a fan site. https://web.archive.org/ web/20220414190238/https://jurassicpark.fandom.com/wiki/Lost-world.com. Accessed April 14, 2022.

84 [No Author], "MMWIREWEBWire—Internet and Online News," *Multimedia Wire* 4:90 (1997).

85 *CBS This Morning,* May 23, 7 a.m. ET, 1997.

86 M. Browne, "Dinosaurs at the Museum: Art Imitating Art Imitating Life," *New York Times,* May 23, 1997.

87 H. Levins, "Newsmakers," *St. Louis Post-Dispatch* (Missouri), August 8, 1999, 2.

88 J. Portman, "T-rex Finally Meets His Match: Dinosaurs Get Bigger, Scarier in Jurassic Park III," *The Gazette (*Montreal, Quebec), July 14, 2001.

89 This may of course be a limit to the methodology.

90 C. Puig, "Humans in 'Jurassic III' Relish Their 'Reduced' Roles," *USA Today,* Life, July 12, 2001.

91 T. Howard, "For Movie Tie-Ins This Year Marketers Say 'Cut!' Summer Movie Season Quieter," *USA Today,* Money, May 3, 2001.

92 Rose M. Matzer, "Studios Taking Cautious Tack in Marketing," '*Hollywood Reporter* 368:23 (2001): 1.

93 J. Druckenmiller and L. V. Harris, "eLIVING," *Atlanta Journal and Constitution,* December 4, 2000, 2.

94 B. Minzesheimer, "Read Any Good Movies Lately? You're in Luck," *USA Today,* Life, May 24, 2001.

95 M. Megna, "Meaner than Barney," *Daily News* (New York), 2001.
96 C. Puig, "Humans in 'Jurassic III' Relish Their 'Reduced' Roles."
97 J. P Telotte, "The 'Blair Witch Project' Project: Film and the Internet," *Film Quarterly* 54:3 (2001): 32–9.
98 M. Bretherton, "Audiences Online Introduced to Films," *Courier Mail* (Queensland), June 9, 2001, 17.
99 J. McKay "Spielberg's Jurassic Park Eats Its Way into Homes," *Prince George Citizen* (British Columbia), Entertainment, October 12, 2000, 27; and M. Janusonis, "VIDEO – Court-martial Drama, Martial-Arts Comed,y" *Providence Journal-Bulletin* (Rhode Island), October 13, 2000.
100 Bretherton, "Audiences Online Introduced to Films," 17.
101 C. Puig, "Humans in 'Jurassic III' Relish Their 'Reduced' Roles."
102 R. Salas, "DVD Notebook," 4.
103 J. Tuckman, "Chan's 'Noon' Full of Humor and Adventure," *Chicago Daily Herald,* Time Out!, Video Reviews, October 13, 2000.
104 J. Druckenmiller and L. V. Harris, "eLIVING," 2.
105 C. Puig, J. Chetwynd, and B. Kevenkey, "'Jurassic Park III' Will Send Shivers with Spinosaurus," *USA Today*, Life, November 24, 2000.
106 D. Giles, "Seasoned Bergen's on a Roll—Over There," *Sunday Telegraph* (Sydney, Australia), December 10, 2000, 150.
107 C. Puig, "Humans in 'Jurassic III' Relish Their 'Reduced' Roles."
108 R. Singh, "Jurassic Park III," *News of the World,* February 4, 2001.
109 Craft D., "Summer Movie Preview," *The Pantagraph* (Bloomington, IL), May 10, 2001, 10.
110 D. R Harris, "Arts Online," *Atlanta Journal-Constitution*, June 17, 2001.

PART TWO

Critical Perspectives and Interpretation

8

Jew-rassic Park

Nathan Abrams
Bangor University, UK

Introduction

Steven Spielberg openly stated "that with *Jurassic* [*Park*] I was really just trying to make a good sequel to *Jaws*. On land."[1] I have argued elsewhere that *Jaws* (1975) can be read as Jewish.[2] Here I wish to extend that argument to *Jurassic Park*: like the shark lurking beneath the waters of his earlier film, Jewishness prowls the undergrowth of all of Spielberg's films, regardless of their explicit subject matter. This chapter will seek to show how *Jurassic Park* can be read as Jewish. Based on Spielberg's background,[3] it will go digging for clues to support a Jewish reading of the film. It will operate as a form of archaeology by excavating for items that are buried below the topsoil of the film, to uncover the hidden history and artefacts that lie beneath. Key factors are not just its production that coincides with the making of Spielberg's *Schindler's List* (1993) and the telling casting of Jeff Goldblum as the scientist-savior-mensch, but also the subtextual codes that are playing in the film not least the homophone inherent in its title.

Consciously or otherwise, Spielberg inserted "a hidden Jewish sub stratum" beneath the surface of the film.[4] Minority ethnic-cultural texts are frequently marked by specialist knowledge unavailable to majority audiences.[5] Such an approach relies on the director; the writer (of source material and/or the screenplay); and often the actors placing, both consciously and unconsciously, characteristics, behaviors, beliefs, and other tics—all of which require a prerequisite and prior knowledge of Jews, Jewishness, or Judaism. In this way, directors, screenwriters, actors/actresses, and other creative personnel encode clues that can be read in terms of Jewish specificity, producing what has been called "Jewish moments" but which a general audience decodes as universal.[6] This requires a "complex of codes that cross-check each other" of which the Jewish identities of the performers are a key but by no means the only part.[7] Other important clues include historical, traditional, and cultural references; appearance; intellect; profession; names; physiognomy; foods; verbal and body language; phenotype; aural, visual, or emotional/genre signs; speech patterns and accents; hairstyles; anxieties; neuroses; and conflicts. This strategy of "directing" or "acting Jewish" relies on the viewer to locate, identify, and decode those clues that can be both textual and extratextual. Consequently, the individual viewer is given the possibility of "reading Jewish" but not with certainty, and with positing varying degrees of pertinence, in such a reading, to the film's overall meaning.[8] This approach will be applied to *Jurassic Park* to argue that Spielberg allowed us the possibility, albeit not the certainty, of reading Jewishness in the film.

Jurassic *Lager*

Michael Crichton's *Jurassic Park* was offered exclusively to Steven Spielberg who blazed through the (still unpublished) novel in a single evening and, for the first time in his career, attached himself to a picture that was unfinanced and had yet to receive a studio green light. Something in the novel manifestly appealed to Spielberg. But it was not Jewish material as none of that or any extant Jews or Jewishness is evident in the source text (unlike Peter Benchley's novel *Jaws*). There are only hints and metaphors that can be mined for Jewish meaning. But this is purely *interpretative*. For example, when describing the park, Crichton wrote: "Each division was separated from the road by a concrete moat. Outside each moat was a fence with a little lightning sign alongside it. That mystified them until they were finally able to figure out it meant the fences were electrified." Twenty pages later, a character says, "Christ, it looks like Alcatraz."[9] Yet, the use of electrified fencing to hem in life considered dangerous very much evokes Auschwitz-Birkenau and the other Nazi death camps.

This may seem a stretch, but *Jurassic Park* was released less than six months before *Schindler's List*. As scholar of Holocaust films, Rich Brownstein, writes, "There was colossal nervousness in the Jewish community at the prospect that the Holocaust would be turned into *Raiders of the Lost Ark* (1981) or *Jurassic Park*."[10] What Brownstein missed, though, is that it was not so much that the Holocaust was turned into *Jurassic Park*, but that *Jurassic Park* was turned into the Holocaust. And this was no doubt because filming *Schindler's List* overlapped with postproduction on *Jurassic Park*.

In February 1993, with postproduction on *Jurassic Park* underway in the United States, Spielberg began filming *Schindler's List* in Poland.

Meanwhile, Industrial Light and Magic had developed cutting-edge software to deliver *Jurassic Park*'s visual effects to Poland via satellite. The software sent a video signal "over high-speed phone lines, then satellited [the signal] to Spielberg's office overseas," allowing the director to view dailies and computer-animated dinosaurs composited with actors, and to communicate with computer artists visible at the bottom of his computer screen.[11] By March, the director was shooting brutal blood-soaked footage of the Holocaust during the day and editing brutal blood-soaked footage of dinosaurs chasing jeeps by night, communicating via satellite uplink with Industrial Light and Magic in San Francisco at night, and making final decisions over how the *T-Rex* ought to roar and whether a *Brachiosaurus* should rise on its back legs when eating. "When I finally started shooting ... in Poland, I had to go home about two or three times a week and get on a very crude satellite feed to northern California ... to be able to approve *T-Rex* shots," Spielberg remembered at an anniversary screening of *Schindler's List* at Tribeca Film Festival.[12] So, returning from the violent Polish concentration camp set each evening, Spielberg went home to edit violent *Velociraptor* footage.

This led to remarkable uncanny plot similarities between the two films. They were both, in the words of Dara Horn, emotional rollercoasters tales of

> a wealthy and eccentric businessman who decides to risk everything to save those who are utterly different from him trapped behind electrified barbed wire and threatened with complete annihilation, filmed with beautiful cinematography and a soaring emotional score by the composer John Williams.[13]

Horn went on to say that both featured

> people trapped in an entirely unnatural and immoral facility surrounded by barbed wire. They find themselves in the position of helpless animals, whimpering and cowering in fear while caught up in a terrifying struggle to survive against a senseless enemy. Some of the scenes felt almost identical to the scenes in *Schindler's List* like the ones of trembling children hiding from the predators and managing split second escapes.[14]

Jurassic Park, she concluded, "even has the same ending with weathered but happy survivors enjoying peace at last. In the end, they only survived because of a kindly gesture by a powerful predator—a *Tyrannosaurus Rex*—who randomly and ungraciously helps them to escape."[15]

In this reading, what Michael Crichton called "domesticated dinosaurs"[16] are the Jews, extinct yet resurrected for public entertainment. It may be just a mere coincidence that Stanley Kubrick chose Joseph Mazzello to play Maciek in his never-to-be-made Holocaust film, *Aryan Papers*, which was in preproduction while Spielberg was making *Jurassic Park* until the imminent release of *Schindler's List* put Warner Bros. and Kubrick off the idea, but the choice suggests a close connection. Critic Molly Haskell compared John Hammond to Oskar Schindler: "The genial but morally enigmatic entertainer, the artist-showman with his stable of workers and performers who do his bidding: if Attenborough's parkmeister fits this description, so does Herr Direktor Oscar Schindler."[17]

The dinosaur park, then, uncannily echoes the centuries of Jewish artistic and historical objects, which were preserved by Nazi Germany, to create a so-called "Museum of an Extinct Race." The dinosaurs are clearly ghettoized, and the dominant colors of red and yellow used to brand the park are those that have historically been used to code Jewishness, including the blood libel through to the yellow stars that the Nazis forced Jews to wear during the Holocaust. The Creation Museum, the brainchild of the Christian apologetics ministry, "Answers in Genesis," for example, has produced a narrative that connects Jews and dinosaurs whereby the Jewish people come to embody fossils of a bygone age.[18] The museum's depiction of Jews as "fossils" echoes the British historian Arnold J. Toynbee's controversial assessment of Judaism's continued presence in the world in his *A Study of History*, the first three volumes of which were initially published in 1934, in which he claimed that Jews constitute "fossils" of a distinct "Syriac Society."[19]

To an extent, popular culture has also connected Jewishness with dinosaurs. Consider the lead singer of the British Glam rock band T-Rex—the Jewish Marc Bolan. The toy dinosaur Rex in the *Toy Story* franchise (1995–2019) is voiced by the Jewish actor Wallace Shawn. Certainly, the idea of Jews as predators is not a new one. In his fourth-century sermon, *Adversus Iudaeos*, John Chrysostom frequently depicted Jews as lascivious predators in pursuit of innocent Christians.[20] That innocent children were frequently cited as the target of Jewish predatory behavior is, perhaps unwittingly, echoed in the storyline of *Jurassic Park*. Manohla Dargis, for example, was "struck by how the most skillfully directed and sadistic scenes involve children, including the kitchen homage to Kubrick's 'The Shining' and its terrorized tot."[21]

And just like the Nazis, the scientists in *Jurassic Park* practice eugenics.

"None of our animals is capable of breeding. That's why we have this nursery. It's the only way to replace stock in Jurassic Park ... there are two independent reasons why the animals can't breed. First of all, they're sterile, because we irradiate them with X-rays ... All the animals in Jurassic Park are female," [Dr] Wu said, with a pleased smile.[22]

It was in 1938, during the Nazi regime, that Hans Spemann, a German scientist, first suggested the prospect of cloning, by removing the nucleus from an unfertilized egg and replacing it with the nucleus from an adult cell in his book *Embryonic Development and Induction* (1938). In *Jurassic Park*, Dr. Wu explains how "these animals are genetically engineered to be unable to survive in the real world. They can only live here in Jurassic Park. They are not free at all. They are essentially our prisoners."[23] The treatment itself evokes the notorious pseudo-scientific medical experiments of Dr. Josef Mengele at Auschwitz. Mengele was obsessed with finding out what triggers twin births, as a means to fulfill Adolf Hitler's demand for a highly fertile Aryan race. The 1978 movie, *The Boys from Brazil* (dir. Franklin J. Schaffner), starred Gregory Peck as Mengele, who has created clones of the Fuhrer in South America in an attempt to establish the Fourth Reich.

On the other hand, as Dara Horn has perceptively picked up, the dinosaurs may also represent the Nazis. When describing the Jewish characters in *Schindler's List*, the *New York Times* critic Frank Richard wrote how they "have the generic feel of composites, are as forgettable as the chorus in a touring company of 'Fiddler on the Roof,' or, for that matter, the human dino-fodder of 'Jurassic Park.'"[24] Molly Haskell described the film as a "*Jaws* of the Jungle, with children as dinosaur prey."[25] Les White has also written how

> Schindler does come off like a super-human Indiana Jones or the archaeologists in *Jurassic Park*. The Nazis can be compared to the dinosaurs running loose in *Jurassic Park* or to the shark in *Jaws*: nature that cannot be wholly controlled, but nature that can be explained as primitive. The Jews—the pitiful Jews showing fear—represent the child in us, like the Indian children rescued by Indiana Jones or the children scared by dinosaurs in *Jurassic Park*.[26]

Thus, just as Art Spiegelman's *Maus: A Survivor's Tale* (1991) allegorized the Jewish experience during the Holocaust as mice, Spielberg allegorizes it as children.[27] "The theme of children at risks crops up in a startlingly high percentage of his films, and reaches a fine climax when Tyrannosaurus rex chomps on a car with the kiddies inside," Haskell writes.[28] Consciously or otherwise, Peter Biskind tapped into this when he described how the *T-Rex* reclined on "an enormous dolly, like the gun carriage of an old World War II howitzer that runs on tracks."[29]

Whether Spielberg picked up on these textual referents in the way I have above is, of course, open to debate. But given that since 1992 he was juggling both *Jurassic Park* and *Schindler's List*, it is not a stretch to argue that the latter may well have influenced the former in oblique ways even if Thomas Schatz writes that *Jurassic Park* and *Schindler's List* were "utterly antithetical pictures that evinced the yin and yang of Spielberg's—and Hollywood's—capacity for unabashed commercial entertainment and for thoughtful, compelling drama."[30]

Malcolm the Macho Mensch

Underpinning the narrative of the film is a binary opposition between Jewish values and goyische (Yiddish: non-Jewish) values. *Menschlikayt* is the Yiddish expression referring to ethical responsibility, social justice, and decency for others expressed in kindness. The Yiddish writer Leo Rosten described a *mensch* as "1. A human being. 'After all, he is a *mensh*, not an animal.' 2. An upright, honorable, decent person. 'Come on, act like a *mensh*!' 3. Someone of consequence; someone to admire and emulate: someone of noble character. 'Now, there is a real *mensch*!'"[31] In the words of scholar Rebecca Alpert, a *mensch* is "an ethical human being who displays his virtues through gentility and kindness."[32] *Menschlikayt* rejected "*goyim naches*," a phrase that "broadly describes non-Jewish activities and pursuits supposedly antithetical to a Jewish sensibility and temperament."[33] Literally meaning "pleasure for/of the gentiles," its root is the Hebrew word *goy* (singular of *goyim*, meaning gentiles) but which also derives from the word for "body" [*geviyah*]. It can therefore also be interpreted to mean a preoccupation with the body, sensuality, rashness, and ruthless force, as manifested in such physical activities as bearing arms, horse-riding, dueling, jousting, archery, wrestling, hunting, orgies, and sports in general.[34] Denied the right to participate in such activities, Jews instead denigrated them, consequently also disparaging those very characteristics that in European culture defined a man as *manly*: physical strength, martial activity, competitive drive, and aggression. *Goyim naches*, therefore, in Daniel Boyarin's words, was "the contemptuous Jewish term for the prevailing ideology of 'manliness' dominant in Europe."[35] Since toughness was downgraded in normative rabbinic culture, physical, martial, and bodily virtues, which flowered in natural surroundings, were rejected in favor of a scholarliness that thrived indoors.

Spielberg invests two rival groups of characters with these values. On the side of *menschlikayt* are the two paleo-scientists Alan Grant (Sam Neill) and Ellie Sattler (Laura Dern) along with the chaotician Ian Malcolm (Jeff Goldblum). On the side of *goyim naches* stand the park developer John Hammond (Richard Attenborough), lawyer Donald Gennaro (Martin Ferrero), and computer programmer Dennis Nedry (Wayne Knight).

Malcolm is what scholar Michael Rogin called a "neurasthenic hysteric" Jew.[36] As played by Jeff Goldblum, who excels at personifying such characters, Malcolm is an eccentric, hipster, intellectual, scientist, and talker, or "Jew is mouth as nervous brain" in Michael Rogin's words referring to his character in *Independence Day* some five years later but just as apt for the one he plays in *Jurassic Park*.[37] Indeed, both of Goldblum's characters recite the same line while escaping alien and dinosaur enemies, respectively, toward the end of each film ("Must go faster").

Spielberg uses Malcolm as a mouthpiece to voice a social perspective. Of the three scientists present, Malcolm proves to be the most skeptical. As Gabriel Sanders has observed,

> Though the name sounds as though it could be borne by a Scottish bagpipe champion, there's little question that Malcolm is there to play a traditionally Jewish role: that of the skeptical wisenheimer—Groucho Marx with a degree in chaos theory. Malcolm serves as the film's voice of reason—and caution. "The lack of humility before nature that's being displayed here staggers me," he scolds. And though he clearly fancies himself a cool, dispassionate man of science, it's Malcolm who expresses the film's underlying theology: "God creates dinosaurs. God destroys dinosaurs. God creates man. Man destroys God. Man creates dinosaurs."[38]

It is from Malcolm's mouth that the crucial ethical question is raised. "Your scientists were so preoccupied with whether or not they could, they didn't stop to think if they should." He thus embodies a tradition of intellectual inquiry, respect for learning, and intense involvement with morality and law. In this way, Malcolm exemplifies best the uniquely Jewish code of *menschlikayt*.

But Malcolm is more than just a mensch, he is macho, too. Writing in the *New York Times*, critic Manohla Dargis described what she called "the most astonishing image in the film," which is, of course

> Jeff Goldblum's injured "chaotician" (hoot!), Dr. Malcolm, lying back with his black shirt unbuttoned to expose his lightly furred musculature. Consciously or not, Spielberg turns Goldblum into a sexualized spectacle, complete with dark shades and come-hither mien, a framing that seems dedicated to destroying a noxious ethnic stereotype. Goldblum has suggested in interviews that this great unbuttoning was spontaneous, but whether it is, the effect is the same. It's as if Spielberg were saying, You want hot Jewish guys? I'll give you hot Jewish guys![39]

Replying to Dargis, her colleague A. O. Scott wrote, "Goldblum got to be both the movie's conscience and its libido."[40] Malcolm is sexualized. As he admits, he is constantly seeking "the next ex-Mrs Malcolm." But when the going gets tough, he and Alan Grant step up to save Hammond's grandchildren at considerable risk to their own safety.

If Malcolm represents macho *menschlikayt*, then Hammond is, at first, the embodiment of its polar opposite: *goyim naches*. One might even play on the implicit *treyf*-ness (that is, as explicitly non-kosher) of the name of the film's villain—Hammond as in Ham(mond)—suggesting that actually this film is *Jurassic Pork*. Punning aside, Hammond is presented as treyf in that he initially puts commerce before human life, endangering not only his workers and guests but also his grandchildren. It says much that the gift shop is completed before the security systems. "John Hammond," says film scholar Lester D. Friedman, "represents a broader corporate perspective that values increased profits over communal safety and moral responsibilities."[41] "Generated by capitalistic greed, corporate corruption, and lack of concern for the public good," Friedman adds, "modern monsters do not emerge from gloomy caverns or secluded laboratories; instead, they lumber out of brightly lit operating rooms and richly funded research centers, such as Hammond's on Isla Nublar."[42] Intentionally, or otherwise, Friedman and hence Spielberg invoke Hannah Arendt's famous notion of the "banality of evil." And, as Gabriel Sanders points out, "when his creations start to run amok and his paradise devolves into a reptilian hell, Hammond is exposed as a false prophet."[43]

Overall, Spielberg's choices reinforce the message of the film that "greed isn't good," harking back to the priorities of the mayor who wants to keep the beaches open in *Jaws*. In the words of Sean T. Collins, "*Jurassic Park* warned us against the carnivorous capitalists" as "capitalist rapaciousness is embedded in *Jurassic Park*'s DNA," in which profits are prioritized over safety concerns. "Money is the real monster of Steven Spielberg's creature feature," he explains.[44] The whole reason that the experts—Alan Grant, Ellie Sattler, and Ian Malcolm—are even hired to inspect the park, is to reassure the skittish insurers and investors after the family of a worker killed by a dinosaur in the opening scene of the movie and his family launches a lawsuit against the parent company InGen for twenty million dollars.

Computer programmer Dennis Nedry, even more than Hammond, is the embodiment of *goyim naches*, motivated by money almost down to the molecular level. As played by Knight, he is instantly recognizable to viewers of the sitcom *Seinfeld* (NBC, 1989–98) as Jerry's arch-nemesis from his first appearance in 1991 and onward, and thus almost automatically posited as the bad guy. He is also "the film's most blatantly negative and thoroughly corrupt character," Lester D. Friedman writes, "Stamped as fat, messy, and greedy—sure signs of ravenous evil in Hollywood's pantheon of stereotypes."[45] The shutdown of the park's security systems that leads to the escape of the dinosaurs is rooted in greed. Believing he is overworked and underpaid, Nedry requests a raise but Hammond refuses because he does not believe in paying Nedry more than Hammond feels he deserves. Hammond's refusal to spend a tiny amount more then, unwittingly, sets into motion a chain of events that are his downfall. Furious, Nedry accepts a bribe from an industrial rival to InGen to steal the dinosaur embryos and smuggle them off the island in a shaving foam can of all things. To do so, Nedry disables the largely automated safety systems to give him a window by which he can sneak the embryos off the island. This temporarily immobilizes the locking mechanisms and electrified perimeter fencing to the dinosaurs' paddock enclosures. At the same time, a tropical storm sweeps across the island and the simultaneity of these occurrences results in the dinosaurs escaping and attacking the humans trapped on the island. Here one can see echoes of the Jewish director Stanley Kubrick's *Dr. Strangelove or, How I Learned to Stop Worrying and Love the Bomb* (1964) in which "human error" undermines the safety systems designed to prevent a nuclear holocaust.

It is ironic, from a Jewish perspective, that the window is only eighteen minutes long for the numerical value of that number equates to the Hebrew word for "life." Nedry's greed is coded visually. He is seen to be subject to his appetites. Surely it is no coincidence that Nedry meets Lewis Dodgson of BioSyn at a restaurant or that Dennis Nedry's name is an anagram of a famous eatery, Denny's Diner.

Donald Gennaro is just as bad. Initially as skittish as the investors he represents, he quickly changes his tune about the island the minute he sees his first dinosaur and says, "We're gonna make a fortune with this place." Suddenly, he conjures visions of "coupon days" for the less well-off. "The only one I've got on my side is the bloodsucking lawyer," Hammond laments, using a long-established historic trope for Jewishness if ever there was one. Luckily, though, the lawyer has a Celtic given name and an Italian family name. Gennaro is cowardly, which is emphasized when the *T-Rex* attacks: it is Gennaro who abandons Hammond's grandchildren to their fate and seeks refuge in a nearby bathroom. It is there that his fate is sealed, and, like Nedry, he is eaten alive by a rampaging dinosaur in a humiliating fashion when the "T-Rex rips him off the toilet seat and devours him like a wriggling worm, a blackly comic demise for a man consumed by 'filthy lucre,'" as Lester D. Friedman notes.[46] Here, Spielberg comes down on the side of the mensches—all of whom survive—versus those on the other side, two of whom die.

Spielberg softened the character of Hammond making him gentle, charming, and even maternal. He is allowed to live because, like the character of Oskar Schindler, he undergoes a moral reevaluation. In a reversal of Schindler, though, he sets out with good intentions when he brings his grandchildren to the park, whereas Schindler is motivated by profit and greed. As the film makes clear, he was hoping to provide them with a good time during their parents' stressful divorce, which distinguishes him from *Jaws*' Mayor Vaughn (Murray Hamilton) who is blithely unconcerned with the lives of others at best and outright murderous at worst. Hammond never wanted this to happen to his grandkids, or to anyone else for that matter, as his increasingly morose demeanor throughout the ordeal communicates. "But," Sean T. Collins points out, "this simply demonstrates the way dollar signs have blinded him to virtually every other consideration. What kind of maniac sends two little kids into the middle of a dinosaur hot zone during an information-gathering tour intended to determine whether the park is even operable, all the while his most trusted employees are telling him the park isn't ready for guests?"[47]

Jurassic Golems

"*Jurassic* [*Park*] had a classic horror-movie moral: Mad scientists mess with God's work at their peril," Peter Biskind wrote in *Premiere* in May 1997.[48] In other words, *Jurassic Park* taps into the Hebrew tradition of the Tower of Babel or the later Golem, an artificial homunculus created by magic that, over time, has become a metaphor for something impossible to fully control and hence a danger to its creator. The Golem of Prague has inspired more novelists, playwrights, artists, and filmmakers than any other Golem legend beforehand or since. One of the most influential adaptations was Mary Shelley's novel *Frankenstein* (1818), a cautionary tale warning against playing God in which an unorthodox scientific experiment that creates life only to reap the horrifying results when the achievement goes horribly wrong. While the specificities of the settings and characters may differ, the story shares many points of similarity: Dr. Frankenstein, like the golem's original creator Rabbi Loew, sets out to create life from dead matter, only to lose control of his creation. Both stories end with the creature waging brutal violence on innocents. From then on, the legend of the Golem and the story of Frankenstein became inextricably intertwined and it was through Shelley's *Frankenstein* that the myth of the Golem began to enter wider, non-Jewish popular culture. The legend also stood as a metaphor for modern science, technology, and war. It was used to warn about how creation without control is a formula for catastrophe and that scientific progress cannot be detached from moral and ethical considerations. But even then, our creations will become uncontrollable at the cost of placing humanity in danger of universal annihilation.

John Hammond, like Dr. Frankenstein and Rabbi Loew, creates life from dead, even extinct, matter, only to lose control of his creation. But it is not just the dinosaurs that are the golems, but the very technology used to clone and birth them as well as to navigate and contain the natural world. The system governing the park itself is one preventable-but-as-of-yet-unprevented glitch after another. Nothing seems to work right. Tim is menaced by the dinosaurs and technology. He is nearly crushed to death by the automated jeep in which he and the other visitors take their abortive tour of the park, first when it is pressed into the mud by the *T-Rex*, and second when the jeep plunges through the branches of a tree, coming very close to squashing him before it comes to a halt. Later in the film, he is electrocuted by the 10,000-volt fence meant to keep the *T-Rex* from escaping, saved only by Alan Grant's resuscitative efforts.

Here Hammond may be a stand-in for Spielberg's own absent father, Arnold, who was a pioneer in computer research at RCA and IBM with several patents to his credit. Spielberg adds another oblique hint by showing Nedry taping J. Robert Oppenheimer's portrait to his computer screen. Not only does this introduce an indirect Jewish element but it also shows an awareness of what he has unleashed: the German-Jewish Oppenheimer was the wartime head of the Los Alamos Laboratory and is among those who are credited with being the "father of the atomic bomb" for his role in the Manhattan Project—the Second World War undertaking that developed the first nuclear weapons. Oppenheimer was among those who observed the Trinity test in New Mexico, where the first atomic bomb was successfully detonated on July 16, 1945. He later remarked that the explosion brought to mind words from the *Bhagavad Gita*: "Now I become Death, the destroyer of worlds."

Conclusion

In his adaptation of Michael Crichton's novel that completely lacked any extant or implicit Jewishness, whether consciously or otherwise, Steven Spielberg infused a subsurface Jewish sensibility into the story that produced a film that introduced a Holocaust subtext that chimed remarkably and uncannily with his *Schindler's List* on which he was working simultaneously. This sensibility was also expressed in the storyline that pitted the *goyim naches* of grasping rapacious capitalism against the Jewish code of *menschlikayt*, especially as relayed by the conceptually Jewish character of Malcolm as embodied by Jeff Goldblum. Finally, in constructing a morality tale about the consequences of scientific hubris messing with nature, Spielberg drew upon the centuries-old Jewish legend of the Golem.

Notes

1 Steven Spielberg, quoted in Joseph McBride, *Steven Spielberg: A Biography*, 3rd edition (London: Faber and Faber, 2012), 418.

2 Nathan Abrams, "Jaws as Jewish," in I. Q. Hunter and Matthew Melia (eds.) *The Jaws Book: New Perspectives on the Classic Summer Blockbuster* (New York: Bloomsbury Academic, 2020), 115–31.

3 For more on Spielberg's Jewish upbringing, see my "Jaws as Jewish"; McBride, *Steven Spielberg*; and Bernard Weinraub, "Steven Spielberg Faces the Holocaust," *New York Times,* December 12, 1993, Section 2, 1.

4 Ella Shohat, "Ethnicities-in-Relation: Toward a Multicultural Reading of American Cinema," in Lester D. Friedman (ed.) *Unspeakable Images: Ethnicity and the American Cinema* (Urbana: University of Illinois Press, 1991), 220.

5 See Henry Bial, *Acting Jewish: Negotiating Ethnicity on the American Stage and Screen* (Ann Arbor: University of Michigan Press, 2005) and Nathan Abrams, *The New Jew in Film: Exploring Jewishness and Judaism in Contemporary Cinema* (New Brunswick, NJ: Rutgers University Press, 2012).

6   Jon Stratton, *Coming Out Jewish* (London: Routledge, 2000), 300.
7   Bial, *Acting Jewish*, 70. See also Joel Rosenberg, "Jewish Experience on Film—An American Overview," in David Singer (ed.) *American Jewish Year Book, 1996* (New York: American Jewish Committee, 1996), 26.
8   Bial, *Acting Jewish*, 70.
9   Michael Crichton, *Jurassic Park* (London: BCA, 1991), 55, 79, 110.
10 Rich Brownstein, *Holocaust Cinema Complete: A History and Analysis of 400 Films, with a Teaching Guide* (Jefferson, NC: McFarland, 2021), 117.
11 *Daily Variety*, March 29, 1993.
12 "Steven Spielberg Resented Jurassic Park while He Was Filming It," *Hollywood.com*, April 30, 2018. https://www.hollywood.com/general/steven-spielberg-resented-jurassic-park-while-he-was-filming-it-60720672. Accessed June 17, 2022.
13 Dara Horn, "Shooting Jews," Episode 3 of *the Adventures with Dead Jews* podcast, September 17, 2021. https://www.tabletmag.com/podcasts/adventures-with-dead-jews/episode-three-shooting-jews-auschwitz-jurassic-park-schindlers-list-steven-spielberg. Accessed December 14, 2021. Spielberg shared with Jewish director Irwin Allen an appreciation for the music of composer John Williams. Known as the "Master of Disaster," Allen had commissioned Williams to write the music for his television shows *Lost in Space* and *Land of the Giants*, as well as his films *The Poseidon Adventure* (1972) and *The Towering Inferno* (1974). This was prior to Williams beginning his long association with Spielberg.
14 Horn, "Shooting Jews."
15 Ibid.
16 Crichton, *Jurassic Park*, 123.
17 Molly Haskell, *Steven Spielberg: A Life in Films* (New Haven, CT: Yale University Press, 2017), 141.
18 D. Nash, "Fossilized Jews and Witnessing Dinosaurs at the Creation Museum: Public Remembering and Forgetting at a Young Earth Creationist 'Memory Place'," *Studies in Christian-Jewish Relations* 14:1 (2019), 1–25.
19 Arnold J. Toynbee, *A Study of History*, vol. 2 (Oxford: Oxford University Press, 1945), 234–48.
20 Susanna Drake, *Slandering the Jew: Sexuality and Difference in Early Christian Texts* (Philadelphia: University of Pennsylvania Press, 2013).
21 A. O. Scott and Manohla Dargis, "'Jurassic Park': Where the Wild Things Are," July 2, 2020. https://www.nytimes.com/2020/07/02/movies/jurassic-park.html?searchResultPosition=6. Accessed December 14, 2021.
22 Crichton, *Jurassic Park*, 115.
23 Ibid.
24 Frank Rich, "Extras in the Shadows," *New York Times*, January 2, 1994, Section 4, 9.

25 Haskell, *Steven Spielberg*, 139.
26 Les White, "*Schindler's List*: My Father Is a Schindler Jew," *Jump Cut* 39 (June 1994): 3–6, reprinted at http://www.ejumpcut.org/archive/onlinessays/JC39fol der/schindlersList.html. Accessed August 24, 2022.
27 Art Spiegelman, *Maus: A Survivor's Tale* (New York: Pantheon Books, 1991).
28 Haskell, *Steven Spielberg*, 139.
29 Peter Biskind, quoted in Lester D. Friedman and Brent Notbohm (eds.), *Steven Spielberg: Interviews, Revised and Updated* (Jackson: University Press of Mississippi, 2019), 201.
30 Thomas Schatz, "Industry and Agency: Spielberg as Director, Producer, and Movie Mogul," in Nigel Morris (ed.) *A Companion to Steven Spielberg* (Chichester, West Sussex: John Wiley & Sons, 2017), 33.
31 Leo Rosten, *The Joys of Yiddish* (London: Penguin, 1972), 240.
32 Rebecca Alpert, "The Macho-Mensch: Modeling American Jewish Masculinity and the Heroes of Baseball," in Raanan Rein and David M. K. Sheinin (eds.) *Muscling in on New Worlds: Jews, Sport, and the Making of the Americas* (Leiden: Brill, 2014),109.
33 Alpert, "The Macho-Mensch," 109.
34 See Laurence Roth, *Inspecting Jews: American Jewish Detective Stories* (New Brunswick: Rutgers University Press, 2004), 31; Jeffrey T. Sammons, *Beyond the Ring: The Role of Boxing in American Society* (Urbana: University of Illinois Press, 1990), 91.
35 Daniel Boyarin, *Unheroic Conduct: The Rise of Heterosexuality and the Invention of the Jewish Man* (Berkeley: University of California Press, 1997), 23, 78.
36 Michael Rogin, *Independence Day* (London: BFI, 1998), 49.
37 Ibid.
38 Gabriel Sanders, "The Theology of 'Jurassic Park,' " *Tablet*, July 8, 2014. https://www.tabletmag.com/sections/news/articles/the-theology-of-juras sic-park. Accessed August 24, 2022.
39 Dargis, "Jurassic Park."
40 Scott, "Jurassic Park."
41 Lester D. Friedman, *Citizen Spielberg*, 2nd edn. (Urbana: University of Illinois Press, 2022), 134.
42 Friedman, *Citizen Spielberg*, 134.
43 Sanders, "The Theology of 'Jurassic Park.' "
44 Sean T. Collins, "*Jurassic Park* Warned Us Against the Carnivorous Capitalists: Money Is the Real Monster of Steven Spielberg's Creature Feature," *Polygon*, August 12, 2020. https://www.polygon.com/platform/ amp/2020/8/12/21362915/jurassic-park-review-where-to-watch-charact ers-covid-pandemic-parallels?__twitter_impression=true. Accessed December 14, 2021.

45 Friedman, *Citizen Spielberg*, 141.
46 Ibid., 132–3.
47 Collins, "*Jurassic Park* Warned Us Against the Carnivorous Capitalists."
48 Peter Biskind, "A 'World' Apart," *Premiere* (May 1997), reprinted in Brent Notbohm and Lester D. Friedman, *Steven Spielberg: Interviews*, revised and updated edition (Jackson: University Press of Mississippi, 2019), 137.

9

Virility, Venality, and Victory: Three Faces of Masculinity in *Jurassic Park*

Katie Barnett
University of Chester, UK

Introduction

In *Jurassic Park*'s most iconic line of dialogue, when Dr. Ian Malcolm (Jeff Goldblum) discovers that the InGen scientists have eliminated the possibility of reproduction by engineering the dinosaurs' chromosomes to create an all-female population, he suggests presciently that "life, uh … finds a way." As well as serving as the film's tagline (and, in 2018, the tagline to *Jurassic World: Fallen Kingdom*), the line is echoed by Dr. Alan Grant (Sam Neill) when he discovers a cache of hatched dinosaur eggs that proves Dr. Malcolm's hypothesis. "Malcolm was right," he says. "Life found a way." The repetition and echo of this phrase and its attendant warning succinctly captures one of the film's central thematic tensions: between the excessive hubris of humans who believe they can control nature, and nature itself.

Far beyond its echoed dialogue and the recycled tagline, repetition is encoded into the very DNA of *Jurassic Park*. Living dinosaurs are created by replicating long-extinct genetic sequences, while the dinosaurs find ways to reproduce still further—a repetition of the formidable survival instinct that fueled their original millennia-long dominance. In a video outlining the scientific process behind the dinosaurs' (re)realization, an image of park director John Hammond (Richard Attenborough) is repeated and multiplied to emphasize the replication taking place. And, on a meta scale, the film repeats various Spielbergian motifs and techniques—from the delayed monster reveal to elements of character function and costume design—that recall (among others) *Jaws* (1975) and the *Indiana Jones* franchise (1981–present), as noted later in this chapter.

There is another repeated phrase in the film that is afforded much less significance than Malcolm's declaration and yet is equally useful as a way of understanding a fundamental aspect of *Jurassic Park*. That is when Hammond's granddaughter Lex (Ariana Richards), on two separate occasions, cries: "He left us! He left us!" The first of these is when Donald Gennaro (Martin Ferrero) flees the tour vehicle and abandons Lex and her brother Tim (Joseph Mazzello) during the *Tyrannosaurus Rex*'s escape. She later repeats these words as Alan rescues the children after the attack. Her cries are an indictment of the multiple men who have not only failed to stay but failed to protect the two children. Most obviously, she is referring to Gennaro, but it is revealed in passing at the beginning of the film that Lex's parents are divorcing, suggesting that Lex may also—consciously or not—be referring to her father.[1] Likewise, the grandfather entrusted with her care has, in sending the children out into the park, also failed to keep Lex safe. It falls to Alan to restore Lex's faith and offer a robust model of paternal protection, reversing rather than repeating the pattern of abandonment that has so shaken her.

As much as *Jurassic Park* is a film about dinosaurs, then, it is also resolutely a film about men. In the same way that *Jaws* reflects on the state of contemporary American masculinity in a decade beleaguered by the Vietnam War and Watergate, revealing a vision of manhood that is both "out of its depth"[2] but ultimately redemptive, *Jurassic Park* is best understood within its wider sociopolitical context. Unlike *Jaws*, however, it is much more critical of the myth of heroic American manhood and reluctant to redeem those men who cling to such notions. Hollywood spent much of the 1990s grappling with the shifting contours and expectations of American masculinity, and especially in relation to straight, white men. The fault lines of what Susan Faludi characterized as a "domestic apocalypse,"[3] referring to the shifting and crumbling certainties of manhood, are clearly visible across much of Hollywood's output during the decade. As a microcosm of 1990s Hollywood cinema, *Jurassic Park* reflects the technological advances, high-concept filmmaking, and auxiliary marketing practices characteristic of the period.[4] Like many films of the decade, it also reflects a common thematic preoccupation with the question of how to be a (modern) man in the cultural space between the perceived certainty of the Reagan era and the unknown of the new millennium.[5] It is this facet of the film that this chapter explores, examining the film's fractured states of masculinity through the representation of various male characters—among them Alan Grant, Ian Malcolm, Donald Gennaro, and Dennis Nedry (Wayne Knight)—and tracing the parameters of their survival through the prism of contemporaneous anxieties about men and masculinity in the United States at the end of the twentieth century.

"I'm a ... and You're a ...": Clever Girls Inherit the Earth

If masculinities are increasingly understood to be always mutable, in flux, and unstable—perennially, perhaps, in *crisis*, to borrow a well-worn concept—then it is nevertheless the case that such crisis was particularly pronounced in the United States in the 1990s. Michael Kimmel points to the "multiplicity of masculinities" and the often "parallel and competing versions" of masculinity that exist in reality, which are frequently at odds with dominant hegemonic constructions of a mythical, singular masculinity.[6] This incongruity lies at the root of much masculine uncertainty during this period. Such uncertainty was compounded by changing cultural and social factors in the United States that altered the workplace, the family, the home, and the body, and with them shifted the expectations of, and experiences of, many American men. The resulting masculine anxieties that erupted on screens, in popular self-help literature, in newspapers, on talk shows, and in presidential declarations were commonly characterized as a "crisis of masculinity."[7] This state of crisis is captured in an early exchange between Malcolm and Dr. Ellie Sattler (Laura Dern). Malcolm reflects on the role of humans in nature, observing that "God creates dinosaurs. God destroys dinosaurs. God creates man. Man destroys God. Man creates dinosaurs." Presciently, Ellie responds, "Dinosaurs eat man. Woman inherits the earth." Though the film reserves being eaten by a dinosaur for its most objectionable man, there is little triumph to be found in most of the versions of masculinity performed by *Jurassic Park*'s male characters.

Intelligence, progress, and determination are coded persistently as female in *Jurassic Park*. Early in the film, game warden Muldoon (Bob Peck) speaks to the intelligence of the (female) dinosaurs and their ability to learn and adapt quickly within their new surroundings, posing a potential problem for the park's (predominantly male) keepers. While Alan is described as "not machine compatible" by Ellie due to his technological aversion, it is Lex's computing skills that enable their eventual escape from the visitor center and the island. Malcolm refers to Ellie as being "tenacious" when she insists on digging through the ailing *Triceratops*' dung, and the same tenacity is ascribed to the *Velociraptors*, who have developed a strategy for testing the weaknesses in the park's fences, systematically attacking different parts each time.

The failure of male characters to appreciate such skill and commitment is at best ill-advised and at worst fatal. Nedry's dismissal of the *Dilophosaurus*, whom he misgenders (and mischaracterizes) as a "nice boy," results in a swift poison-drenched death. Muldoon, fully cognizant of the dinosaurs' intelligence, is nevertheless outsmarted by a *Velociraptor* and has time for a final admiring statement – "clever girl' – before being ambushed. Meanwhile, Hammond, a grandfather with a walking stick, believes he, not Ellie, should accompany Muldoon through the storm-ridden jungle to switch the power back on. "Because I'm a ... and you're a ...," he blusters, to be met only with disdain for his clumsy sexism. The dinosaur in this scenario, it turns out, is Hammond, convinced that the very fact of his maleness grants him superiority over the young female scientist in front of him. Successfully turning on the power relies on both Ellie's intelligence and athleticism, while Lex's hacking is crucial in being able to control the doors, phones, and security systems that map the remaining characters' eventual escape.

Lex's technological savvy is the preserve of her brother Tim in Michael Crichton's original novel, with Lex herself characterized as whiny and timid, frequently complaining or shrieking.[8] In the film, however, Lex is reimagined as smart, capable, and astute. Casting Lex, Spielberg was keen to find an actor who could conjure a scream akin to those of cinema's original Scream Queen, Fay Wray, in *King Kong* (1933).[9] Lex does emit an impressive scream when confronted by the *T-Rex* after its escape, but Lex is not *just* a screaming girl; she is also integral to the humans' survival.

While success and survival are associated firmly with *Jurassic Park*'s female characters, the film's male characters fare less well. This chapter now turns to examining four of these men, whose own survival—or indeed lack thereof—is shaped by the extent to which they can adapt and, crucially, embody a softer, more nurturing model of masculinity that relies significantly on a turn towards the paternal.

Venality

Though the disaster in *Jurassic Park* is distinctly dinosaur-shaped, its origins are resolutely human. As far as culprits goes, there are no shortage of candidates. It may be Hammond whose vision the park brings to life, but he is aided by a host of scientists, including Dr. Henry Wu (B. D. Wong), and abetted by his investors, represented here by Gennaro. Like the government scientists in *E.T. the Extra-Terrestrial* (1982) or Professor Hobby (William Hurt) in *A.I. Artificial Intelligence* (2001), Wu is another of Spielberg's dubious scientist characters, possessing the same desire to play God that drives Hobby to create his mecha children. Wu's experimental approach to gene-splicing sets the disaster in motion, a practice that causes further disaster in *Jurassic World* when Wu engineers the lethal *Indominus rex*, though in *Jurassic Park* it is those with economic, rather than scientific, preoccupations for whom the harshest criticism is reserved. Beyond individual blame, however, lies a cluster of venal human traits. Mark Lacy notes that the "spectacle of destruction" unleashed in *Jurassic Park* results from "technological accidents, natural disasters and greed,"[10] while Robin Andersen similarly identifies "a storm, corruption, and human arrogance" as the root of the disaster.[11] Natural phenomena aside, the human capacity for greed and corruption is the clue to both the park's creation and destruction. This venality is embodied in two of the film's secondary characters—Nedry and Gennaro. Otherwise separated by age, class, appearance, social status, and self-perception, they are united by their inability to see beyond the potential for profit and power afforded by their involvement with the park. Nedry, the park's computer programmer, is an unpleasant, self-important man who arranges to smuggle dinosaur embryos to a rival company in exchange for money. The cowardly Gennaro, a lawyer acting on behalf of the park's investors, is also revealed as corruptible, as his initial skepticism is quickly superseded by his realization that there is astronomical profit to be made. Both men are ultimately destroyed by that which they seek to exploit, as Nedry is killed by a venomous *Dilophosaurus* and Gennaro is eaten by the escaped *T-Rex*.

Gennaro begins the film as a cautious, rather fussy man. He is evidently more at home in the office than in the unfamiliar environs of the amber mine in the Dominican Republic and, later, the park itself. When he arrives at the mine looking for Hammond, he stands awkwardly on a raft, wearing a suit and tie, and carrying a briefcase. There is a hint of the yuppie about Gennaro, a man who in the original script is described as a "city man" with a "hundred dollar haircut."[12] The mine foreman, Rostagno (Miguel Sandoval), draws an immediate distinction between Gennaro and Alan, whom the investors want to assess the viability of the park. He tells Gennaro that Alan will never agree to it "because Grant's like me. He's a digger." Here "digger" works as shorthand for straightforward, hardworking, and incorruptible; in failing to understand this simple fact, Gennaro, it is implied, lacks such virtues.

Initially, Gennaro is unenthusiastic about the park and convinced—with a certain degree of anticipatory glee—that it will not pass the necessary inspections. "I'll shut you down, John," he promises Hammond, who remains optimistic that Gennaro will soon be offering an apology instead. That Gennaro's mind is changed, however, has nothing to do with the safety assessment and everything to do with the potential to make money. The first significant glimmers of Gennaro's venal nature emerge during Hammond's big reveal of the *Brachiosaurus* herd. While Alan and Ellie are suitably overcome with distinctly Spielbergian wonder and Malcolm expresses an incredulous and begrudging admiration, Gennaro remains seated in the car and murmurs, "We're going to make a fortune with this place." Never mind that in front of him, a huge sauropod, millions of years extinct, is raising up on its back legs to strip leaves from a tree. All Gennaro sees are dollar signs. Later, while Malcolm lectures Hammond on scientific responsibility,

Gennaro speculates on the potential ticket prices. "We can charge anything we want," he says, his own wonder reserved not for the dinosaur hatchlings but for the huge sums of money Hammond (and by extension, his investors) can charge for entry to Jurassic Park. When Hammond protests that he does not want the park to be only for the "super-rich," Gennaro smirks, "we'll have a coupon day." One of his last contributions before being killed is to admonish Tim for playing with the night vision goggles in the tour vehicle. "Are they heavy? Then they're expensive. Put them back," he snaps. If Gennaro had any remaining soul to lose, it is here—as an adult man unable to understand a child's curiosity and enthusiasm—that he is condemned utterly. In Spielberg's films, the endangered child—what Linda Ruth Williams refers to as the use of "children as bait," seen in both *Jaws* and *Jurassic Park*—is most often made vulnerable through an adult's "failure to protect" them.[13] Even before he fails to keep Lex and Tim safe, however, Gennaro has failed to empathize with them. It is here, before he ever sets foot outside the vehicle, that his fate is sealed. Discussing Spielberg's cinematic children, Adrian Schober observes that they typically reflect a Romantic belief in "the child as a repository of inborn wisdom which in the adult has been largely sublimated, repressed, or denied."[14] While child-like adults are not without criticism, the adult who refuses to acknowledge any trace of their youthful innocence is afforded little sympathy.

As noted above, Gennaro's appearance, combined with his worship of wealth and profit, orients him toward the cultural figure of the yuppie so reminiscent of the 1980s and early 1990s. His city roots, his prestigious career, and his aspirations for "recognition," "power," and "money" recall Piesman and Hartley's definition of the yuppie in their satirical 1984 handbook for young urban professionals.[15] Certainly, Gennaro appears wedded to a version of manhood heavy on success and prosperity and light on emotion and empathy.

In the 1980s, constructions of hegemonic masculinity around financial power, individualism, dominance, and a competitive approach to business and life was enshrined in American culture. On the big screen, this became evident in the physical heroics of screen stars such as Sylvester Stallone, Bruce Willis, and Arnold Schwarzenegger.[16] More broadly, it could also be seen in the renewed military aspirations of President Reagan, as well as in the rise of financial journalism and the popularity of publications such as Ivan Boesky's *Merger Mania* (1985), Donald Trump's *The Art of the Deal* (1987), and Tom Peters's *Thriving on Chaos* (1987).[17] Boesky memorably described greed as "healthy" and informed the character of Gordon Gekko (Michael Douglas) in *Wall Street* (1987).[18] Hammond refers to Gennaro as a "bloodsucking lawyer," reinforcing the suggestion that Gennaro is a necessary evil, possessed of the required mercenary legal mind and mindful of the investors' financial risk, but lacking human warmth. In Spielbergian terms, Gennaro is the equivalent of Amity Island's Mayor Vaughn (Murray

Hamilton) in *Jaws*, a man committed to keeping the beaches open to secure valuable summer tourist dollars despite evidence of a proximate marauding shark.

By the 1990s, however, this vision of hegemonic American masculinity had undergone some modification. The bullish, "greed is good" ethos that thrived during the Reagan era floundered as the new decade dawned and the economy faltered under the leadership of George H. W. Bush. The "fascination with upward mobility, financial prosperity, materialism, and consumerism" that had found a natural home in Reaganite ideology was ultimately untenable.[19] As such, Gennaro reflects the disconnect between materialism and the means of production that ensures "the American brand of material yuppism ... [is] culturally unsustainable and unethical."[20] Gennaro sees only the material gain to be made from Jurassic Park and its prehistoric inhabitants. His failure to connect this gain to the actual creatures who sustain it becomes his downfall. As Rostagno predicted, Gennaro is resolutely *not* a digger and does not want to get his hands dirty, which is why at the first sight of the *T-Rex* he bolts and leaves Lex and Tim behind. For this egregious act, he suffers the film's most humiliating death, plucked from a toilet seat and devoured in one messy bite. Later, Ellie and Muldoon discover the partial remains of Gennaro strewn among the ruins of the portable toilet. In sacrificing his ethics and his empathy, Gennaro— and the outdated image of corporate masculinity he embodies—is deemed faintly ridiculous and certainly unworthy of saving.

Like Gennaro, Nedry is motivated primarily by money, though the characters are otherwise dissimilar. Success, and thus the recognition he craves and believes is his due, has eluded Nedry. Played by Wayne Knight with a similar gleeful meanness to his stalwart *Seinfeld* character, Newman, Nedry is first introduced at a beachside café in San Jose, Costa Rica, where he is meeting Lewis Dodgson (Cameron Thor). Dodgson has engaged Nedry in corporate espionage on behalf of InGen's rival company Biosyn and to that end presents him with a large bag of money and a set of fake Barbasol shaving foam cans in which Nedry is instructed to hide the cache of stolen dinosaur embryos. Everything about this scene is constructed to convey Nedry's greed and excess, from the ample plates of food in front of him to his garish aloha shirt and clashing patterned shorts, and especially the way he clutches the leather bag of money to his body. "Don't get cheap on me, Dodgson," he warns when his bill arrives, echoing his motivations for betraying InGen and Hammond. Where Nedry's ruthless pursuit of power, money, and control may have grown out of the expectations of the previous decade, there is little space for such flagrantly self-serving motivations here.

Jurassic Park ultimately has little sympathy for Nedry, whose financial problems are blamed firmly on himself, reflecting the prevailing neoliberalism of the time: "I'm sorry about your financial problems, Dennis," Hammond tells him wearily, "but they are *your* problems." Inevitably, Nedry's greed is his undoing. Caught in the storm on his way to deliver the stolen embryos, he becomes lost and encounters a young *Dilophosaurus* in the jungle. A lack of intelligence and foresight, underlined visually by the loss of his glasses, becomes fatal when combined with the single-minded intelligence of the *Dilophosaurus*. Nedry is dismissive of the creature, first trying to placate it with murmurs of "nice boy, nice boy" and then calling it "stupid" when it refuses to chase the stick he throws. What Nedry fails to understand is that he is not facing a "nice boy" or even a "stupid" boy, but another "clever girl." The *Dilophosaurus* outsmarts Nedry by climbing into his jeep and paralyzing him with venom, while the fake can of Barbasol—Nedry's ticket to wealth—rolls uselessly into a torrent of floodwater and is washed away. Greed, the film suggests, is no longer healthy or good, but liable to get you killed. In failing to cast off outdated constructions of power and masculinity, both Gennaro and Nedry also fail to survive.

Virility

If *Jurassic Park* is replete with men who blunder—unseeing—towards danger, downfall, and death, then Dr. Malcolm is the observant antidote. His leather jacket and tinted glasses give him an air of cool glamour, an image further compounded by Hammond's mildly disapproving assessment. "I bring scientists," he grumbles at Gennaro as the helicopter approaches Isla Nublar, "you bring a rock star." The "rock star" label overlooks the fact that Malcolm is himself a brilliant mathematician—specifically, a chaos theoretician—but more importantly it belies Malcolm's function as the wise corrective to Hammond's hubris. As discussed above in relation to Gennaro, the first sighting of the *Brachiosaurus* herd provides an insight into the film's main players. In Malcolm's case, he is suitably impressed but resists succumbing to absolute wonder like Alan and Ellie. They both immediately sweep off their sunglasses, all the better to see the dinosaurs, but Malcolm keeps his (actual and metaphorical) glasses on, his admiration tempered by caution. He sees not only the dinosaurs but the scientific achievements—and sacrifices—behind their existence. "The crazy son of a bitch did it," he murmurs, and the question of whether Hammond is "crazy" to have unleashed a population of genetically engineered dinosaurs is one that Malcolm returns to not only in *Jurassic Park*, but repeatedly in its franchise-extended life.[21]

Malcolm's primary concern is one of responsibility. He accuses Hammond and InGen of "standing on the shoulders of geniuses," using the available scientific knowledge without earning it themselves, thus breaking a chain of ethical accountability in pursuit of profit and glory. As a chaos theoretician, he is preoccupied with cause and effect, retaining a clear-eyed view of the potential consequences of the park. However, this in itself cannot save

Malcolm from those same consequences. In the same *T-Rex* attack that kills Gennaro, Malcolm is injured and knocked unconscious as he and Alan attempt to lure the *T-Rex* away from vehicle containing the children. Here, it is possible to glimpse the film's intervention into shifting ideas of masculine heroism, as Malcolm—the confident, capable, desirable "rock star"—spends the rest of the film incapacitated.

In another time, Malcolm would be *Jurassic Park*'s uncontested hero. Certainly, he would eventually occupy that role in its sequel, *The Lost World* (1997). If Gennaro's Spielbergian equivalent is *Jaws*' Mayor Vaughn, then Malcolm's is surely Indiana Jones (Harrison Ford). Indiana Jones is similarly a character possessing both intellect and virile charm: as Dr. Jones, he is an accomplished professor of archaeology, while as Indy he is charismatic, adventurous, and resolutely skeptical, not unlike Malcolm. Chris Yogerst draws a parallel between Indy in *Indiana Jones and the Temple of Doom* (1984) and Rick Blaine (Humphrey Bogart) in *Casablanca* (1942), noting the visual echo in *Temple*'s opening Shanghai nightclub scenes, where both the setting and the costuming are reminiscent of Bogart's classic role.[22] This comparison speaks to the charisma and appeal—and a certain reluctant heroism—present in Indy's character, elements that reappear in the characterization of Malcolm. Like Indy, Malcolm is supremely intelligent, wryly observant, and desirable. The latter of these traits is encapsulated in the contemporary widespread usage of a GIF showing a reclining, injured Malcolm with his shirt undone, an image that has become, as Rebecca Williams observes, "a short-hand ... used to connote sexiness" on numerous online platforms.[23] Indeed, Malcolm has transcended *Jurassic Park* more so than any other character, including Alan Grant, and his endurance both within the franchise (to date, appearing in all three films from the first trilogy as well as having a cameo in *Jurassic World: Fallen Kingdom* and a significant role in *Jurassic World: Dominion* [2022]) and in its extratextual universe confers an importance that might reasonably be expected of a screen hero. Malcolm's incapacitation and consequent sidelining in *Jurassic Park*, therefore, is significant.

The key to understanding the demotion of Malcolm lies in his repudiation of personal responsibility. If Malcolm is aware of the importance of scientific accountability, this sense of commitment and duty does not extend to his personal life. Noting that Spielberg's depictions of children and childhood are often informed by a certain darkness, Schober observes that irresponsible adults are not looked upon kindly in the director's work[24] and quotes Spielberg's biographer Joseph McBride, who identifies a common protagonist as "a child-like adult whose attempts to escape a grown-up's responsibilities are viewed by [Spielberg] with deep ambivalence".[25] Here, then, is the vital clue to Malcolm's muted survival in *Jurassic Park*. Unlike Alan, he professes to "love kids" and has three of his own, a revelation that serves as shorthand for red-blooded vitality. He has, however, also been married multiple times and jokes that he is "always on the lookout for a future ex-Mrs. Malcolm." Clearly, Malcolm's private life is tumultuous and his repeated efforts to flirt with Ellie only underline his status as a charming, if opportunistic, philanderer. In a period in which the AIDS epidemic had fundamentally transformed attitudes toward promiscuity and sex, record numbers of families were experiencing the effects of separation, divorce and single-parenthood, and cultural narratives of contemporary masculinity increasingly emphasized problems of uncertainty and instability, the uncommitted single man became a figure in need of redemption, not least in Hollywood. The father detached from his own children likewise required redirecting toward familial commitment, in what quickly became a well-worn narrative trope of mainstream 1990s cinema.[26] As such, Malcolm is an imperfect hero for the time, not least because he is cheerfully unrepentant about his checkered romantic and paternal history. His injury and subsequent marginalizing in the narrative suggest that the film considers his brand of swaggering masculinity incompatible with a more reflective and nurturing ideal of masculinity. Consequently, the way is paved for the reluctant, understated heroism of another.

Victory

The characters' time on Isla Nublar is bookended by helicopter journeys that deposit them on, and later rescue them from, the island. On the first journey, Malcolm is confident and at ease, flirtatious toward Ellie and mildly amused by Alan's discomfort. Alan's feeling of being out of place is visually underscored by his inability to connect his seatbelt; improvising, he ties together the incompatible ends, foreshadowing Malcolm's later prediction that the all-female population of dinosaurs may still find a way to reproduce. However, the helicopter journey that closes the film marks a role reversal. Now, it is Malcolm who is subdued while Alan is serene and quietly triumphant, his arms around the sleeping children. This moment marks the culmination of Alan's redemptive journey and the validation of a heroism that is informed significantly by a turn toward a softer, more paternal imagining of masculinity, the defining features of which are "vulnerability, devotion, and care."[27]

Crucially, it is not that Alan possesses these characteristics before the film begins, but rather that he embraces this vision of evolved masculinity as it progresses. Alan's initial characterization rests on his own dinosaur-like status. A man preoccupied with the prehistoric past, he is resolutely old-school and notably technophobic. Paleontology is a convenient foil for Alan, who is more comfortable with interpreting the past than navigating the future. It is precisely this orientation that Alan must correct to survive the film, as he is compelled to trade his measured, certain existence for the messy, unpredictable job of protecting Lex and Tim.

If Ian Malcolm's character is comparable to Indiana Jones, then Alan Grant provides a further echo of Spielberg's 1980s hero through his attire. Alan wears a light brown fedora not unlike Indy's, and certainly too similar to be accidental. On the latter, this hat is symbolic of the character's daring and quest for adventure. Indeed, it is so significant to Indy that he memorably risks his arm to retrieve it in *Temple of Doom*, swiping it from beneath a rapidly closing stone door. Giving Alan the same hat draws a parallel between the two men, creating an expectation that Alan will be cut from the same lone adventurer cloth. However, while Indiana Jones goes to great lengths to save his hat, Alan loses his when shielding the children from the *T-Rex* and does not give it a second thought.[28] That which has been representative of a particular kind of masculine heroism—independent, macho, reckless—is suddenly expendable. Instead, Alan begins to pivot toward a more paternal vision of heroism, trading individual feats of bravado for caution, care, and reassurance. It is this that secures Alan's survival and ultimate sense of victory, as the other men around him flounder or fall.

For this to occur, Alan must amend his own outlook and behavior, specifically around his feelings toward children. It is notable that, just as Lex's character undergoes a shift from the novel to the film, so too does Alan, specifically in relation to Ellie. In the novel, although characters speculate about the nature of their relationship, Ellie is his graduate student. In the film, Ellie is slightly older and more clearly Alan's girlfriend, removing any ambiguity and sense of impropriety and framing Alan as the steadfast, upstanding alternative to Malcolm. Unlike Malcolm, however, Alan is not predisposed toward family life. Although Ellie is interested in having children, Alan is skeptical of babies and condemns them as "noisy," "expensive," and "smelly." On a dig in Montana prior to Hammond's summons, he is positively gleeful when describing to a young boy how a *Velociraptor* would go about disemboweling him. Toward Hammond's grandchildren, meanwhile, he is barely tolerant and actively avoids their company on the ill-fated tour of the park. *Jurassic Park* is certainly not unusual in featuring a male protagonist who is reluctant about fatherhood—Hollywood during this period was awash with such redemption-ready characters—but the film's backdrop of questions about evolution and reproduction gives added potency to Alan's necessary transformation.

As the second half of the film progresses, Alan learns to encourage and reassure Lex and Tim, and crucially restore their trust in a father figure. He verbalizes this when Lex, again, frets (ostensibly in reference to Gennaro), "He left us! He left us!" Alan responds, "But that's not what I'm going to do." Tasked with breaking this trend of paternal—or pseudo-paternal—abandonment, Alan first rescues Tim from the suspended jeep and then guides both children to relative safety, before watching over them all night as they sleep in a tree. This moment is reflective of a wider sociocultural narrative that gained momentum in the 1990s, as the role of the father and particularly the perceived damage caused by absent fatherhood became frequent topics of discussion. Popular magazines such as *Newsweek* and *People* ran stories on so-called "deadbeat dads"; the May 1992 issue of *Newsweek* memorably mocked up a Wanted poster of Frederick Grimaldi, alleged to owe over $22,000 in unpaid child support.[29] The tabloid talk show *Maury* (1991–present) made a regular feature of paternity testing, and it and similar shows found success in declarations of shirked paternal responsibility or deceived men. On the political stage, President Clinton referred to absent fathers in numerous speeches and signed into law the Deadbeat Parents' Punishment Act (1998), criminalizing child support avoidance. The changing parameters of the American nuclear family, along with shifting gendered experiences and expectations of work, breadwinning, and childcare, made fatherhood visible in ways it had not been before. Within this cultural moment—and recognizing too Spielberg's own personal preoccupation with issues of divorce and fatherhood—Alan's pledge to stay awake while Lex and Tim sleep is not only practical but symbolic of the protection and commitment they have previously been denied. It is a quiet promise, rather than a bombastic feat of daring or endurance, but it is a crucial moment in Alan's journey to being *Jurassic Park*'s undisputed hero.

As noted earlier in this chapter, Alan is described by Rostagno as a "digger," an admirable designation that sets him apart from men such as Gennaro. Following this scene, Alan is told by one of his younger colleagues that in a few more years "we won't even have to dig anymore," such are the technological advances in the field of paleontology. Though men like Rostagno and Alan value the hands-on nature of the dig, and the sense of authenticity that this suggests, technology is changing both the methods and the results. While Alan's initial response is to dismiss these new tools and lament the loss of the old methods, when settled with Lex and Tim in the tree he acknowledges the importance of adaptation. Now InGen has succeeded in recreating dinosaurs, Lex asks what Alan will do if he and Ellie no longer need to dig up dinosaurs. "I don't know," he says. "I guess we'll just have to evolve too." This realization underscores Alan's newfound heroism. Once admired for being a "digger," Alan's mistake would be to cleave to this version of himself forever. In recognizing that he can be something else too—protector, survivor, father—he becomes the only man who leaves *Jurassic Park* with any vestige of victory.

Conclusion

Randy Laist characterizes the 1990s as a "lost decade," an undefined period lacking a narrative through-line.[30] This perception of instability and change is echoed in claims that the 1990s were a decade in a "state of flux," a *fin de siècle* characterized in the United States by social, cultural, political, economic, militaristic, and technological change.³¹ These often destabilizing shifts, however, arguably *become* the narrative. In Hollywood, a persistent narrative was established precisely around those men who also found themselves in a flux state. This was a narrative of adaptability, of evolution, and of a turn toward the paternal. Such a narrative is embodied in the character arc of Alan Grant, a technophobic, child-averse man focused on the past who ends *Jurassic Park* with his arms around Lex and Tim, staring out at the birds on the horizon and contemplating the future.

Like *Jaws*, *Jurassic Park* is a film ostensibly about a potentially monstrous creature that is, beneath the surface, a film about much more than that.³² In both cases, these are as much films about men as they are about monsters. Just as the unreconstructed Quint (Robert Shaw) perishes aboard the *Orca*, those men in *Jurassic Park* who remain relics of a previous masculine age do not survive. Malcolm and Hammond, meanwhile, are left shaken by their experience, their hubris and misplaced confidence no longer redolent of success. Tim, it appears, chose correctly when he directed his earlier hero-worship toward Alan Grant.

That the final shot of *Jurassic Park* is not of a dinosaur—say, the triumphant *T-Rex* last seen among the detritus of the visitor center—but a flock of birds that is significant and underscores both Alan's personal and professional victory. The image is a reminder of the fact that birds are the only living descendants of dinosaurs, confirming Alan's controversial paleontological hypothesis. It also acts as a visual reminder of Alan's earlier acknowledgment of the importance of evolving as a person, which for Alan means cultivating a more nurturing model of masculinity. The birds signify a future that, thanks to this realization, is now accessible to Alan due to his embrace of that equally potent symbol of the future, the children. The extraordinary heroics of *Jurassic Park* may include near-misses, daring escapes, and acts of bravery, yet they also extend to a very straightforward promise to two traumatized children: to be the man who doesn't leave.

Notes

1 Katie Barnett, *Fathers on Film: Paternity and Masculinity in 1990s Hollywood* (London: Bloomsbury Academic, 2020), 44.
2 I. Q. Hunter and Matthew Melia, "Introduction," in Hunter and Melia (eds.) *The Jaws Book: New Perspectives on the Classic Summer Blockbuster* (London: Bloomsbury Academic, 2020), 9.
3 Susan Faludi, *Stiffed: The Betrayal of the Modern Man* (London: Chatto & Windus, 1999), 5.
4 For discussion of the changing technological and economic landscape of Hollywood in the 1990s, see Winston Wheeler Dixon, "Twenty-Five Reasons Why It's All Over," in Jon Lewis (ed.) *The End of Cinema as We Know*

It: American Film in the Nineties (New York: New York University Press, 2001), 356–66; Chuck Kleinhans, "1993: Movies and the New Economics of Blockbusters and Indies," in Chris Holmund (ed.) *American Cinema of the 1990s: Themes and Variations* (New Brunswick, NJ: Rutgers University Press, 2008), 91–114.

5   Randy Laist, *Cinema of Simulation: Hyperreal Hollywood in the Long 1990s* (London: Bloomsbury Academic, 2015).

6   Michael Kimmel, *Manhood in America: A Cultural History* (Oxford: Oxford University Press, 2012), 4.

7   For comprehensive discussions of a crisis of masculinity in the 1990s, see particularly Faludi, *Stiffed*, and Brenton J. Malin, *American Masculinity under Clinton: Popular Media and the Nineties Crisis of Masculinity* (New York: Peter Lang, 2005).

8   Michael Crichton, *Jurassic Park* (New York: Knopf, 1990).

9   Steven Awalt, "The Evolution of Lex," January 1, 2020. https://amblin.com/article/the-evolution-of-lex/. Accessed December 14, 2021.

10 Mark J. Lacy, "Cinema and Ecopolitics: Existence in *Jurassic Park*," *Millennium: Journal of International Studies* 30:1 (2001): 639.

11 Robin Andersen, "Learning to Love Biomimetic Killing: How *Jurassic World* Embraces Life Forms as Weapons," *American Journal of Economics and Sociology* 76:2 (2017): 468.

12 David Koepp, *Jurassic Park,* original screenplay. http://www.dailyscript.com/scripts/jurassicpark_script_final_12_92.html. Accessed December 14, 2021.

13 Linda Ruth Williams, "Children as Bait," in Hunter and Melia (eds.) *The Jaws Book: New Perspectives on the Classic Summer Blockbuster* (London: Bloomsbury Academic, 2020), 138.

14 Adrian Schober, "Introduction," in Adrian Schober and Debbie Olson (eds.) *Children in the Films of Steven Spielberg* (Lanham, MD: Lexington Books, 2016), 5.

15 Marissa Piesman and Marilee Hartley, *The Yuppie Handbook: The State-of-the-Art Manual for Young Urban Professionals* (New York: Pocket Books, 1984), 12.

16 Susan Jeffords, *Hard Bodies: Hollywood Masculinity in the Reagan Era* (New Brunswick, NJ: Rutgers University Press, 1994).

17 Leigh Claire La Berge, "The Men Who Make the Killings: *American Psycho*, Financial Masculinity, and 1980s Financial Print Culture," *Studies in American Fiction* 37:2 (2010): 273–96.

18 Thomas Gabor, *Everybody Does It!: Crime by the Public* (Toronto: University of Toronto Press, 1994), 116.

19 Richard Lowy, "Yuppie Racism: Race Relations in the 1980s," *Journal of Black Studies* 21:4 (1991): 448.

20 Mattius Rischard, "Masculine Capital / Yuppie Patriarchy: Visualizing the Noir Commodity in *American Psycho*," *Texas Studies in Literature and Language* 62:4 (2020): 458.

21 In *Jurassic World: Fallen Kingdom* (2018), at a hearing to determine the fate of the dinosaurs stranded on Isla Nublar, Malcolm observes: "We altered the course of our natural history. This is a correction," as he advocates for the dinosaurs to be left to perish in an impending volcanic eruption.

22 Chris Yogerst, "Faith under the Fedora: Indiana Jones and the Heroic Journey Towards God," *Journal of Religion and Film* 18:2 (2014): 17.

23 Rebecca Williams, "The Goldblum That Keeps on GIF-ing: *Jurassic Park*'s Afterlife in Meme Culture," 25 Years of *Jurassic Park* Conference, University of Cardiff, June 8, 2018.

24 Schober, "Introduction," 1.

25 Joseph McBride, *Steven Spielberg: A Biography* (London: Faber and Faber), 17.

26 Barnett, *Fathers on Film*, 34.

27 Tatiana Prorokova, "Between Vietnam and 9/11: Arnold Schwarzenegger and a New Type of Masculinity in *Twins* and *Kindergarten Cop*," *MCS: Masculinities and Social Change* 6:1 (2017): 22.

28 Further discussion of the parallels between Indy and Alan's hats can be found in Barnett, *Fathers on Film*, 41–2.

29 Anon., "Deadbeat Dads," *Newsweek*, May 4, 1992.

30 Laist, *Cinema of Simulation*, 2–3.

31 Anna Everett, *Pretty People: Movie Stars of the 1990s* (New Brunswick, NJ: Rutgers University Press, 2012), 2.

32 I. Q. Hunter and Matthew Melia, *The Jaws Book*, 6.

10

Jurassic Park and Spielberg's Scientists

James Kendrick
Baylor University, USA

Introduction

It would be the apex of understatement to say that *Jurassic Park* was one of Steven Spielberg's most highly anticipated films. Released after months of increasing media hype in June 1993, it heralded Spielberg's return to the realm of the summer blockbuster that had helped define his public persona with *Jaws* (1975) nearly twenty years earlier. Anticipation was heightened by the fact that it followed a rare string of critical and commercial disappointments for Spielberg, including his romantic fantasy *Always* (1989) and his big-budget Peter Pan sequel *Hook* (1991). *Jurassic Park* was already a known entity before it reached theaters, having been based on the best-selling novel of the same name by Michael Crichton. Word had been swirling for months about the new computer-generated effects the film would use to bring its hordes of dinosaurs to cinematic life, and more than a hundred American and international companies had already lined up to produce officially licensed tie-in merchandise six months before the film hit screens.[1]

Jurassic Park was featured on the covers of both *Time* (April 26, 1993) and *Newsweek* (June 14, 1993), thus giving it the kind of widespread coverage and advance publicity that precious few films enjoy. And, while both articles trumpeted the significant advances in special effects technologies the film promised, they also alluded to how its success would ultimately hinge not just on dinosaur effects, but on finding a working balance between reality and fantasy. The *Time* article described *Jurassic Park* as being "At the boundary between science and science fiction—in that twilight area where the imaginative sleuthing of paleontology meets the storytelling craft of filmmaking,"[2] while the *Newsweek* article argued that "special effects alone can't persuade audiences to pretend that dinosaurs have burst the coffin of extinction. There is only one hidden persuader in science fiction: a solid kernel of scientific plausibility."[3]

That "kernel of scientific plausibility" became the centerpiece of what turned into a significant debate within the scientific community about *Jurassic Park*. And that debate focused not just on the realities of extracting ancient DNA and using it to clone long extinct species, but also about the manner in which that science was dramatized and how the scientists themselves were portrayed. In both newsletters and publications within the scientific community and in the pages of such mass market publications as the *New York Times*, a fight emerged over *Jurassic Park* and the effects its depiction of science and scientists might have culturally, politically, and ideologically.

This chapter will examine *Jurassic Park*'s depiction of science and put it in dialogue with Spielberg's numerous other films that depict scientists as either heroes, villains, or something in between. It is well documented that Spielberg was an avid consumer of science fiction as a child—on television, in pulp magazines, and at the movies—and his father was an early computer engineer, thus giving him a great deal of exposure to science and technology and their depictions in popular culture. It is not surprising, then, that he would so frequently turn to not just the genre of science fiction (seven of his feature films are science fiction, and numerous others incorporate science fiction, fantasy, or horror elements), but to particular narratives that depict scientists and the dangers involved—to themselves and others—of the scientific enterprise, especially when it is unmoored from the goal of advancing humanity and is instead put to personal goals of ego-building or financial enrichment.

These depictions of science and scientists are by no means consistent in Spielberg's films, but there is a clear, recurring thematic strain about scientists trying and failing to control things that are inherently (or destined to be) out of their control, a staple narrative theme in science fiction dating back to Mary Shelly's *Frankenstein* (1818). However, Shelley's novel, like *Jurassic Park*, is often misunderstood as a simple condemnation of science out of control, when in fact both narratives present opposing models of science that create a critical interplay of how science can be done well and how it can be done badly. As with all of Spielberg's films, there is inherent tension in his depiction of scientists and science across these films, which reflects the thematic and narrative complexity throughout his body of work. *Jurassic Park* dramatizes this tension in depicting scientists who are both respectful and contemptuous of the power of nature and humankind's ability to harness it.

Spielberg's Depictions of Scientists

Spielberg's films are replete with fascinating scientific figures whose various aspirations and failings create a rich tapestry of drama regarding the long-standing human desire to understand, but also to conquer and control. Of the fourteen theatrical feature films he directed prior to *Jurassic Park*, more than half of them feature major characters who are scientists: *Jaws* (1975), *Close Encounters of the Third Kind* (1977), *Poltergeist* (1982), *E.T. the Extra-Terrestrial* (1982), and the first three Indiana Jones films: *Raiders of the Lost Ark* (1981), *Indiana Jones and the Temple of Doom* (1984), and *Indiana Jones and the Last Crusade* (1989).

Matt Hooper (Richard Dreyfuss), the ichthyologist from the Oceanographic Institute in *Jaws*, is the first significant scientist to appear in a Spielberg film, and in many ways he set the mold for the director's positive approach to the scientific enterprise. Young and enthusiastic, he is empowered by earned knowledge that puts him both in awe of the sharks he studies and aware of the potential dangers they present. Like many Spielberg protagonists, he is also a perennial outsider, brought in from "the mainland" to the fictional Amity Island to help the island's beleaguered Chief Brody (Roy Scheider) manage a series of shark attacks off the island's beaches.

Yet, as much as he is shunned by the islanders, he is repeatedly proved correct in his assertions, which are always based on scientific information, observation, and reason. In this regard, Hooper plays two crucial narrative functions in the film: first, he is an important source of scientifically accurate information about shark behavior for the other characters (and, by proxy, the audience), which gives the film's horrors an edge of informed realism, and second, as a voice of reason to counter the politically and financially motivated Mayor Vaughn (Murray Hamilton), whose chief concern is Amity's fiscal prosperity, especially leading up to the coveted Fourth of July weekend. Therefore, Hooper the scientist stands in for knowledge and reason and the importance of applying them in difficult situations, and his being ignored repeatedly leads to further deaths. After performing his own medical examination on the remains of the shark's first victim, Hooper confronts the ethically challenged medical examiner who was willing to change his initial assessment and write the death off as a boating accident.

It is worth noting that Spielberg came to view Dreyfuss as "his alter ego," casting him as the protagonist in two subsequent films, *Close Encounters of the Third Kind* and *Always*. As Joseph McBride shows, Spielberg reshaped Matt Hooper's character "to reflect his own sensibilities,"[4] making him substantially different from the much less sympathetic character in Peter Benchley's source novel.

Using him as a mouthpiece, Spielberg and [*Jaws* co-screenwriter Carl] Gottlieb were able to elevate *Jaws* from a formulaic monster melodrama to a film with a modestly stated, yet clearly defined social perspective. As "an American Jew with clearly defined ethnic roots," Dreyfuss exemplified what Gottlieb defined as "a tradition of intellectual inquiry, respect for learning, and intense involvement with morality and law." Those qualities are abundantly present in the film's Matt Hooper, the voice of scientific reason and civic responsibility.[5]

Thus, Matt Hooper can be seen as the ideal scientist figure in Spielberg's body of work, a character who unambiguously merges science with an ethically defined concern for others.

Spielberg's next film, *Close Encounters of the Third Kind*, also prominently features a scientist character, in this case Claude Lacombe (François Truffaut), a French government scientist who spends most of the film tracking evidence of extraterrestrial visitors. Throughout the film he plays the role of investigator, showing up at various places around the world (the Sonoran Desert in Mexico, the Gobi Desert in East Asia, the mountains of India) to observe firsthand the aftermath of direct contact with extraterrestrials. Thus, even though we know virtually nothing about him, Lacombe becomes one of the film's most important audience surrogates, taking us from place to place and wondering the same questions we might have. Although he is clearly part of a huge, multinational government operation that eventually engages in a massive cover-up and directly lies to the public to hide the landing of an alien spacecraft at Devil's Tower in Wyoming, he is never directly implicated in the kind of dark government activities and corruption that one might imagine being associated with a government scientist in the years just after Watergate and Vietnam.

Instead, Lacombe is depicted as a man of gentleness and humility, a kind of dreamer who uses science to pursue the great mysteries of the world. As Spielberg put it:

> For the Lacombe character I wanted a humanitarian and not a military officer. I wanted someone who would be more of a *mensch* than a militant. Truffaut struck me as the wise child. He has a lot of wonder in him and I liked that more than someone with narrow eyes and a pragmatic outlook on life.[6]

The fact that Lacombe is French is also directly connected to Spielberg's desire for the character to be one of openness and enthusiasm for discovery and knowledge: "We're [Americans] still very ego-centered about the possibility of life elsewhere. The French are much more optimistic."[7]

Lacombe is directly connected with Keys (Peter Coyote), the unnamed government scientist in *E.T. the Extra-Terrestrial*, who stands out from the other scientists and military officials because of his sense of wonder and desire to experience and understand, rather than control. Although he is initially depicted in ways that make him seem ominous (his first appearance on screen is his elongated shadow darkening the driveway of the home where the abandoned alien E.T. is taken in), he is eventually revealed to be a sympathetic character who shares many characteristics with Elliott (Henry Thomas), the young boy who befriends E.T. In fact, one could argue that Keys is an adult version of Elliott, as he tells the boy that E.T.'s arrival was a "miracle" that he has been waiting for since he was a "ten-year-old boy." That sense of wonder also defines the trio of paranormal researchers in *Poltergeist*, who pursue their study of ghosts with a clear sense of both enthusiasm and respect for the afterlife—a rare combination of the technological and the spiritual that is also reflected in *Close Encounters*.

All of these scientists are positive characters who represent the potential for good in their melding of scientific knowledge and understanding with engagement and responsibility toward their fellow human beings. This is not to say that there are not some morally questionable scientists and dubious uses of science in Spielberg's films. Chief among these is Dr. Iris Hineman (Lois Smith) in *Minority Report* (2002), the person most directly responsible for creating "Precrime," the near-future justice system in which murders are detected and stopped before they can occur. The system utilizes a combination of advanced technology and a threesome of clairvoyant humans known as "Precogs," who are held in a near comatose state, their only purpose being to alert authorities if they see a future murder. A seemingly "perfect" system, it is actually a bastardization of Dr. Hineman's original work, which involved genetic research to treat the severely brain-damaged children of drug addicts, especially those born to addicts of a particularly toxic street drug called neuroin. She describes Precrime as "the unintended consequences of a series of genetic mistakes and science gone haywire," and when told that she doesn't "seem all that proud," she immediately snaps back, "I'm not." Living in complete isolation on a rural farm, she surrounds herself with plants—a visual rebuke to all the screens and digital technologies that otherwise define the film's hypermediated and controlled futuristic world—many of which she has modified and engineered. Far from embracing Precrime, she rejects it, although without taking any direct steps to counter it or dismantle it. Although the development of Precrime is a tragic distortion of her original, humane scientific work, Dr. Hineman has responded not by fighting the wrong, but by retreating into her own world, abandoning the Precogs she once tried to heal to the system born of "genetic mistakes and science gone haywire," where they float in a shallow vat of "photon milk" and are fed a constant supply of dopamine and endorphins and exist a netherworld hovering between sleep and wakefulness.

The most morally compromised scientist in Spielberg's body of work is, on the surface at least, the most unlikely: Dr. Hobby (William Hurt), the robotics engineer in *A.I. Artificial Intelligence* (2001) who designs and builds a robot boy named David (Haley Joel Osment) that is programmed to love a human being. Dr. Hobby's goal, as he puts it, is to "fulfill a great human need" by supplying loving children at a time in the near future when childbirth is strictly limited due to a global climate catastrophe. Dr. Hobby's cruelty stems from how shockingly unreflective he is about the potential consequences of designing an artificial child (a "mecha" in the film's terminology) who, rather than simply mimicking the distinctly human emotion of love, literally experiences it and, once activated, is incapable of stopping. The film introduces Dr. Hobby during a meeting with other scientists and engineers, where he declares, as thunder rolls on the soundtrack, that "to create an artificial being has been the dream of man since the birth of science," thus immediately aligning him with the dangerous hubris of humankind desiring to play God. Dr. Hobby's casual cruelty toward his creations is immediately apparent when he stabs a female mecha in the hand with a pen to illustrate her "pain memory response." The audience of scientists and engineers are unfazed by his actions and even laugh when the mecha recoils when he tries to stab her hand again, although there is one scientist who challenges him by posing the moral quandary of what responsibility a person has to the mecha that is programmed to love them.

Later in the film, Dr. Hobby shows in no uncertain terms that he feels no responsibility toward his creation and rather views David as little more than a fascinating experiment, despite the fact that David literally feels human emotion and was physically fashioned after his own deceased child. When David arrives at Cybertronics after a torturous journey through a dangerous and hostile world in his pursuit of the Blue Fairy that he erroneously believes has the magical power to turn him into a "real boy," he finds only Dr. Hobby. In the film's most quietly disturbing scene, Dr. Hobby ignores how much David has suffered in his journey both physically and psychologically and expresses exhilaration at how successful he has been as an experiment in robotics. While Dr. Hobby speaks to David in a soft, gentle voice—the way a caring father might speak to a troubled son— what he says to him is disturbing in the way it reveals the depth of Dr. Hobby's recognition of David's suffering and his simultaneous refusal to take responsibility for it:

> Until you were born, robots didn't dream, robots didn't desire unless we told them what to want. David, do you have any idea what a success story you've become? You found a fairy tale and inspired by love, fueled by desire, you set out on a journey to make her real. And, most remarkable of all, no one taught you how …. Where would your self-motivated reasoning take you? To the logical conclusion … that Blue Fairy is part of the great human flaw to wish for things that don't exist, or the greatest single human gift—the ability to chase down our dreams. And that is something no machine has ever done until you.

Thus, while Dr. Hobby is able to see and articulate David's "desire" and "love," for him they are just facets of a successful technological experiment. He recognizes that David shares in a fundamental aspect of humanity: "wish[ing] for things that don't exist," which is "part of the great human flaw ... or the greatest single human gift." That humanity begets tragedy because David is, in Dr. Hobby's words, "a perfect child caught in a freeze-frame, always loving, never ill, never changing," even though the object of his love will, as all human do, grow old and die. Thus, Dr. Hobby either never took into account or actively ignores the inherent cruelty in creating a mecha that is programmed to love someone who might reject him and will eventually die, leaving the mecha alone with an unmitigated love that can only be resolved by death. Yet, for Dr. Hobby, David's humanity and his suffering, which eventually drives him to attempt suicide, are just components of an elaborate research project. Dr. Hobby, despite his benign, middle-aged exterior and gentle demeanor, is an exemplar of the horrors that follow when science is shorn of human context and a moral framework. Whether his own grief over his son has numbed him or whether he has simply buried himself so deeply in his own work that he cannot see beyond it, Dr. Hobby has become a monster, even if he doesn't recognize it.

Debate in the Scientific Community around *Jurassic Park*'s Science and Scientists

Unlike the films discussed above, which caused no real stir or controversy regarding their depiction of science and scientists, there was active debate within the scientific community about *Jurassic Park* months before the film reached screens. This debate was driven by both the nature of the science being portrayed and the recognition that the combination of the popularity of Crichton's novel, the allure of the film's pioneering special effects, and Spielberg's immense marquee value all but ensured that *Jurassic Park* would be a massive blockbuster that had a high probability of influencing the general public's understanding of ancient genetic research and what is and is not scientifically possible within that realm.

The debate arguably kicked off with an editorial by molecular biologist Russell Higuchi in the second issue of the *Ancient DNA Newsletter* in December 1992, a full seven months before the film's premiere. Roughly a decade earlier, Higuchi had helped pioneer the real-life procedure of extracting ancient DNA when he and a team of researchers successfully extracted, sequenced, and analyzed DNA from the dried muscle of a quagga, a zebra-like species that had been declared extinct since 1883.[8] He was also instrumental in the development of polymerase chain reaction (PCR), a technique that could exponentially increase the copying of specific DNA samples and was quickly applied to the analysis of ancient DNA. These successes gave official scientific credence to what became known as "Ancient DNA Studies," a field that grew significantly in the decades that followed.[9]

As Elizabeth D. Jones has noted, the desire to extract and study DNA from fossil remains and potentially employ it to resurrect extinct species emerged from a confluence of independent sources, from "futurists and enthusiasts to scientists and the popular press."[10] This particular confluence of molecular biology and paleontology became a "celebrity-driven" scientific practice, due in no small part to its narrative employment in Crichton's novel and Spielberg's film adaptation. The idea of extracting dinosaur DNA from blood samples inside the bodies of biting insects preserved in amber originated with Dr. George O. Poinar Jr., a paleontologist at the University of California at Berkeley, who speculated on such possibilities in the mid-1980s after he and his wife, Dr. Roberta Hess, examined a forty-million-year-old chunk of amber inside of which was embedded a perfectly preserved female fungus gnat.[11]

Almost from the outset the practice was deemed controversial within the scientific community. Robust debate ensued on the possibilities of extracting useful DNA, much less using said DNA to bring back to life extinct species, and Crichton's novel enflamed those divisions by taking the technique and extrapolating from it a thriller premise that, on the page, would seem entirely plausible to the general reader. Spielberg's turning that thriller premise into a blockbuster movie promised to complicate the issue further, leading to Higuchi's trying to get out in front of the problem by requesting that his colleagues not entertain the hypothetical possibility of cloning dinosaurs from ancient DNA:

> When you get asked (and in the wake of *Jurassic Park*, the movie, it seems inevitable that some of you will) whether the resurrection of dinosaurs from ancient DNA is possible, I hope you will say it is not. Although it is fun to say, "in theory, it may be possible (nudge, nudge—wink, wink)", let's get real ... I myself have been guilty of allowing this romantic—if not Gothic—notion, the resurrection of extinct species, to colour reports of our work (it *is* hard to keep the Media from focusing on that). It now seems clear to me that the responsible thing to do is to try as much as possible not to overstate the power of new technology, in the field of ancient DNA or elsewhere.[12]

As the film's release drew closer, the debate about how it might depict science and scientists spilled over into the mainstream press, including several articles and opinion pieces in the *New York Times*. The headline of Michael W. Browne's May 11, 1993, article is telling of the overall narrative: "In New Spielberg Film, a Dim View of Science." The article notes:

Some scientists are ... uneasy about what they perceive as an anti-science bias in the plot, a charge that [Michael Crichton] himself acknowledges. In its attack on biotechnology, they say, "Jurassic Park" revives the Frankenstein image of amoral scientists unleashing forces they cannot control.[13]

The article quotes directly from Higuchi's column in the *Ancient DNA Newsletter*, which it characterized as a "condemnation" of the film: "Both the book and movie, he wrote, contain 'gross overstatements of the capabilities of DNA technology' that 'lead to unreasonable fear' of it. According to this line or reasoning, he said, 'If dinosaurs can be brought back to life, who knows what other evils'."[14] The article goes on to note that microbiologists viewed the film as "a veiled attack on science," a view that is corroborated by both Crichton, who is quoted as being skeptical of the "growing tendency toward scientism—unthinking acceptance of scientific ideas, and a tendency to discount ideas that science can't address" and Spielberg, who is quoted as saying, "Every gain in science involves an equal and opposite reaction—a loss, usually a loss of the environment .... Science is intrusive. I wouldn't ban molecular biology altogether, because it's useful in finding cures for AIDS, cancer and other diseases. But it's also dangerous and that's the theme of 'Jurassic Park'."[15]

On June 11, the day of the film's US release, the *New York Times* published "Evil Science Runs Amok—Again!," an op-ed by Carol Muske Dukes, a poet and professor of English at the University of Southern California. Muske Dukes placed the film squarely within the "mad scientist" tradition, which she argued "has historically embodied public anxiety over science's role in industrialization. And the development of the Bomb. And the invention of thalidomide. Today, he [the mad scientist] has come to represent our anxiety about knowledge itself."[16] For Muske Dukes, *Jurassic Park* was just one part of a much larger issue of distorted representation of scientists on screen, where they are either "sellouts" who make deals with corporations, military, and the government, or "kooks, misfits or loners."[17]

Of course, it is more complicated than that. For example, as Christopher Frayling points out, even though the 1930s produced a veritable onslaught of movies featuring mad scientists, at the same time Hollywood produced "a parallel cycle of films based on the lives of real-life scientists" that were part of a general trend at that time of "inspiring biographies of individuals who challenged accepted conventions and did better than outmoded traditions."[18] Frayling also cites Jacques Jouhaneau's study of the cinematic depiction of scientists in 520 films released between 1910 and 1990, which concludes that such representation is a mixed bag "that mad scientists have become more and more stereotypical (today appearing in cartoons and comedies rather than dramas), that there used to be more of them about, and that today there is an increasing emphasis on surface realism."[19]

Nevertheless, the fear of the cinematic "mad scientist" and its negative public effect was palpable in the scientific community around *Jurassic Park*'s release. The tumult about the film's representation of science spilled out into the foreign press, as well, with a June 25 feature story in London's *The Times* reporting that the film was "stirring up an anti-science fervour in America" by depicting scientists as "the most frightening monsters of all."[20] The article notes that Muske Dukes's *New York Times* op-ed "evolved into a full-scale battle in the letters pages of newspapers, on television and in the scientific press, with Spielberg's supporters insisting that the film might actually encourage young people to go to museums while his detractors complain that science has again been undermined and undervalued." The article is most likely referring to a Letter to the Editor written in response to Muske Dukes's op-ed by Robert Boland, an assistant professor of psychiatry at Brown University School of Medicine, who argued that "our children don't avoid science because they think it's morally bereft, 'intrusive' or 'dangerous.' They avoid it because they think it's boring. Ultimately, such films as 'Jurassic Park' may do science more good than harm by glamorizing it .... Kids leaving 'Jurassic Park' won't be pondering the moral ambiguities of science—they'll be dreaming about the dinosaurs."[21]

Misunderstanding Frankenstein

It is telling that virtually every critical article and opinion piece published around the release of *Jurassic Park* mentioned Mary Shelley's *Frankenstein*. Muske Dukes's take-down of the film notes how "a group of scientists recently accused the creators of the film of a Frankenstein-like distortion of reality,"[22] while Michael W. Browne's *New York Times* article ends by quoting Dr. Eugene S. Gaffney, the curator of vertebrate paleontology at the American Museum of Natural History in New York: "'Jurassic Park' has a Frankenstein aspect ... I'm not too happy about that. Unfortunately, though, the Frankenstein view of science has become very strong in our society."[23]

It should come as no surprise that scientists would use *Frankenstein* to frame their concerns because the name has become synonymous in popular culture with any depiction of a mad scientist or one who perversely yearns to challenge the natural order and play God or any depiction of science that has ill-intended effects. This has been especially true since the release of James Whale's 1931 film adaptation, which lodged the Frankenstein mythos in the cultural unconscious, even more so than Shelley's novel and its many nineteenth- and early twentieth-century stage adaptations. As Christopher Frayling notes, the film created "a simple Faustian morality tale about the social responsibility of science, and the transgressions of God's/nature's laws, at a time—just after the Wall Street Crash of 1929—when scientists and 'experts' were being regularly vilified in the popular press for all their broken promises of the 1920s."[24]

The problem with deploying *Frankenstein* to characterize negative depictions of science or scientists is that it ignores the thematic richness of Shelley's novel, which does not castigate science so much as it interrogates its nature, both good and bad. Paul O'Flinn has charted the distillation of the novel's complex narrative and thematic structure in favor of something simpler and more direct in the 1931 film version, demonstrating how meanings in the original text were substantially changed, especially those involving science. The original novel is told through three interrelated sources: a series of letters written by an Arctic explorer, Captain Robert Walton, to his sister, which create a frame for the reminiscences of Victor Frankenstein and those of the creature he creates. Most adaptations, whether to stage or screen, eliminate the Captain Walton frame story, arguably because it is narratively unnecessary (when Stephen King recounts the novel's plot over three and a half pages in *Danse Macabre*, he doesn't even mention Captain Walton until the final sentence). As Steven Earl Forry notes in his critical catalogue of *Frankenstein* stage adaptations,

> pre-Karloffian dramatizations played an important role in disseminating popular conceptions—and misconceptions—of Mary Shelley's novel ... the early melodramas developed solely the romance (or gothic) roots of the story ... and simplified the plot by removing Walton's narrative.[25]

This was true of most film adaptations, as well, including Whale's 1931 version, which "brought the movie image of the mad scientist into focus and in the process launched a thousand imitations."[26]

However, as O'Flinn makes clear in his critical assessment of the novel-to-screen adaptation, the loss of the Captain Walton frame significantly impacts the story's depiction of science because Walton is himself an ambitious scientist and explorer, one who says he would "sacrifice my fortune, my existence, my every hope, to the furtherance of my enterprise. One man's life or death were but a small price to pay for the acquirement of the knowledge which I sought, for the dominion I should acquire and transmit over the elemental foes of our race"[27]. Shelley's interest in scientific questions is built into the "very narrative structure of the novel" through the twin narratives of Captain Walton and Frankenstein, which "presents two models of scientific progress. Both men are obsessed by the urge to discover and both pursue that obsession, enticed by the possibility of 'immortality and power' that success would bring. In the end the pursuit kills Frankenstein whereas Walton survives."[28] O'Flinn attributes the difference between the two men's fates to their relationship to others; whereas Captain Walton must ultimately take his ship's crew and their threat of mutiny into account in determining whether or not to continue forth on his potentially deadly exploration, Frankenstein works alone and is accountable only to himself. Thus, two models of scientific enterprise are dramatized, one in which science "is subject to some form of strong democratic control" and one in which science is "pursued for private motives and with no reining and directing social control or sense of social responsibility."[29] The former potentially saves lives, while the latter ultimately leads to catastrophe. The removal of the Captain Walton frame story from any adaptation of *Frankenstein* thus leads to the simplified myth of dangerous science so often associated with it:

> The work collapses into Frankenstein's experience alone which can then be presented as a universal model, replete with the sort of reactionary moralizing about the dangers of meddling with the unknown .... The film can then more easily slide towards a wider statement about the perils of any kind of progress and change, feeding fears of the unknown that change brings and reinforcing those conservative values that stand in its way.[30]

This is precisely the view that so many took of *Jurassic Park* and is born out in their concerns that the film would feed into generalized fears about the ramifications of genetic research and make genetic researchers into modern monsters of science—deranged Frankensteins of the 1990s. In fact, quite the opposite is true, as *Jurassic Park*, just like Mary Shelley's novel, presents differing models of science and allows them to play off each other as a means of dramatizing both the dangers that scientific exploration can create and the reins necessary for enforcing ethical boundaries.

In *Jurassic Park*, there are two conflicting groups of scientists. The first group is composed of the film's protagonists: Dr. Alan Grant (Sam Neill), a paleontologist; Dr. Ellie Sattler (Laura Dern), a paleobotanist; and Dr. Ian Malcolm (Jeff Goldblum), a theoretical mathematician whose strong belief in chaos theory portends the disaster that ensues. Grant, Sattler, and Malcolm are invited to spend a weekend at the titular park, where billionaire entrepreneur John Hammond (Richard Attenborough) has successfully brought back from extinction a wide range of dinosaurs who now populate a private island on which he has built the equivalent of a massive zoo. The purpose of their visit to the park is to assess it for legal and financial purposes, to assure a lawyer representing Hammond's investors that the park is stable and poses no major risks. Their presence at the park, then, is purely formal and evaluative in nature, as they had no hand in creating it and, prior to Hammond visiting them, did not even know of its existence.

The second group of scientists are those who work for Hammond—who he calls "the real miracle workers of Jurassic Park"—and who are, for the most part, simply implied, rather than dramatized (their on-screen presence is limited to a few seconds of footage in an in-park educational film about how dinosaurs were cloned and a scene in which generally nondescript men and women wearing white protective coveralls peer into electron microscopes, look at clipboards, and mill about a laboratory where the dinosaurs are incubated and hatched). The only Jurassic Park scientist given any substantial screen time and dialogue is Dr. Wu (B. D. Wong), whose primary purpose is to dispense information about the operations of Jurassic Park, specifically how the park achieves "population control" by purposefully breeding all the dinosaurs to be female. Dr. Wu is depicted as friendly and gentle, although his smiling confidence in assuring Malcolm that the dinosaurs cannot breed in the wild is ultimately proved to be wrong, thus setting him up as an example of scientific ego crashing against the relentless march of nature. There is nothing overtly evil or deranged about Dr. Wu (he is hardly a clear descendent of Frankenstein's progeny of "mad scientists"), although his very mildness arguably plays into critiques that the film presents science not as overtly, manifestly evil, but rather as simply misguided in its hubris and too absorbed in its own endeavors to recognize the dangers it is creating.

That lack of understanding on the part of the Jurassic Park scientists and Hammond, the mastermind behind the park and its greatest advocate, is central to one of the film's most overt depictions of scientific debate, where Malcolm butts heads with Hammond over the dangers the park presents. Although the lawyer, who is first depicted as skeptical of the park, seems more than assuaged by what he has seen so far, Malcolm contends that things are "a lot worse" than he initially feared. In response to Hammond and the lawyer's back-and-forth about entrance fees and merchandising potential, Malcolm throws cold water on the conversation by quietly declaring, "The lack of humility before nature that's being displayed here staggers me." The dialogue immediately preceding Malcolm's statement is rooted entirely in the economics of the park, which suggests that the hubris of the Jurassic Park scientists is inextricable connected to the profit motive, thus making them prime examples of Muske Dukes's "sellout" scientists who make deals with corporations.[31] Science, in this instance, appears to be just another extension of the capitalist enterprise. But, Malcolm's concerns also implicate the nature of the scientific enterprise itself:

> Don't you see the danger, John, inherent in what you're doing here? Genetic power is the most awesome force the planet has ever seen, but you wield it like a kid that's found his dad's gun. If I may, I'll tell you the problem with the scientific power that you're using here: It didn't require any discipline to attain it. You know, you read what others had done and you took the next step. You didn't earn the knowledge for yourselves, so you don't take any responsibility for it. You stood on the shoulders of geniuses to accomplish something as fast as you could, and before you even knew what you had, you patented it, and packaged it, and slapped it on a plastic lunchbox, and now you're selling it. You want to sell it.

When Hammond argues that Malcolm isn't being fair to the park's scientists, who have done things no one has ever before accomplished, Malcolm delivers the film's most damning critique of science "pursued for private motives and with no reining and directing social control or sense of social responsibility"[32]: "Yeah, but your scientists were so preoccupied with whether or not they *could*, they didn't stop to think if they *should*."

So, at this point, it is clear that the film is taking to task the scientists who rushed into a new domain with little attention being paid to the dangers it might present and the businessmen who seek to profit from it, which would seem to suggest that the film is as blatantly anti-science, or at least leery of science and progress and its involvement with profiteering corporations, as its detractors would suggest. This perspective is enflamed even further with Malcolm's subsequent argument in the same scene about the nature of scientific discovery—"What's so great about discovery? It's a violent, penetrative act that scars what it explores. What you call discovery I call the rape of the natural world"—which falls in line with Spielberg's assertion regarding the film's theme: "Every gain in science involves an equal and opposite reaction—a loss, usually a loss of the environment .... Science is intrusive."[33]

Yet, as clearly as the film seems to be damning science for its many sins, it is crucial to note that the people drawing attention to these issues are *other scientists*. In other words, Malcolm's criticisms are sharp indeed, but they are not necessarily criticisms of science itself, but rather particular instances of how science has been used. Grant, Sattler, and Malcolm bring a different, and no less scientific perspective that ultimately reveals why the park was destined for chaos and why the dinosaurs would not stay locked up in their electrified paddocks. "The question is, how can you know anything about an extinct eco-system?" Sattler asks. "And therefore, how could you ever assume that you can control it? ... These are aggressive living things that have no idea what century they're living in, and they'll defend themselves, violently if necessary." This sentiment is reinforced by Grant, who intones, "I don't want to jump to any conclusions, but dinosaurs and man, two species separated by 65 million years of evolution, have just been suddenly thrown back into the mix together. How can we possibly have the slightest idea what to expect?" At all times in the film these scientists are depicted as level-headed, reasonable, and articulate in their concerns (even the irascible Malcolm, whose black leather clothes and sunglasses cause Hammond to dismiss him at one point as a "rock star"). They are a far cry from "sellouts ... kooks, misfits or loners" that concerned Muske Dukes, but rather likeable, intelligent, thoughtful protagonists who get the rare opportunity to engage in both hard science and action heroics. Thus, unlike *Frankenstein*, which dramatizes the reining in of overly ambitious and dangerous science by those outside the scientific realm in Captain Walton's bowing to the demands of his mutinous crew, the scientists and their corporate enablers in

Jurassic Park are brought to heel by other scientists who articulate a set of reasonable concerns about the park stability.

It is also important to note that Grant, Sattler, and Malcolm are not just one-note critics of the science being employed in *Jurassic Park*. Spielberg depicts them as ardent practitioners of their fields who display a genuine love of science and are initially in awe of what has been done in Jurassic Park. We see this particularly in the scene in which they first see the dinosaurs—in this case, a *Brachiosaurus* moving across a grassy plain and eating leaves from nearby treetops—to which they respond with wide, incredulous eyes and gaping mouths. This is, not incidentally, also the first time the audience sees the dinosaurs in all their photorealistic, computer-generated glory, and many a viewer in theaters that summer likely responded in a similar manner, thus aligning them experientially with the scientist-protagonists. More importantly, though, is how Grant and Sattler respond after the initial shock of seeing a living, breathing dinosaur: They immediately go into scientist-observation mode, noting that the creature is warm-blooded, not cold-blooded as previously assumed, which fits in Grant's previously derided theory that dinosaurs have more in common with modern-day birds than reptiles. Grant begins estimating the *Brachiosaur*'s neck length, inquiring about their speed, and noting their movement in herds. Their response to seeing the dinosaurs is one of both rapture and fascination, quickly stoking their thirst for knowledge. This stands in stark contrast to both Hammond's childlike glee at the spectacle of it all and the lawyer's single-minded pursuit of profit: "We're gonna make a fortune with this place," he says breathlessly. It also stands in stark contrast to Spielberg's depiction of Professor Hobby in *A.I.*, whose barely contained excitement over David's successful journey illustrates the depths of his unfeeling and his inability to connect with anything outside of his own desire for technological success.

Grant and Sattler's euphoric fascination with the dinosaurs is soon tempered by their scientific reason and recognition of the dangers involved in the very enterprise that they initially found so overwhelming in its majesty. They are, then, directly in line with the positive depictions of scientists found in Spielberg's earlier films, notably Matt Hooper in *Jaws*, whose self-professed obsession with sharks ("I love sharks, I love them," he says at one point) melds scientific curiosity with a healthy recognition of their danger. And, while we learn little about Claude Lacombe from *Close Encounters of the Third Kind*, we do see that he clearly maintains an open mind about the possibilities of life outside of Earth and doggedly pursues the clues of its existence. Grant and Sattler, and to some degree Malcolm, are, like Hooper and Lacombe, ideal scientists, people who endeavor to better understand the world and its history while paying appropriate heed to potential negative outcomes and the necessity of braking scientific progress with ethical boundaries when necessary. When, at the end of *Jurassic Park*, Grant declares, "Mr. Hammond, after careful consideration, I've decided not to endorse your park," it is humorous because it is delivered just after he and Sattler and Hammond's grandchildren have barely escaped yet another dinosaur encounter. However, the groundwork had already been laid for why his endorsement, which functions as a "reining and directing social control or sense of social responsibility,"[34] might be withheld.

Like *Jaws* did nearly two decades earlier, *Jurassic Park* reminds us that, despite all our intelligence and technological prowess, we are ultimately at the mercy of the forces of nature, a point that is recognized and articulated by scientists. Thus, far from condemning science out of hand, *Jurassic Park* instead presents, as Shelley did in *Frankenstein*, a nuanced perspective on a complex subject, rendering both its inherent dangers and the manner in which it can be ethically and socially bounded for the betterment of humankind.

Notes

1. Terry Lefton, "Behemoths Line up to License on 'Park' Row," *Brandweek (New York, N.Y.)* 34:3 (1993): 1.
2. Richard Corliss and Andrea Dorfman, "Behind the Magic of Jurassic Park. (Cover Story)," *TIME Magazine* 141, no. 17 (April 26, 1993): 49.
3. Sharon Begley and Anthony Duignan-Cabrera., "Here Come the DNAsaurs. (Cover Story)," *Newsweek* 121:24 (June 14, 1993): 60.
4. Joseph McBride, *Steven Spielberg: A Biography*, 2nd edition (Jackson: University Press of Mississippi, 2010), 236.
5. McBride, *Steven Spielberg: A Biography*, 236.
6. Thomas Durwood (ed.), *Close Encounters of the Third Kind: A Document of the Film* (Kansas City, MO: Ariel Books, 1978), 121.
7. Ibid., 61.
8. Russell Higuchi et al., "DNA Sequences from the Quagga, an Extinct Member of the Horse Family," *Nature* 312:5991 (November 1984): 282–4. https://doi.org/10.1038/312282a0.
9. Erika Hagelberg, Michael Hofreiter, and Christine Keyser, "Ancient DNA: The First Three Decades," *Philosophical Transactions of the Royal Society B: Biological Sciences* 370:1660 (January 19, 2015): 20130371. https://doi.org/10.1098/rstb.2013.0371.
10. Elizabeth D. Jones, "Ancient Genetics to Ancient Genomics: Celebrity and Credibility in Data-Driven Practice," *Biology & Philosophy* 34:2 (April 2019): 7. https://doi.org/10.1007/s10539-019-9675-1.
11. Malcolm W. Browne, "Scientists Study Ancient DNA for Glimpses of Past Worlds," *New York Times*, June 25, 1991.
12. Russell Higuchi, "Dr. Russ' Problem Corner," *Ancient DNA Newsletter*, December 1992, 6–7.

13 "In New Spielberg Film, a Dim View of Science," *New York Times*, May 11, 1993, sec. Science Times, C1.
14 Ibid., C10.
15 Ibid.
16 "Evil Science Runs Amok—Again!," *New York Times*, June 10, 1993, A27.
17 Ibid.
18 Christopher Frayling, *Mad, Bad and Dangerous?: The Scientist and the Cinema* (London: Reaktion Books, 2013), 133.
19 Ibid., 43.
20 Ben Macintyre, "Mad Scientists on the Loose," *The Times*, June 25, 1993, sec. Features.
21 Robert Boland., "Letter to the Editor: 'Jurassic Park' Won't Turn Kids against Science," *New York Times*, June 22, 1993, sec. Editorials/Letters, A22.
22 "Evil Science Runs Amok—Again!," A27.
23 "In New Spielberg Film, a Dim View of Science," A10.
24 Frayling, *Mad, Bad and Dangerous?*, 116.
25 "Dramatizations of Frankenstein, 1821–1986: A Comprehensive List," *English Language Notes* 25:2 (December 1987): 64. http://knarf.english.upenn.edu/Articles/forry2.html#par4.
26 Frayling, *Mad, Bad and Dangerous?*, 114.
27 Mary Wollstonecraft Shelley, *Frankenstein, or The Modern Prometheus* (1818), 15.
28 Paul O'Flinn, "Production and Reproduction: The Case of Frankenstein," in Mark Jancovich (ed.) *Horror: The Film Reader* (London: Routledge, 2002), 107.
29 Ibid., 108.
30 Ibid., 110.
31 "Evil Science Runs Amok—Again!," A27.
32 O'Flinn, "Production and Reproduction: The Case of Frankenstein," 108.
33 Browne, "In New Spielberg Film, a Dim View of Science," C10.
34 O'Flinn, "Production and Reproduction: The Case of Frankenstein," 108.

11

The Dinosaurs of *Jurassic Park* and the Portrayal of Prehistoric Life and Paleontology in Film

Ali Nabavizadeh
University of Pennsylvania School of Veterinary Medicine, USA

Introduction

Jurassic Park is an iconic film that, upon its release, delivered a cinematic experience unlike any other up to that point. Its special effects were unlike anything seen in film, captivating audiences for decades to follow, thanks to its portrayal of its real star players—the dinosaurs. For over a century, science fiction and fantasy films have portrayed dinosaurs and other prehistoric animals in many different ways, including hand-drawn and stop-motion animation, filming living animals dressed up as prehistoric creatures, puppetry, robotics, and CGI. Winsor McCay's 1914 film *Gertie the Dinosaur* was the first animated film depicting a dinosaur, portraying a *Brontosaurus* named Gertie walking around and doing comedic tricks. This was no simple feat (especially in its time) because, of course, no one had ever seen a dinosaur walking, speaking to the brilliance of McCay as a cartoonist.

Filmmakers have nearly always taken inspiration from relevant museum exhibits and paleontological scientific illustrations (or "paleoart") of their time. Illustrations by world-renowned paleoartists Charles R. Knight and Zdeněk Burian inspired many aspects of prehistoric creature designs created by special effects artists, including stop-motion artists Willis O'Brien (who worked on films such as *The Lost World* [1925] and *King Kong* [1933]) and Ray Harryhausen (who worked on films such as *The Beast from 20,000 Fathoms* [1953], *One Million Years B.C.* [1966], and *The Valley of Gwangi* [1969]). The 1925 film *The Lost World*, based on Arthur Conan Doyle's classic novel of the same name, was especially remarkable in the way that it portrayed a variety of stop-motion-animated dinosaurs as living, breathing creatures instead of mere monsters on the big screen. Of particular note is how this film depicts a *Triceratops* mother interacting with and caring for its baby in a realistic manner.

Other early movies involving dinosaurs and other prehistoric animals include *A Journey to the Beginning of Time* (1955) (*Cesta do Pravěku* in Czech), *Journey to the Center of the Earth* (1959), *When Dinosaurs Ruled the Earth* (1970), *The Land That Time Forgot* (1974), and *Planet of Dinosaurs* (1977), among many others. Many of these movies often show fantastical portrayals of dinosaurs interacting with humans in unthinkable ways. They are often seen spending a lot of their time roaring, bellowing, hissing, and posing in unusual ways not seen in living animals. Their anatomy is oftentimes poorly designed, and extinct animals are shown as nothing more than monsters hell-bent on eating anything that gets in their way. This, of course, is taken to the extreme with *Godzilla* (1955—Japanese: *Gojira*) and other Kaiju movies showing incredible oversized dinosaur-like monsters with exaggerated features. As a result, many of these films present a hazy view among the general audience of how to distinguish between monstrous, mythological creatures and the actual extinct animal that is intended to be portrayed.

As unnerving and even comical as some earlier film portrayals were, however, many films strived to meet the science of their time with continued improvements in portrayals of prehistoric animals made with the advancement of scientific discovery. Walt Disney's classic animated anthology *Fantasia* (1940) was the first film to depict dinosaurs in their natural habitat (without anachronistic human interaction) in a segment set to composer Igor Stravinsky's *Rite of Spring* (1913). In creating this segment, animators asked paleontologists for guidance in their reconstructions to make them as scientifically accurate as possible. Although the depictions are now wildly out of date and many of the dinosaurs and other prehistoric animals portrayed lived many millions of years apart from each other, it is still a monumental achievement that set a standard for dinosaur movies in the decades that followed.

From the late 1960s onward, a phenomenon in the world of paleontology known as the "Dinosaur Renaissance" played a major role in influencing our understanding of dinosaur biology, creating the idea that dinosaurs were not slow, lumbering animals but were, in fact, highly active, dynamic, intelligent, and possibly warm-blooded creatures in many cases and should be depicted as such both in the studies that followed as well as in different media.[1] It also saw new studies in dinosaur behavior, such as the possibility of parental care,[2] and jump-started studies showing how today's birds are, in fact, living descendants of extinct theropod dinosaurs.[3] Films such as Universal Pictures' *The Land before Time* (1988), Disney's *Dinosaur* (2000), and 20th Century Fox's *Walking with Dinosaurs: The Movie* (2013) are all stellar examples of films that went above and beyond to make sure their dinosaurs were portrayed accurately while staying within their storytelling parameters. Of course, none of these movies have even come close to being as influential to the general public's perception of dinosaurs as living, breathing animals as with the release of *Jurassic Park* in 1993.

From that monumental scene featuring a gargantuan *Brachiosaurus* rearing up on its hind limbs to reach a meal, to the memorable up-close and personal view of a sick *Triceratops*, to the terrifying encounters with *Dilophosaurus*, *Velociraptor*, and, of course, the infamous *Tyrannosaurus*, the dinosaurs portrayed in *Jurassic Park* are some of the most realistic and (in its time) scientifically accurate in a science fiction movie. The dinosaur designs of Mark 'Crash' McCreery, the initial outstanding stop-motion animations of Phil Tippett, and the animatronic masterpieces of Stan Winston and his crew all contributed to the masterpieces that are the dinosaurs we see in this iconic Steven Spielberg film. Of course, some artistic license was also implemented, including coloration of the animals as well as, in some cases, the addition of extraneous anatomical structures. These types of speculative depictions have created much debate among paleontologists as to what would have been possible or not, but the fact remains that *Jurassic Park* was a revolutionary film that went to great heights in depicting the latest scientific understanding of dinosaurs. This film emphasized the active lifestyle of dinosaurs, it portrayed plausible social behaviors, and it even discussed the relationship of modern birds with extinct dinosaurs.

Although a vast majority of audience members know a dinosaur when they see one, it is important to understand what a dinosaur is and how they are broadly related to one another to really appreciate the level of detail that went into their depiction in *Jurassic Park*. For starters, although the movie is named *Jurassic Park*, many of the dinosaurs are, in fact, from the Cretaceous Period. The Mesozoic Era (~250 to 66 million years ago) is known as the age of dinosaurs and was divided into the Triassic, Jurassic, and Cretaceous Periods. Collectively, dinosaurs are characterized by several features—the most prominent being that their hind limbs stood erect directly beneath their bodies (rather than sprawling outward like their close relatives—the crocodilians). Dinosaurs (or Dinosauria) are made up of three main lineages, including Sauropodomorpha (long-necked dinosaurs including the herbivorous sauropods like *Brachiosaurus*), Theropoda (including largely all carnivorous dinosaurs like *Tyrannosaurus* and *Velociraptor*), and Ornithischia (including diverse herbivores such as *Triceratops*, *Stegosaurus*,

Ankylosaurus, Parasaurolophus, Pachycephalosaurus, and all their respective kin). The following will be an examination of the portrayal of dinosaurs in the *Jurassic Park* franchise, with dinosaurs representing all three lineages.

Brachiosaurus and the Sauropods

The first full reveal of a dinosaur in *Jurassic Park* is a significant moment in film history, and the audience's sense of awe is reflected in the response of the two lead characters as Alan Grant (Sam Neill) and Ellie Sattler (Laura Dern), who pull up in a Jeep and look up in utter, jaw-dropping astonishment and wonder of what stands before them: a Gargantuan, full-size *Brachiosaurus*—a sauropod dinosaur (Figure 11.1). Sauropods are four-legged dinosaurs known for their extremely long necks with relatively tiny heads, their massive, long tails, their pillar-like limbs, and, in many cases, enormous body size. In fact, some sauropods were undoubtedly the largest, most massive, tallest, and/or longest-bodied terrestrial animals to have ever lived. Although the basic body plan is somewhat consistent across sauropods, they did come in a variety of shapes, sizes, and postures. For instance, *Brachiosaurus* is a member of a major group of sauropods known as macronarians that typically show a relatively larger, bulkier body, boxier skull, and likely stood taller with a more erect neck. In contrast, another major sauropod group known as diplodocoids, which includes *Apatosaurus* (mentioned below), typically show longer tails and more gracile skulls and bodies and may have held their necks lower down or more horizontally.

FIGURE 11.1 *The sauropod dinosaur* Brachiosaurus *rearing up to feed from a tall tree*

Sauropods were herbivores, as portrayed in this scene with the *Brachiosaurus*. This massive animal is seen enjoying a nice meal using its long neck to reach leaves from the tops of very tall trees. As it walks up to the trees with its massive tail swaying from side to side, we notice its forelimbs are taller than its hind limbs, adding to the amount of height this animal can get to with its long neck. Although the legs and feet are a bit too elephant-like (as is seen with many of the herbivores portrayed in the *Jurassic Park* franchise), its posture and gait are quite accurate and its enormous size is portrayed well.

In taking a bite from the treetops, the *Brachiosaurus* extends its neck up vertically and, at times, holds it in a slightly curved, s-shaped posture. The extent to which it would have been able to hold its neck vertically is a matter that has been debated for decades. Some paleontologists argue that brachiosaurs would have, indeed, been able to hold their necks vertically, as seen in *Jurassic Park*.[4] Other paleontologists, however, suggest that the anatomy of its neck vertebrae do not support an upright neck posture and that brachiosaurs likely held their necks at more of an angle.[5] Of course, this distinction would have an impact on exactly how high the animal would have been able to reach for consuming vegetation, with an upright neck posture possibly reaching up to forty feet high. To get up even higher, the *Brachiosaurus* in the film rears up on its hind limbs in a tripodal stance supported by its tail and with its forelimbs in the air, curving its neck even more to reach the leaves. Although it is argued that this tripodal stance is less likely to have been possible in brachiosaurs than in other sauropods, it is still a reasonable behavior to reconstruct that only just adds to the sense of wonder that both the characters and the viewers at home experience while watching it.

As the scene pans out, we see that there are two *Brachiosaurus* individuals wading in a lake next to a herd of duck-billed hadrosaurs known as *Parasaurolophus*. Decades ago, it was suggested that sauropods were water-wading, amphibious animals because it was thought the water would have supported their massive weight better.[6] However, many anatomical and biomechanical studies argue against this notion and strongly suggest that sauropods were indeed terrestrial animals; although they could still swim.[7]

In a later scene, Alan Grant as well as park owner John Hammond's (Richard Attenborough's) grandchildren, Lex and Tim, have climbed up a tree to go to sleep. In the distance they see multiple craning necks of brachiosaurs as they hear them "singing." Suddenly, a large *Brachiosaurus* head pops up in front of them. Grant takes a big tree branch and feeds it to the dinosaur and we see it chewing the vegetation from side to side like a cow. This sort of mammal-like chewing was not possible in sauropods. Instead, brachiosaurs cropped their food mainly with an up-and-down motion of the jaw and initially crushed the food with its spoon-like teeth before it swallowed and let its enormous gut system do the rest of the digestive work.

We also get a very clear look at the distinctive hump on the top of its head, which is a trait that makes it instantly recognizable as a brachiosaur. A pair of nostrils are visible higher up in this hump and, although at the time this reconstruction was plausible due to narial opening of the skull being pulled back in the skull in brachiosaurs, a study that came out a few years after the movie's release suggested the nostrils would have been further down and forward. The shape of the hump itself is also worthy of note because, at the time, it was believed that the specimen that this reconstruction was based on was referred to the genus *Brachiosaurus*. However, a later study suggested that this specimen was actually another member of the brachiosaur family and named it *Giraffatitan*, noting that *Brachiosaurus* had a relatively smaller hump on its head and was slightly smaller in body size.[8]

Although *Brachiosaurus* was the only sauropod shown in the original *Jurassic Park*, other sauropods were depicted in later movies in the franchise. The recent film *Jurassic World Dominion* (2022) introduces *Dreadnoughtus*, one of the largest sauropods to have ever lived (part of a subgroup of macronarians called titanosaurs). In *The Lost World: Jurassic Park* (1997), we see a pair of *Mamenchisaurus*, widely known for having an incredibly long neck that is longer than its tail. The diplodocoid *Apatosaurus* is a sauropod introduced in *Jurassic World* (2015). In a close-up scene of a dying apatosaur in *Jurassic World*, its teeth are noticeably too sharp and conical. In reality, its teeth would have been thinner, pencil-like, and restricted to the front of the mouth (typical of *Diplodocoids*), and were likely used to strip leaves off branches in a raking motion.

Triceratops and the Ornithischians

Following the iconic *Brachiosaurus* reveal scene, the second dinosaur we get a complete look at in *Jurassic Park* is a sick *Triceratops* that has been tranquilized and is lying down in a field (Figure 11.2). We see Alan Grant, Ellie Sattler, Ian Malcolm (Jeff Goldblum), Lex (Ariana Richards), and Tim (Joseph Mazzello) all walking up to the animal in astonishment as they place their hands upon it in awe.

Triceratops is an ornithischian dinosaur—specifically, a ceratopsian. Most ceratopsians are quadrupedal (four-legged) herbivores that are known for possessing various assortments of long and short horns above their eyes and nose as well as elaborate bony frills decorating the back of their heads. Ceratopsians primarily lived throughout the Cretaceous Period and *Triceratops* is known as one of the very last ceratopsians to have lived (up until the end of the Late Cretaceous sixty-six million years ago) and is one of the largest, most well-known ceratopsians.

The name *Triceratops* means 'three-horned face' and, as the name implies, its stand-out features are indeed its two enormous brow horns (one above

FIGURE 11.2 *The ornithischian dinosaur* Triceratops *lying down sick*

each eye) and one shorter horn above its nose. These horns were covered by a keratinous sheath, such as that seen in today's bovids (including antelope, cattle, sheep, and goats). As the camera first pans over this animal in *Jurassic Park*, its horns are protruding toward the camera as we get a glimpse of its enormous head. In fact, the head alone of *Triceratops* accounted for about one-third of its thirty-foot body length. It sports an expansive, solid, round frill with several small sharp horns jutting out all along its circumference (which are variable in size and shape across ceratopsian species). Although the frill was thin, it would have still made it difficult for a predator like *Tyrannosaurus* to get its mouth around it as long as the *Triceratops* was facing it head on.

We also see its large, "parrot-like" beak, which would have been used for plucking vegetation to eat. The sides of its mouth are covered by a thick flap of skin acting like a large mammal-like cheek. Although the presence of this flap of skin is plausible (and many have argued that it would have helped keep food in the mouth), it is unlikely that it was covering a large mammal-like cheek muscle.[9] Instead, it may have added protection for enlarged jaw muscles that have been rearranged to extend further forward on the jaw for more complex feeding mechanisms.[10] Its mouth was filled with columns of packed teeth ideal for a highly efficient food processing system.

We also see the *Triceratops*' massive torso moving up and down as it takes enormous breaths, and the scaling pattern on the skin is well reconstructed. We see its large front and hind feet, which are recreated to look like elephant feet with flat bottoms; however, the anatomy suggests it would have stood more on its toes. Furthermore, it is revealed that a possible reason for its sickness is that it had been eating poisonous West Indian lilac and, although the park ranger notes it wouldn't have eaten them, it is likely that the berries of the plant were ingested when the animal picked up stones from the dirt to assist with internal digestion. These stones are known as gastroliths and, although there is no evidence that ceratopsians used them to digest plant material in the gut system, possible evidence of gastroliths has been found associated with other dinosaurs such as sauropods. We then see an enormous pile of dung that was presumably from the *Triceratops*; however, given that the pile was much taller than Ian Malcolm in the shot, this would have been an unlikely sight.

Triceratops has been portrayed as a more active animal in the movies that followed *Jurassic Park* within the franchise. In *The Lost World: Jurassic Park*, it is shown wrecking a base camp tent with the use of its horns after being released from its cage. It is indeed very likely that *Triceratops* would have used its large horns for self-defense against *Tyrannosaurus* or any other dinosaur that might have attacked. It is also likely that it would have used its horns in combat with another *Triceratops*—maybe in competition for a mate or territory. After it attacks the tent, we get a full glimpse of the animal on all fours, showing very good stance with the legs mostly directly underneath the body (albeit with very short front limbs) and a very large, round frill. A baby *Triceratops* is also seen in a cage prior to the attack with horns that are still growing in, which we know from fossil evidence would have been the case; although, the horns would have been more curved. Other appearances of *Triceratops* include in *Jurassic Park III* as well as the following *Jurassic World* films. Of note is a scene in *Jurassic World* where it is seen galloping quite fast in a meadow when it likely was a relatively slower animal.

Triceratops was indeed the only ceratopsian in *Jurassic Park*; however, other ceratopsians have shown up in later films. In *Jurassic World: Fallen Kingdom* (2018), *Sinoceratops* is seen in multiple scenes. *Sinoceratops* possessed one large horn coming out of its nose like a rhinoceros. Additional small horns are also seen curving downward from its frill as well. One glaring flaw in its design is the two large holes seen in the frill. Although these holes are seen in the fossil skull (as in many ceratopsians), in life, it would have been covered over completely with skin. Another beautiful ceratopsian seen in *Jurassic World: Dominion* is *Nasutoceratops*—accurately portrayed with its two large curved brow horns like a bull's as well as a more rectangular frill.

Although *Triceratops* is the most prominent ornithischian in the original *Jurassic Park*, another ornithischian makes a brief appearance earlier on in the movie. In the above-mentioned shot of the two *Brachiosaurus* individuals wading through a lake, a herd of *Parasaurolophus* is seen standing along the edge of the lake drinking water and feeding. *Parasaurolophus* was a hadrosaur—a group colloquially known as the "duck-billed dinosaurs." Hadrosaurs (which are themselves part of larger group known as ornithopods) were large herbivores that, as the nickname implies, sported an elongate, broadened bill that has been loosely likened to that of a duck. They used their bills to strip tough plant material to eat with their powerful jaws that were filled with hundreds of packed teeth situated in many columns in the mouth. It, too, is portrayed with cheeks and, although it can be seen chewing its food side-to-side like a mammal in *Jurassic World*, in life it would have chewed up-and-down and backward, as has been shown with tooth wear studies. Additionally, in the original *Jurassic Park* and subsequent films of the franchise, *Parasaurolophus* is often shown with an s-shaped neck which, at the time, was thought to be an accurate depiction. A more recent study, however, has argued that the neck would have been much thicker due to the presence of an elastic nuchal ligament that would have aided in energy storage during feeding and locomotion.

Typically, hadrosaurs are portrayed in films as peaceful herbivores that typically do not cause any trouble and that is certainly the case as well as in the entire *Jurassic Park* franchise. While they are drinking, they are shown standing quadrupedally, which is currently hypothesized as the primary locomotor stance of hadrosaurs. Hadrosaurs were graceful animals that possessed long, slender forelimbs; larger, powerful hind limbs; and a muscular, stiffened tail ideal for this style of gait. It is possible they could have run bipedally as well. This is shown in a chase scene in *The Lost World: Jurassic Park*, for example, where viewers get a very clear view of the large size and great strength of the animal as it struggles to free itself from being tied down.

Parasaurolophus belongs to a subgroup of hadrosaurs called lambeosaurines known for possessing diverse shapes of hollow crests on their heads. Paleontologists have argued that the hollow tube-like nature of these crests would have made expansive resonating chambers used while honking in communication.[11] The distinctive crest of *Parasaurolophus* is long and tubular, extending backward from the head, likely amplifying a loud, bellowing honking noise. Another lambeosaurine hadrosaur known as *Corythosaurus* is briefly seen running in a herd with *Parasaurolophus* in *Jurassic Park III*. Instead of a long tubular crest, *Corythosaurus* sported a crest in the shape of a circular hump—much like a Corinthian helmet for which it is named. Outside of hadrosaurs, the only other ornithopod to appear in a *Jurassic Park* franchise movie is *Iguanodon*, which appears in *Jurassic World Dominion*. *Iguanodon* was also a large ornithopod that was one of the first dinosaurs to have ever been described in the 1800s and is known for a specialized thumb spike on its hand.

Outside of the original *Jurassic Park*, other ornithischian groups are portrayed in the following films. Pachycephalosaurs, such as *Pachycephalosaurus*, are introduced in *The Lost World: Jurassic Park*. Pachycephalosaurs were typically bipedal ornithischians with nine-to-ten-inch-thick dome-shaped skull roofs that sported knobs and spikes. In the movie, it is undersized and seen bashing its head through a car. They were likely more herbivorous; although, it is possible they may have been generally omnivores. *Stygimoloch* is another pachycephalosaur that is introduced in *Jurassic World: Fallen Kingdom* that sports much longer spikes coming out of its head. Some paleontologists have argued that *Stygimoloch* may have just been a younger individual of *Pachycephalosaurus*; however, this is still being debated.

The Lost World: Jurassic Park also introduced the first armored ornithischian dinosaur into the franchise—*Stegosaurus*. *Stegosaurus* was a late Jurassic quadrupedal herbivore well-known for its large, diamond-shaped plates running in two parallel rows alternating along its back (possibly used in regulating body heat). It is also known for its four long, bony spikes on its tail. In the movie, *Stegosaurus* is shown to be quite large with a relatively decent posture showing its tail raised up near horizontal. Studies have recently shown that it likely would have held its tail up even more horizontally, which would have given *Stegosaurus* a direct shot for swinging its tail spikes at a predator should one have tried to attack it.[12] The subsequent *Jurassic World* films reverted to more outdated depictions of *Stegosaurus* with a more arched back and dragging its tail on the ground. This would have created more of a waddling locomotor style as opposed to the relatively more accurate agile posture seen in *The Lost World: Jurassic Park*. Furthermore, in *Jurassic World: Fallen Kingdom*, a close-up view shows it depicted with cheeks and a view inside its mouth shows what look like inaccurate mammalian, cusped teeth. *Stegosaurus* possessed "leaf-shaped" teeth (as did many ornithischians) that would have been ideal for a herbivorous lifestyle.

Ankylosaurus is another armored dinosaur introduced in *Jurassic Park III*. Ankylosaurs were herbivorous quadrupeds that are known as "living tanks" (as noted in *Jurassic World: Fallen Kingdom*) due to their elaborate armored bodies and, in the case of some ankylosaurs like *Ankylosaurus*, large tail clubs. Bony ossifications created by many scutes and spikes covered the head, back, and tail of *Ankylosaurus* creating what looks like a solid armored shell, loosely reminiscent of that of a turtle. This is portrayed in the movie; although, the sequence, shapes, and sizes of the scutes and spikes seen on the *Ankylosaurus* are not true to that seen in the actual animal. Still, the flatter nature of its body is reasonably accurate as is the size and shape of its tail club that would have been used to cause serious damage to anything trying to attack it. *Ankylosaurus* was one of the largest of the ankylosaurs and was also the last to exist before the extinction of the dinosaurs at the end of the Late Cretaceous sixty-six million years ago.

Tyrannosaurus, *Velociraptor*, and the Theropods

Without question, the most thrilling scenes in *Jurassic Park* are those that involve theropods—the group including all carnivorous dinosaurs.

THE DINOSAURS OF *JURASSIC PARK*

FIGURE 11.3 *The theropod dinosaur* Tyrannosaurus *escaping its enclosure*

Theropods are primarily bipedal animals with, in many cases, sharp teeth and claws, powerful jaws, and muscular hind limbs and tails. They are also the group that led to the evolution of today's birds—something alluded to by Alan Grant in the beginning of *Jurassic Park*. Still, the theropods featured in *Jurassic Park* posed threats far greater than any birds we see today and what better way to introduce the villainous dinosaurs than with the grand entrance of the most iconic theropod to have ever lived: *Tyrannosaurus* (Figure 11.3).

Tyrannosaurus was among the largest theropods known today, surviving through the end of the Late Cretaceous. The first we see of it, it is shown breaking through an unpowered gate onto a platform with two stalled vehicles along with Alan Grant, Ian Malcolm, Lex, Tim, and Donald Gennaro (the lawyer). The *Tyrannosaurus* is shown stomping in with an enormous head with menacing teeth, a large torso, two-fingered hands on rather short forelimbs, powerful hind limbs with large claws, and a massive tail swaying back and forth as it walks.

Jurassic Park's *Tyrannosaurus* head design is incredibly distinctive and instantly recognizable. It is largely accurate albeit with mild exaggerations of certain features. For example, osteoderms along its brow ridge make it seem as it has very prominent brows over its eyes. Alan Grant also mentions that its eyesight is based on movement, which is highly unlikely, especially because, as a predator, it had stereoscopic vision that would have allowed it to focus well on prey items standing in front of it. It also would have had an incredible sense of smell, as evidenced by large olfactory bulbs in its brain. It is often depicted roaring loudly, especially before attacking a prey. Although it may have made a loud rumbling noise, roaring was less likely and especially in times of prey capture where the prey item would be easily alerted of its presence.

Tyrannosaurus has a compressed but very broad muzzle and an enormous chamber within its skull housing powerful jaw muscles. In fact, computer modeling studies suggest that *Tyrannosaurus* possessed one of the highest bite forces to have ever existed in nature—powerful enough to easily crush bone with its enormous, stake-like teeth reaching up to a foot long including the roots. There is no doubt that it would have used its head to grab and subdue its prey, especially given its short forelimbs. This is well portrayed in a scene where *Tyrannosaurus* comes out of the trees and grabs a *Gallimimus* by biting down forcefully and then shaking its head violently to knock it out. Still, its forelimbs were certainly powerful enough to latch onto any prey it may have captured. The *Tyrannosaurus*' teeth are somewhat visible from the outside, which may have been possible, although some argue that "lip-like" extraoral tissues may have covered its teeth completely like any lizard today.[13]

The *Tyrannosaurus* is accurately shown standing on its two legs directly underneath its body and its torso in a more horizontal orientation with its muscular tail used to counterbalance its body weight. It stands on three large toes on each foot, each with large, sharp claws that seem to clutch the ground with every step. Its torso would have been much bulkier in life; although, at the time of filming, this was not as widely believed. Also, its short arms are shown with its wrist flopped in front (like how a bunny holds its wrists) when it would have held them against its body more like a bird. We later see the *Tyrannosaurus* running and chasing a Jeep at one point and appears to gain on it rather well. John Hammond mentions that the *Tyrannosaurus* could run thirty-two miles an hour; however, this looks to be a significantly overestimated number according to recent biomechanical research showing it likely was not a very fast runner after all. Last, recent discoveries of various theropods (including close relatives of *Tyrannosaurus* possessing feathers) has led to speculation that *Tyrannosaurus* itself had feathers.[14] This is highly plausible; although, if true, it would have only had feathers covering certain parts of the body.

While computer programmer Dennis Nedry is driving in the rain at night, we see a small *Dilophosaurus* hopping around and chirping—a gracile theropod with two large, parallel crests over its eyes. *Dilophosaurus* has, over the years, become known as the "spitting dinosaur" specifically due to its portrayal in *Jurassic Park*. In the film, it opens a colorful neck frill and spits out a black tar-like venom at Nedry supposedly causing blindness and paralysis. This is a case where artistic license was imposed as there is no evidence that *Dilophosaurus* was venomous in any way. There is also no evidence that it had any frill on its neck (like a frilled lizard); although, in fairness, most soft tissues are not preserved in the fossil record, so it is difficult to tell what kinds of extravagant soft tissue structures dinosaurs might have had in general. Beyond this, it is shown to be no bigger than a dog when, in fact, they could reach up to seven meters in length. *Dilophosaurus* was one of the major predators in its ecosystem in the Early Jurassic, long before dinosaurs like *Tyrannosaurus* showed up.

While Alan Grant, Lex, and Tim are walking through a field, they see a "flock" of *Gallimimus* running toward them from a distance. *Gallimimus* was an ornithomimosaur—a bipedal, toothless, "ostrich-mimic" group of theropods. Likely herbivorous, ornithomimosaurs have narrow skulls with a beak, long, s-shaped necks, and long hind limbs fit for faster running speeds. Standing over two meters tall with an outstretched neck, *Gallimimus* is one of the larger known ornithomimosaurs and their size is well represented in *Jurassic Park*. The ostrich-like running behavior portrayed in the movie is also highly plausible given their overall morphology. Additionally, although not known at the time *Jurassic Park* was created, we are now confident that ornithomimosaurs were covered in a coat of feathers (as discussed below with other closely related theropods).

Many clues in non-bird theropod anatomy have led paleontologists to conclude definitively that birds are, in fact, theropod dinosaurs themselves. Birds are part of a group of theropods known as maniraptorans. Maniraptorans are known for several distinguishing features—a prominent one being a half-moon-shaped wrist bone, which is what Alan Grant refers to when looking at the skeleton of a *Velociraptor* and comparing it to a bird. Other features he rightly mentions are a backward-facing pubis (hip bone) and vertebrae full of hollows and air sacs. He also notes that the term "raptor" itself means "bird of prey."

Aside from its similarities to birds, *Velociraptor* itself is part of a group of maniraptorans known as dromaeosaurs. Dromaeosaurs are bipedal predators with elongate muzzles, s-shaped necks, gracile bodies with long hind limbs and tails that range from the size of a small bird to a few meters in length depending on the genus. Although *Velociraptor* is shown in *Jurassic Park* to be nearly two meters tall and three meters long, it was, in truth, much smaller measuring only two meters long and only half a meter tall. The size of the *Velociraptor* depicted in *Jurassic Park* is more comparable to that of *Utahraptor*, which was a much larger animal. Additionally, the elongated head of *Velociraptor* was more gracile than the deeper skull shape shown in the film (which is more like that of the dromaeosaur *Deinonychus*). Its eyes are shown with a slit-like pupil, which is unlikely considering a vast majority of birds have a round pupil. Additionally, some shots of the *Velociraptor* show them slightly curling their lips (like a snarl) as they growl to a degree that is unlikely considering a lack of muscles in their lips.

Like many Dromaeosaurs, *Velociraptor* possessed a long, sickle-shaped claw on its second toe which was undoubtedly used to help subdue prey by using it to pin its prey to the ground. In one of the most memorable scenes of *Jurassic Park*, two *Velociraptors* are walking through a kitchen and jumping on countertops looking for Lex and Tim (Figure 11.4). We get a clear look

FIGURE 11.4 *A pair of the theropod dinosaurs* Velociraptor *in a kitchen*

at the *Velociraptors* as a whole, including their large size. Their hands and wrists are clearly shown as incorrectly hanging pronated (as with the *Tyrannosaurus* above) when they should be held against the body like a bird. At one point, a *Velociraptor* is even shown successfully opening the latch of a door, even though the true anatomy of its wrists would not have allowed it to do so. The portrayal of its problem-solving skills and pack hunting abilities are also notable, especially with the film's constant comparisons to birds. Dromaeosaurs were indeed quite intelligent relative to other dinosaurs as shown by the relative size of their brains compared to their bodies.

It is likely the *Velociraptor* (and dromaeosaurs in general) used its powerful long hind limbs to jump high and capture prey in a lethal attack as shown in the film. Although likely not as fast as a cheetah as suggested in the film, the *Velociraptor* would have still been a very swift runner and it is possible its larger relatives could have reached close to ostrich-like speeds. It is also noted in the film that the animals were homeothermic (warm-blooded), just as in birds and mammals, and recent studies have continued to suggest that this was likely the case for many non-bird dinosaurs. One major flaw in the film design of the *Velociraptor*, however, is the fact that it is not covered in feathers. Granted, it was not yet known that *Velociraptor* would have had feathers during the filming of *Jurassic Park* in 1993. Since then, however, many dromaeosaur skeletons have revealed fully feathered coats. Although *Jurassic Park III* started to implement some quills on their *Velociraptor* designs (as well as round pupils), the more recent *Jurassic World* movies unfortunately did not give the *Velociraptors* any feathers at all, even though the science has confirmed it. Still, the *Jurassic Park Velociraptors* remain instantly recognizable and have become very well known to the general public. Other dromaeosaurs introduced in *Jurassic World Dominion* include the deeper-skulled *Atrociraptor* as well as *Pyroraptor*, the latter of which is correctly depicted with a full coat of feathers.

A number of other theropods appear in the *Jurassic Park* franchise as well. One of the most well-known is *Spinosaurus* from *Jurassic Park III*. *Spinosaurus* was an exceptionally large carnivore of comparable or even possibly larger size than *Tyrannosaurus*. *Spinosaurus* is best known for the large sail on its back and elongate, somewhat crocodilian skull. Contrary to much that is shown in *Jurassic Park III*, however, it was likely a fish eater and spent its time in or near water catching prey with its large claws (as it is shown in one of its final scenes). Furthermore, more recent discoveries have shown that it may have been quadrupedal and that its tail was more paddle-like, adding to the assertion that it may have spent more time along the water. Other enormous theropods include those introduced in the recent *Jurassic World: Dominion*, including *Giganotosaurus* (a huge theropod of comparable or slightly larger size than *Tyrannosaurus* with a massive head but smaller teeth) and *Therizinosaurus*, a likely herbivorous theropod known for its large body, small head, and its highly elongate, massive claws on its hands.

Medium-sized theropods have appeared in the *Jurassic Park* franchise as well (all of which are shown to be much larger than they were in real life). *Ceratosaurus*, a carnivorous theropod with a single horn on its nose and osteoderms, appears briefly in *Jurassic Park III*. *Baryonyx*, a smaller relative of *Spinosaurus*, appears in *Jurassic World: Fallen Kingdom*—a species that looks similar to its larger relative but without a sail on its back. Other species that first appear in *Jurassic World: Fallen Kingdom* are *Carnotaurus*, a blunt-muzzled carnivore known for the two horns above its eyes and incredibly short forelimbs, and *Allosaurus*, a carnivore with a more elongate muzzle and small crests above its eyes. Smaller theropods include the chicken-sized *Compsognathus* from *The Lost World: Jurassic Park* (which are shown featherless hopping around on long hind limbs), *Moros* (a small relative of *Tyrannosaurus*), and *Oviraptor* (a beaked, herbivorous maniraptoran) in *Jurassic World Dominion*. As the massive hybrid dinosaurs called "Indominus rex" (in *Jurassic World*) and "Indoraptor" (in *Jurassic World: Fallen Kingdom*) are fictional, they will not be discussed here except to say that their hybridization of multiple theropod species as well as other animals is a fascinating thought experiment that was implemented well in this franchise.

Beyond Dinosaurs and the Portrayal of Paleontology

Paleontology as a field of study examines the entire history of all life on earth, which means many paleontologists study other animals, including flying reptiles, marine reptiles, mammals, amphibians, fish, and invertebrates. Some paleontologists known as paleobotanists (like Ellie Sattler) even study plants. Although not the case for the original *Jurassic Park* film, the franchise has introduced non-dinosaurian prehistoric animals in the films that followed.

Most notably, *The Lost World: Jurassic Park* was the first of the franchise to introduce pterosaurs, a group of flying reptiles with wing membranes extending from a super elongated finger on each hand down to its lower limbs. Pterosaurs are frequently viewed by the general public as being dinosaurs themselves; however, they are, in fact, a separate group closely related to dinosaurs. *Pteranodon* is distinguished by a long, narrow crest extending back from its head. It is accurately portrayed with a long toothless beak in most cases except in *Jurassic Park III*, where it is shown with small sharp teeth. As shown in the films, pterosaurs used powered flight, or wing-flapping, to fly high in the air for long distances. Many times, it is portrayed as picking people up with its feet as they fly; however, its feet were not built for such a mode of prey capture. They likely swooped down and caught ocean fish with their mouths. Other pterosaurs featured in the franchise are the tiny, toothed pterosaur *Dimorphodon* as well the one of the largest pterosaurs of all, *Quetzalcoatlus*—a pterosaur that was taller than a giraffe with an enormous, jet-sized wingspan—accurately portrayed with hair-like feathers covering its body in *Jurassic World: Dominion*.

A highly overgrown *Mosasaurus* is also portrayed in the *Jurassic World* movies. Mosasaurs were the largest predatory marine lizards to have ever lived. It could reach up to fifty feet in length and swam with enormous flippers and paddle-like tails. In *Jurassic World*, it is seen breaching to grab a shark that it is being fed. Here, we get a view of just how overgrown the animal is in the movie with an extra wide head and many scales along its back. The inside of the mouth is notably quite accurate with extra teeth shown on its palate, which would have been extra useful in acquiring prey and not letting it escape its mouth.

The recent *Jurassic World Dominion* also includes two quadrupedal precursors of mammals that are portrayed with relatively decent anatomy. *Lystrosaurus* is a small dicynodont, which was a group of herbivorous animals with bizarre-looking head, big jaw muscles, and a toothless, parrot-like beak. *Dimetrodon* is a sprawling, predatory animal known for the tall sail along its back often mistaken for a dinosaur. Both animals lived well before dinosaurs even existed, which speaks to the breadth of time the mammalian lineage was sustained before evolving many more forms and taking over numerous ecological niches following the demise of the dinosaurs.

In *Jurassic Park*, Tim references the dinosaur extinction, noting how a meteor (asteroid) hit the earth sixty-six million years ago. This created a large crater in the Yucatán Peninsula in Mexico and set off a series of events drastically changing global climate and ultimately killing off all non-avian dinosaurs. In bringing dinosaurs back to life, scientists like Henry Wu (B. D. Wong) in *Jurassic Park* acquired DNA from within mosquitoes trapped in amber that supposedly drank the blood of dinosaurs before fossilization. This is largely agreed as likely impossible as the blood would have broken down quickly along with the contamination of mosquito DNA over millions of years. They then filled in holes in the genome with frog DNA. Furthermore, the scientists denied the animals the hormone for male chromosomes, intending to breed only females. When Alan Grant finds dinosaur eggs that showed the animals were in fact breeding, he realizes that some must have changed sex from female to male given the pressures of an all-female environment—something known to occur in some frog species.

With John Hammond's success in bringing dinosaurs back to life, major characters like Chaotician Ian Malcolm bring up the dangers inherent in doing so, pointing out that dinosaurs were naturally selected against. Furthermore, Ellie Sattler argues that animals that are not supposed to live in today's ecosystems will defend themselves any way they can in an unfit environment. We see this throughout the franchise, with various large theropods rampaging around, sometimes killing everything in sight and it shows how we would not really get a good grasp of these animals as they truly would have behaved in their own times and environments.

Of course, *Jurassic Park* would not have made any sense without the perspectives of Alan Grant and Ellie Sattler—the paleontologists. Although previous films have portrayed paleontologists in much smaller roles, *Jurassic Park* was the first major motion picture to truly put a spotlight on the profession. In fact, some younger paleontologists, including myself, have referred to *Jurassic Park* as one of their inspirations for entering the field. In the beginning of the film, we see them working at a quarry in Montana digging up a *Velociraptor*. Many at the dig site are seen easily using brushes to clean off the dirt on top of the fossil—a method that would not typically work quite as well in the field as the tough dirt and rock usually requires more powerful tools and effort. Additionally, we see a perfectly articulated, 100 percent complete skeleton in the ground, which is a highly unlikely occurrence and would be considered by paleontologists as a truly miraculous find. Dinosaur skeletons of similar size are typically disarticulated in the ground with bones spread out all over and, in most cases, a majority of the specimen eroded or washed away completely.

Although paleontologists are portrayed digging, that is not all they do. Many spend their time in museum collections analyzing specimens, analyzing data in labs and with computer programs, and educating the public in a variety of different ways, whether it be at a museum or in a school. Also, while working in the quarry, Alan Grant is seen wearing a fedora, denim shirt, red scarf, khakis, and hiking boots. Although there are paleontologists that use aspects of this type of ensemble, it is mainly a trope carried on in general media involving paleontologists. During the 1990s and before, paleontologists have been generally perceived as an Indiana Jones type (although many times with the addition of a large beard). This could not be further from the truth now, however, due to the ever-growing diversity of paleontologists of all different backgrounds, genders, and abilities.

Since its release thirty years ago, *Jurassic Park* has inspired an entire generation of paleontologists and dinosaur enthusiasts. Its breathtaking imagery of animals once thought of as nothing more than mythical beasts by many has created a world of endless possibilities in cinema. The beauty portrayed in *Jurassic Park*'s recreation of the anatomy and biology of its dinosaurs is a testament to the care and great attention to detail put into their design. *Jurassic Park* has set a high standard in recreating prehistoric animals that will hopefully be carried on for generations to come in film.

Notes

1 Robert T. Bakker, "Dinosaur Renaissance," *Scientific American* 232:4 (1975): 58–79.
2 John R. Horner and Robert Makela, "Nest of Juveniles Provides Evidence of Family Structure among Dinosaurs," *Nature* 282:5736 (1979): 296–8.
3 John H. Ostrom, *Osteology of* Deinonychus antirrhopus, *an Unusual Theropod from the Lower Cretaceous of Montana* (New Haven, CT: Yale University Press, 1969); John H. Ostrom, "Archaeopteryx and the Origin of Flight," *Quarterly Review of Biology* 49:1 (1974): 27–47.
4 Andreas Christian and Gordon Dzemski, "Reconstruction of the Cervical Skeleton Posture of *Brachiosaurus brancai Janensch*, 1914 by an Analysis of the Intervertebral Stress along the Neck and a Comparison with the Results of Different Approaches," *Fossil Record* 10:1 (2007): 38–49; Andreas Christian and W-D. Heinrich, "The Neck Posture of *Brachiosaurus brancai*," *Fossil Record* 1:1 (1998): 73–80.
5 Kent A. Stevens and J. Michael Parrish, "Neck Posture and Feeding Habits of two Jurassic Sauropod Dinosaurs," *Science* 284:5415 (1999): 798–800; Kent A. Stevens, "The Articulation of Sauropod Necks: Methodology and Mythology," *PLoS One* 8:10 (2013): e78572.
6 Henry Fairfield Osborn and Charles Craig Mook, "Camarasaurus, Amphicoelias, and Other Sauropods of Cope," *Bulletin of the Geological Society of America* 30:1 (1919): 379–88.
7 Walter P. Coombs Jr., "Sauropod Habits and Habitats," *Palaeogeography, Palaeoclimatology, Palaeoecology* 17:1 (1975): 1–33; Donald M. Henderson, "Tipsy Punters: Sauropod Dinosaur Pneumaticity, Buoyancy and Aquatic Habits," *Proceedings of the Royal Society of London. Series B: Biological Sciences* 271: no. sup. 4 (2004): S180–S183.

8 Michael P. Taylor, "A Re-evaluation of Brachiosaurus altithorax Riggs 1903 (Dinosauria, Sauropoda) and Its Generic Separation from Giraffatitan brancai (Janensch 1914)," *Journal of vertebrate Paleontology* 29:3 (2009): 787–806.
9 Peter M. Galton, "The Cheeks of Ornithischian Dinosaurs," *Lethaia* 6:1 (1973): 67–89.
10 Ali Nabavizadeh, "New Reconstruction of Cranial Musculature in Ornithischian Dinosaurs: Implications for Feeding Mechanisms and Buccal Anatomy," *Anatomical Record* 303:2 (2020): 347–62.
11 David B. Weishampel, "Acoustic Analyses of Potential Vocalization in Lambeosaurine Dinosaurs (Reptilia: Ornithischia)," *Paleobiology* 7:2 (1981): 252–61.
12 Heinrich Mallison, "Defense Capabilities of Kentrosaurus aethiopicus Hennig, 1915," *Palaeontologia Electronica* 14:2; 10A (2011): 1–25.
13 Ashley C. Morhardt, *Dinosaur Smiles: Do the Texture and Morphology of The Premaxilla, Maxilla, and Dentary Bones of Sauropsids Provide Osteological Correlates for Inferring Extra-Oral Structures Reliably in Dinosaurs?* (Macomb, IL: Western Illinois University, 2009).
14 Xu Xing, Kebai Wang, Ke Zhang, Qingyu Ma, Lida Xing, Corwin Sullivan, Dongyu Hu, Shuqing Cheng, and Shuo Wang, "A Gigantic Feathered Dinosaur from the Lower Cretaceous of China," *Nature* 484:7392 (2012): 92–5.

12

From Creatures to Companions: Representations of Dinosaur Violence in the *Jurassic Park* and *Jurassic World* Films

Jennifer Schell
University of Alaska Fairbanks, USA

Introduction

All of the *Jurassic Park* (1993–2001) and *Jurassic World* films (2015–22) contain suspenseful moments of animal violence in which the protagonists are attacked by aggressive, predatory dinosaurs.[1] The list of rapacious reptiles is long and includes representatives from various actual and fictional genera: *Giganotosaurus*, *Indominus*, *Indoraptor*, *Mosasaurus*, *Spinosaurus*, *Therizinosaurus*, *Tyrannosaurus*, and *Velociraptor* (for example). Significantly, the humans in these films often find themselves saved from certain death, not by powerful weapons or superior intelligence, but by other carnivorous dinosaurs.[2] At the very end of *Jurassic Park* (1993), the *Tyrannosaurus* arrives at the visitor center just in time to rescue Alan (Sam Neill), Ellie (Laura Dern), Lex (Ariana Richards), and Tim (Joseph Mazzello) from the two crafty *Velociraptors* circling around them. Meanwhile, in the final moments of *Jurassic World* (2015), the *Mosasaurus*—aided by one cantankerous *Tyrannosaurus* and three clicker-trained *Velociraptors*—saves Owen (Chris Pratt), Claire (Bryce Dallas Howard), Gray (Ty Simpkins), and Zach (Nick Robinson) from the rampaging *Indominus Rex*. In these scenes, as well as many others from across the franchises, humans cannot fend off the depredations of the dinosaurs on their own; they need the help of reptilian reinforcements.

This tendency serves to differentiate the *Jurassic Park* and *Jurassic World* movies from other creature feature and animal horror films, which typically involve more direct confrontations between humans and animals.[3] Examples include, among others, *Jaws* (1975), *Grizzly* (1976), *Alligator* (1980), *Razorback* (1984), *Lake Placid* (1999), *Rogue* (2007), *The Grey* (2011), *Crawl* (2019), and *The Meg* (2018). In most of these movies, the intrepid heroes (typically white men from the Global North) slaughter their monstrous nonhuman adversaries in dramatic fashion. Not coincidentally, many of them employ the same tactic as Martin Brody (Roy Scheider) in *Jaws*, namely detonating a massive explosion that kills the animal and scatters pieces of flesh everywhere. Taken together, then, animal horror movies tend to elaborate what Val Plumwood calls a "masculinist monster myth," a "master narrative" that is grounded on a "dualistic vision of human mastery over the planet in which we are predators but we can never be prey."[4] In so doing, they cater to the notions of human exceptionalism and supremacy that have been integral to Euro-American thought for centuries.

As I argue, the *Jurassic Park* and *Jurassic World* films also express anxiety about the relationship between humans and dangerous, predatory animals, but they differ from the horror movies with respect to their representations of dinosaur violence, because they draw on different storytelling traditions. Produced in regular intervals between 1993 and 2001, the *Jurassic Park* films tend to rehash the tropes of *Lost World* fiction and cinema established by *Journey to the Centre of the Earth* (1864), *The Lost World* (1912), and *The Lost World* (1925). Thus, they characterize carnivorous dinosaurs as monstrous creatures, driven by their primeval instincts to violently attack other animals whenever they encounter them. Although the dinosaurs also attempt to kill the human protagonists, these films—much like their *Lost World* predecessors—prefer to invest in the spectacle of dinosaur violence, regaling viewers with titanic battle sequences in which prehistoric reptiles duel to the death. Generally speaking, humans, in the *Jurassic Park* universe, tend to function as terrified victims or amazed bystanders.

Released between 2015 and 2022, the *Jurassic World* movies tend to rely less upon *Lost World* tropes and more on the narrative traditions established by popular Boy-and-Dog novels, such as *Big Red* (1945), *Old Yeller* (1956), and *Where the Red Fern Grows* (1961). Thus, these films depict some dinosaurs—the three *Velociraptors* that Owen trains for InGen—as companion animals, a category that Donna Haraway argues includes "horses, dogs, cats, or a range of other beings willing to make the leap to the biosociality of service dogs, family members, or team members in cross-species sports."[5] Just like the canine companions in the Boy-and-Dog books, these predatory dinosaurs possess emotions, intelligence, and agency. They are also devoted to their humans, risking their lives to defend them from the violent onslaught of other reptiles. As I contend, though, the movies reinvent the narrative paradigm manifested in the novels. They ground their depictions of dinosaur sentience on recent scientific developments regarding the intellectual and emotional capacities of reptiles. They tell stirring stories of multispecies cooperation and survival instead of sentimental tales of animal sacrifice and death. And they focus on adults in addition to children, thereby demonstrating that all humans—regardless of age or gender—are capable of forming intimate and meaningful bonds with other species.

Monstrous Creatures: Dinosaur Violence in *Lost World* Fiction and Film

As a genre, *Lost World* fiction emerged in Euro-American culture in the early nineteenth century and proliferated across time. In addition to the aforementioned texts, the list includes the anonymously authored *Symzonia: A Voyage of Discovery* (1820), as well as H. Rider Haggard's *King Solomon's Mines* (1885), James De Mille's *A Strange Manuscript Found in a Copper Cylinder* (1888), and Edgar Rice Burroughs' *The Land That Time Forgot* (1918).[6] All of these novels revolve around the exploits of enterprising white men, who embark on voyages of exploration to isolated, inaccessible corners of the globe. Over the course of their travels, these individuals "discover" lost civilizations, whose members seem barbaric because they engage in unfamiliar or objectionable cultural practices. Sometimes, but not always, the protagonists also stumble across remnant populations of long extinct organisms: *Plesiosaurus*, *Pterodactylus*, and *Allosaurus*. Since these books revolve around the hostilities that arise between the white adventurers and the various other life forms they encounter, they tend to express themes that address Euro-American anxieties about empire, eugenics, and evolution.[7]

Fascinated by and preoccupied with prehistoric reptiles, *Lost World* novels almost always characterize them as monstrous creatures, cold-blooded and instinct-driven behemoths who violently attack any human or nonhuman organism daring to trespass in their territory. Art historian, W. J. T. Mitchell attributes this tendency to late-nineteenth-century visions of the natural world as "red in tooth and claw" ruled by the doctrine of the "survival of the fittest."[8] While this insight is astute, I would add that contemporary scientific views about extant reptiles also likely contributed to this view. According to a number of late-nineteenth-century naturalists and zoologists (George Romanes, James Baskett, and Raymond Ditmars) these animals possessed small, primitive brains and operated according to mechanistic instincts, not conscious thoughts.[9] In *Life and Evolution* (1906), Frederick Headley summarizes the majority opinion, declaring that "reptiles are singularly wanting in intelligence," because the "mind is not of a high order: the forehead is low and the cerebral hemispheres are very little developed." To add insult to injury, he criticizes their lack of interest in play and "their indifference to the fate of their young."[10] Influenced by these ideas, many late-nineteenth-century authors characterized the dinosaurs of the Mesozoic Era as just as ferocious and stupid as their evolutionary successors.

Although they menace humans—especially anachronistic white adventurers—the dinosaurs in *Lost World* novels tend to be far more interested in attacking each other. In *Journey to the Centre of the Earth*, the *Plesiosaurus* and the *Ichthyosaurus* are so involved in their duel to the death that they fail to notice Axel and his companions floating beside them on the raft:

> Those huge creatures attacked each other with the greatest animosity. They heaved around them liquid mountains, which rolled even to our raft and rocked it perilously. Twenty times we were near capsizing. Hissings of prodigious force are heard. The two beasts are fast locked together; I cannot distinguish the one from the other. The probable rage of the conqueror inspires us with intense fear.
>
> One hour, two hours, pass away. The struggle continues with unabated ferocity. The combatants alternately approach and recede from our raft. We remain motionless, ready to fire. Suddenly the ichthyosaurus and the plesiosaurus disappear below, leaving a whirlpool eddying in the water. Several minutes pass by while the fight goes on under water.
>
> All at once an enormous head is darted up, the head of the plesiosaurus. The monster is wounded to death. I no longer see his scaly armour. Only his long neck shoots up, drops again, coils and uncoils, droops, lashes the waters like a gigantic whip, and writhes like a worm that you tread on. The water is splashed for a long way around. The spray almost blinds us. But soon the reptile's agony draws to an end; its movements become fainter, its contortions cease to be so violent, and the long serpentine form lies a lifeless log on the labouring deep.[11]

In these paragraphs, Axel generates suspense and excitement by using evocative imagery, vivid verbs, and striking similes. Ignoring the possibility that these titanic apex predators might possess some form of intelligence, he emphasizes their physicality—their tremendous size, spectacular strength, and incredible endurance. Importantly, Axel and his friends witness but do not participate in this combat sequence. Never are they threatened by the reptiles, and never do they fire their weapons at them. While this passivity might seem strange, it furnishes more evidence for Allen Debus's claim that the novel represents "a fictionalized paleontological treatise" in which the underground cavern functions like "a subterranean museum" containing different dioramas of prehistoric life.[12] Here, the adventurers represent patrons, and the reptiles represent something akin to taxidermy specimens staged to maximize their sensational appeal.

After the publication of *Journey to the Centre of the Earth*, dinosaurian combat sequences emerged as a staple of *Lost World* novels and films. Authors did not always employ the same representational strategies, however. In *The Lost World*, Arthur Conan Doyle depicts scenes of dinosaur violence that involve desperate predator/prey—not predator/predator—conflicts. He also privileges suspense over spectacle, locating the action offstage far from human witnesses. On their third night on the plateau, Edward Malone and his companions hear the "most frightful cries and screams," but they only learn the "source of the hideous uproar" in the morning when they discover the bloody aftermath of an epic contest between an *Allosaurus* and an *Iguanodon*.[13] Introducing the bloodthirsty carnivore in absentia enables Doyle to create an atmosphere of apprehension that persists until the animal finally materializes, ambushing Malone and chasing him through the forest. Throughout this sequence, Doyle regales readers with contemporary scientific theories about dinosaurs, explaining that these reptiles might be brutally efficient killing machines, but they are also "brainless" beasts, who "disappeared from the rest of the world" as a result of "their own stupidity."[14]

If Doyle eschews dinosaur battle sequences, then Harry Hoyt—the director of the 1925 silent film version of *The Lost World*—revels in them. As Stefan Lampadius explains, the movie "focuses much more on the dinosaurs, especially their struggle for survival as a constant mortal battle among the different dinosaur species."[15] While accurate, this assessment of the film understates the extremities of its representations of dinosaur ferocity. In its first combat scene, the members of the expedition watch from the safe confines of their campsite as an *Allosaurus* approaches and attacks an unidentified, foraging hadrosaurid. After a desperate contest, the predator proves victorious, killing his prey with a bite to the neck. Instead of consuming the carcass, the *Allosaurus* immediately launches an assault on four nearby *Triceratops*, three adults and one juvenile. Once they nudge their progeny into a safe hiding place, the herbivores turn to confront their carnivorous foe, who then retreats into the forest in search of other victims. As a whole, this scene—and the many others that follow—characterizes predatory dinosaurs as impressive physical specimens and cold-blooded killing machines, driven not by hunger but by instinct to slaughter every single organism they encounter in the forest. In this way, this film sets the stage for its numerous cinematic successors—*King Kong* (1933), *One Million B.C.* (1940), *The Land Unknown* (1957), and *One Million Years B.C.* (1966)—most of which depict prehistoric reptiles in a similar manner.

Monstrous Creatures, Continued: Dinosaur Violence in the *Jurassic Park* Film

Influenced by *Lost World* books and films, *Jurassic Park* tends to portray life in the Mesozoic Era as marked by violent confrontations among various species of prehistoric reptiles. Notably, though, the film combines some of the different representational strategies adopted by its antecedents. If the opening scene creates suspense by refusing to reveal the identity of dangerous animal in the crate, the subsequent scenes indulge in spectacle by using stunning special effects to depict the *Tyrannosaurus*'s brutal attacks on the tour group, *Gallimimus* herd, and *Velociraptor* pack. Some of these sequences pit predator against prey, and some of them pit predator against predator. All of them depict humans as powerless victims—or stupefied spectators—and reinforce the idea that carnivorous dinosaurs are inherently and instinctively violent animals.

Insofar as *Jurassic Park* is concerned, scholars tend to address either anthropocentric themes, involving the decline of American procreative capacities and capitalist hegemony, or ecocentric themes, regarding the perils of experimental genetic technology and mass extinction.[16] Although these discussions are insightful, I am more interested in the characterizations of the carnivorous dinosaurs that appear in *Jurassic Park*, because they demonstrate the pronounced influence of *Lost World* texts on the film. Much like the *Allosaurus* and the *Pterodactylus* in the 1925 film adaptation of *The Lost World*, the *Tyrannosaurus* represents a monstrous creature, armed with sharp teeth and giant claws, which she uses to attack any organism she encounters in her travels through the park.[17] Her inherent ferocity—not to mention her colossal size and tremendous strength—more than make up for her deficient visual, olfactory, and cognitive capacities. For their part, the *Velociraptors* also possess impressive physical attributes, namely their speed, agility, and dexterity. Similar to the warm-blooded, pack-hunting dinosaurs described by paleontologists John Ostrom and Robert Bakker, they are capable of exercising certain forms of reasoning ability and social intelligence.[18] Still, they are ultimately just as subject to the dictates of their vicious instincts as the *Tyrannosaurus*.

As indicated, *Jurassic Park* combines the representational strategies of different *Lost World* texts, regaling viewers with suspenseful *and* spectacular scenes of dinosaur violence. Importantly, though, the function and intensity of these sequences shifts as the film progresses. At first, the dinosaurs direct their animosity toward their human captors, the park employees and visitors. After they escape the confines of their cages, they begin launching attacks against each in an effort to reestablish the primordial predator/prey relationships inherent in prehistoric food webs. To assert their dominance in this new environment, the apex carnivores—the *Tyrannosaurus* and the

Velociraptors—engage in a ferocious territorial dispute in the visitor center atrium that inadvertently allows Alan, Ellie, Lex, and Tim to escape the island.

Suspenseful, but not spectacular, the very first scene of the movie establishes the park's carnivorous dinosaurs as violent animals, who instinctively lash out against their human captors at every opportunity. In this sequence, a large group of armed, uniformed men attempt to transfer a mysterious, unidentified animal from a large metal crate into an adjacent building. As they do so, one of them—a worker named Jophery (Jophery Brown)—is brutally attacked and killed. Perhaps not surprisingly, Spielberg creates tension and anticipation by employing many of the same techniques that he used in the opening sequence of *Jaws*. Instead of revealing Jophery's animal attacker, he focuses the camera on the crowd of workers, occasionally zooming in on their frightened faces. He intercuts this footage with point-of-view shots taken from the perspective of the *Velociraptor* as she glares at her captors through the holes in the crate. And he splices in a few tight close-ups on her yellow eyes.

Suspense soon turns to spectacle when the *Tyrannosaurus*—released from her pen by the power outage—assaults the tour group as they attempt to return to the visitor center. Lasting approximately six full minutes, the scene employs stupendous special effects to create an astounding display of dinosaur violence in which the *Tyrannosaurus* stomps, roars, and chomps at every obstacle in her path. Close-ups on her jaws, claws, and eyes serve to showcase both her ferocity and malevolence. Much like the raptor in the first scene, she instinctively attempts to attack her human captors, targeting both employees of and visitors to the park. As she does so, she destroys key elements of park infrastructure, namely the electric fences, sport utility vehicles, and bathroom facilities. Although they use their ingenuity to temporarily distract her with emergency flares, the humans in this scene—Alan, Lex, Tim, Malcom (Jeff Goldblum), and Gennaro (Martin Ferrero)—spend most of their time running and hiding from their much larger foe.

From here, the dinosaur violence shifts in purpose but increases in intensity. Freed from their cages and abandoned by their keepers, the dinosaurs roam the park in search of sustenance, territory, and novelty. As the members of the various species interact, they rapidly establish their own primeval ecosystem with the apex predators—*Tyrannosaurus* and *Velociraptor*—occupying niches at the top of the food web. *Jurassic Park* showcases this newly developed dinosaurian hierarchy in spectacular fashion in the scene in which Alan, Lex, and Tim spy a herd of *Gallimimus* stampeding toward them across a broad, open plain. Taking shelter behind a gigantic, fallen tree, the three human interlopers watch with breathless anticipation as the *Tyrannosaurus* bursts from a nearby cluster of trees onto the plain. After roaring and bellowing a few times, she grabs a *Gallimimus* in her jaws and crushes it to death. Vigorously shaking her head back and forth, she rips off a shred of flesh and devours it, while Alan, Lex, and Tim maintain their peripheral position as enraptured—and aghast—onlookers. Much like those appearing in *Lost World* texts, this scene serves to characterize the *Tyrannosaurus* as a monstrous creature, who possesses a natural instinct for violence.

If the *Gallimimus* sequence illustrates the brutality of predator/prey relationships, the final battle between the *Tyrannosaurus* and the *Velociraptors* showcases the ferocity of predator/predator conflicts. What is at stake here is not food, but territorial dominance over the visitor center and, by extension, the entire ecosystem. As in the first scene with the *Tyrannosaurus*, the human characters tend function as helpless victims, fleeing rather than fighting the aggressive dinosaurs that threaten them. After crawling through the ductwork, Alan, Ellie, Lex, and Tim emerge from a panel in the ceiling of the visitor center. Confronted by one *Velociraptor*, they descend—or fall—to the floor only to be accosted by another. Just as the two predators corner the humans, the *Tyrannosaurus* arrives on the scene. Snarling and growling, she instinctively attacks the other reptiles, grabbing one of them in her mouth and tossing the carcass to the ground. Instead of fleeing, the remaining *Velociraptor* screeches in anger and runs toward the *Tyrannosaurus*, jumping on her back and biting her neck with reckless abandon. As she bellows and lurches about the atrium, the larger dinosaur manages to shake her smaller foe to the ground and crush her in her jaws. Flinging the carcass of the *Velociraptor* into an half-assembled dinosaur skeleton, the *Tyrannosaurus* celebrates her victory—and flaunts her newly acquired ecosystemic supremacy—by indulging in a triumphant roar. Meanwhile, in the midst of the fray, Alan, Ellie, Lex, and Tim run out of the building, where they find a vehicle waiting to transport them to safety. Along with its predecessors, then, this scene presents a vision of carnivorous dinosaurs as inherently violent, instinct-driven machines, who cannot resist attacking other prehistoric predators whenever they have the opportunity to do so.

Given that it is the first film in the franchise, *Jurassic Park* sets important precedents for its sequels, especially with respect to dinosaurian combat sequences. In *The Lost World: Jurassic Park* (1997), Sarah (Julianne Moore) slides off a roof and lands between two skirmishing *Velociraptors*. Too distracted by each other to care about the human in their midst, they ignore her and allow her to escape. Meanwhile, in *Jurassic Park III* (2001), Alan and his colleagues flee from a hostile *Tyrannosaurus*, inadvertently leading her straight into the path of an aggressive *Spinosaurus*. As the two prehistoric titans duel to the death, the humans escape unharmed into the jungle. Thus, these two films serve to reinforce the representations of the dinosaurs that appear in both *Jurassic Park* and its *Lost World* predecessors.

Loyal Companions: Animal Violence in Boy-and-Dog Stories

Many of the carnivorous dinosaurs in the *Jurassic World* films—*Giganotosaurus, Indominus, Indoraptor, Mosasaurus*, and *Tyrannosaurus*—resemble those in *Jurassic Park*, at least insofar as their inherent predilection for violence is concerned. Significantly, though, *Jurassic World* and its sequels portray the *Velociraptors* as intelligent, emotional animals, who are capable of learning complex skills, making important decisions, and forging intimate bonds with human beings. To account for this representational shift, I argue that these films draw on the tropes of the Boy-and-Dog novel, a subgenre of children's literature, which emerged in the 1940s with the publication of Jim Kjelgaard's *Big Red* and peaked in popularity in subsequent decades with the publication of Fred Gipson's *Old Yeller* and Wilson Rawls's *Where the Red Fern Grows*.

Generically speaking, Boy-and-Dog novels are rite-of-passage stories that revolve around the outdoor adventures of adolescent boys—most of whom hail from poor, rural communities—and their beloved dogs. As both working and companion animals, these canines perform important services for and form intense bonds with their owners.[19] While some of them are pampered purebreds from champion kennels and others are neglected strays of unknown ancestry, all of them are exceptional animals, who command incredible physical, emotional, and intellectual abilities. Most of them also possess an uncanny capacity for intuitive communication, conversing with their owners through nonverbal utterances, facial expressions, and body language.

These novels are both intensely emotional and incredibly formulaic. In all of the aforementioned texts, the dogs risk their lives to defend their adolescent companions from the aggressive onslaughts of carnivorous animals—wolverines, bears, wolves, and cougars. Most are killed in a brutally violent manner. Though traumatic for the boys, the dog deaths serve as catalysts for their maturation into full-fledged adults, teaching them difficult but important lessons about selflessness, loyalty, and loss.[20] Note that, more often than not, these novels present human–animal relationships in anthropocentric terms. Thus, as Karla Armbruster explains, they tend to "reinforce prevailing assumptions regarding the superiority of the human species and the rightness of the human battle to dominate nature, while also affirming the notion that domesticated animals exist to serve the interests of human beings rather than to pursue their own."[21]

As one of the first Boy-and-Dog books, *Big Red* establishes many of the key tropes employed by later examples. At the beginning of the novel, Danny Pickett—a teenage boy from an impoverished background—befriends Red—a prize-winning Irish setter owned by a wealthy dog-breeder. Forming an intense, cross-class bond, the two roam the wilderness together, hunting partridges and running traplines. Importantly, Red represents an exemplary individual. A magnificent physical specimen with superior scenting abilities, he also possesses intelligence, pride, courage, nobility, and untold "depths of feeling and sensitivity."[22] In a telling early moment in the novel, Danny describes Red as "almost human."[23] Though the pair experience many challenges over the course of the book, none are as life-altering as their climactic encounter with a rogue black bear named Old Majesty. At one point, Danny finds himself cornered by the bear, and Red leaps to his defense, protecting his human companion but incurring several severe injuries in the process. In the end, the boy kills Old Majesty and saves his dog with several well-placed shots from his rifle. Victory comes at a price, however, for the two are forever altered by their involvement in the deadly contest. Red recovers from his injuries but loses his status as a prize-winning show dog, while Danny leaves behind the innocence of childhood and matures into manhood.

Other Boy-and-Dog books are far more tragic and traumatic than *Big Red*. In *Old Yeller*, the titular dog develops a deep bond with Travis Coates and the other members of his family, rescuing them from an angry bear, an aggressive boar, and a rabid wolf. Although Yeller does not receive any serious injuries in the last encounter, he is bitten by the crazed canine. After an emotionally wrenching conversation with his mother, Travis shoots and kills his dog to prevent him from contracting an incurable disease and suffering a torturous death. Meanwhile, in *Where the Red Fern Grows*, Billy Coleman forms an intense attachment to his two redbone coonhounds, Old Dan and Little Ann. Their idyllic world is shattered when they encounter a cougar while hunting late one night in the woods. Though they survive the horrific fight that ensues, Old Dan eventually succumbs to the devastating injuries he incurs while defending Billy. Shortly thereafter, Little Ann loses the will to live and dies of a broken heart. Much like *Big Red*, these books portray the incredible sacrifices of the dogs as necessary because they enable their adolescent owners to mature into men.

Animal Violence in the *Jurassic World* Films

In many respects, the *Jurassic World* movies follow the narrative paradigm established by Boy-and-Dog novels. They present Owen Grady as developing an intimate, loving bond with his *Velociraptors*, which allows them to communicate with a variety of nonverbal sounds, gestures, and gazes. They also contain dramatic climactic scenes in which the dinosaurs choose to defend Owen and his friends from the violent assaults of other predatory reptiles. Importantly, though, the *Jurassic World* films eliminate some of the problematic features of this paradigm, updating it for contemporary audiences. If, as Walter Hogan argues, the books promote the "reactionary message that loyal and affectionate attachments to animals must be violently broken to 'kill the child' and 'make the man'," then the movies indicate that this need not be the case.[24] Although some of the *Velociraptors* perish in their contest with the *Tyrannosaurus* and the *Indominus*, Blue survives all three films, together with her offspring. Along the way, she forms and maintains lasting, meaningful relationships with both adults—Owen and Claire—and adolescents—Zach, Gray, and Maisie. These details are important to mark, for they serve to support Gail Melton's claim that adults need not abandon their "fascination with animals as a childish thing."[25]

Although *Jurassic World* has not inspired as much scholarship as *Jurassic Park*, some critics have examined the contradictions inherent in the film's contrast between "natural" and "hybrid" dinosaurs.[26] Others have discussed Owen and his relationship with the *Velociraptors* that he trains for the InGen security team. Likening him to Tarzan, Richard Dyer argues that "he may be with the animals, but he is in a commanding relationship to them."[27] Though astute with respect to the opening scenes of *Jurassic World*, I would suggest that this observation fails to account for the evolution of Owen's relationship with Blue over the course of the film and its sequels. Initially just trainer and trainee, the two eventually form a more intimate bond, grounded on care, respect, trust, mutuality, and reciprocity. Much like the characters in the Boy-and-Dog books, they become companions.

Because dinosaurs are so different from dogs, both in terms of their anatomy and reputation, *Velociraptors* might not seem like ideal companion animals. To make the idea more plausible, the *Jurassic World* films take advantage of recent scientific discoveries about extant reptiles and their cognitive capacities. As G. A. Bradshaw, quoting neurobiologist Erich Jarvis, explains, "a reptile brain is similar to a bird brain and both are similar to mammalian brains which implies that reptiles may have parallel capacities to think, feel, experience consciousness, and related abilities to mentally function."[28] Shortly thereafter, she observes that many reptile predators—snakes, alligators, and crocodiles—possess certain forms of emotional intelligence—self-awareness, empathy, and self-regulation—that are integral to their hunting practices.[29] She even speculates about dinosaur intelligence, positing that "brontosaurus and pterodactyls weren't less smart than humans or other contemporary species are today. They were able to thrive and survive in conditions that would have killed off most modern-day species."[30] In so doing, Bradshaw makes the depictions of *Velociraptors* as companion animals that appear in the *Jurassic World* films seem more compelling than not.

As the first film in the franchise, *Jurassic World* introduces Owen as an animal behaviorist and Navy veteran, hired by park security to train its raptors and explore their potential as military assets. In his first appearance in the film, he is presented as an authority figure, who possesses amazing control of his animals. Shown in silhouette backlit by the sun, Owen stands on a catwalk above the *Velociraptor* pen with his arms raised and his training clicker in his hand. Issuing terse commands and rapid clicks, he instructs the members of his pack—Blue, Charlie, Delta, and Echo—to stop chasing a pig and pay attention to him instead. The fact that they resist temptation and obey orders attests to both Owen's ability as a trainer and his dominance over his animals.

Throughout the film, though, Owen tends to oscillate between two extremes whenever he attempts to describe his relationship with the *Velociraptors* to the other characters. Sometimes, he emphasizes respect and trust, as he does in his conversations with Claire. When the two meet to talk about the *Indominus*, Owen explains, "I don't control the Raptors. It's a relationship. It's based on mutual respect." At other times, though, he stresses dominance and control, as he does in his conversations with Zach and Gray. When introducing the members of the *Velociraptor* pack to the brothers, Owen employs outdated scientific ideas about wolf pack hierarchies, observing, "This one's called Blue. She's the beta."[31] In response to Gray's question about the identity of the alpha, Owen declares with a confident smile, "You're looking at him, kid."

Tellingly, in the final scene of the film, Owen opts for trust and respect as opposed to control and dominance. In a touching moment, he releases Blue from her tracking headgear, thereby allowing her to choose whether her loyalties lie with the humans or the *Indominus*. After pausing to study each party and assess the situation, Blue decides to defend her trainer and his friends from the rampaging carnivore. Knowing that the *Velociraptors* are no match for the *Indominus*, Claire runs to the *Tyrannosaurus* pen to fetch "more teeth." Taking advantage of her instinctive penchant for violence—established by the previous *Jurassic Park* films—Claire lures her from confinement with an emergency road flare, which she tosses in the general direction of the *Indominus*. As soon as she catches sight of her rival predator, the *Tyrannosaurus* joins the *Velociraptors* and the humans in their desperate struggle for survival. Just as the *Indominus* is about to prove herself the victor in the spectacularly violent contest, the *Mosasaurus* leaps from her pool and drags her into the water to her death. As the scene ends, Owen and Blue make eye contact, recognizing their mutual affection, intimacy, and gratefulness. Then, she runs away from the humans and into the park to enjoy her newfound freedom.

Jurassic World: Fallen Kingdom (2018) further develops Owen's relationship with Blue, by depicting the mutuality of the love and companionship that the two share. Most of this information is conveyed, not in flashbacks, but in Owen's training videos, which show him working with Blue as a hatchling. In the first of these, Owen discovers that Blue is a special dinosaur, for she follows his commands, and she convinces her siblings to do the same. The second video provides more evidence for this conclusion, for it contrasts Delta's and Blue's interactions with Owen. When he crouches on the ground and whimpers to show his vulnerability, the former bites his arm, but the latter nuzzles his face. In his post-session comments, Owen explains that Blue exhibits "levels of interest, concern, hyper-intelligence, cognitive bonding." As the two continue to interact, he exclaims, "See that? She's tilting her head, she's craning forward. Increased eye movement. She's curious. She's showing empathy." Importantly, the scene concludes with footage of the two bonding, staring lovingly into each other's eyes.

Given their history, it is perhaps not surprising that Blue leaps to Owen's defense when he, Claire, and Maisie are threatened by the *Indoraptor* in the final scenes of *Fallen Kingdom*. Much like the canines in the Boy-and-Dog novels, Blue throws herself at her much larger and fiercer antagonist, while the humans escape out the window onto the ridgeline of the roof. Shaking off his diminutive adversary, the *Indoraptor* stalks and corners Owen. Just as the superpredator readies himself for the slaughter, Blue roars and jumps on him, using her momentum to knock them both off the ridgeline and through the glass roof. As the writhing tangle of dinosaurs falls into the great hall, the *Indoraptor* is impaled on the horns of the *Triceratops* skull positioned below them. More fortunate than the companion animals in the Boy-and-Dog novels, Blue survives unhurt.

Perhaps the most poignant moment of the movie occurs when Owen reunites with Blue after Maisie releases all of the dinosaurs. Approaching Blue, Owen reaches out his hand and rubs her snout while she purrs. He, then, offers to take her to "a safe place" so that they can stay together. First, she cocks her head at him, and then she glances back at one of the open cages behind them. Finally, she makes her choice, turning away from Owen and running off into the distance. Tellingly, the parting is difficult for both the human and the dinosaur. Owen looks utterly devastated, but he does not try to persuade or stop her from embracing her freedom. Though her expression is more difficult to interpret, Blue stops and looks back at her trainer one last time, chittering at him before leaving for good.

Blue is not a prominent character in *Jurassic World: Dominion* (2022). Nevertheless, the movie does contain a few key scenes that showcase the mutuality and reciprocity of the bond that she shares with Owen. Just after her daughter Beta is kidnapped by poachers working for Biosyn, Owen swears that he will return her to her mother. Later in the film, when his human companions protest his plan to rescue Beta before leaving the Biosyn facility, he remains undeterred, insisting that "I made a promise we would bring her home." At the very end of the film—after many near-death experiences—Owen finally manages to reunite mother and daughter. Just before the two dinosaurs run off in the forest together, Blue demonstrates her gratitude, returning to thank Owen with a single meaningful look.

Taken altogether, this evidence indicates that the *Jurassic Park* and the *Jurassic World* films draw on different generic forms—*Lost World* texts and

Boy-and-Dog novels—in order to tell different stories about prehistoric reptiles. Influenced by novels and films, such as *Journey to the Centre of the Earth* and *The Lost World*, the former portray dinosaurs as violent killing machines. They indicate the impossibility of living with ferocious predatory animals. Influenced by books, such as *Big Red* and *Old Yeller*, the latter represent prehistoric reptiles as intelligent, emotional beings. They offer an important contrast to their predecessors insofar as they gesture toward the possibility of coexisting with dangerous carnivorous creatures.

Notes

1 Although humans are animals, they are not generally referred to as such in Euro-American discourse; therefore, I use the term "animal" both here and elsewhere as shorthand for the more cumbersome phrase "nonhuman animal."

2 I recognize that "human" is an imprecise and problematic word, but I employ it both here and elsewhere to describe the protagonists in the films—most of whom are white, upper-middle-class men, women, and children from the Global North—and differentiate them from their dinosaur antagonists.

3 Some scholars classify the *Jurassic Park* and *Jurassic World* movies as animal horror, while others categorize them as adventure fiction or science fiction. See Ursula Heise, "From Extinction to Electronics: Dead Frogs, Live Dinosaurs, and Electric Sheep," in Cary Wolfe (ed.) *Zoontologies: The Question of the Animal* (Minneapolis: University of Minnesota Press, 2003), 61; Randy Laist, "Hypersaurus Rex: Recombinant Reality in Jurassic Park," in Andrea Wood and Brandy Schillace (eds.) *Unnatural Reproductions and Monstrosity: The Birth of the Monster in Literature, Film, and Media* (Amherst, NY: Cambria, 2013), 214; Dominic Lennard, *Brute Force: Animal Horror Movies* (Albany: State University of New York Press, 2019), 129–35; and Christy Tidwell, "'Life Finds a Way': Jurassic Park, Jurassic World, and Extinction Anxiety," in Jonathan Elmore (ed.) *Fiction and the Sixth Mass Extinction: Narrative in an Era of Loss* (Lanham, MD: Lexington, 2020), 33.

4 Val Plumwood, "Being Prey," in David Rothenberg and Marta Ulvaeus (eds.) *The New Earth Reader: The Best of Terra Nova* (Cambridge: Massachusetts Institute of Technology Press, 1999), 85–8.

5 Donna Haraway, "The Companion Species Manifesto," in *Manifestly Haraway* (Minneapolis: University of Minnesota Press, 2016), 106.

6 Since they describe underground Lost Worlds, many of these texts also qualify as Hollow Earth fiction. For more on this genre, see David Standish, *Hollow Earth: The Long and Curious History of Imagining Strange Lands, Fantastical Creatures, Advanced Civilizations, and Marvelous Machines Below the Earth's Surface* (Cambridge, MA: Da Capo, 2006), 12–13.

7 W. J. T. Mitchell, *The Last Dinosaur Book: The Life and Times of a Cultural Icon* (Chicago: University of Chicago Press, 1998), 169; Elana Gomel, "Lost

and Found: The Lost World Novel and the Shape of the Past," *Genre* 40:1–2 (2007): 106–7.
8 Mitchell, *Last Dinosaur Book*, 146.
9 George Romanes, *Animal Intelligence* (New York: Appleton's, 1901), 255; James Baskett and Raymond Ditmar, *The Story of the Amphibians and the Reptiles* (New York: Appleton's, 1902), 205.
10 Frederick Headley, *Life and Evolution* (London: Duckworth, 1906), 92–4. Only recently have these ideas about reptiles begun to change. See G. A. Bradshaw, *Carnivore Minds: Who These Fearsome Animals Really Are* (New Haven, CT: Yale University Press, 2017), 119–20.
11 Jules Verne, *Journey to the Centre of the Earth* (Ware: Wordsworth, 2012), 134–5.
12 Allen Debus, *Dinosaurs in Fantastic Fiction: A Thematic Survey* (Jefferson, NC: McFarland, 2006), 17–18.
13 Ibid., 124.
14 Ibid., 145. For more on Doyle's interest in paleontology, see Stefan Lampadius, "Evolutionary Ideas in Arthur Conan Doyle's *The Lost World*," in Dieter Petzold (ed.) *Inklings Yearbook* (Frankfurt: Peter Lang, 2012), 77–81; Roy Pilot and Alvin Rodin, "Introduction," in Roy Pilot and Alvin Rodin (eds.) *The Annotated* Lost World: *The Classic Adventure Novel* (Indianapolis: Wessex, 1996), xi–xii.
15 Lampadius, "Evolutionary Ideas," 90.
16 See Laura Briggs and Jodi Kelber-Kaye, "'There Is No Unauthorized Breeding in Jurassic Park': Gender and the Uses of Genetics," *NWSA Journal* 12:3 (2000): 92; Heise, "From Extinction to Electronics," 64; Paul Lauter, *From Walden Pond to Jurassic Park: Activism, Culture, and American Studies* (Durham, NC: Duke University Press, 2001), 103–4; Lennard, *Brute Force*, 129; Mitchell, *Last Dinosaur Book*, 80, 100; and Tidwell, "Life Finds a Way," 36–44.
17 In postproduction interviews, Spielberg stressed, "I wanted my dinosaurs to be animals. I wouldn't even let anyone call them monsters or creatures." Don Shay and Jody Duncan, *The Making of Jurassic Park* (New York: Ballantine, 1993), 15–16. Nevertheless, "creature" is a vague term that can refer to human or nonhuman animals. Also, the dinosaurs in the film certainly possess monstrous characteristics insofar as they represent menacing Frankensteinian creations.
18 John Ostrom, "Osteology of *Deinonychus antirrhopus,* an Unusual Theropod from the Lower Cretaceous of Montana," in *Bulletin of the Peabody Museum of Natural History* 30 (1969): 144; Robert Bakker, *The Dinosaur Heresies: New Theories Unlocking the Mystery of the Dinosaurs and Their Extinction* (New York: William Morrow, 1986), 371. For information on *Jurassic Park*'s scientific inaccuracies, see Brian Switek, *My Beloved Brontosaurus: On the Road with Old Bones, New Science, and Our Favorite Dinosaurs* (New York: Scientific American, 2013), 120–2, 139–40; Steve

Brusatte, *The Rise and Fall of the Dinosaurs: A New History of a Lost World* (New York: William Morrow, 2016), 216–25.

19 Walter Hogan, *Animals in Young Adult Fiction* (Lanham, MD: Scarecrow, 2009), 118.

20 See Kathleen Johnson, "The Ambiguous Terrain of Petkeeping in Children's Realistic Animal Stories," *Society and Animals: Journal of Human-Animal Studies* 4:1 (1996): 12; Eric Tribunella, "A Boy and His Dog: Canine Companions and the Proto-Erotics of Youth," *Children's Literature Association Quarterly* 29:3 (2004): 153.

21 Karla Armbruster, "Dog Stories and Why They Matter," in *Tydskrif vir Letterkunde* 55:3 (2018): 7.

22 Jim Kjelgaard, *Big Red* (New York: Bantam Skylark, 1992), 7, 67, 212.

23 Ibid., 7.

24 Hogan, *Animals in Young Adult Fiction*, 161.

25 Gail Melson, *Why the Wild Things Are: Animals in the Lives of Children* (Cambridge: Harvard University Press, 2001), 199.

26 See Lennard, *Brute Force*, 134–5; Damian O'Byrne, "The Mosasaurus and Immediacy in *Jurassic World*," in Jon Hackett and Seán Harrington (eds.) *Beasts of the Deep: Sea Creatures and Popular Culture* (East Barnet: John Libbey, 2018), 210–11.

27 Richard Dyer, "*Jurassic World* and Procreation Anxiety," *Film Quarterly* 69:2 (2015): 21.

28 Bradshaw, *Carnivore Minds*, 117.

29 Ibid., 127–30.

30 Ibid., 121. See also Brusatte, *Rise and Fall of the Dinosaurs*, 216–25.

31 Jane Packard, "Wolf Behavior: Reproductive, Social, Intelligent." in L. David Mech and Luigi Boitani (eds.)*Wolves: Behavior, Ecology, and Conservation* (Chicago: University of Chicago Press, 2003), 53–5.

13

Jurassic Park: Disaster, Chaos, and Existential Threat

Matthew Melia
Kingston University, UK

Introduction: Disaster Cinema

In the countdown to the end of the twentieth century, popular, commercial cinema saw the reemergence of a genre that for some time had been deemed to be extinct: the disaster movie. *Jurassic Park*, released in June 1993, is historically positioned at the start of a new wave of spectacular, big budget disaster movies that came to define the final decade of twentieth-century Hollywood cinema. The ways in which Spielberg's film anticipated the renaissance of disaster cinema have, however, been critically overlooked. This chapter proposes that is a film which incorporates, articulates (or at least is synergistic with), and anticipates a set of global, existential, and apocalyptic anxieties that were increasingly prescient as the twenty-first century loomed ever closer. The chapter considers *Jurassic Park* as a disaster film and observes how Spielberg's epic dinosaur film may be mapped against the generic criteria for disaster cinema (as this chapter will do) established by the film-scholar and critic Maurice Yacowar in his essay "The Bug in The Rug: Notes on the Disaster Genre"[1]—a benchmark genre analysis that unpacks disaster cinema into a set of subcategories/subgenres. *Jurassic Park* visually and textually quotes from, and looks back to, earlier forms of genre cinema (as Jennifer Schell has saliently observed earlier in Chapter 12) with the disaster movie present at the forefront of this reflection.

Disaster cinema had been a phenomenon of the 1970s, during which time (according to Stephen Keane—citing the now defunct website "Disaster Online") "a veritable swarm of 53 disaster movies were released."[2] While the quality of these films was often variable, among the most notable and celebrated examples of films depicting large-scale spectacular death and destruction were *Meteor* (1979), *The Poseidon Adventure* (1972), and *Earthquake* (1974). Helen Wood proposes that 1974 was the year that genre really broke with a triple whammy of big-budget disaster blockbusters including not only *Earthquake* but also *Airport 1975* and *The Towering Inferno*.[3] As Stephen Keane also observes, disaster cinema was also commonly dismissed as,

> Formulaic and spectatorial, with ingenious moments of destruction inevitably wasted on cardboard characters. These movies came and went because the narrative possibilities were limited and the law of diminishing returns was such that, after numerous planes in peril, an overturned ship, a burning skyscraper and Los Angeles laid to waste by earthquakes, there was nowhere left to go.[4]

From the mid- to late 1990s, however, cinema was again overwhelmed with images of Armageddon, apocalypse, and existential threat. Subgeneric disaster categories included films depicting natural disasters and reawakened dormant Volcanoes (*Twister* [1996],[5] *Volcano* [1997], *Dante's Peak* [1997]), giant monsters and other antagonistic creatures rampaging through the Urban metropolis (*The Lost World: Jurassic Park* [1997], *Godzilla* [1998], and even *Gremlins 2: The New Batch* [1990]),[6] alien invasions (*Independence Day* [1996], *Mars Attacks* [1996], *Men in Black* [1998], *The X-Files: I Want to Believe* [1998], *Predator 2* [1990]), and planet-killing meteors on collision course with earth (*Deep Impact* [1998], *Armageddon* [1998], *Judgement Day* [TV Movie, 1998]).[7] Extinction events and ancient, atavistic and alien threats returning to imperil humanity and its way of life became part of the premillennial cinematic landscape and vocabulary—a cultural response to the zeitgeist of mounting existential (and millenarian) uncertainty felt by many in the lead up to the end of the century.

This mounting premillennium angst is perhaps summed up by the disaster anxiety surrounding the "Y2K Threat" or "Millennium Bug" (the "narrative" of which might have been taken straight from a disaster movie). This was based around the idea that every electronic item would fail on the count of midnight December 31, 1999, as a result of an inbuilt failure to recognize the changeover to the year 2000 (misinterpreting it as 1900)—a technical oversight in all electronic machines, which threatened the worldwide collapse of all computer systems and technology leading (potentially) to the collapse of banking systems and the stock market, would cause food shortages, planes falling from the skies, and the collapse of civilization as we know it. This "existential threat" turned out to be as much of a fiction as the cinematic disasters that preceded it. The failure of computer systems, however, and the collapse of technological infrastructure *is* central to the disaster scenario of *Jurassic Park*—a film that deals with the breakdown of technology and systems of containment—resulting in unleashing an ancient, predatory, and prehistoric force within the park. Although the Y2K scare didn't begin to enter the cultural consciousness till around two years after *Jurassic Park* in 1995, we might view the film's techno-anxieties as anticipatory of later real-life panics. *Jurassic Park* stands as a preeminent disaster movie of the 1990s as it dramatized the realization, as the twentieth century came to an end, that our sense of control over our own environment was an illusion and that human error and oversight would win out.

As with its 1990s counterpart, there has been surprisingly little critical attention paid to disaster cinema of the 1970s, despite it having a prominent, culturally mainstream position—and there has been little in the way of critical consensus surrounding it as well. For instance, whether disaster cinema was classified as either a genre or a cycle of films has been the subject of some academic dispute. In his essay "Only the Stars Survive: Disaster Cinema and the 1970s" (written in 1980 at the tale-end of the genre's initial popularity with audiences) Nick Roddick alluded to the problems in bringing definition to a genre that was "never a true generic label like the Western or Horror movie" but that was "nevertheless in fairly current use and endowed for a time with a definite, if imprecise, meaning by the cinema-going public."[8]

Offering a counterpoint to this, Yacowar maintained that "disaster films constitute a sufficiently numerous, old and conventionally organized group to be considered a genre rather than a popular cycle that comes and goes"[9] (the present chapter adopts this thesis and will refer from here on in to the disaster *genre*). Roddick also contends that the heyday of disaster cinema came to an end *ca.* 1977 (after *Airport, 1977*) while others have noted that it was the "Master of Disaster," Irwin Allen's calamitous *The Swarm* (1978) that really brought the genre to its knees: a film dealing with a swarm (the size of Texas) of "African Killer Bees" which threaten the white heartland of suburban United States.[10] Despite the film's rather xenophobic subtext, it dramatizes the uncontainable out-of-control violence of the natural world (as dealt with in *Jurassic Park*). *The Swarm* was a commercial and critical failure and commenting on the efficacy of the swarm of bees as a global threat, Janet Maslin wrote that "Mr. Allen might just as well have devoted his talents to man-eating goldfish, poodles on the rampage or carnivorous canaries."[11]

Allen would go on to produce two more films for theatrical release: *Beyond the Poseidon Adventure* (1979) and *When Time Ran Out* (1980) before retreating to work in television (these are, however, largely viewed as a coda to the first wave of disaster cinema). However, despite its narrative and technical deficiencies, *The Swarm* forms part of subgeneric trend in disaster cinema from which *Jurassic Park* descends—a narrative of nature beyond the control of man. The monstrous depiction of nature that we see in *Jurassic Park* may also be traced back, perhaps more pertinently, to American postwar sci-fi B pictures such as *Them!* (1954), *It Came from Beneath the Sea!* (1955), or *The Beast from 5000 Fathoms* (1953) in which dormant prehistoric beasts are either roused from their ancient slumber by nuclear testing or—as in the case of *Them!*—microscopic creatures (in this case ants) monstrously mutated to a terrifying, colossal size by radiation. Heather Hendershot observes:

> In splitting the atom, these films show, humankind has released forces it can neither control nor understand. Though humans are responsible for the advent of giant, murderous bugs and other animals, these films do not posit any means for humans to take responsibility for their actions. Nature takes revenge on the atomic age in the bug movies, even if American military forces usually win a temporary victory.[12]

These texts find their way into the DNA of *Jurassic Park* also and its narrative of man's hubristic interference in the natural order via the misuse of science and technology. The dinosaurs of *Jurassic Park* occupy a similar cinematic space as these earlier radioactive monsters. As Raymond J. Haberski Jr. observes, Spielberg's debt to the era of 1950s B movies was also noted in a rather derisory review of *Jaws* in the *New York Times* by Stephen Faber. *Jaws*, Faber claimed, was "nothing more than a creaky, old fashioned monster picture, reminiscent of 'Creature From the Black Lagoon' … and a whole rash of grade B movies about giant ants, tarantulas, and rats on the warpath."[13] However, if these tarantulas, ants, and other mutated atomic creatures were a response to cold war nuclear anxiety, then Spielberg's dinosaurs respond to a different set of cultural concerns appropriate to the end of the twentieth century with the rise of artificial intelligence, genetic research, DNA cloning (three years later the world was witness to the birth of Dolly—not a cloned dinosaur but a much tamer sheep) and the exploitative effects of neoliberalism and globalization.

That these things might also be seen as evidence of progress, discovery, and technological, social, economic, and environmental change is neatly countered by the chaotician Ian Malcom (Jeff Goldblum) responding to park owner John Hammond (Richard Attenborough) when Hammond suggests that he and his scientists have been acting in the interests of progress and discovery: "What's so great about discovery? it's a violent penetrative act. What you call discovery I call the rape of the natural world," Malcom counters. It's worth noting here that in Michael Crichton's novel, Hammond is an unrepentant capitalist monster who is finally devoured by his own creations. Spielberg softens the character dramatically turning him into a naïve if well-meaning fool who, at the end of the film, when Grant tells him of his decision not to endorse his park, responds, "So have I." Stephen Keane notes how in *The Towering Inferno*, William Holden's building developer Jim Duncan goes through a similar reversal of position:

FIGURE 13.1 *Arriving at* Jurassic Park   **FIGURE 13.2** *Helicopter shot,* The Towering Inferno

For his part Holden survives exactly so he can go on to build a better, safer world. As he says to his grieving daughter: "All I can do now is pray to God that I can stop this from happening again." Disaster movies do not always play fair but even in death there are life lessons to be learned ... Only the repentant survive.[14]

Despite the somewhat muted end to his career, Irwin Allen had been *the* catalyzing force behind the emergence of the disaster genre from the late 1960s—as director, writer, and producer of some of its major successes—not least *The Towering Inferno* (in which capacity he worked as producer). It is to Allen's pioneering work within the genre that *Jurassic Park* is largely indebted. The sequence toward the start of the film (Figure 13.1) in which the film's protagonists approach Isla Nublar via helicopter recalls and quotes the opening sequence of a helicopter flying over San Francisco Bay in *The Towering Inferno* (Figure 13.2).

While this comparison may seem at first glance superficial, it is, however, reinforced by the use of two rousing and musically similar scores by the same composer: John Williams. From the earliest moments of the film, therefore, Spielberg homages the work of Irwin Allen, embedding an awareness of the disaster genre within his own film, and (more broadly speaking) the "golden age" of disaster cinema itself. Furthermore, both the park and the skyscraper in *Towering Inferno* are examples of what Maurice Yacowar terms "The Ship of Fools" in his generic deconstruction of the genre (and will be discussed in more detail later in this chapter).

From the end of the 1970s and into the 1980s the disaster genre's DNA started had to become absorbed or hybridized into other forms of popular cinema. Roddick observed that "Disaster Movies ... are now part of cultural history. Their narrative strategies and devices, on the other hand, are still very much current: they exemplify a trend in popular—or dominant—cinema."[15] In other words, the form, aesthetics, and tropes of the disaster film were appropriated into emerging trends in the popular cinema of the 1980s, merging (for example) with the high concept blockbuster (as Keane notes with regard to *Die Hard* [1988]).[16]

Spielberg, *Jurassic Park*, and the Disaster Movie

If Irwin Allen is widely considered to be the "founding father" of the disaster film, Spielberg is both responsible for the transitioning and hybridization of the genre from the mid-1970s (and its revitalization during the 1990s)—*Jurassic Park*, whetting the cultural appetite for the spectacular cinematic disasters that followed. Film scholar Frederick Wasser has positioned *Jaws* (1975), *Jurassic Park's* closest relation in the Spielberg canon (and the film to which it was immediately compared with in the press—see the introduction to this book), as the film that brought the disaster cycle (as he refers to it) to a close. He observes:

> *Jaws* is the end of the disaster film cycle. The contrast between *Jaws* and its immediate predecessor *The Towering Inferno* (John Guillermin), released six months earlier in the Christmas season of 1974, supports the thesis that *Jaws* gave the audience a new thrill that allowed them to reject the disaster film. While *The Towering Inferno* was a smash hit, each post-*Jaws* disaster movie declined in box office even as Spielberg and Lucas films continued to earn spectacular amounts.[17]

Jaws exhibited key aspects of disaster cinema (the town put under existential threat by a terrifying and primeval, animalistic threat; the necessity for someone to heroically rise above themselves; the failure of official leadership). It is also, Wasser argues, the film that (along with *Star Wars*) brings the mainstream dominance of the genre to an end with audiences wanting less and less to see spectacular studio-created disaster movies and more and more spectacular Spielberg and Lucas movies.

Those disaster movies produced in the wake of *Jaws* were released to diminishing box office returns, and while *Jaws* contains aspects of disaster cinema, it is part of a wider generic matrix that structures the film. Furthermore, its intermedial position between both the new wave of American cinema ("the New Hollywood") and the subsequent era of the Hollywood blockbuster, which it would usher in, places it on the peripheries of the disaster genre. Both Spielberg and George Lucas, Wasser proposes, borrowed the spectacular aesthetics (and narratives) of the genre, but at the same time displace it within a new form of "high concept" blockbuster that would become a defining (popular) cinematic form into the 1980s.

If, as Wasser claims, *Jaws* signified the beginning of the end for the disaster movie in the 1970s, then it is with some irony that *Jurassic Park* (a much needed blockbuster hit for Spielberg and a rejuvenation of the Spielberg brand after the relative disasters *Always* [1989] and *Hook* [1991])—along with *Terminator 2* (1991)—paved the way for the emergence of the digital, spectacular, and apocalyptic cinema from the mid-1990s. This reached its

FIGURE 13.3 *White House explosion in* Independence Day

peak with the runaway success of the alien invasion film *Independence Day* in 1997 and is exemplified by the sequence in which the White House is blown up to spectacular effect (Figure 13.3). Disaster cinema is defined in terms of scale and enormity (colossal threats and images of destruction)—it is an experiential form of cinema intended to be viewed on the largest screen possible. Furthermore, *Jurassic Park* was released five months after Frank Marshall's *Alive* (1993)—an adaptation of Piers Paul Read's true account of a Uruguayan Rugby Team stranded in the Andes Mountains and forced to resort to cannibalism to survive. The opening sequence of that film contains a devastating and spectacular plane crash. Subsequently the film then goes on to depict images of human devastation, flesh eating, and the struggle to survive. Prior to the explosion of disaster narratives from the mid-1990s, therefore, there was already a growing cultural appetite for such spectacular cinematic catastrophes and *Jurassic Park* is at the center of a moment which consolidated the subsequent fully fledged return of the genre.

Like *Terminator 2*, the disaster-spectacle of *Jurassic Park* provided a way of unveiling new and cutting-edge advances in digital imagery. Both films engage humanity's precarious relationship with technology and the unleashing of destructive forces it is unable to reconcile with—be they futuristic and technological or primal and prehistoric. The advent of digital SFX (of which Spielberg's company Industrial Light and Magic was at the forefront) in the 1990s expanded the possibilities and scale of the disaster genre even further—and provided the ideal forum and cinematic environment to resurrect the dinosaurs. In the final film of the *Jurassic World* trilogy, *Jurassic World: Dominion* (2022), the T-Rex is, at one point, framed in front of a drive-in cinema screen during an attack sequence (Figure 13.4)—a self-reflexive commentary on the colossal cinematic nature of Spielberg's original film (and its own dramatic *T-Rex* attack sequence).[18]

FIGURE 13.4 T-Rex *in* Jurassic World: Dominion

Furthermore, the film's dinosaurs represent the return of the primal and prehistoric. Popular cinema became preoccupied with the sudden return of the primal—be it Spielberg's dinosaurs, the meteor hurtling toward Earth in *Armageddon* (at the beginning of which New York is laid waste in spectacular fashion by a meteor shower), or the sudden appearance of an ancient dormant volcano from beneath the streets of L.A in in *Volcano* (to name a few examples). These threats were rendered using new and innovative digital technology and depicted a world increasingly untethered from any surety of itself. Furthermore, it's worth noting that *Dante's Peak* the *other* 1990s disaster film (and direct competitor to *Volcano*) was "essentially a remake of *Jaws* with the role of the shark being played by a Volcano"[19] showing not only how the disaster movie was embedded in Spielberg's work but how Spielberg was embedded in the disaster genre itself.

What, perhaps, differentiates *Jurassic Park* from these spectacular disasters is itself containedness—the films events are contained within a single locale rather than transgressing into wider, global society. That is not to say that the disaster narrative is not borne out globally across the franchise—in the *Jurassic World* films the dinosaurs escape into the world becoming part of its natural order again (in *Dominion* we are given a final montage that pairs them coexisting with their natural descendants); in *The Lost World: Jurassic Park*, T-Rex and its infant are transported, Kong-like, to San Diego where they run riot on its streets in traditional monster-movie fashion. It's worth noting here that a sequence from Crichton's novel in which a group of raptors almost reach the mainland by boat was omitted from the first film (this is repurposed in its sequel).

During its 1970s heyday the disaster genre had run parallel with the emergent New Wave of American cinema. This might (to some extent) explain the relative lack of contemporary critical discourse surrounding it—with critical, cultural, and academic attention turning increasingly toward the artistry and political seriousness of the New Hollywood and away from a form of cinema that (appeared to) pander to a more populist taste for cinematic spectacle and thrills. The cultural positioning of disaster cinema is also alluded to by Nikita Mathias who observes that the persistent reference to this body of films as Disaster "movies" and the "terminological shift from film to movie" indicates a "semantic change reflecting the rather low artistic value ascribed to these commercially produced Hollywood films."[20]

It would, however, be a mistake to suggest that disaster cinema was devoid of political seriousness or merit. As Keane (and others) have indicated the disaster movie did respond to the various social, economic, and political pressures of the 1970s—whether it be a post-Kennedy (and post- / Vietnam) failure of leadership and responsibility and the economic and class-based stratification of society (both of which are clear and present themes in *The Poseidon Adventure*, for instance—it is the overturning of this "ship of fools" which levels the playing field and forces the different representatives of US society to work together to survive).

Environmental Catastrophe

The 1990s, which were bookended by two highly controversial and catastrophic US/UK military incursions into the Persian Gulf, were also a decade defined through a variety of global catastrophes and anxieties.[21] These included race riots in the United States, genocide in Rwanda, global economic collapse (especially in the Asian markets), the irradiated legacy of Chernobyl, and growing, conspiratorial, anxieties over the impending millennium. A decade that had started on a note of optimism with the collapse of Communism and the toppling of the Berlin Wall gave way to an era increasingly affected by anxiety, paranoia, and conflict (e.g., in the Balkan States). The emergence of post-Soviet globalization also provides a framework for understanding *Jurassic Park*'s own status as a disaster film. Catalyzed by the arrival of the internet, the 1990s played host to a variety of bizarre conspiracy theories regarding perceived (and imagined) existential threats to humanity; one conspiracy that gathered cultural momentum (and which has its roots in the anti-Semitic 1903 text "The Protocols of the Elders of Zion" as well as early twentieth-century science fiction and was brought to the cultural fore) is the presence of an all-powerful, global cabal of world leaders, media barons, corporate leaders, and politicians who are really alien reptiles masquerading as humans (as in the 1980s sci-fi TV series *V* [1984])—a theory popularized by Coventry

FIGURE 13.5 *Dennis Nedry's Barbasol can*

City goalkeeper-turned self-proclaimed Messiah, David Icke, at the turn of the millennium. It's interesting to consider that giant lizards and alien invasions have such a presence in mid-1990s popular cinema (especially given these film's roots in early science fiction too). As Jewish scholar Nathan Abrams[22] noted in an email with this author, these ideas were circulating in the cultural ether during the 1990s and were "available as a reading to those who know it."[23]

There was also a growing sense of climate emergence and environmental anxiety—instigated by damage done to the ozone layer by harmful chlorofluorocarbons (CFCs) used as propellants in aerosols[24]—the type used by Dennis Nedry (Wayne Knight) to steal the dinosaur embryos. Nedry's aerosol plays a prominent role as a catalyst in the film's disaster scenario and is left polluting the natural environment of the park after he is devoured by *Dilophosaurus*. The close-up shot of Nedry's can of "Barbosol" shaving cream/dinosaur embryos lying in the mud is a conative reminder of such impending ecological disaster (Figure 13.5) and is embedded in the film's visual articulation of disaster and existential crisis and "the rape of the natural world" (to quote Malcom).[25]

Artificial Intelligence and "The Singularity"

The 1990s also gave rise to a particular existential anxiety over the evolution and potential of artificial intelligence (A.I.), termed "The Singularity." The

"Technological Singularity" as proposed by Vernor Vinge in 1993, the year of *Jurassic Park*'s release, centered around the idea that technology and A.I. would evolve to the point that it would displace humanity and human control. Vinge maintained, "We are on the edge of change comparable to the rise of human life on Earth. The precise cause of this change is the imminent creation by technology of entities with greater-than-human intelligence." [26] "The Singularity" as defined by Vinge implies the emergence and evolution of a new form of life and intelligence—a reset to Year Zero. Verge writes:

> When greater-than-human intelligence drives progress, that progress will be much more rapid. In fact, there seems no reason why progress itself would not involve the creation of still more intelligent entities—on a still-shorter time scale.[27]

He continues,

> We humans have the ability to internalize the world and conduct what-if's in our heads; we can solve many problems thousands of times faster than natural selection could. Now, by creating the means to execute those simulations at much higher speeds, we are entering a regime as radically different from our human past as we humans are from the lower animals ... This change will be a throwing-away of all the human rules, perhaps in the blink of an eye—an exponential runaway beyond any hope of control ... It's fair to call this event a singularity ("the Singularity" for the purposes of this piece). It is a point where our old models must be discarded and a new reality rules.[28]

Jurassic Park's disaster scenario (the technological breakdown of the park and the loss of control over an evolving A.I.—in this case the dinosaurs) articulates the anxieties prompted by the technological singularity. The film's artificial park environment and locale provides a simulation of the "evolutionary past" where the humans (through hubristic oversight) place themselves at the bottom of the food chain. It embodies the Year Zero point to which the singularity will eventually consign an increasingly obsolete humanity. *Jurassic Park*'s prehistoric dinosaurs are both a manufactured A.I. struggling to adapt and evolve (Ellie Sattler [Laura Dern] tells Hammond: "You have plants in this building that are poisonous, you picked them because they look good, but these are aggressive living things that have no idea what century they're in, and they'll defend themselves, violently if necessary.") and a visual reminder of the potential for humanity to be left behind in the evolutionary race. Embedded within Vinge's discourse are debates over evolution, man's relationship to technology and the hubristic assumption (and illusion) of control. Ian Malcom's celebrated statement "Life finds a way" articulates the anxieties over "The Singularity" in which the emergence of a new evolutionary era in which "God creates dinosaurs, God destroys dinosaurs. God creates Man, man destroys God. Man creates dinosaurs ... Dinosaurs eat man." Here is a narrative that presents an A.I, which, like Frankenstein's monster, is beyond the control of its naive creator—a child that (in a Kubrickian sense also) has broken its programming (a fact demonstrated in the film by the fact that the dinosaurs can, contrary to their design, adapt, change sex, and reproduce—due to the aforementioned inevitable human error, an oversight in using amphibian DNA in their programming).

Amid the vast amount of literature surrounding Spielberg's career, only a handful of commentators have really engaged with the generic presence of disaster in his work, primarily locating its nexus points as both *Jaws* (as Wasser does) and *War of the Worlds* (2003), a film that responds to, and emerges out of, the post-9/11 era, the Bush Jr. presidency and anxieties over Al-Qaeda, terrorism, and a compromised homeland security. Furthermore, Nigel Morris comments that *War of the Worlds* "retreads familiar Spielberg concerns, combining large-scale disaster-movie spectacle, science fiction fantasy involving alien contact, technological trauma, technical virtuosity, cinematic self-reflexivity and auto-citation, with family psychodrama"[29]—all of which, of course, are genetic components of *Jurassic Park*.

Disaster narratives proliferate and are hybridized *within* many of Spielberg's films. Charles-Antoine Courcoux observes: "*Jaws* represented a productive hybridization between the codes of the disaster film and those of the horror film";[30] *A.I. Artificial Intelligence* (2001) opens on a statement of ecological and environmental collapse (Medhi Achouche notes how the film recalls 1970s dystopian, post-apocalyptic narratives);[31] *Schindler's List* (1993), *Saving Private Ryan* (1998), and latterly *Bridge of Spies* (2015) turn to real historical disaster (the Holocaust, the D-Day Landings, and the construction of the Berlin Wall, respectively). *Saving Private Ryan*'s opening sequence graphically depicts the massacre of US troops as they disembark from the landing craft on Omaha Beach on D-Day. It combines spectacular vistas of chaos, catastrophe, and human annihilation (identifying markers of the disaster genre) with real-world, historical trauma.

Why then has *Jurassic Park* not more often been included in critical discourse around the 1990s disaster movie? Is it because it never spawned a major cycle of prehistoric monster films outside of its own franchise?[32] Could *Jurassic Park*'s omission from such critical study be due to the film's hybridizing (its devouring) of *other* genres and film cycles (not least the prehistoric "Lost world" thriller—as discussed by Jennifer Schell in Chapter 12 in this book)? In his study of pre-millennial and spectacular cinema (which draws on *Godzilla*, *Deep Impact*, and *Armageddon*), Geoff King also omits reference to *Jurassic Park* as anticipatory of the genre's return. King does cite *Terminator 2*, noting: "Apocalypse haunts the margins of the two *Terminator* films rather than forming the central action, but the way it is approached here makes explicit a tendency found widely in the contemporary disaster movie."[33] In *Terminator 2* (and as King has noted), a film which shares similar concerns around A.I as *Jurassic Park*, the central disaster—a nuclear apocalypse and the subsequent rise of the machines brought on by the computer Skynet—is displaced via the film's time-travel narrative, deferring its status as bona-fide "disaster movie." This is a film not about the experience of disaster but the effort to prevent it from happening in the first place. James Cameron's later 1990s mega-blockbuster *Titanic* (1998) also draws upon the disaster genre but incorporates it within a wider matrix of genres (historical drama, romantic melodrama). King notes: "The principal targets for destruction are symbols of luxury, decadence, arrogance and the smothering of 'nature.' It is no accident that disaster strikes the luxurious cruise liner in *The Poseidon Adventure* (1972) and *Titanic* (1997)."[34]

Globalization

Jurassic Park was released just over three years after the collapse of the Soviet Union. This collapse was followed by the start of the colonizing process of globalization and the dissolution of national and economic borders. Communism was replaced by unchecked and rampant free-marketeering and neoliberalism: a global culture of "survival of the fittest" in which stronger and more market-driven economies devoured weaker ones. This may be a rather simplistic summary of the process of post-Soviet globalization (and certainly *Jurassic Park*'s articulation of the processes of early 1990s globalization deserves a fuller discussion than there is space for here), but it allows us to see how this era of global economic competition and its attendant anxieties over the power of emerging global corporations might be articulated by Spielberg's film. That *Jurassic Park* is a metaphor or allegory for globalization has, so far, gone undiscussed in critical discourse around the film, The collapse of the park system and the removal of its barriers—the powering down of the fences that keep the dinosaurs in place allows the more powerful and aggressive dinosaurs (carnivores) to transgress their demarcated areas and devour the more passive dinosaurs (the herbivores)—as seen in the sequence in which the *T-Rex* suddenly appears from the trees to tuck into a flock of stampeding *Gallimimus* (while Grant, Lex, and Tim look on in horror and wonder). The film articulates a globalization-as-disaster scenario from the start, with powerful corporations exploiting the natural resources and environments of developing nations: in the sequence at the start of the film, corporate lawyer Donald Gennaro (Martin Ferrero) commandingly rides a raft up a Dominican river to where the amber is being mined on behalf of the corporation, INGEN; Dennis Nedry and the head of the rival firm "Biosyn," Lewis Dodgson (Cameron Thor), conduct their clandestine meeting on Costa

Rican soil as two economic, corporate imperialists from North America exploiting their economically beleaguered continental neighbor to the South; indigenous manual laborers are expendable (such as the construction worker devoured by a *Velociraptor* at the start of the film). The film's later emphasis on merchandising and the gift shop present further evidence of how the film articulates the "disaster" of globalization.

Jurassic Park deals with the processes of "Disneyfication," which "implies the internationalisation of the entertainment values of US mass culture. It is the idea of bigger, faster, and better entertainment with an overarching sense of uniformity worldwide ... Disneyfication is regarded as spectacle, theming, hybrid consumption, and emotional labour."[35] It does so in a highly self-aware and self-referential manner (the film includes park merchandise that was also merchandise used to promote the film itself—everything seen in the park gift shop was available in stores across the United States and elsewhere). The film's (self) awareness of "Disneyfication" is developed in *Jurassic World* in which Hammond's original statement that he "spared no expense" turning science into entertainment is taken to its natural conclusion. Humanity has become so inured and bored by cloned dinosaurs that the new park is forced to invent a new one, the *Indominus Rex* (a hybrid of *Velociraptor* and *T-Rex*), which is "bigger, scarier ... cooler." Hence Science, innovation, and progress are subordinated to the demands of the market, entertainment, and consumerism.

Ian Malcom

It's the contention of this chapter that *Jurassic Park*'s articulation (or at least the reading it offers) of the effects of globalization are central to positioning it as a disaster film apposite to the socioeconomic, financial, and political climate of the 1990s—during which time the building blocks for the current and very real environmental crisis, global economic inequality, and Western exploitation of "developing nations" were laid. In a key sequence in the film, Chaotician Ian Malcom states: "The lack of humility before nature that's being displayed here, ... uh stagger's me." Malcom's role is to be a mouthpiece for articulating the existential crises and anxieties at the heart of the film. Many of the films produced and conceived by Irwin Allen over the course of his career involved disasters arising out of man's hubristic tendencies: the Gargantuan Titanic-esque Ocean liner of *The Poseidon Adventure* and Paul Newman's impossible skyscraper in *The Towering Inferno* are two of the most striking examples. Spielberg encodes *Jurassic Park* with a variety of intertextual and thematic references to the genre for which Malcom becomes a spokesperson and means of articulation. In *The Towering Inferno*, for instance, Steve McQueen's Fire chief, O'Halloran, admonishes Newman's architect, Doug Roberts, telling him, "Now, you know there's no sure way for us to fight a fire in anything over the seventh floor, but you guys just keep building 'em as high as you can"—this dialogue resonates clearly with Malcom's oft quoted statement to John Hammond in *Jurassic Park* that "Your scientists were so pre-occupied with whether they could, they didn't stop to think whether they should." The chaotician's prophetic arguments and criticisms anchor the film to the disaster genre and articulate, for us, the many of causes of the film's breakdown of order: from a "lack of humility before nature" to neoliberalism, "Disneyfication" and rampant consumerism ("You stood on the shoulders of geniuses to accomplish something as fast as you could, and before you even knew what you had, you patented it, and packaged it, and slapped it on a plastic lunchbox") to a fundamental inability to understand the power and enormity of the scientific power being wielded ("Don't you see the danger, John, inherent in what you're doing here? Genetic power is the most awesome force the planet's ever seen, but you wield it like a kid that's found his dad's gun.").

As Katie Barnett notes, he provides a counterpoint to the naïve hubris of John Hammond:

> Malcom's primary concern is one of responsibility. He accuses Hammond and InGen of "standing on the shoulders of geniuses," using the available scientific knowledge without earning it themselves, thus breaking a chain of ethical accountability in pursuit of profit and glory. As a chaos theoretician, he is preoccupied with cause and effect, retaining a clear-eyed view of the potential consequences of the park. However, this in itself cannot save Malcom from those same consequences.[36]

Furthermore, Malcom declares of Hammond at one point: "The Crazy son of a bitch did it," a line which recalls Charlton Heston's final agonized line of dialogue in 1968s *Planet of the Apes* (a precursor of sorts to the 1970s disaster film) when on seeing the Statue of Liberty half buried in the sand famously declares "You finally really did it! You maniacs!"

Malcom's position as a chaotician and the film's emphasis on chaos theory is also a useful lens for textually framing the idea of "disaster." Chaos is at the heart of both novel and film and it is the fulcrum upon which the text's expression of disaster operates—and how our understanding of the *Jurassic Park* as a disaster film/text is mediated. Chaos theory, as Malcom demonstrates to Sattler toward the start of the film (illustrating his point via droplets of water navigating the fine hairs on her skin) rests on the idea of unpredictability in sets of complex systems, and he draws on the "Butterfly effect" analogy given by scientist Edward Lorenz in 1972—that "the flap of a butterfly's wings in Japan could create a small change in the atmosphere that might eventually lead to a tornado in Texas."[37] As Malcom explains it, "the shorthand is 'the butterfly effect.' A butterfly can flap its wings in Peking, and in Central Park, you get rain instead of sunshine." Originally conceived as a way of understanding weather systems, the "Butterfly Effect" has been reappropriated to understand and to predict within all manner of different systems—financial, technological, environmental, and the like. John Edwards uses it to try and understand financial markets within the system of globalization, for instance.[38] It rests on the idea that we cannot predict the outcome of any one event due to an infinite number of variables. *Jurassic Park* presents a complex techno/eco system in crisis. In Crichton's novel, Malcom tells Gennaro:

> I gave all this information to Hammond before he broke ground on this place. You're going to engineer a bunch of prehistoric animals and set them on an island? Fine. A lovely dream. Charming. But it won't go as planned. It is inherently unpredictable. Just as the weather is.[39]

He later tells Grant on their initial tour through the park, prior to the breakdown of the park systems:

> We have soothed ourselves into imagining sudden change as something that happens outside the normal order of things. An accident, like a car crash. Or beyond our control, like a fatal illness. We do not conceive a sudden, radical, irrational change as built into the very fabric of existence. Yet it is, And chaos theory teaches us that.[40]

In the film, as the visitors begin their tour, Malcom comments on the lack of visible dinosaurs that "the *Tyrannosaur* doesn't obey any set patterns or park schedules—the essence of chaos!" The *T-Rex*'s status as the embodiment of chaos is reinforced at the end of the film when it suddenly appears without warning to "rescue" Sattler, Grant, and the children from the encircling *Velociraptors* in the visitor's center. It is uncontainable and unpredictable, an embodiment of the living ecosystem of the park itself—a system hubristically built to be contained and controlled by Hammond. Such systems, however, are irrational and do not follow linear patterns—they are prone to "sudden, radical and irrational change" and will inevitably break down and break free from human control.

Conclusion: Maurice Yacowar and the Typology of Disaster

The breakdown and unpredictability of man-made systems is a key trope of disaster cinema dating back to its 1970s heyday. Like overturned liner in *The Poseidon Adventure* or the burning skyscraper in *The Towering Inferno*, *Jurassic Park* itself is a version what Maurice Yacowar refers to as "The

Ship of Fools" in his typology of the disaster film.⁴¹ In "The Ship of Fools" narrative, a group of disparate strangers, undertaking a dangerous journey together, must learn to work together in order to survive. As Stephen Keane notes, the "ship" is allegorical, it takes different forms. In The *Towering Inferno*, "the ship" takes the form of a luxury towering megastructure (a modern-day "Tower of Babel"). *The Poseidon Adventure* presents a literal ship—an overturned luxury ocean liner through which a party of survivors led by Gene Hackman's radical priest make their way up through the upside-down hull to safety.

In *Jurassic Park*, this "Ship" is the park itself, through which the survivors must travel (in pairs and groups). It is an unpredictable system which they must attempt to navigate and work together to restore order and human technological control. Disaster cinema is, of course, not simply about the overpowering spectacle of disaster but about the need to step up to a position of leadership from a position of reluctance (Ernest Borgnine's Grogo in *The Poseidon* adventure, for instance), as well as heroic self-sacrifice (as in the heroic death of the ageing Belle Rosen [Shelley Winters] in *The Poseidon* adventure). In *Jurassic Park*, Alan Grant's heroic arc and "journey" and his assumption of parent/guardian role to Tim and Lex (leading them to safety through the park) begins from a pedophobic position at the start of the film—established by the scare tactics he applies to a disrespectful young brat at the opening archaeological dig; big game hunter/park game Keeper Muldoon's (Bob Peck) own self-sacrifice (distracting the raptor's and allowing Sattler to reach the bunker in order to return power to the park systems) also fulfils this criteria. Is Muldoon's "heroism" altruistic or yet another example in the film of a hubristic attempt at control and mastery over nature? "Run," he tells Sattler as they are hunted by the raptors, "I've got her"—cocking his gun with a glint in his eye. The hunter however, turns out to be the hunted.

In his own analysis of the politics of disaster cinema, Keane cites Michael Ryan and Douglas Kellner's discussion of the genre's conservatism:

> [It] exhibit a return to more traditional generic conventions and depict a society in crisis attempting to solve its social and cultural problems through the ritualised legitimation of strong male leadership, the renewal of traditional values and the regeneration of institutions like the patriarchal family.⁴²

While *Jurassic Park* appears to also support this depiction of male leadership, like *Jaws*, it both looks back to romantic myths of maleness while also critiquing them.⁴³ John Hammond's performative grandfatherly-ness, for instance, is countered by the way he sends his young wards out, alone with strangers, into the untested park while he stays behind. The film is more progressive than many earlier disaster films though—Ellie Sattler never takes up a particularly maternal position in relation to the two endangered children, this is also left to Grant.

Jurassic Park can be further mapped against Yacowar's disaster criteria. He also lists "natural attack films"[44] (in which a "Human Community is pitted against a destructive force of nature") and the "city fails" narrative (in which "people are most dramatically punished for placing their faith in their own works and losing sight of their maker.").[45] *Jurassic Park* clearly falls into both categories (as detailed above). In a literal sense, the failure of the man-made technological systems that control the park and contain the animals is indicative of the "city failing." It's important to remember, however, that human greed and avarice too are at the center of this system failure—in Nedry's shutting down of the park systems while making off with the stolen embryos. Other subcategories of disaster cinema offered by Yacowar include "the Monster" narrative—in which humanity is threatened by natural, man-made, or alien creatures, incorporating variations on the Frankenstein and Golem myths and the irradiated monsters of Japanese *Kaiju* cinema.[46] *Jurassic Park* has, of course, been frequently discussed in terms of its Golem/Frankenstein narrative (not least by Nathan Abrams in Chapter 8 in this book). Earlier on in this chapter I considered the premillennial anxieties over A.I. and "the Singularity"—ideas which incorporate aspects of the Frankenstein mythology, and which can be mapped onto Spielberg's film.

Yacowar offers further categorization, citing "War" narratives as a subdivision of disaster cinema: "The war film becomes a disaster film when the imagery of carnage and destruction predominates over the elements of human conflict,"[47] he proposes. This is perhaps less immediately applicable in the case of *Jurassic Park*; the film however does present its own set of internal human conflicts that are subsumed within the carnage and destruction of the dino-narrative. Furthermore, in the final sequence we are also presented with the violent battle between *T-Rex* and the *Velociraptors*, after which the triumphant *T-Rex* asserts its dominant position at the top of the park's food chain with a terrifying roar—announcing also that it is reclaiming its position as the apex predator on the planet (displacing man). Perhaps, as Abrams does, we might also consider the "War" narrative as "The Historical" (another subcategory of disaster cinema, according to Yacowar).[48] Here, the trauma of history is framed as a disaster—certainly this is applicable to other Spielberg films such as *Schindler's List* (1993), *Saving Private Ryan* (1998), *Amistad* (1997), *Munich* (2005), and *Bridge of Spies* (2015). Abrams notes how Spielberg embeds Holocaust imagery in the film, hypothesizing that this was catalyzed by the fact that the film's production overlapped with the production of *Schindler's List* (in Poland).[49] Furthermore, in terms of "The Historical," in the simulated environment of the park, Spielberg engages with a "pre-historical" disaster narrative, confronting both the technological present with the atavistic past.

Finally, Yacowar presents "The Comic" as his final disaster subcategory. Here disaster is mitigated through absurdity, parody, self-reflexivity, and humor.⁵⁰ *Jurassic Park*'s sense of disaster and trauma is leavened by humor and comedy—primarily via the character of the Menschlichkeit Ian Malcom who, through comic dialogue and nebbishness, also draws our attention to the serious moral and ethical dilemmas at the heart of the narrative.⁵¹

To conclude then, Yacowar's analysis of the disaster genre presents a lens through which to reflect on this chapter's own analysis of *Jurassic Park* as "Disaster" movie. Spielberg's film provides a multivalent, textual space for reading the anxieties, discourses, and "disaster narratives" apposite to the end of the twentieth century. This chapter is by no means a comprehensive analysis and there is much more to be said, for instance, about *Jurassic Park* as an allegory for the more disastrous effects of globalization as well as anxieties over the rise of A.I. Jurassic Park is not only offers space to read these contemporary disaster narratives but is also anchored textually and referentially to the "golden era" of 1970s disaster films (and a reading of Yacowar helps to support this). At the same time, *Jurassic Park* anticipated and opened the way for the return of colossal existential threats in popular 1990s cinema. It was in the wake of the film that the disaster genre reclaimed its position of dominance—not unlike the *T-Rex* in the film's final moments (Figure 13.4).

Notes

1 Maurice Yacowar, "The Bug in the Rug. Notes on the Disaster Gere," in Barry Keith Grant (ed.) *Film Genre Reader IV* (Austin: University of Texas Press, 2012), 313–32.
2 Stephen Keane, *Disaster Movies: The Cinema of Catastrophe* (Camden: Wallflower Press, 2001), 18.
3 Helen Wood, "How 1974 Became the Year of the Disaster Movie," *Den of Geek*, March 15, 2018 [Online]. https://www.denofgeek.com/movies/how-1974-became-the-year-of-the-disaster-movie/. Accessed September 7, 2022.
4 Keane, *Disaster Movies*, 1.
5 The original screenplay for which was written by Michael Crichton and Anne-Marie Martin.
6 Joe Dante's *Gremlins 2* was produced by Spielberg's Amblin Entertainment. The original 1984 film *Gremlins* had also been produced by Spielberg.
7 Some of these films cited, including *Gremlins 2* and *Mars Attacks*, may be considered as disaster film–adjacent movies as they present as self-aware comic takes on the genre—demonstrating that the cultural currency of disaster cinema in mid- to late 1990s Hollywood.

8   Nick Roddick, "Only the Stars Survive: Disaster Movies in the Seventies," in David Bradby, Louis James, and Bernard Sharratt (eds.) *Performance and Politics in Popular Drama: Aspects of Popular Entertainment in Theatre, Film and Television* (Cambridge: Cambridge University Press, 1980), 243.
9   Yacowar, "The Bug in the Rug," 313.
10 Tim Brayton, "Bee Afraid," Alternate *Ending: Discovering Good Movies and Bad*, June 12, 2016 [Online]. https://www.alternateending.com/2016/06/bee-afraid.html. Accessed December 14, 2022.
11 Janet Maslin, "'The Swam' by Allen Flies onto Screens," *New York Times*, July 15, 1978 [Online]. https://www.nytimes.com/1978/07/15/archives/the-swarm-by-allen-flies-onto-screens.html. Accessed November 18, 2022.
12 Heather Hendershot, "The Golden Age of the 1950s," Date Unspecified [Online]. http://www.filmreference.com/encyclopedia/Romantic-Comedy-Yugoslavia/Science-Fiction-THE-GOLDEN-AGE-OF-THE-1950s.html. Accessed December 6, 2022.
13 Raymond J. Haberski Jr., "Sharks, Aliens and Nazis: The Crisis of Film Criticism and the Rise of Steven Spielberg," in Nigel Morris (ed.) *A Companion to Steven Spielberg* (Sussex: Wiley Blackwell, 2017), 580.
14 Keane, *Disaster Movies*, 48.
15 Roddick, Only the Stars Survive," 243.
16 Keane, *Disaster Movies*, 56–72.
17 Frederick Wasser, "Spielberg's *Jaws* and the Disaster Film," *Il Cinema E Le Altre Arti*, 7 (2015): 46.
18 The use of the drive-in reenforces the film's recognition of the franchises' b-movie heritage.
19 Hunter, Stephen, "Dante's Peaks & Valleys Acting and Plot Are a Near-Disaster, but When the Lava Flows, Film Sizzles." *Baltimore Sun*, February 6, 1997.
20 Nikita Mathias, *Disaster Cinema in Historical Perspective: Mediations of the Sublime* (Amsterdam: Amsterdam University Press 2020), 29.
21 Keane has provided the most comprehensive and reflective twenty-first-century study of the disaster film (again, however, *Jurassic Park* is an omission from his discussion) in his book *Disaster Movies: The Cinema of Catastrophe*.
22 Abrams contributes a reading of *Jurassic Park*'s Jewish subtexts in Chapter 8 in this book.
23 Private email correspondence with author, December 3, 2022.
24 CFCs in aerosol cans were banned in the latter half of the 1990s.
25 The lost Barbasol can returns and plays the central role of the McGuffin in John Sayles's unmade script for *Jurassic Park IV*.
26 Vernor Vinge, "Technological Singularity," presented at Vision-21 Symposium, March 30, 1993 [Online]. https://frc.ri.cmu.edu/~hpm/book98/com.ch1/vinge.singularity.html. Accessed December 14, 2022.

27 Ibid.
28 Ibid.
29 Nigel Morris, *The Cinema of Steven Spielberg: Empire of Light* (London: Wallflower Press), 352.
30 Charles-Antoine Courcoux, "To Be or Not to Be (Born): The Spielbergian Hero and the Uterine Challenge of the Digital Revolution," in David Roche (ed.) *Steven Spielberg: Hollywood WunderKind and Humanist* (Montpellier: Presses Universitaires de la Méditerranée 2018), 235–52.
31 Mehdi Achouche, "From *E.T.* to *A.I.*: The Evolution of Steven Spielberg's Science Fiction Fairy Tales," in David Roche (ed.) *Steven Spielberg: Hollywood WunderKind and Humanist* (Montpellier: Presses Universitaires de la Méditerranée, 2018), 129–48.
32 It did however spawn, a la the "Jawsploitation" film, a series of Roger Corman-produced B-movie/exploitation films—the *Carnosaur* series (1993, 1995, 1996).
33 Geoff King, *Spectacular Narratives: Contemporary Hollywood and Frontier Mythology* (London: I.B. Tauris, 2000), 145.
34 Ibid.
35 Jonathan Matusitz and Lauren Palermo, "The Disneyfication of the World: A Grobalisation Perspective," *Journal of Organisational Transformation & Social Change* 11:2 (2014): 91–107.
36 Barnett, Katie, "Virility, Venality and Victory: Three Faces of Masculinity in *Jurassic Park*," in Matthew Melia (ed.) *The Jurassic Park Book: Thirty Years of Spielberg's Dinosaurs* (London: Bloomsbury, 2023).
37 John Edwards, "Globalisation and the Butterfly Effect," *Finance Group Accounting and Consulting* August 22, 2017 [Online]. https://finance-group.az/en/globalization-butterfly-effect/. Accessed December 7, 2022.
38 Ibid.
39 Michael Crichton, *Jurassic Park* (London: BCA, 1991), 160.
40 Ibid., 172.
41 Yacowar, "The Bug in the Rug," 315.
42 Michael Ryan and Doug Kellner, *Camera Politica: The Politics and Ideology of Contemporary Hollywood Film* (Bloomington and Indianapolis: Indiana University Press, 1988) 23. In Keane, *Disaster Movies*, 26.
43 Matthew Melia, "Relocating the Western in *Jaws*," in I. Q. Hunter and Matthew Melia (eds.) *The Jaws Book* (London: Bloomsbury, 2020), 185–99.
44 Yacowar, "The Bug in the Rug," 313–14.
45 Ibid., 315–16.
46 Ibid., 316–17.
47 Ibid., 318.
48 Ibid.

49 Nathan Abrams, "Jew-Rassic Park," in Matthew Melia (ed.) *The Jurassic Park Book: Thirty Years of Spielberg's Dinosaurs* (London: Bloomsbury, 2023).
50 Yacowar, "The Bug in the Rug," 318.
51 Ibid.

PART THREE

Beyond *Jurassic Park*

14

Smoke and Mirrors: The 3D Reimaginings of *Jurassic Park*

Allison Whitney
Texas Tech University, USA

Introduction

Jurassic Park 3D, a stereo conversion of the 1993 original, was released theatrically in 2013 to mark the film's twentieth anniversary. In a behind-the-scenes featurette on the subsequent Blu-ray release, Steven Spielberg begins his production narrative:

> *Jurassic Park* was shot, in a sense, in my mind, in 3D, with shots of animals coming into the lens and a lot of visual foreground/background dynamics...I call them trombone effects where suddenly people and creatures are running towards the camera. There was a lot of, I think, subconscious 3D etiquette in my first approach to the material a long time ago.[1]

While Spielberg immediately clarifies that he did not literally plan *Jurassic Park* as a 3D film, (asserting that 3D was not "ready for prime time" in 1993) his opening statement frames the film's conversion as an expression of an innate spatial logic, excavated through a process of methodically re-viewing the film with a team of stereoscopy experts to generate a collective viewing experience fitting the tastes of a twenty-first-century audience. The video continues with the 3D conversion team sitting down in a screening room together, and while scenes of filmmakers watching dailies are fairly typical in behind-the-scenes content, the production narrative presented here both reinforces Spielberg's authorial imprimatur on what might otherwise be construed as a sensationalistic gimmick and locates the nostalgic appreciation of *Jurassic Park* in the theatrical setting, one that had not been available to audiences for decades.

Meanwhile, in the reception of *Jurassic Park 3D*, critics continually express surprise at its effectiveness and its avoiding the stereotypical pitfalls of 3D cinema. Even those who had dismissed *Jurassic Park* in the past not only praise its "more-impressive-than-usual-3D" but also acknowledge that, rather than merely an empty lure to sell movie tickets, the conversion cultivates a deeper admiration for the original film.[2] In his *Guardian* review, Philip French admitted that revisiting the film in IMAX 3D "and in light of the endless inferior epics I've endured over the past 20 years ... I loved every fascinating, suspenseful, frightening, skillfully calibrated minute of it."[3] Critics continually differentiate *Jurassic Park 3D* from "unnecessary post-conversion rereleases," noting that Spielberg's deep-space visual compositions not only lend themselves to the visual logic of 3D, but also reward repeat viewers by "breathing fresh excitement and immersion into scenes that many moviegoers already know by heart."[4] Indeed, in his *Screen Rant* review, Ben Kendrick comments that the film's CGI elements seem even more "realistic" in the 3D version, and while this observation glosses over the extensive digital interventions in the conversion processes that would bring the film in line with contemporary aesthetic norms, it speaks to the rhetorical power of Spielberg's premise that this version of *Jurassic Park*, with its new level of sensory engagement, allows viewers to perceive the film in its ideal state.

Jurassic Park 3D capitalizes on the original's legendary status in the history of CGI and blockbuster spectacle, while asserting that the next generation of digital technologies, including remastering and projection systems, can allow successive generations of filmgoers to not only enjoy the social experience of theatrical viewing, but to ground that experience in ever-regenerating technical novelties. *Jurassic Park 3D* accomplishes this through careful consideration of the compositional potential of 3D, and by adapting the film's self-reflexive properties, where it meditates on the implications of computerization, spectacle, and the means by which we imagine dinosaurs, in a manner that incorporates the unique sensory and spatial logic of stereoscopy and theatrical exhibition.

The Conversion Process

Stereoscopic movies create illusions by mimicking some, but not all, properties of human binocular vision, essentially projecting two films at once, one for each of the viewer's eyes. The filtering properties of 3D glasses keep the left- and right-eye images distinct, and depending on the degree of parallax, that is, the displacement of each cinematic "eye," the resulting image will appear to have varying degrees of volume, depth, and/ or emergence. Negative parallax results in the illusion that objects are in the space of the auditorium, while positive parallax places objects in depth beyond the plane of the screen. Live-action films shot in 3D typically involve camera rigs with two lenses, each one recording a slightly different image, but in the case of 3D conversion, that displacement needs to be created from a single 2D image. Stereographers will plan the spatial arrangement of each shot, generating what is akin to a topographical map indicating where each element will be located in 3D space. Once these elements are mapped out, the software generates paired images with the necessary degree of parallax to create the desired illusion, thereby transforming the spatial relationships among objects, characters, and spaces, while also impacting not only the compositional function of the frame, but also the perception of the screen as both a physical presence and a conceptual barrier between the audience and the diegetic realm.

While *Jurassic Park 3D* was exhibited with a variety of 3D projection systems, IMAX 3D deserves particular attention. The IMAX brand includes a number of theater configurations, screen sizes and shapes (including Dome screens), and both film and digital projection systems, but for the purposes of this discussion, IMAX entails exceptionally large screens, a complex sound system, and an extended history of 3D film production from 1985 to the present. Traditional IMAX screens are not just wide but also emphatically tall, with an aspect ratio of 1.43:1, and while many more recent IMAX facilities have wider aspect ratios, it remains that they are taller than most conventional screens. These dimensions are significant because feelings of sensory immersion, motion simulation, and vertigo depend in part on IMAX's engaging with the top and bottom portions of viewers' peripheral vision. While the IMAX version of *Jurassic Park 3D* retained its original aspect ratio of 1.85:1, it remains that the geometry of IMAX facilities capitalizes on feelings of vertical magnitude. For example, traditional IMAX theater design has audiences enter at the foot of the screen, allowing its towering form to impress upon them before they take their seat. While much of the IMAX filmography consists of documentary films, in 2002 they launched a digital remastering system (abbreviated DMR), which allowed for films shot on 35 mm to be transformed for screening in IMAX facilities. IMAX 15/70 film is roughly ten times that of conventional 35 mm, so DMR uses proprietary software to analyze the original image and add sufficient detail such that giant screen projection will not result in a noticeable loss of image quality.[5]

One must also situate *Jurassic Park 3D* in the historical context of the early 2010s, when both 3D and IMAX became increasingly common in mainstream film production and exhibition, including a proliferation of transformed versions of blockbuster films from decades past, marketed as both nostalgic revisitation and an opportunity for younger generations to experience canonical spectacles engineered to twenty-first-century tastes. These included 2012 releases of *Star Wars: The Phantom Menace* (1999) in 3D, *Raiders of the Lost Ark* (1981) in IMAX, and *Titanic* (1997) in both 3D and IMAX, followed in 2013 by IMAX 3D releases of *The Wizard of Oz* (1939) and *Top Gun* (1986), among many others. While theatrical and home-video releases of restored or remastered films are nothing new, the 3D and IMAX iterations of these trends are necessarily theatrical: IMAX entails immense purpose-built cinemas, while 3D requires projector and glasses systems that, with the exception of the niche market of 3D televisions and home projectors, require a cinema's apparatus.[6] The examples listed above share the characteristics of having a core audience of repeat viewers during their original runs, and subsequent fans who have committed them to memory through televised and home video releases. The 3D and IMAX iterations employ a paradoxical premise of presenting movies "as they were meant to be seen" but also "as they have never been seen before," using the intersection of nostalgia and new exhibition technologies to assert the cultural value of theatrical moviegoing. As Nell Minow exhorts in her review on RogerEbert.com, "Go see *Jurassic Park* in 3-D. Go to take your kids who were not born when it was released. Go to see it the way it should be seen, on a big screen in a theater filled with happily terrified fans."[7]

The Formal Logic of 3D

With these intersecting technological and promotional discourses in mind, let us turn to how Spielberg's notion of "subconscious 3D etiquette" manifests in both the original and its conversion. In *Jurassic Park*'s opening sequence, park workers attempt to transport a mostly unseen dinosaur, but things go awry, resulting in the violent end of one of their colleagues. The scene not only establishes themes of scientific hubris and the fragility of containment and control, but it also demonstrates a formal logic of deep perspectival compositions, strategic use of off-screen space and sound design, and atmospheric effects of darkness, foliage, mist, and shadow. The opening shots of the forest, its moving trees anticipating a commotion, are quickly followed by a group of men gazing in astonishment, setting up an editing strategy that persists throughout the film where characters stop to stare, cueing the viewer for a visual spectacle rendered through special effects. Meanwhile, the sequence employs cinematographic techniques consistent with a particular rhetoric of photographic realism embraced by Industrial Light and Magic, where hand-held camera, rack focus, and lens flares assert the presence of the profilmic camera.[8] The 3D conversion process selectively emphasizes these formal and thematic properties, and in a way that is conscious of the audiences' likely knowledge of the film, making the result both different enough to warrant a return to the cinema, while retaining a critical mass of *Jurassic Park*'s original properties. This strategy is consistent with Nick Jones's observation that contemporary Hollywood 3D releases use stereoscopy to convey novelty and "freshness" while remaining comfortably within the established norms of familiar cinematic style.[9]

The first shot of *Jurassic Park* shows jungle foliage, with a soft-focus branch in the upper portion of the frame. In the original composition this branch establishes a sense of immersion while also directing the viewer's attention to the center of the image, inspiring curiosity about what the forest may reveal. In the 3D conversion, this branch becomes not only a spatial marker but a volumetric form, one that appears suspended not only close to, but *over* the audience, an effect that is especially powerful in IMAX 3D. While one might assume that this newly volumetric branch would create a disruptive pop-out effect, its remaining out-of-focus allows it to perform its necessary spatial functions while remaining consistent with the blurred outer edges of human binocular vision. Moments later, when the camera pushes in on Muldoon (Bob Peck), a man in the foreground holds an electric prod. Not unlike the branch, the prod lapses out of focus before leaving the frame, but once rendered in 3D it becomes prominent enough to be noticed, even to the point of being comically phallic, especially given the ensuing breakdown in gendered fantasies of "man vs. Nature", but not enough to disrupt the narrative cohesion of the scene. In both of these instances, blurred objects interacting with the frame are rendered in terms that both capitalize on the 3D space while avoiding a common problem of 3D composition, where emergent objects can appear strangely amputated when they run into the rectangular edges of the screen. Moments later, when the unseen dinosaur grabs a doomed worker, the 3D conversion emphasizes one of Spielberg's "trombone effects" where the man is rapidly dragged away from the camera, using speed, distance, and perspectival space to denote the dinosaur's physical power and predatory acumen, thereby establishing another formal and thematic connection that will persist throughout the film. In each of these instances, the stereo conversion assigns portions of the image with varying degrees of parallax in order to establish the formal and thematic norms for the rest of the film, taking compositional elements that are familiar to the audience, whether from repeat viewings of *Jurassic Park* or simply Hollywood convention, and making them noticeable enough to expand on their original function. This makes the 3D conversion appear consequential, but not so much that it disrupts the original's spatial logic.

At the same time, there are moments in *Jurassic Park 3D* that do push the boundaries of 3D's more eccentric formal capabilities. One of the paradoxical features of stereoscopy is that it engages in a rhetoric of replicating natural vision even while many of its cinematic applications are markedly inconsistent with perceptual realism. For example, consider the moment in the opening sequence when the camera briefly assumes the point of view of the dinosaur inside the shipping container, peering out through rectangular slits in the walls. This moment affirms the consciousness of the as-yet-unseen dinosaur, draws upon notions of immersion and realism connected to handheld cinematography, cultivates sympathy for the frightened animal, and in an act of foreshadowing, assumes a canted angle when looking at the person the dinosaur will soon attack. In its 3D version, this scene provides a visual spectacle that is optically impossible, for while the perspective through the small slits in the container represents a point of view from a single eye, the space beyond is rendered with stereoscopic parallax. Putting aside the fact that a dinosaur's eye placement would create a visual field quite unlike a human's, the notion of using stereoscopy to create impossible images has long been part of the discourse on 3D. For example, in John Norling's 1952 description of using matching masks on a 3D image to represent looking through a keyhole, he notes that this is "an anomalous effect since key-holes are so small that real-life peering through one is limited to one eye."[10] The evocation of the keyhole effect in *Jurassic Park 3D* creates a disorienting visual experience, where a 3D frame within the frame bobs against a dark screen that seems to function both as background and foreground. This shot introduces a moment of perceptual strangeness that is brief enough to maintain narrative continuity but jarring enough to assert the film's promise of 3D offering new ways of seeing, and then associate that novelty with the visual and cognitive perspective of the dinosaur. *Jurassic Park 3D* not only assigns the viewer the task of anticipating expressive uses of depth and volume, but it also explicitly connects stereoscopy to *Jurassic Park*'s reflexivity regarding its novel visual effects and their awe-inspiring rendering of the figure of the dinosaur.

Reflexivity and Apparatus

Jurassic Park overtly positions itself as a watershed in the history of dinosaur visualization, best summarized in the concluding scene where the *T-Rex* smashes the fossilized skeleton of its ancestor, roaring as a banner reading "When Dinosaurs Ruled the Earth" flutters from the ceiling. Further, the film's constant emphasis on the powers and perils of computerization allows for significant reflexivity on its uses of CGI. *Jurassic Park 3D* inherits these reflexive modes, with the added challenge of encouraging audience reflection on the implications of stereoscopy and the state of cinematic spectacle in 2013. While common sense notions of film spectatorship maintain that any reminder of the cinematic apparatus necessarily shatters the illusion, and thus the pleasures of filmgoing, it is also true that simultaneous wonder at the amazing image and astonishment at the technical skill behind it can be compatible with viewer engagement. With this in mind, it is interesting to consider how *Jurassic Park*'s less obvious attractions are rendered in 3D, and the kinds of reflexivity they might inspire. Indeed, Alan Scherstuhl's *Village Voice* review titled "How Does *Jurassic Park 3D* Play When You Can't Fast-Forward?" acknowledges that viewer memories of the original film crystallize around the most spectacular sequences of dinosaur action, reinforced by the selective viewing made possible by home-video technologies.[11] While Scherstuhl's observations tend to focus more on issues of narrative, suspense, and metaphor, some of the most interesting implications of the 3D conversion are found in scenes that are less dependent on dinosaur effects but still manage to use 3D to raise questions about technology and spectatorship.

For example, consider the dinner scene where the main characters debate the ethical implications of the biological resurrection of extinct flora and fauna and their commercialization in the park. They sit at a table in a dark room surrounded by projection screens, a configuration that recalls the slide shows typical of museum interpretive material and multiscreen immersive media spaces common to theme park attractions. This unusual layout, with beams of light crisscrossing the dinner table, allows for persistent and prominent lens flares throughout the sequence. As Julie Turnock has argued, the presence of this kind of cinematographic artifact, particularly in films whose promotional rhetoric leans on the marvels of CGI, emerges from a rhetoric of cinematic realism grounded in 1970s American independent cinema. Produced by excess light bouncing around inside the mechanism of the camera, lens flares encode the camera's presence and indexical relationship to the represented objects, and thus they can function as a shorthand for cinematic realism even in computer-generated images generated with no camera at all.[12] The flares are particularly visible in shots where Malcolm (Jeff Goldblum) asserts his objections to the very premise of Jurassic Park with his now-iconic line of dialogue, "your scientists were so preoccupied with whether or not they could, they didn't stop to think if they should."

In the original film, the emphatic use of lens flares supports the film's reflexivity by underlining the image-projection apparatus caused by not just any bright light source, but specifically slide projectors that recall the apparatus of cinema. However, once rendered in 3D, the flares take on a strange spatial property, appearing like glowing volumetric objects suspended in space. These 3D flares not only draw attention to the original film's brand of realism, but do so in a way that, not unlike the keyhole phenomenon, deploys the paradoxical qualities of 3D cinema for both sensory and rhetorical effect. As Nick Jones explains in *Spaces Mapped and Monstrous: Digital 3D Cinema and Visual Culture*, this reimagining of "screen-based codes of realism" as volumetric forms demonstrates "how the screen plane is paradoxically retained and confirmed, even as it is also transformed .... Lens-based artifacts navigate the liminal terrain not only between analog and digital cinema but also between planar and stereoscopic exhibition, and they highlight the extent to which the screen quite literally changes shape in digital 3D."[13] The inherent reflexivity of the dialogue in the scene, where, for example, they comment on the Park's commercialization in a way that playfully ironizes the film's own promotion and merchandising, is clearly supported by the optical artifacts and their assertion of the apparatus of cinema. Once rendered in 3D, these now-volumetric artifacts allow this commentary to extend to the apparatus of twenty-first-century cinema, reflecting on the possibilities of digital technologies, their particular application in 3D, and the transforming cultural and technical significance of theatrical exhibition.

Geometry and Sensation

While the appeal of 3D movies often involves sensations of forward or lateral movement through immersive spaces, *Jurassic Park 3D* further plays with the geometry of cinematic space, both in the diegesis and in the large-screen space of the movie theater, in the ways it responds to the original film's vertical dynamics of scale. In *Spectacular Digital Effects: CGI and Contemporary Cinema*, Kristen Whissel describes how filmmakers have used digital technologies to explore the possibilities of the vertical axis, whether through gravity-defying set pieces or by emphasizing vertical magnitude, citing *Jurassic Park*'s "towering photorealistic dinosaurs" as a prime example.[14] Indeed, when the main characters arrive at Jurassic Park, their first dinosaur encounter is with a long-necked brachiosaur. While the dialogue briefly mentions the fearsome *T-Rex*, hinting at sequences to come, the brachiosaur reveal cultivates an affective position of astonishment—all presented within the relative safety of encountering a gentle herbivore.

This scene uses multiple strategies to emphasize verticality. First, the characters' gazes are directed upward, including Grant (Sam Neill) physically turning Ellie's (Laura Dern) head to look up at the dinosaur. Second, the dinosaur walks among very tall trees, stopping to eat the foliage at their highest branches. Third, once the humans leave their vehicle to get closer, their bodies provide an immediately intelligible scale marker, while the camera tilts to photograph them from an emphatically low angle, with Ellie and Grant in the foreground and the dinosaur's neck extending high above them, accompanied by dialogue about its vast dimensions. In *Jurassic Park 3D*, this dramatic staging of the act of looking up encourages the viewer to approach the scene with a suitable level of wonder, but it also demonstrates how stereoscopy's particular manipulations of perspective, volume, and bodily experience can play with the geometry of cinematic and theatrical space. The low-angle shot with Ellie and Grant in particular has the unusual effect of creating huge volumetric human bodies that appear close to the viewer, while also tying the dinosaur's vertical enormity to stereoscopic depth. This effect is even more acutely felt in IMAX 3D, where the rhetoric of vertical immensity concerning the IMAX screen further underlines the film's convergence of deep 3D space and vertigo-inducing magnitude. The dynamics of scale in this scene are particularly interesting when one considers the use of human bodies as points of reference, both as tiny figures at the foot of the dinosaur, and as bulging proxies for the audience, the latter emphasized by Ellie and Grant's volume and proximity to the viewer in the low-angle shot.

Jurassic Park 3D's strategy in connecting the spatial and sensory impact of perspectival depth and verticality comes across in low-angle shots of dinosaurs, but it also contributes to the film's themes of barriers and containment, with similarly towering/deep images looking up and through walls, fences, and partitions. For example, consider the sequence where Grant and the children Lex (Ariana Richards) and Tim (Joseph Mazzello) are climbing over the temporarily deactivated electric fence. The camera follows them as they climb, emphasizing their precarity, while the film crosscuts to Ellie's attempts to reactivate the park's power system, generating suspense through risks of falling, electrocution, and on Ellie's part, a lurking *Velociraptor*. As the characters reach the top of the fence, the camera passes underneath it while pointed directly upward, emphasizing its geometric properties as a vertical barrier. The 3D rendering of this scene creates a dramatic sensation of the fence as a planar structure, which appears to pass simultaneously in front of, above, and "at" the viewer. This moment is highly effective in the original film, but in 3D the simultaneous feelings of closeness and distance are particularly vertigo-inducing, further enhancing the feelings of suspense through sensations unique to stereoscopy. Meanwhile, in the parallel scene with Ellie, multiple shots place the camera behind metal grate partitions, furthering the themes of containment and permeability, and hinting at the point of view of the *Velociraptor* that will soon burst from the shadows. Once rendered in 3D, the spatial functions of these visual barriers become even more marked, further emphasizing the play of boundaries in the diegesis, but also attuning the viewer to the spatial layout of the scene. With these elements in place, the 3D conversion underlines the geometric complexity of the scene to such an extent that the ensuing jump scare, where the *Velociraptor* finally lunges at Ellie from behind some pipes, manages to both utilize the 3D conceit of emergent creatures threatening the audience, while also manifesting a logical extension of the film's formal sophistication.

Bodies and Binoculars

Jurassic Park 3D's integration of stereoscopic effects, reflexivity, and the film's thematic concerns extends to several more of the common phenomenological and spatial particularities of 3D, including tropes where characters use visual devices to evoke the audience's 3D glasses, the ambiguous status of the screen both as a point from which parallax extends or recedes and as a physical plane in the cinema, and the use of diffuse subjects like smoke, mist, and rain, to generate immersion and haptic sensation. Each of these is well expressed in the sequence when the characters first encounter the *T-Rex*, newly escaped from the Park's enclosure. While on a tour of the park, their vehicles stall by the *T-Rex* enclosure due to a system-wide computer failure caused by Nedry's (Wayne Knight) sabotage. As nightfall and heavy rain obscure visibility, Tim discovers a pair of night-vision binoculars under his seat, and he begins to use them to scan the area. The presence of the binoculars serves several functions: by calling attention to the act of looking it signals that a spectacle is soon to begin, while it also introduces an irony, since for all this technological sophistication, the device pointedly does not reveal the dinosaur, but only the fact that the unfortunate goat that was tethered as bait to attract the predator is now disappeared. This play of visibility is a common technique in horror and suspense films, where long takes encourage the viewer to look closely, both desiring visual information and fearing that what they might see. Meanwhile, it is important to recall that *Jurassic Park*, in a pattern that is common in effects-heavy films, often draws attention to acts of looking, as in the earlier brachiosaur reveal, which includes characters emphatically taking off their sunglasses to get a better view. In this case, however, the tone of the scene is significantly darker, both literally and thematically, as the *T-Rex*'s physical power and predatory instincts, combined with the darkness and rain, make it a source of terror. *Jurassic Park* uses these techniques to set the stage for the spectacular and terrifying appearance of the *T-Rex*, but once converted to 3D, the binoculars also evoke a tradition in 3D cinema where characters put on glasses to cue the audience for stereoscopic spectacle.[15]

When the camera assumes Tim's night-vision viewpoint, the 3D conversion extends the visual irony of the dinosaur's persistent invisibility by having this footage appear flat, choosing not to introduce any parallax in spite of its explicitly binocular origins. This might seem like an oversight, but it picks up on a dynamic established earlier in the film, where technologies of visualization are placed in contrast with the volumetric and textural properties of "real" dinosaurs, whether as fossils or living bodies. For example, early in the film at Grant and Ellie's paleontological dig site, the scene begins with close-up shots of excavators' brushes gently removing dust from fossils. This painstaking and tactile process starkly contrasts with the ensuing scene of ground-penetrating radar rendering an image of a buried fossil on a computer screen. This comparison establishes the film's thematic tension between technophobia and the awe-inspiring powers of computerization, while in the 3D conversion, this distinction comes to be marked through a contrast of volume and flatness. The texture of the fossils, the dust, the bristles on the brushes, and the hands of the paleontologists are all accentuated in 3D, while the surface of the computer screen, and the clearly digital image upon it, appears artificial and flat. This pattern repeats in the *T-Rex* sequence, where the flatness of mediated vision contrasts with the volumetric properties of the dinosaur, and the tactility of the off-screen sound cues that signal its arrival. Indeed, Tim is the first to notice the *T-Rex*'s footfalls, putting down his binoculars to ask his sister, "Did you feel that?" As he crawls toward the front of the vehicle, he notices the vibration in the glasses of water on the dashboard. This drawn-out introduction of the *T-Rex*'s physical properties generates suspense, while also remaining consistent with the film's themes of scientific hubris, where the technological viewing device fails to warn of the dinosaur's physical proximity. As the occupants in the vehicle start to hear and feel the vibration, Gennaro (Martin Ferrero) looks in the rear-view mirror, which itself vibrates, such that the haptic quite literally destabilizes the visual. Tim's night-vision view reveals the absence of the goat, soon followed by the gruesome sight of its severed leg falling onto the vehicle's sunroof.

As the scene continues, the *T-Rex* emerges from the forest, breaking through the now-deactivated electric fence. The effectiveness of the scene in part rests on the strategic use of darkness, rain, and the fragile boundaries of the vehicles' windows, which, covered in raindrops and fogged with humidity, both obscure the view of the dinosaur and mark the disintegration of the boundaries separating the humans from the predator. In the 3D conversion, these windows further accentuate the play of flatness and volume and help to enact the 3D conceit of creatures bursting from the planar surface of the screen. The most dramatic example occurs when the *T-Rex* dislodges the sunroof as it tries to extract the children from the vehicle, the children screaming as they desperately hold the glass surface separating them from the penetrating jaws. This moment is another example of Spielberg's "3D etiquette" manifesting in the spatial arrangement of the scene, where the transparency of the window allows for terrifying shots of the *T-Rex* from the children's point of view, while also evoking discourses of immersion where the cinema screen is at once barrier, window, and portal. Once rendered in actual 3D, the scene further enacts this spatial dynamic, now within the framework of flatness and volume. This conceit will persist throughout the film in predatory attack sequences, including the kitchen scene where the *Velociraptor* is briefly foiled by Lex's reflection and crashes into her rectangular image, soon followed by the moment when the humans try to escape through the building's ductwork, pursued by a *Velociraptor* who lunges upward, centered in the frame-within-the-frame of a rectangular ceiling tile.

Mirrors and Rain

Another crucial factor in this sequence is the strategic use of rain. Not only does the rainfall evoke the tradition of the dark and stormy night, while adding contingencies of mud and loss of traction to the human's attempts at self-preservation, but in the original film it also contributed to the effective merging of practical and digital effects, at once highlighting the dinosaur's texture in the low lighting, but also obscuring the seams of the image. Once rendered in 3D, however, the visual impact of the rain required interventions that transformed its spatial functions. In *The World of Jurassic Park 3D*, they mention that in their initial attempt at stereo conversion, the shift from planar to parallax composition made the rain appear to have a sharp cutoff, as if a flat curtain of water formed a barrier between the film and the audience. They addressed this by generating additional raindrops in negative parallax, such that the rain would appear to be falling throughout the auditorium. As Miriam Ross explains in *3D Cinema: Optical Illusions and Tactile Experiences*, filmmakers will often utilize rain as a bridge between areas of positive and negative parallax, the droplets providing a type of spatial coherence, in that the same rain that falls "through auditorium space … can also be seen at the back of the scene behind characters."[16] Similar interventions appear in the digital enhancement of smoke and mist, and in the scene where the *T-Rex* bursts through the wall of the bathroom, a spray of debris flying toward the viewer. In these cases, the 3D conversion capitalizes on the spatial properties of diffuse materials, originally intended to support the aesthetic coherence of practical and digital effects, to extend the play of flatness and volume into the theatrical space, the very viewing location made obligatory by *Jurassic Park 3D*'s technical specificities.

As the *T-Rex* sequence continues, survivors drive away from the charging dinosaur, only to glimpse it in the rear-view mirror bearing the standard disclaimer that "objects in mirror are closer than they appear". This moment is emblematic of Spielberg's approach to tone, the levity of the ironic reference offering a temporary release of tension in the midst of a suspenseful sequence. At the same time, given film's the persistent attention to visual devices, a mirror-based joke also acknowledges the way such technologies distort our spatial and sensory orientation. In *The World of Jurassic Park 3D*, producer Kathleen Kennedy remarks that the rear-view mirror shot takes on new meaning in 3D, referring to the way the stereographic conversion extrapolates from the spatial relationships among the viewer, the screen, and the diegetic dinosaurs. Indeed, an advertising poster for the IMAX version of *Jurassic Park 3D* cites this exact moment, with most of the poster taken up by a rear-view mirror, reflecting the *T-Rex*'s open jaws just above the "objects may be closer" warning, and with the tagline "Experience it in IMAX 3D" at the bottom of the image. While this poster reminds experienced viewers of an iconic moment in the original film, the poster does not replicate that image's composition. Rather, the dinosaur's nose obscures the edge of the mirror, as though it is emerging from the reflection. This image, like several of the 3D effects in *Jurassic Park 3D*, presents the viewer with a paradox wherein the dinosaur bears down on the viewer from two directions, both rushing up behind them and emerging from the mirror before them. This poster adapts the irony of the mirror's sensory distortion and translates it into the spatial discourse of stereoscopic cinema, doing so in a manner that both activates nostalgic affection for the original film's sensory thrills, while also asserting that the new technological capacities of IMAX 3D will offer a revitalized experience.

Twentieth Anniversary/Twenty-First Century

As a twentieth anniversary theatrical event, *Jurassic Park 3D* offered viewers an experience that made a powerful assertion about the film's legacy. Through careful extrapolation from the original's spatial and thematic logic, effective adjustments to its visual effects and sound design, and exhibition formats that require a return to the cinema, the 3D version makes *Jurassic Park* appear not only compatible with contemporary standards of cinematic spectacle, but even anticipatory of the most advanced forms of cinema production and exhibition. In many respects the IMAX 3D poster encapsulates this constellation of ideas, particularly since the dinosaur's paradoxical ability to obscure the edge of the mirror is both striking enough to attract and hold viewer attention, but subtle enough to avoid the stereotypes of crude sensationalism associated with the history of 3D filmmaking. By bringing *Jurassic Park*'s "subconscious 3D etiquette" into consciousness, *Jurassic Park 3D* makes the case that not only does it "hold up" to the twenty intervening years of advances in CGI and exhibition technology, but also that *Jurassic Park* laid the groundwork for viewers' contemporary sensibilities, both in the creation of images and in their consumption.[17]

Notes

1 *The World of Jurassic Park 3D*, directed by Laurent Bouzereau, *Jurassic Park 3D*, Universal Home Video, 2013, Blu-Ray.
2 Alan Scherstuhl, "How Does Jurassic Park 3D Play When You Can't Fast-Forward?," *Village Voice*, April 2, 2013. https://www.villagevoice.com/2013/04/02/how-does-jurassic-park-3d-play-when-you-cant-fast-forward/. Accessed October 4, 2021.
3 Philip French, "Jurassic Park 3D Review," *The Guardian*, August 24, 2013. https://www.theguardian.com/film/2013/aug/25/jurassic-park-3d-review-spielberg. Accessed May 5, 2021.
4 Ben Kendrick, "Jurassic Park 3D Review," *Screen Rant*, April 3, 2013. https://screenrant.com/jurassic-park-3d-reviews-imax/. Accessed August 8, 2021.

5   Note that while *Jurassic Park 3D* was exhibited in digital 3D in most conventional cinemas, in 2013 many IMAX 3D theatres were still using 15/70-mm film. Furthermore, the remastered IMAX version of *Jurassic Park* was exhibited in 2D in some venues, as the connection to paleontology made the film a viable programming option for IMAX facilities in museums, science centers, and other theaters with an educational mandate.

6   It is important to note that "restoration" and "remastering" are neither synonymous nor are they necessarily applicable to all re-releases, but it is fair to say that these terms are often conflated in promotional discourse.

7   Nell Minow, "*Jurassic Park 3D* Movie Review—Objects in 3D Are Closer Than They Appear," *RogerEbert.com*, April 2, 2013. https://www.rogerebert.com/reviews/jurassic-park-3d-2013. Accessed September 12, 2021.

8   Julie Turnock, "The ILM Version: Recent Digital Effects and the Aesthetics of 1970s Cinematography," *Film History* 24:2 (2012): 162.

9   Nick Jones, "Variation within Stability: Digital 3D and Film Style," *Cinema Journal* 55:1 (2015): 72.

10 John Norling, "The Stereoscopic Art," *PSA Journal: The Journal of the Photographic Society of America* (January–February 1952): 8.

11 Scherstuhl, "How Does Jurassic Park 3D Play When You Can't Fast-Forward?"

12 Turnock, "The ILM Version," 162.

13 Nick Jones., *Spaces Mapped and Monstrous: Digital 3D Cinema and Visual Culture* (New York: Columbia University Press, 2020), 163.

14 Kristen Whissel, *Spectacular Digital Effects: CGI and Contemporary Cinema* (Durham, NC: Duke University Press, 2014), 25.

15 Examples include *Spy Kids 3-D* (Robert Rodriguez, 2003) and *Avatar* (James Cameron, 2009), among others.

16 Miriam Ross, *3D Cinema: Optical Illusions and Tactile Experiences* (New York: Palgrave Macmillan, 2015), 102.

17 While *Jurassic Park* is a milestone in CGI, computerization also had a significant impact on many of the film's practical effects, including go-motion and animatronics. See Oliver Gaycken, "'Don't You Mean Extinct?': On the Circulation of Knowledge in *Jurassic Park*," in Dan North, Bob Rehak, and Michael S. Duffy (eds.) *Special Effects: New Histories/Theories/Contexts* (London: British Film Institute, 2015), 241–53.

15

The *Jurassic* Joke

Janet Staiger
University of Texas, at Austin

Introduction

Two Sunday comic strip cartoons from July 1993 are the starting point for this inquiry into the cultural implications of *Jurassic Park* (1993). In one, *Outland*, by Berkeley Breathed, "the half-cat, half-billionaire Bill the Gates prepares for a final, desperate attempt to separate the cat DNA from his own." The experiment works, and Bill declares, "Cool. Let IBM try that." However, the experiment is not totally successful since Bill's DNA and characteristics are also beamed into a television set. Bill says, "Ya mean my habit of swallowing up my enemies whole? We've created a horrible mutant!" Indeed, the final panel shows Barney, the dinosaur, on the PBS children's show eating the show's small child Heather.[1]

In the second comic strip, *Doonesbury*, by G. B. Trudeau, in the first panel Mike and Zonker are on hillside being shot at by people in a helicopter; they leap over the cliff's edge and land on a dinosaur. In the fourth panel, they jump onto a car driving by and then, pursued by the dinosaur, fly off another cliff over and into a lake. In the last panel, while surrounded by sharks, Mike thinks, "Boy, I'll be glad when summer's over," while Zonker cries, "where's the sub? Where's the sub?"[2]

These comic strips demonstrate the seepage of *Jurassic Park* into wider culture. They are also examples of what Sigmund Freud calls a tendentious joke—a joke that involves aggression. Taking a critical interest in these sorts of jokes allows an analysis of culture, especially, here, a culture surrounding the social functions of movies and television.

Indeed, Freud writes at the start of his book, *Jokes and Their Relation to the Unconscious,* that two reasons exist to study jokes: first, he believes in "an intimate connection between all mental happenings" and, second, "a new joke acts almost like an event of universal interest; it is passed from one person to another like the news of the latest victory."[3]

Two aspects of this latter reason—"person to person" and "news of the latest victory"—matter in studying the history of culture, not just culture. The processes of social change are important. Thus, explanations for circulation of cultural discourses—for example, person to person—need studying. Moreover, not only is a victory announced in a joke, but the circulating news (or in this case the joke) also implies a vicarious social participation in the event. As cultural historian Robert Darnton puts it about a joke played by printers against their bourgeois employers, studying the joke does not prove the workers hated their bosses (a truism), but it helps to "see how workers made their experience meaningful by playing with themes of their culture."[4] The case of *Jurassic Park* jokes is valuable because of their quantitative status. According to a *U.S. News and World Report* writer, one month after the opening of Steven Spielberg's movie, the phrase "Jurassic Park" turned up more than two hundred times in a Nexis search of newspapers and magazines. In contrast, the writer pointed out that "even 'the mother of all cliches,' derived from the contemporaneous Gulf War's 'mother of all battles,' appeared only 92 times in a comparable time period."[5] A similar search carried out for this chapter revealed that the word "Jurassic" by itself or in combination with another word occurred 2,631 times in the same time span.[6] Obviously, this numerical comparison suggests some major "victories" being socially shared (as well as the victory of the Hollywood publicist).

A second reason to examine the *Jurassic* joke is that while the movie *Jurassic Park* is easily linked to both the melodrama and horror genres (one reviewer describes it as being about families and the undead), the film seems to have provoked an unusual outpouring of jokes out of line with the genres for the film's content. Moreover, although the film was criticized for possibly scaring young children, children were ready to play with its elements, taking up the roles of the terrifying dinosaurs. So its cultural anomalies are pertinent to thinking about how films interact with society and our culture, becoming part of our wider social and media discourse.

In fact, a third stimulus for this study came from watching two young boys returning from seeing the movie. The elder brother was playing at pretending that he was the spitting *Dilophosaurus* that attacks the computer whiz Dennis Nedry (Wayne Knight). The boy did this by opening and closing an umbrella in front of him. Both boys were giggling tremendously over the analogy. This identification pattern of the children with the powerful dinosaur rather than the human victim is also evident in children assuming the roles of dinosaurs in video games. Beyond these real-life examples, children's identification with dinosaurs was a running motif in the extremely popular "Calvin and Hobbes" cartoon[7] but even appeared for the daughter, Hilary, in the "Sally Forth" family series in fall 1993.[8] As any parent of the era knows, the Barney costume (the sweet PBS television dinosaur version) was particularly ubiquitous for very young children at Halloween in the mid-1990s. Thus, the cultural pervasiveness, the connections of melodrama and horror to jokes, and questions of identification and power motivate this investigation.

This chapter will briefly review Freud's description, categorization, and analysis of jokes because his work provides several helpful distinctions about these actions.[9] It will provide a database for considering what happens culturally with jokes related to *Jurassic Park*. I will provide thirty-two instances of the comic or joking use of the term "Jurassic" that occurred in the public news between June 10, 1993, and December 31, 1993. The chapter will then propose some hypotheses about how the jokes functioned in promoting certain possibilities of identification. These hypotheses will be of use in understanding the economy of jokes using current cultural material: our latest news of "victories," the fluidity of identification for children (and other people), and the importance of thinking about the interconnections between affect and genres (here melodrama and horror).

Jokes and *Jurassic Park*

In his 1905 book on jokes and a 1927 essay on "Humour," Freud splits the concept of laughter into three categories: humor, comic, and jokes.[10] Humor is a process that involves an affective response such as anger or pity, but the story saves that affect from happening. Examples here would be "gallows" humor or the type of stories told by Mark Twain. The comic occurs when one person sees in another person or a situation an unintended discovery about relations. Freud lists mimicry, caricature, and parody as typical instances in this category (although he notes that parody may edge into the third category of jokes). Jokes offer pleasure through the process or technique of the telling. Freud makes further distinctions among these three in the discussion below:

Chart 1

Freud on Laughter

A. Techniques of Construction Based on:		
Humor	Comic	Jokes
Displacement	Comparison	Multiple
[1] Purposes		
Pleasure in affect	Pleasure in ideation	Multiple
[2] Number of people involved		Multiple
1 or 2	2	2 or 3
[3] Economies of expenditure in		
<u>affect</u>: avoid anger, pity, horror, disgust	<u>ideation</u> (upon cathexis): if difference is unutilizable and capable of discharge	<u>inhibition</u>: prevent from being constructed or circumvent
[4] Based in		
preconscious (superego consoling the ego)[b]; ego refuses to be distressed by reality	preconscious	unconscious
[5] "Intensity" of pleasure		
lowest	middle	greatest

II. General Techniques of Construction Based on Psychic Work

Verbal Jokes—Condensation produces a substitute-formation

> Composite words
>
> Same work/phrase used two ways, but both ways are meaningful
>
> Double meanings

Conceptual Jokes

> Displacement
>
> Absurdity
>
> Faulty reasoning
>
> Representation by the opposite or overstatement (irony)
>
> Indirect representation (allusion or analogy)

III. Purposes Based on Psychic Aims

Non-tendentious jokes (innocent jokes)—aim is in itself

Tendentious Jokes—aim is aggression through exposure

> Obscene (smut)—sexual aggression against a person
>
> Hostile—against a person
>
> Cynical—against an institution
>
> Skeptical—against our certainty of knowledge (truth)
>
> - The hope is to "bribe" the third person (the hearer) with the pleasure of laughter to function as an ally with the first person (the joke-teller) against the second person/institution/belief against whom the aggression is directed.
>
> - The aggression is indirect, protecting the joke partners.

- The effect on the joke-teller and hearer should be the same: overcoming inhibitions, but for the joke-teller the inhibition is internal, for the hearer the inhibition is external. Moreover, the pleasure should be greater for the hearer.

IV. Psychogenesis of Jokes

Play—child plays with words and thoughts to produce pleasure until child is interested in avoiding criticism for failing to make sense.

Jest—child's ability to say something without being forbidden by criticism.

Joke—when jest's content has substance or value, jest becomes a joke; jokes are still framed to avoid criticism.

[a] In "Humor" Freud changes the number of people involved from one to one or two.

[b] Freud adds the ego/superego model in "Humor."

Humor is the least aggressive method of provoking laughter while the most aggressive, jokes, may be non-tendentious or purposefully hostile and antagonistic. In the latter case, Freud argues that the teller of the joke seeks a "neutral" hearer of it to become complicit in the aggression being pursued against the object of the joke. These tendentious jokes run from attacks on the person ("obscene," which is a sexual aggression, or "hostile"), to those against an institution ("cynical"), and, finally, against our certainty of knowledge ("skeptical").

In reviewing jokes during the first month after the release of *Jurassic Park* and more occasionally for the following five months, a set of thirty-two examples provide good instances by which to follow the possibilities.

Chart 2

Selected Jurassic Jokes in Mid- to End of 1993

#	Date	Text	Teller	Comic or Joke Type
1	6–21	Do you like dinosaurs? You bet Jurassic!	David Letterman	O

2	6–22	1980s bosses are willing to unleash environmental disasters	citizen	H—1980s bosses of finance, government, science
3	6–24	Democrats are creating a "taxaurus"	Sen. Robert Dole	H—Democrats
4	6–25	Rangers' new stadium is a Jurassic Park	sportswriter	H—Texas Rangers
5	6–25	Barney's is a "prissy little purple dinosaur" (ad campaign)	LA clothing competitor	H—NYC clothing competitor
6	6–25	Supercollider is devouring everything—Jurassic Pork	US Rep. Sherrod Brown	H—Supercollider
7	6–25	Breeder technology is expensive, scary for environment and big fantasy—Jurassic Pork [later used for many entitlement programs]	Environmental activist group	H—Breeder technology
8	6–28	His savings institution makes kinds of loans considered extinct by others—Jurassic Savings	Savings vice president	C—Savings & Loan
9	6–28	White House aides do not recognize threat of old media (dinosaurs)	*Newsweek* journalist	H—White House aides
10	6–29	Senators are extinct population to be kept alive to feed on public	citizen	C—Canadian Senate
11	6–30	Congresspeople are fossils: tax us to death in Geriatric Park	citizen	C—U.S. Congress
12	6–30	Politicians are small-brained creatures in a fantasy land	citizen	H—Politicians

13	6–30	Justice O'Connor is digging and cloning monster (old Southern voting rights)—*Jurassic Park* jurisprudence	*New York Times* writer	H—Justice Sandra Day O'Connor
14	7–4	Cher and other old singers—Jurassic Rock	*Newsweek* critic	H—Cher, older rock stars
15	7–4	Developers are always devouring	Business columnist	H—Developers of new Shea stadium
16	7–5	Networks' selling rules no longer operating in new cable world— Networsic Park Upfrontasaurus is dying	President of Turner Broadcasting Sales	H—Networks
17	7–5 to 7–11	Hollywood sequels to *Jurassic Park*:	Knight-Ridder writers and *Philadelphia Daily* writers	H—filmmakers

Barefoot in Jurassic Park

Sunday in Jurassic Park with George

Jurassic Gorky Park

Jurassic MacArthur Park

Jurassic Good Man, Charlie Brown

Geriatric Park

Jurassic Hyde Park

Jurassic Shibe Park

You Bet Your Assic Park

Giraffic Park

THE *JURASSIC* JOKE

Gastric Park

Gymnastic Park

18	7–6	NEA is out-of-date—" an aesthetic Jurassic Park"	attorney for NEA	C—NEA
19	7–6	Filmmakers may confuse kids about dinosaurs; threat to family	Shari Lewis and Lamb Chop	H—*Jurassic Park* filmmakers
20	7–7	IBM is "a high-tech theme park full of dinosaurs"	Microsoft	H—IBM
21	7–12	Perks from dinosaur merchandise—Jurassic Perks	*Orlando Sentinel*	H—Merchandisers
22	7–12	Cloning dead leaders— Jurassic White House	*Washington Post*	H—Government leaders
23	7–12	Lawyers are scarier than (and like) dinosaurs in "The Firm," a Juristic Park	*NY Times* film critic James Gorman	H—lawyers
24	7–19	Bill Gates gobbles up competitors	Berkley Breathed ("Outland")	H—Microsoft
25	7–24	Thriller movies are exhausting	G. B. Trudeau ("Doonesbury")	C—Hollywood thrill movies
26	8–22	AT&T is like Jurassic dinosaur-- fleet at devouring, master of domain, reborn	business commentator	Comic
27	9–10	Aircraft carriers are large and inefficient—Jurassic Fleet	*Mother Jones*	H—US naval aircraft carriers
28	9–22	Pope's hat blocks viewing *Jurassic Park*	Gary Larsen ("Far Side")	Comic

29	9–28	Bette Midler is "jurassified" at Radio City Hall concert	Michael Musto	H—Bette Midler
30	10–12	Ziggy's dog saw *Jurassic Park*; now afraid of Barney	Tom Wilson("Ziggy")	H—*Jurassic Park* filmmakers
31	10–17	Caveman admits to poaching in *Jurassic Park*	Wagner ("Grin and Bear It")	Comic
32	12–6	Dinosaurs try to park— Jurassic parking	Gary Larsen("Far Side")	C—parking lots

Object of the Comic or Joke (the labeling of "hostile" versus "cynical" is based on content): If tendentious joke, type is O = obscene, H = hostile, C = cynical, and S = skeptical.

These jokes range from the slightly off-color David Letterman joke (Chart 2, joke #1)—you bet Jurassic!—to much more aggression such as lawyers being more scary than dinosaurs—a "juristic" park (#23). In all, much is available for thinking about the cultural invasion of the film.

Hypothesis 1: The (Political) Economy of Jurassic Jokes

To consider economies of these jokes, some patterns to their structure are worth observing. For the first month after the film's release, two stand out:

Chart 3

Tellers and Types of Dinosaurs

According to teller, what is the threat or bad object?	Type of Dinosaur		
	Devouring	Fossilized	Total
1. Dinosaurs	4	9	13

2.	Enemies of dinosaurs	4	0	4
3.	Creators of dinosaurs	5	3	8
Total		13	12	25

The first pattern of these early jokes has to do with how the dinosaurs are represented. Are they aggressive and cunning or are they fossilized and old? A second pattern involves how the joke teller characterizes where the threat exists. Is it the dinosaur itself? Perhaps, conversely, is it the enemies of the dinosaur? Or could it be the creators of the dinosaurs?

Notice that when dinosaurs are the threat, their threat lies twice as often with being fossilized, old, clumsy, small-brained, or undead. Conversely, when the threat is the enemies of the dinosaurs, dinosaurs are routinely characterized as devouring, strong, or aggressive. Overall, dinosaurs are characterized equally as fossilized (12) or devouring (13).

What can these observations tell us about the cultural functions of Jurassic jokes? Depending upon the epistemological theory of how people process movies (cognitive psychology or semiology), dinosaurs seem to fit easily into several schemata or have multiple signifieds. The sources for the schemata or signifieds are cultural and contextual. The wide extratextual diversity of characterizing dinosaurs, from PBS's Barney to Calvin's *Tyrannosaurus Rex*, is obvious. Moreover, *Jurassic Park*—while probably not much of a player in this portion of the game since audiences come to the film with these schemata or signifying systems—also represents dinosaurs as having a range of characteristics. The herbivores are depicted as gentle, potential pets while the *Velociraptors* are vicious, cunning animal eaters.

To understand the media and cultural pervasiveness of Jurassic jokes, perhaps one explanation might be how suitable dinosaurs are for a variety of identifications and allegiances. Looking at the possibilities in Chart 3, minimally, a massive permutation set is ready for joke-tellers to construct objects for jocular attacks on an array of grounds from being fossilized—a geriatric park—to aggressive—the juristic park.

What is perhaps more valuable to notice, however, are the patterns involving who is telling what type of joke. In cases of four tellers who identified with the dinosaurs against their enemies, all the tellers might be said to be in the positions of some power. The four cases are a Los Angeles clothing store (#5), a savings-and-loan vice president (#8), a *Newsweek* journalist (#9), and a business commentator (#26). In Jurassic jokes, the tellers who were inclined to joke by adapting the persona of the dinosaur are those already in power.

In many other cases, the joke-tellers might be considered the equals of those they target—although the tellers may also adopt roles of being victims to those they accuse of being either dinosaurs or creators of dinosaurs. Examples would include U.S. Representative Sherrod Brown calling the supercollider "Jurassic Pork" (#6) or the *New York Times* suggesting Supreme Court Justice Sandra Day O'Connor was digging up and cloning an extinct voting rights act with her *Jurassic Park* jurisprudence (#13) or even music critics accusing Cher of performing Jurassic rock (#14). A choice one occurs in #20. The actual joke reported to be circulating at Microsoft in its email goes as follows: "What's the difference between *Jurassic Park* and IBM? One is a high-tech theme park full of dinosaurs and the other is a Steven Spielberg movie."[11]

A third situation does exist. In some cases the average citizen or activists gain a lick at those in power. Examples include the liberal journal *Mother Jones* accusing the U.S. Navy of having a Jurassic Fleet (#27) or citizens comparing politicians to small-brained, old dinosaurs (#12). Often comedians stand in for citizens. A good instance of this is the Shari Lewis and Lamb Chop joke (#19). The joke was reported: "After Lamb Chop noted that she was anxious to see the movie 'Jurassic Park,' Lewis inquired as to whether her sheepish [sic] sidekick was really familiar with the subject matter of the film. 'Sure' she snapped back, 'It's Barney goes ballistic.' 'No,' corrected Lewis, 'Barney is a domesticated dinosaur. Do you know what that means?' 'Yeh,' said Lamb Chop, 'he only eats families.'"[12]

In lovely and convoluted displacement and indirect allusion, Lewis expresses the fears of several parents who condemned the film for the possible negative associations it might produce toward PBS's Barney. Of course, other parents who were sick of the sugar-sweet repetitious Barney applauded a Don Wright cartoon of June 15, 1993, in which *Jurassic Park* dinosaurs apparently gave Barney what some parents thought he deserved.[13] This is a case in which parents as disempowered—at least in the case of their children's attachment to Barney—identified with and was empowered by dinosaurs against other dinosaurs.

As Freud put it so well, if tendentious jokes function as oblique attacks on our enemies, the circulation of those jokes announce the brief victory of the teller and those who laugh along with the teller. However, as scholars such as Mick Eaton have noted, jokes come from those in positions of power as well as those without it.[14] Thus, it is important to avoid the tendency in so many applications of Freud of assuming essential power relations, including gender, sexuality, class, or ethnicity, and dominance/power versus subordination. Although some jokes may be signs of resistance (e.g., Lewis pitting parents without access to media against the Spielberg powerhouse at Universal), those jokes can only be considered light tactical glances. Moreover, at least among those Jurassic jokes reported in the media, the blows were more often from the powerful against other powerful competitors. That aggressors attacked other aggressors seems uncannily appropriate for this set of jokes, for they derive from a movie constructed not only to be a blockbuster but also to be a merchandising and amusement landslide.[15] This is dinosaurs and theme parks as big business, and nobody was confused about that.

Hypothesis 2: The Fluidity and Fun of Identification

By now, the argument about the identification of children with dinosaurs should be foreseen. From the point of view of a child, parents and other adults have very similar-scale relations to dinosaurs. Moreover, parents can be both "fossils" and "aggressive." To take on the roles of dinosaurs turns children into equals with adults, with all those individuals' apparent power *and* their inexplicable variety of personalities—affectionate to threatening. Sometimes Calvin fights dinosaurs; sometimes he is one. Sometimes the two boys jesting with the umbrella can suggest that they, too, are able to be scary.

Here, the issue of sex and gender needs to be considered. At least in a basic-response schema, in our larger culture, dinosaurs seem to be sexed and gendered stereotypically: *T-Rexes* are obviously male rather than female. (The term "Rex" may help produce this.) Other dinosaurs seem to be of either sex or gender. However, the film *Jurassic Park* is quite specific and rather assertive about allocating the sexes and genders of its dinosaurs. According to the park's creators, they are all females. The range of female dinosaur behavior, however, is part of the plot's development that the conventions of the horror genre and the movie's advertising led audiences to anticipate. Although the film starts off with the cow-like *Brachiosaurus* grazing pastorally in a meadow, the story ends up in the kitchen with cunning and angry *Velociraptors* hunting down the children.

Moreover, as these beasts become more threatening, they rise up on their hind legs and grow tremendously sharp teeth and claws. Barbara Creed argues that horror films can depict not only the horror of the "castrated" woman but also other terrors: the woman in relation to her reproductive and maternal functions and the woman as castrating.[16] *Jurassic Park* seems willing to run the gamut of such threats especially when the computer expert drops the dinosaur eggs, and they wash into the mud and out into the ocean (oh no! a sequel). The chaos expert predicts that these animals will not be content to remain infertile. The dinosaurs will indiscriminately mutate so they can reproduce. The paleontologist speculates that these dinosaurs can fly (like witches?). And the vagina dentata display in the final kitchen chase scene is hardly a subtext.

Again, the *Tyrannosaurus Rex* seems male so that the end of the movie appears to be the victory of patriarchy over the feminine, especially in relation to the melodrama that interweaves with the horror plotline. That, however, is a subjective interpretation. No matter what *T-Rex*'s sex is,

Barney is a *Tyrannosaurus Rex*, and Calvin's and Hilary's costumes are also of that species. Considered the most threatening and powerful dinosaur, the *T-Rex* is the dinosaur of choice when children play. Although some ambiguity about that choice exists in terms of sex and gender identification, no ambiguity remains about the projection of power. When the child chooses to identify with Jurassic dinosaurs, the Jurassic joke is on the mothers and fathers whom the child fears and hopes to defend against if not replaced.

Hypothesis 3: Genres and Affect

These observations bring out the third and last set of hypotheses around the Jurassic jokes: the connections of genre to bursts of laughter. That probably as much laughing as gasping occurred during the screenings of *Jurassic Park* that I attended in its first six months of release is not unusual for many post-1960s horror films as the genre conventions changed to incorporate comedy and jokes as routine.[17] Although, for *Jurassic Park*, the affective order was generally from laughing (the death of the lawyer on the toilet) to bodily reactions against threats (the chase by the raptors), other classics in the horror genre—*The Texas Chain Saw Massacre* (Toby Hooper, 1974) or *Nightmare on Elm Street* (Wes Craven, 1984)—solicit mixes of these responses throughout the movies. Recent horror films are much more duplicitous than they are sometimes analyzed to be.

Moreover, *Jurassic Park* might also be categorized as a melodrama. The motif of finding proper fathers permeates the narrative. Thus, the connection between joking and other affects is very linked, both psychically and culturally. One possible argument might be that the emotions of laughter and terror seem paired in an inverse relation of power: the aggression and dominance of the joke-tellers and hearers versus the powerlessness for the one threatened by the monstrous. For those taking on the power role of laughing, being scared is delayed or staved off.

If Jurassic jokes entered our cultural currency in an unusually powerful way through a blockbuster movie, could it also be because the symbolism was particularly flexible in relation to horror and its inhibitions? Throughout *Jokes and Their Relation to the Unconscious*, Freud remarks about evaluating jokes. For him, the better jokes are the ones with the greater psychic economy manifested by the more bodily laugh. Freud writes, "joking analogies are very seldom able to provoke the explosive laugh which signals a good joke" and "a non-tendentious joke scarcely ever achieves the sudden burst of laughter which makes tendentious ones so irresistible."[18]

In a 1985 essay about affective genres, Richard Dyer writes: "[Porn] is like genres such as the weepie and the thriller, and also low or vulgar comedy. Like all of these, it is supposed to have an effect that is registered in the spectator's body—s/he weeps, gets goose bumps, rolls about laughing, comes."[19] Dyer wisely emphasizes the spectator's physical response as critically important as well as the lower cultural status of such affective experiences as a consequence. Linda Williams's 1991 essay, "Film Bodies," duplicates Dyer's argument, presenting a typology for what she labels as the "gross-out" genres of pornography, horror, and melodrama with each solved by originary fantasies: for pornography, seduction solves the problem of the origin of sexual desire; for horror, castration solves the problem of sexual difference; for melodrama, the family romance and return to origins solves the problem of the self.[20] Comedy is not included in her list although some forms of jokes might well be considered "gross-out" jokes. See, for example, the contemporaneous "sick jokes" circulating around Christa McAuliffe after the 1986 Challenger rocket disaster that Constance Penley and Patricia Mellencamp have analyzed.[21]

Although it is tempting to argue for inserting a new grouping to Williams's schema, comedy, or more specifically tendentious jokes, it is not a genre but somewhat like melodrama—both broader and yet more specific. While it might be possible to speak of a humorous, comic, or joking movie, scholars would be hard-pressed to describe its conventions unless they connected those conventions to some other standard genre such as the romance or adventure plot structure. Then the film's label would become screwball comedy or the comic quest, with adjectives modifying the genre's noun. Additionally, of course, any film might incorporate joking moments.[22]

Moreover, Williams's argument requires the physical representation of bodily excess and ecstasy to be shown within the movie, with an equivalent bodily response hopefully duplicated by the spectator watching the movie. This works well for the three genres Williams describes, but it will not work for comedy. Rather the spectator's bodily response—the burst of laughter—may be quite at odds with the affect being represented on the screen. Moreover, jokes do not derive directly from originary fantasies, which is part of Williams's argument about the three gross-out ones. According to Freud, jokes are related to economies around inhibitions. It is these differences that makes necessary the rejection of adding comedy to Williams's list as well as propelling further inquiry into what is going on. Of course, Dyer's argument about bodily effects of films on spectators still stands; he was considering a different question: that of the relation between affect and cultural categorizations between low and high culture.

Indeed, laughter sometimes occurs while watching pornographic, horror, and melodramatic movies, and it certainly occurred for audiences of *Jurassic Park*. Why this happened depends upon whether the laughter was a consequence of, in Freudian categorization, humor, the comic, or a joke. In the case of a tendentious joke in which the movie is the joke-teller, the spectator's reaction might constitute a declaration of alliance with the film, a willingness to be bribed to participate in the array of affects about to be strung in the amusement chain, priming the audience members, as it were, to rid themselves of particular inhibitions and open themselves to the various affective reactions about to be solicited.[23] It appears that that is the case for *Jurassic Park*.

Two scenes from *Jurassic Park* are illustrative and supportive of the thesis that the humor involved solicitations of allegiance with the filmmakers: the deaths of the lawyer, Donald Genarro (Martin Ferrero), and Dennis Nedry, the computer expert. The plot has already invited antipathy toward them. If someone must go (and someone does in a horror movie), those two people seem ready to be the first sacrifices. The abject conditions of their death—the implied excrement, the spitting dinosaur—increase the disgust and their defeat. An audience laugh adds another bodily expulsion. The audience is "with" the joke-teller in conquering death through the vehicle of the loss of the two "unnecessary" characters. Audiences laugh—here in the horror genre—in the face of death, the death of someone other than them. The joking relation has placed them in collusion with the maker of the movie, the powerful, the immortal, the undead.

While writing *Jokes and Their Relation to the Unconscious*, Freud was not yet paying the theoretical attention to aggression that he would later connect to sadomasochism and the death instinct. What the effect of his later thoughts might have had on his work on laughter should he have returned to the question of tendentious jokes is unknown. However, even in 1905, he described the joking process as rebellion against authorities. Although laughing during a pornographic, melodramatic, or horror movie might be due to a spectator finding humor or the comic there, the incorporation of tendentious jokes in films of those genres and the solicitation from the audiences of bursts of laughter should be thought through when critics analyze the particular dynamics of any specific text. This seems particularly necessary in post-1960s genre films that seem such an ambiguous and ambitious network of conventions.

While this chapter has considered the extratextual phenomenon of Jurassic jokes, the argument is that the joke-work of the movie *Jurassic Park* provides the psychic economy and schematic homology for many of the jokes that circulated in the culture surrounding the film upon its release in 1993. For example, the film's plot primes the extratextual, public jokes about lawyers and computer experts. The film is about power, as are all tendentious jokes. Who has it? How can one obtain it? Whom can be bribed to be with the joke's maker? Who needs to be defeated but secretly desired as the Other toward whom this joke is hostilely directed? As Mary Douglas argues, Freud may be right about figuring out jokes from their structures, but to understand them, they need to be considered an utterance within a total situation.[24]

Given this, and returning to the Breathed cartoon about Gates, it seems apt since it is a fine network of many Jurassic motifs: genetic engineering gone amuck; IBM versus Microsoft and both as dangerous; dinosaurs as emotionally unpredictable and a threat to children; and the capricious narrative plot full of surprising twists.

In summary, the three hypotheses about Jurassic jokes are initial thoughts about the plurality of schemata or signifieds circulating with the culture and providing a variety of positions to take up in the joking network. These networks permit a fluidity of subject positions for individuals, including children, which raises further queries about originary fantasies in melodrama and horror, inhibitions, and power relations. Finally, psychic permissions to joke about *Jurassic Park* have in this case been offered by the text itself. This historical fact complicates the assignment of the extratextual jokes to political categories of containment versus resistance. People in power make jokes too. It is this perversity of jokes that reveals their psychic value and permits their complex social functions.

Notes

1 Berkeley Breathed, "Outland," July 19, 1993.
2 G. B. Trudeau, "Doonesbury," July 24, 1993.
3 Sigmund Freud, *Jokes and Their Relation to the Unconscious*, trans. James Strachey (New York: W. W. Norton, 1963), 15.
4 Robert Darnton, *The Great Cat Massacre: And Other Episodes in French Cultural History* (New York: Vintage Books, 1985), 99.
5 Amy Bernstein, 'Eye on the 90s,' *U. S. News and World Report*, July 21, 1993, 20.
6 Lexis/Nexis search for appearances after June 10, 1993, and before July 13, 1993. Accessed June and July 1993.
7 See, for instance, Bill Watterson, "Calvin and Hobbes," October 31, 1993.
8 Greg Howard and Craig MacIntosh, "Sally Forth," October 31, 1993.
9 This chapter uses Freud's categorizations and discussions, but it does not develop any significant psychoanalytic claims.
10 Freud, *Jokes and Their Relation to the Unconscious*; Sigmund Freud, "Humour," in *The Standard Edition of the Complete Psychological Works of Sigmund Freud, Volume XXI* (1927–1931), trans. James Strachey (London: Hogarth Press, 1966), 159–66. Freud only discusses these three terms. I do not know whether he might have thought other categories existed. At the time of writing *Jokes*, the pleasure principle was of major analytical concern for Freud, and he was still using the conscious/unconscious model. Only later would attention to the death instinct and questions of aggression and mastery become more central to his theorizing. This would also occur after he shifts to a libido/ego/superego model. The essay on "Humour" written in 1927 reflects the latter period of work. It is difficult to know how his analysis in *Jokes* might have changed.

11 Stephen H. Dunphy, "The Newsletter," *Seattle Times*, July 7, 1993, D1.
12 Dennis Polkow, "Lewis' Entertainment Menu More Than a Lamb Chop," *Chicago Tribune*, July 6, 1993, 18.
13 Unfortunately, I was unable to locate the original cartoon. Reported in "Letters to the Editor," *Star Tribune*, June 22, 1993.
14 Mick Eaton, "Laughter in the Dark," *Screen* 22:2 (1981): 22.
15 See, for instance, the Golden Book, *Jurassic Park* (1993) which provides pages of dinosaurs to draw and color.
16 Barbara Creed, *The Monstrous-Feminine: Film, Feminism, Psychoanalysis* (London: Routledge, 1993).
17 See, for instance, the ubiquitous mixture of comedy with horror in the slasher movies starting in the 1970s. Of course, humor and jokes occur throughout the history of the horror genre; a historical study of their presence and function throughout the genre's history is needed.
18 Freud, *Jokes*, 82 and 96.
19 Richard Dyer, "Coming to Terms: Male Gay Porn," *Jump Cut*, 30 (1985): 27–9.
20 Linda Williams, "Film Bodies: Gender, Genre, and Excess," *Film Quarterly* 44:4 (Summer 1991): 2–13.
21 Constance Penley, *NASA/Trek: Popular Science and Sex in America* (London: Version, 1997), 11–96; Patricia Mellencamp, 'TV Time and Catastrophe, or *Beyond the Pleasure Principle* of Television,' in Patricia Mellencamp (ed.) *Logics of Television: Essays in Cultural Criticism* (Bloomington: Indiana University Press, 1990), 240–66. Also see Kris Macomber, Christine Mallinson, and Elizabeth Seale, "'Katrina That Bitch!': Hegemonic Representations of Women's Sexuality on Hurricane Katrina Souvenir T-Shirts," June 2011. https://www.researchgate.net/publication/229181580/. Accessed July 19, 2021.
22 For a proposition about reconsidering how we study genres that might permit such a discussion, see Janet Staiger, 'Sound and the Comic/Horror Romance Film: Formula, Affect, and Inflection,' in James Buhler and Hanna Lewis (eds.) *Voicing the Cinema: Film Music and the Integrated Soundtrack* (Urbana: University of Illinois Press, 2020), 245–59.
23 Stephen Neale and Frank Krutnick, *Popular Film and Television Comedy* (London: Routledge, 1990), 80, notes that Jean Guillaumin has linked laughter with expulsion and release of anxiety. The expulsion is a "psychic ejection of the threatening object." This conforms to Freud's notion but does not quite tackle the power alliances operating in agreeing to participate in circumventing an inhibition.
24 Mary Douglas, "Jokes," (1975), reprinted in Chandra Mukerji and Michael Schudson (eds.) *Rethinking Popular Culture: Contemporary Perspectives in Cultural Studies* (Berkeley: University of California Press, 1991), 291–310.

16

"A Chance to Three-Dimensionally Live the Movie": *Jurassic Park* Attractions and Their Influence on Global Themed Experiences

Carissa Baker
University of Central Florida, USA

Introduction

The multibillion dollar global theme park industry has several famous single-intellectual property theme park lands including "*Star Wars:* Galaxy's Edge" at Disneyland (California) and Disney's Hollywood Studios (Florida), "Pandora: The World of *Avatar*" at Disney's Animal Kingdom (Florida), and "The Wizarding World of Harry Potter" at Universal Studios parks in Florida, California, Japan, and China. Before all of these, however, there was *Jurassic Park*. The attraction at Universal Studios Hollywood was an early example of an immersive experience, and *Jurassic Park* would become a powerful franchise for the Universal Studios theme park brand.

The *Jurassic Park* theme park concept in fact predates the movie release (with development beginning right after the book's release in 1990) and some of the built experiences within it were more expensive than the films, yet they are rarely considered of critical significance when discussing the franchise. This chapter contains three main sections that make a case for the importance of the theme park representations of *Jurassic Park*: the first offers a survey of the Universal Studios theme park attractions related to *Jurassic Park*, the second offers a reading of some of these experiences, and the third a discussion of how the franchise changed themed entertainment as a whole through its use of single-intellectual property immersive spaces. For nearly thirty years, *Jurassic Park* attraction iterations have been thrilling guests around the world and have left a lasting legacy on the theme park industry. The spatial, participatory experiences in the theme park provide some of the most compelling entries in the cultural phenomenon that is *Jurassic Park*.

When Dinosaurs Ruled the Theme Park: Universal's Spatial Representations

Even before *Jurassic Park* was released, several people considered turning the 1990 Michael Crichton book into a theme park ride. When creative director Neil Engel first read the book, he thought, "wow, this book was meant to be a ride."[1] Steven Spielberg confirmed, "I had the idea to do a ride even before we shot the movie. Universal trusted us and they said OK. And 18 months before the film was in release, the ride was already on the drawing board."[2] The making of the ride was stalled because of the need for lifelike dinosaurs in the attraction, and the movie debuted first. The earliest iteration of *Jurassic Park* in Universal Studios, and my first encounter, was *Jurassic Park: Behind the Scenes* (1994), a walkthrough exhibit set in a soundstage that lasted for a mere five months. It integrated physical sets with animatronics that recreated cinematic scenes: the sequence with the sick *Triceratops* that is cared for by Ellie Sattler (Laura Dern); the sequence with the raptors in the kitchen; the famous gate and jeep from the movie, and several interactive and informative exhibits. Though there were impressive elements, they seemed antiquated and hearkened back to the kinds of exhibits that explicitly described filmmaking processes and supported the "behind-the-scenes" model of Universal Studios.

Universal Studios Hollywood's next recreation of *Jurassic Park* would be the most influential. Designers worked for six years on engineering components, realistic skin, story, and other factors before finally being ready for construction. Coming right on the heels of the bar-raising and attendance-driving attraction *Indiana Jones Adventure* at Disneyland (1995, an enhanced motion vehicle dark ride), Universal knew they had to deliver something remarkable if only because they "wouldn't dare open anything less after Indy Jones."[3] The dark ride, a usually track- or canal-based enclosed ride with multiple show scenes, is one of the most common amusement and theme park rides, and most *Jurassic Park* rides would end up featuring darkened, narrative show scenes. What would open in 1996 was "*Jurassic Park*—The Ride": a wet boat ride with, at the time, the steepest drop in ride history (at 84 feet). It cost 110 million dollars to build, making it nearly twice as expensive as the film.[4] The ride is based on lengthy scenes in the novel that involve characters taking a sometimes serene, sometimes harrowing raft ride down a river and encountering dinosaurs along the way (a jeep-based attraction was the original concept but became a boat ride for reasons including thrill and the wet factor).

A peaceful ride through the more docile dinosaurs (in Ultrasaur Lagoon, Stegosaur Springs, and Hadrosaur Cove) is thrown off course into the Raptor Containment Area, and then to a *T-Rex* encounter in the Water Treatment Facility. Hosted by Dr. John Hammond (portrayed by Richard Attenborough), the ride presents a sequel story with the basic theme park trope of "something goes wrong" and a very *Jurassic Park* theme of "no worries, we've fixed everything that happened last time." We have seen this story before, and we love it. The story would change, however, when the Hollywood attraction closed in 2018 and reopened in 2019 as *Jurassic World: The Ride*, after the theatrical release of *Jurassic World: Fallen Kingdom*, the second film in the recently extended universe of the franchise. This version kept the same layout but added human characters to the experience—Claire Dearing (Bryce Dallas Howard), Owen Grady (Chris Pratt), and Dr. Henry Wu (B. D. Wong) as well as new dinosaurs from the most recent film series like the *Mosasaurus* and *Indominus rex*. It also increased the level of horror with spatters of blood and dead Pteranodons; added later were the interactive meet and greet *Raptor Encounter* (2015, with "Blue" the raptor arriving in 2018) and the *DinoPlay* playground structure (2019).

The success of the Hollywood experience spawned others at Universal theme parks elsewhere. A similar behind-the-scenes exhibit opened at Universal Studios Florida in 1995. The water ride had been planned even earlier than Hollywood's because of Florida's hot weather and was a "great way to tell a story" that was "straight from the novel."[5] This became a preview to the largest *Jurassic Park* experience, a whole land at the new *Islands of Adventure* theme park in 1999 (the park built next to Universal Studios Florida). Because it was a dedicated area instead of a single ride, landscaping played an even greater role than in the Hollywood park, where to "create a lush tropical jungle along the barren hillside," they imported hundreds of trees.[6] That attraction had been shoehorned into the hillside and the small lower lot area, whereas *Islands of Adventure*, a master-planned park, would need to incorporate foliage across the land's roughly sixteen acres (with "abundant tropical plantings and simulated dirt for paving") and new arrangements of the soundtrack for the background music.[7] The largest of the islands at the park, it was placed in the middle of the site to be an "oasis" where guests could relax and refuel with lush jungle in the day and cool blue light at night. It incorporated several features for children, giving them places to engage in the spirit of exploration.[8]

The fully imagined *Jurassic Park* land in Florida includes a Discovery Center (modeled on the first film's Visitor Center) with kid-friendly, science-based interactive features, a slightly updated version of the ride ("Jurassic Park River Adventure"), a play area ("Camp Jurassic"), a children's roller coaster ("*Pteranodon* Flyers"), and the "Raptor Encounter" (2015, expanded with new dinosaurs later). It also hosted restaurants, shops, and games as well as "*Triceratops* Encounter" (later "*Triceratops* Discovery Trail"): a walkthrough with three animatronic *Triceratops* under vet care. The feature opened in 1999 and closed in 2010. While it was a "cutting-edge attraction," according to designer Phil Hettema it "never really sparked with people."[9]

In 2021, the "*Jurassic World* VelociCoaster" opened. The ride, which introduced the *Jurassic World* storyline and characters to the otherwise *Jurassic Park*-based land, is headlined by the Dearing and Grady characters, with Grady finding it crazy that Dearing would place a roller coaster in the middle of a raptor pen. The queue includes Dr. Wu explaining the science as well as raptors violently trying to escape their rather brutal confinement. The thrilling, multi-launch, multi-inversion ("upside down" elements) roller coaster was instantly placed among the top coasters in the world by coaster fans. Taken together, Jurassic Park at Islands of Adventure is an elaborately detailed, single-intellectual property themed land that predates many of the great examples of this genre.

Jurassic Park-based attractions were developed for Universal's international locations as well. Universal Studios Japan (2001) opened with a small *Jurassic Park* land that includes "*Jurassic Park*—The Ride" (similar to the Florida version), the Discovery Center, a "Dinosaur Wonder" experience show, and "The Flying Dinosaur" (2016): a "flying" roller coaster where the vehicle glides below the track and riders lay prone to simulate and experience the flight of the Pterosaur. Universal Studios Singapore's (2010) attractions in their *Lost World* area are *Jurassic Park* "Rapids Adventure": a river rapids-style ride rather than the "shoot-the-chute" type the others are; "Canopy Flyer" (a family roller coaster); "Dino-Soarin," a children's spinning ride; "Raptor Training School," the interactive meet and greet; the *Jurassic World* "ROAR!" Show; and "Amber Rock Climb," a large rock-climbing wall. Universal's newest property, Universal Beijing Resort (2021), has a *Jurassic World* "Isla Nublar land," the first Universal land developed according to the *Jurassic World* style and incorporating references to the later film's Innovation Center rather than the Discovery Center of the original film. Interestingly, it is also the first not to include the staple of the franchise: a water ride. Instead, the area has a motion-based dark ride through wrecked *Jurassic World* exhibits ("Jurassic World Adventure," a rather metatextual commentary attraction), a high-tech family roller coaster ("Jurassic Flyers"), and a play area in an aviary ("Camp Jurassic"). Like the others, it includes restaurants and retail locations. Now in four countries, Universal's *Jurassic* attractions have strengthened visitor desire to interact with dinosaurs in physical space.

From Beauty to Horror: *Jurassic Park* Attractions as Dimensional Texts

Anyone who saw the original *Jurassic Park* movie remembers that before fear and death, there was wonderment. In Crichton's novel it is the idea of dinosaurs coming back to life that seems incredible. Sattler can only whisper "My God" and Dr. Grant can only laugh. The film relies on visual effects to accomplish this emotion. As Alan Grant and Ellie Sattler have their first Park encounter with the majestic *Brontosaurus*, the sweeping, simulated ancient environment and the iconic John Williams music soars, the audience experiences awe vicariously along with them. Throughout the course of the story in any medium, amazement turns into terror and realization.

"*Jurassic Park*—The Ride" was such a captivating attraction because it mimicked the structure of the film, captured its tone, and reinforced the core metaphors of the story. As the ride begins, the original wonder is replicated. The boat floats up to the wooden *Jurassic Park* gates, the music anticipates arrival, and a narrator speaks with an encouraging voice: "Time, the ever-flowing river. Come with us now to a time before man when the river flowed through a new-born world and giants walked the earth. Welcome to Jurassic Park." At this, the gates open, the theme music crescendos, and mother and child ultrasaurs crane their necks to greet you. These early areas represent that presence of joy in the prehistoric idyll. Soon, a *Parasaurolophus* knocks the boat off course; as with the core story, unintended consequences lead to disaster. The *Velociraptor*, *Dilophosaurus*, and *Tyrannosaurus rex* try to kill you, and an Animal Control crew that attempted to respond has already been eaten. The experience turns jarring, with dark scenes, loud sirens, and warnings about the life-support systems being terminated before riders escape through the "big drop." Humorously, it ends by announcing, "This concludes your tranquil journey through the world of dinosaurs." Like the movie, the ride starts with "domestic tranquility scenes" according to Spielberg.[10] Engel clarifies the transition in tone: "Everything gets stark and industrial and ugly ... from beauty to horror."[11]

Part of the appeal of the attraction lies in the capability of the theme park medium. The theme park presents a form of "spatial transmedia"[12] with dimensionality being one of the essential affordances of the form.[13] Environmental storytelling, where the physical environment has narrative properties (rather than only a narrator telling the story), is a way that theme parks express storyworlds, worlds which have "stories embedded in them."[14] Henry Jenkins defines four principles of environmental storytelling that create "preconditions for an immersive narrative experience"; these are clearly found on "*Jurassic Park*—The Ride."[15] First, spatial stories can "evoke pre-existing narratives" and in the ride, the logos, fonts, architecture, color palettes, music, fauna, and other symbols recall the source material. Next, they provide a "staging ground" for narrative events to be enacted.[16] The continuously moving boats traverse this environment each minute and pass through a narrative landscape and plot devices that reset again and again. In the third concept, narrative information is placed within the mise-en-scène, a hallmark of the design style that created this ride, with architecture, landscaping, sounds, lighting, texture, colors, and props enacting the storyline. Finally, these spaces provide the means for "emergent narratives," which in a medium like video games means those storylines were not written by designers but arise from interaction with systems.[17]

While theme parks have less emergent narratives than other mediums and are only recently starting to play with more experimental forms like interactive theaterand branching narratives, the guest's imagination is activated by the story and a mode of participation is encouraged. Theme park rides often rely on a "bi-narrative structure" where there is both an observable narrative and an experiential one, or, the narrative of the characters' in-ride scenes being witnessed by the visitor and the experience of the visitor going through a ride as a protagonist.[18] "*Jurassic Park*—The Ride" falls into a category where there is little narrative to observe aside from one's own experience. *You* are the one going on this tour of Jurassic Park, *your* boat is thrown off course, and the dinosaurs are after *you*. The tourist is the actor in most theme park settings according to Kokai and Robson, but this ride is a prime example of the power of the theme park medium.[19] In the *Jurassic* themed worlds, the well-known characters are there, but they are talking to *you*. The film's famous dinosaurs are there, but it is *you* they want to harm.

Both book and movie play essential roles in the history of the *Jurassic Park* franchise, but it is in the theme park where the guest is now role-playing as a part of the world. Universal had the tagline "ride the movies"; and as Spielberg noted, "this really is a chance to three-dimensionally live the movie and ride the movie."[20] However, this attraction was unlike prior entries that discussed filmmaking or yelled "cut!" There is no deus ex machina here; the only escape is a literal eighty-foot drop. Ride promotion played up the experiences in the new medium, with advertisements like "see the movie then dare to ride it" and "you'll wish it was just a movie." Promotional spreads before the ride opened revealed that fear was the dominant message, with ads asking guests to "brave it this summer": "Thrilling Chilling! Pure adrenaline rush," "Hang on to your life as a runaway raft brings you face-to-fangs with Spitters, Raptors and the ultimate terror—a roaring, ravenous

T-Rex," and "Visitors to Universal Studios Hollywood will confront the most fearsome predators ever to prowl the Earth as they journey into the living, breathing, three-dimensional world of Steven Spielberg's blockbuster thriller." It is the horror, rather than the beauty, that they employ here, and it is the physical, visceral aspect of the ride that brings it to a greater level of anxiety and authenticity. As an ad for the newer *Jurassic World* version warns, "It just got real." Ads for the VelociCoaster call it a "new species of coaster" and the "apex predator of coasters," connecting it with the raptor theme. Like with the water ride versions, there is an essential materiality that make it "real" regardless of its state of simulation, and that is what sells the experience for guests.

Jurassic Park as theme park ride and then theme park makes perfect sense, as few properties are as plainly metatextual. *Jurassic Park*, in the novel, is a theme park; Hammond chooses the multidimensional format of the theme park to display his discoveries, even using Universal behind-the-scenes style attractions to tell the story. *Jurassic Park* is dubbed by Hammond the "most advanced amusement park in the world" that would not have just rides (which "everybody has") or "animatronic environments" but would be living exhibits.[21] The irony of Universal creating these spaces with rides and animatronic environments is not lost on fans. Like the ride at Universal, there is a "Jungle River Ride" not yet open because of "problems with the control of the animals."[22] When on the raft (in the novel) that inspired the ride, the narrator observes, "The raft was going faster all the time. It was starting to feel like an amusement park ride."[23] The raft would become a self-referential amusement park ride with layers of irony including the control booth for the fake raft ride being the control booth for the actual "*Jurassic Park*—The Ride." It is notable that most later iterations dropped "the ride," the touch that allows riders to know firsthand it is not real and close the gap between simulation and simulacrum. Now the rides go straight to the notion that *this really is a ride inside of Jurassic Park*. This was not possible for the original ride, which sat beside several other rides and attractions, but the more immersive environments chose to stray from Universal's explicit artificiality of the film set trope, a shift that would continue in later attractions. Even the original ride now has a sign on an entry gate that says, "River Adventure Ride." *Jurassic Park*, the "theme park/zoo/natural history museum" also shifts, as by *Jurassic World*, it has "unashamedly become an extravagant theme park."[24]

Jurassic Park and theme parks have clear theoretical connections. The novel draws comparison between John Hammond and Walt Disney, with Dr. Grant saying he is "about as sinister" as him in this case meaning a visionary not meaning to do harm;[25] this would likely carry a double meaning for scholars who worry about the totalizing landscape of artificial fantasy.[26] John Arnold (portrayed by Samuel L Jackson in the film) was a systems engineer who worked at Walt Disney World and opened other theme parks. The narrator explains that Arnold's theme park employment had given him a "somewhat skewed view of reality."[27] Arnold "contended, only half jokingly, that the entire world was increasingly described as the metaphor of the theme park."[28] Immediately recalling the postmodernists who interrogated theme parks (Baudrillard, Eco, Marin, etc.), the book reminded us that simulacra can be hyperreal. When referencing the flea circus in the movie, Hammond says that with this place he "wanted to show them something that wasn't an illusion, something that was real, something that they could see and touch." Despite its physicality, the *Jurassic Parks* are nonetheless not reality as it is supposed to be, and the facades crumble in each subsequent iteration.

Jurassic Park is the "most ambitious theme park in history," and it is plagued with "all the problems of any amusement park" but on a magnified scale.[29] Perhaps the most famous quote to this effect in the film is when Hammond states, "All major theme parks have delays. When Disneyland opened in 1956, nothing worked" (it opened in 1955, so one wonders if the error is intentional). Malcolm responds, "But John, if the Pirates of the Caribbean breaks down, the pirates don't eat the tourists."

The limits of theory here are exposed since the Disneylands of the world will not be fatal in this way, but it can be read as a metaphor. Sherry Turkle's concepts of the Disneyland effect (where the artificial seems more real than the real) and the artificial crocodile effect (where the artificial is more compelling than the real) are relevant.[30] In the book, Dr. Malcolm avows, "Jurassic Park is not the real world. It is intended to be a controlled world that only imitates the natural world. In that sense, it's a true park, rather like a Japanese formal garden. Nature manipulated to be more natural than the real thing, if you will."[31] The Universal theme park is certainly more real than the real thing, as the real thing is both extinct and a never-quite-reality.

Theme park rides are our access to realistic dinosaurs though "*Jurassic Park*—The Ride" is still "essentially a computer-driven machine for telling an immersive story."[32] It is a "technologically produced," "architecturally simulated" version that "takes guests through an environment in the throes of technological malfunction."[33] This is the continued elaborate artifice of the theme park industry, and we are willing to be convinced. In the "immersion-effect," Constance Balides asserts, "a *Jurassic*-literate consumer ... while taking pleasure in simulation, knows that a fake is fake."[34] The purposeful saturation in a simulated space is for the "pleasures of immersion"; it is not a "straightforward substitute of real experience" or simple naivete.[35] If these *Jurassic Parks* were real, they would kill us, but they are not, so we can suspend disbelief and simultaneously immerse ourselves.

The emotional responses audiences have towards these experiences speak to our collective imagination regarding dinosaurs and the irony of our wonder. These are the "monsters of our imagination," lethal and awesome.[36] The monstrous realities lie outside of our human experience, as "dinosaurs can only become 'real' to us via visceral encounters with impressive fakes."[37] When "*Jurassic Park*—The Ride" opened, it allowed guests to escape Los Angeles for five minutes and traverse a primeval landscape, come face to face with the past, get doused in water, and then walk away. The later, more elaborate, spaces permitted greater role-play where the horror lasted only moments and the beauty potentially hours, bringing us closer to the original dreams of John Hammond.

Something Has Survived: Industry Influence

"*Jurassic Park*—The Ride," and the technological competition with Disney it engendered, influenced the future of the theme park industry. Though the film relied on impressive computer graphics, the ride was full of practical sets (ironically, the *Jurassic World* follow-up attraction would add in more screen-based visuals). The use of large, lifelike, expensive animatronics would propel this ride into the spotlight. While Disney created the original theme park audio-animatronics, the *Jurassic Park* dinosaurs were some of the most impressive seen in a theme park to that point. Spielberg called them the "most realistic animatronic actors" he had seen in a park, and this derived from satisfying visitor desires to encounter "full-sized animals."[38] Hettema agreed, noting that guests "want to see this come to life" and that Spielberg's ride "raised the bar on what people expect."[39] Also raising the bar on what people expected, Islands of Adventure was a highly lauded park that heightened competition with Disney and helped propel the single-intellectual property, highly immersive theme park world, into a paradigm for the industry. A decade later, the first section of "Wizarding World of Harry Potter" (Hogsmeade, 2010), in the same theme park, would become one of the most celebrated design achievements in the industry and an immersive space that further raised guest expectations around the world.

Jurassic Park made its way into the visitor attractions space with a proliferation of exhibits. The film inspired many museum exhibits, but one of the first was the American Museum of National History's "Dinosaurs of Jurassic Park" (1993), complete with "jungle setting" and dinosaurs but "highlighting the differences between science fiction and the research done at the Museum."[40] One exhibit blurring the lines between museums/theme parks with immersive narrative and in-situ display[41] as well as scripted space and scenographic design is "*Jurassic World*: The Exhibition" (2016).[42] The traveling exhibit has been showcased at sites in several countries including Australia, China, France, Korea, Spain, and the United States. Developed with paleontologist Jack Horner, the advisor for the films, the exhibit is the "closest simulation of dinosaurs ever created."[43] The arrangement is another experiment in synergy, co-branding, and reciprocal benefit. Museums like the Field Museum in Chicago gain high attendance and "spark imagination" about the dinosaur fossils in the museum through excitement the animatronics generate;[44] Universal finds profit through merchandise, synergy with a current franchise, and brand loyalty. Nonetheless, the exhibits have faced controversy because of their theme park attributes, branding focus, spectacle over education, and mixing of fact and fiction, such as the presence of an *Indominus rex*.[45] Like the theme park experience, though, it is a "real-world, spatialized reimagining of a fictional, cinematic theme park" illustrating the convergence of attraction types.[46]

Another iteration of *Jurassic*-based entertainment developed is by way of "Jurassic World Live" (2019), a traveling show in concert with Feld Entertainment. Complete with a new storyline approved by Spielberg, there is an emphasis on staying "true to the brand and their expectations."[47] The show has dinosaurs that can be controlled mechanically or through puppetry. Over the years, there have been several other synergistic moves to align film, theme parks, video games, and other transmedia nodes. Merchandise itself is synonymous with the brand, again adding to the irony of Malcolm's assertion in the film that Hammond would patent it, package it, and slap it on a "plastic lunchbox." Scholars have discussed the commodification of the property and elements of consumption over the years.[48] The marketing strategies for the original film were planned two years in advance,[49] and it continues to have legs, with new films, television shows (like *Camp Cretaceous*), or products each year; it "continues to be wildly lucrative and shows no sign of falling out of favor with audiences."[50] Over the years, multimedia companies have "relied more and more on the synergy effects of transmedial promotion of specific brands."[51] Though the franchise becomes a theme park and a commercial entity that encourages consumption, the story itself "critiques the theme park mentality" and the commercialization of science for a theme park.[52] While the films continue to critique this aggressive capitalism in the real world, Universal rakes in the profits from film sales, theme park visitation, and merchandise.

Jurassic Park not only "inspired a whole new generation of paleontologists," but also "led to an explosion of public interest in dinosaurs."[53] A lasting effect of *Jurassic Park* goes beyond licensed adaptations to the ubiquitous presence of Dinosauria in entertainment and attractions. This is likely a combination of the theme park iteration and the film sparking a dinomania and parks knowing that dino additions would appeal to visitors. Balides argues, "In an apt postmodern inversion, the world outside the film, moreover, mirrored the world inside the film during the period of dinomania that accompanied *Jurassic Park's* theatrical release."[54] Many exhibits and touring shows exist that are not based on the *Jurassic* license including "Dinosaurs Live!" (going for fifteen years seasonally at the Heard Museum in Texas) and traveling shows "Dinosaur World Live," "Jurassic Quest,"

Dinos Alive, Dino & Dragon Stroll, Dinosaur Invasion, or Expo Dino World (Belgium), which advertised on their website that visitors would feel "as if they were in the mythical *Jurassic Park*."

An important dinosaur iteration in theme parks is "Dinoland, U.S.A." at "Disney's Animal Kingdom" (1998) in Florida. This land includes a dinosaur dig site, play area, carnival rides, and the dark ride "Dinosaur" (formerly "Countdown to Extinction" but changed to share the name of Disney's 2000 movie *Dinosaur*), which shares the same ride system as the aforementioned *Indiana Jones* ride. Opening several years after the *Jurassic Park* ride was supposed to open in Florida and a year before Islands of Adventure, it seems like a response to Universal. Disney had dinosaur content before in their diorama "Primeval World" (at multiple Disney parks and originally from the 1964/65 New York World's Fair) and the scenes in the former Epcot ride "Universe of Energy/Ellen's Energy Adventure" (1982–2017), but this was a timely addition. The storyline for "Dinosaur" is slightly different in that it is based around time travel rather than cloning, but the Dino Institute shares similarities including starting off with sound, credible science and then turning to unscrupulous behavior (in this case, wanting the guests to steal an Iguanodon before the dinosaurs are destroyed) and of course, following the tried-and-true "something goes wrong" motif. Many of the same dinosaurs are portrayed including a *Parasaurolophus*, *Velociraptor*, *Compsognathus*, a flying dinosaur, a sauropod, and a large predator (in this case, *Carnotaurus*). Though likely inspired by *Jurassic Park*, it also recalled the ride that foreshadowed the dinosaur theme park craze, "Kingdom of the Dinosaurs" at Knott's Berry Farm in California (1987–2004).

After the two major players in the theme park industry had prominent dinosaur content, multiple theme parks across the world, amusements parks, and attractions would follow (of which only some will be discussed here). Several attractions are dinosaur themed including "China Dinosaurs Park (2000)," a popular Chinese theme park also known as "Eastern Jurassic Park." "Jurassic Land Kiulu," a family park in Malaysia, was "inspired by the Jurassic Park movie" and created by "avid fans of the Jurassic Park movies."[55] One park ("IMG Worlds of Adventure" in Dubai, 2016) opened with a land called "Lost Valley Dinosaur Adventure." It contains a play area, carousel, two roller coasters ("Predator" and "Velociraptor"), and a dark ride called "Forbidden Territory." The latter is derivative of Disney's dinosaur ride but with a new story and accompanying children's books. In 2014, the Blackgang Chine family park on the Isle of Wight, UK, added "Restricted Area 5," an immersive dinosaur trail. Also in 2014, the family park "Dutch Wonderland" in Pennsylvania added "Exploration Island," which contains a walking trail with animatronic dinosaurs (the "Prehistoric Path") and a "Dino Dig." An executive said at the opening, "Now we can give children the opportunity to experience what it's like to walk with dinosaurs."[56] Their website details, "We just need some young and curious explorers to help us dig up and dust off these amazing fossils so that we can understand their story and educate ourselves about their time here on Earth."[57] Like many dinosaur-related sites, there is an edutainment orientation.

Dinosaur trails became a frequent component of the dinosaur attraction. "Dinosaurs Alive!," a dinosaur trail featuring dozens of dinosaur figures, was created by Dinosaurs Unearthed, a company that had created "multi-sensory experiences" about dinosaurs in museums and sciences centers since 2005.[58] Though a few museum exhibits existed with this name, "Dinosaurs Alive!" attractions were upcharge attractions at eight Cedar Fair-owned amusement parks from 2012 to 2019, with each having unique configurations of dinosaurs. Columbus Zoo's temporary "Dinosaur Island" (where one can see dinosaur animatronics via a boat ride or walking tour) returned after popular demand in 2018. An exhibit with large and quite visually impressive dinosaurs including a 32-foot-tall *Argentinosaurus* in a half-mile stretch of forest is found in "Dino Roar Valley" at Lake George Expedition Park (2019), which also has a sandbox to unearth fossils, a playground, and dino workshops. Parents observed that it "felt like walking onto the set of *Jurassic Park*."[59] McKee Botanical Garden in Florida has integrated dinosaurs into their landscapes several times including Dinosaurs Around the World (2021). Some exhibits, like Dino Roar Valley, have succeeded in still filling my adult self with the wonder that original attraction sparked so many years ago.

Multiple sites have standalone dinosaur rides. "Dino Rampage" (2011 and on), a motion-based dark ride with violent scenes of dinosaurs eating humans and soldiers shooting dinosaurs, is at several Fantawild theme parks in China and became an animated television show. A lesson in copyright infringement, Cinecittà World's immersive tunnel ride "Jurassic War" (2018) has references to the *Jurassic Park* gate, logo, dinosaur egg pile, particular fossils and dinosaurs, and Dr. Grant's dress style, and it even uses extracts of the soundtrack. The film starts similarly to the early shots in *Jurassic Park* but then turns into the Universal ride "Skull Island: Reign of Kong," which is located directly next to *Jurassic Park* at Islands of Adventure. The company that created the movie explains, "'Jurassic War' pays homage to science fiction movies revolving around cloned dinosaurs: a cinematographic genre that has thrilled generations of spectators for a few decades now."[60] The attraction is thus a copy of a copy, an imperfect replica in a long line of *Jurassic* imitations. Some parks have roller coasters that represent dinosaurs, for instance, Story Land's (New Hampshire) "Roar-O-Saurus" (2014) or the defunct "Jurassic Adventure" rollercoaster (2008–15) at Beijing Shijingshan Amusement Park. A boat ride in Tennessee, the "Jurassic Jungle Boat Ride" (2008), is debated as a "tourist trap" or a "beloved icon."[61] Other water-based attractions include "Jurassic Land" at Enakyo Wonderland (Japan), "Jurassic Cruise" at Formosan Aboriginal Cultural Village (Taiwan), and "Jurassic Island" at Trans Studio Cibubur (Indonesia), which utilizes similar boats, logos, and environments to "*Jurassic Park*—The Ride." No matter where one is in the world, chances are there is a dinosaur ride, exhibit, or experience nearby.

Paleontologist Steven Brusatte believes *Jurassic Park* to be "the best thing that's ever happened to dinosaur paleontology."[62] It would be safe to say that *Jurassic Park* also had an indelible mark on the theme park industry. From creating a powerful reproduction of a popular franchise to being one of the first single-intellectual property immersive worlds, *Jurassic Park* helped to set a course that would lead to a participatory kind of dinomania. We don't just want to read about dinosaurs or watch them impressively portrayed on screen. We want to walk with them, live with them, and run from them. The collective imagination about these monsters was dimensionalized in the attraction space. Whether in destination theme parks, family parks, museums, zoos, traveling exhibits, or shows, visitors love confronting material dinosaurs. Much of these representations are imaginative, as they do not necessarily reflect prevailing notions of dinosaurs or are fictionalized because scientists just do not know (for instance, skin color, texture, or pattern). Nonetheless, we enjoy engaging in this fantasy speculation about these long-gone creatures. When considering *Jurassic Park*, it is easy to recognize the legacy of the blockbuster film or best-selling book that began the craze. However, the theme park spaces have proved significant in terms of our relationship with the franchise and the alteration of our desired entertainment. There is nothing quite like hearing "Welcome to *Jurassic Park*" and being completely enveloped in that newborn world, coming face to face with awe-inspiring dinosaurs, worrying as something goes wrong, and then disembarking from that ride drenched, running back in line, and doing it all over again.

Notes

1 Wharton, D., "Creating a Monster; With a $110 Million Budget, Jurassic Park Is This Summer's Most-Anticipated Theme Park Ride. But How Do You Make Dinosaurs True to Life?," *Los Angeles Times*, May 5, 1996.
2 D. Michael, "'Jurassic Park: The Ride' Opens with a Big Splash," *CNN*, June 22, 1996.
3 Tim O'Brien in Wharton, "Creating a Monster."
4 Wharton, "Creating a Monster."
5 Gary Goddard in S. Gennawey, *Universal versus Disney: The Unofficial Guide to American Theme Parks' Greatest Rivalry* (Birmingham, AL: Keen Communications, 2014), 167.
6 Gennawey, *Universal versus Disney*, 170.
7 Ibid., 181.

8   Bob Shreve in Gennawey, *Universal versus Disney*, 192.
9   Hettema in Gennawey, *Universal versus Disney*, 194.
10 Wharton, "Creating a Monster."
11 Ibid.
12 R. Williams, *Theme Park Fandom: Spatial Transmedia, Materiality and Participatory Culture* (Amsterdam: Amsterdam University Press, 2020).
13 C. Baker, "Summary of Exploring a Three-Dimensional Narrative Medium: The Theme Park as 'de Sprookjessprokkelaar,' the Gatherer and Teller of Stories," *Journal of Themed Experience and Attraction Studies* 1 (2018): 1–9.
14 M. J. P. Wolf, *Building Imaginary Worlds: The Theory and History of Subcreation* (New York: Routledge, 2012).
15 H. Jenkins, "Game Design as Narrative Architecture," in N. Wardrip-Fruin and P. Harrigan (eds.) *First Person: New Media as Story, Performance, and Game* (Cambridge, MA: MIT Press, 2004), 118–29, 123.
16 Ibid.
17 Ibid.
18 I. Kay, "Bi-Narrative Structure," *Pure Imagineering: Theme Park Narratology*, September 17, 2013 [Online]. www.pureimagineering.blogspot.com/2013/09/experiential-and-presentational-stories.html. Accessed July 30, 2018.
19 J. Kokai and T. Robson (eds.), *Performance and the Disney Theme Park: The Tourist as Actor* (London: Palgrave Macmillan, 2019).
20 *Making of Jurassic Park: The Ride* [Film]. Dirs. Jeff Cvengross and David Palmer (Silver Spring, MD: Learning Channel, 1996).
21 M. Crichton, *Jurassic Park* (New York: Ballantine Books, 2015 [1990]), 67.
22 Ibid., 147.
23 Ibid., 326.
24 J. Balanzategui and A. Ndalianis, "Hybrid Spaces: Melbourne Museum's *Jurassic World: The Exhibition*," *Australasian Journal of Popular Culture* 7:1 (2018): 69.
25 Crichton, *Jurassic Park*, 45.
26 M. Mitrašinović, *Total Landscape, Theme Parks, Public Space* (New York: Routledge, 2006).
27 Crichton, *Jurassic Park*, 155.
28 Ibid.
29 Ibid.
30 S. Turkle, *Life on the Screen: Identity in the Age of the Internet* (New York: Simon & Schuster, 1995).
31 Crichton, *Jurassic Park*, 149.
32 J. Murray, *Hamlet on the Holodeck: The Future of Narrative in Cyberspace* (Cambridge, MA: MIT Press, 1997).

33 Balanzategui and Ndalianis, "Hybrid Spaces," 66.
34 C. Balides, "Jurassic Post-Fordism: Tall Tales of Economies in the Theme Park," *Screen* 41:1 (2000): 148.
35 Ibid.
36 *Making of Jurassic Park: The Ride*, [Film] Dirs. Jeff Cvengross and David Palmer, USA: The Learning Channel, 1996.
37 Balanzategui and Ndalianis, "Hybrid Spaces," 71.
38 Michael, "'Jurassic Park: The Ride' Opens with a Big Splash."
39 Ibid.
40 C. O'Dowd, "The Dinosaurs of Jurassic Park (Exhibition)," *American Museum of Natural History*, December 7, 2018 [Online]. https://data.library.amnh.org/archives-authorities/id/amnhc_5000450. Accessed December 18, 2021.
41 C. Baker, "The Use of Themed Entertainment Design in Museums and Heritage Sites," *Museum Review* 3 (2018): 1.
42 Balanzategui and Ndalianis, "Hybrid Spaces," 65.
43 "Field Museum to Host Jurassic World: The Exhibition," *Field Museum*, March 23, 2017 [Online] https://www.fieldmuseum.org/about/press/field-museum-host-jurassic-world-exhibition. Accessed December 18, 2021.
44 Ibid.
45 Balanzategui and Ndalianis, "Hybrid Spaces," 58.
46 Ibid., 70.
47 S. Thompson, "Inside the 'Jurassic World Live' Tour and Its Global Aspirations," *Forbes*, December 24, 2019 [Online]. https://www.forbes.com/sites/simonthompson/2019/12/24/inside-the-jurassic-world-live-tour-and-its-global-aspirations/?sh=4c95d9825ccb. Accessed December 18, 2021.
48 e.g., Balides, "Jurassic Post-Fordism," 153; Brigham, A. "Consuming of Re/Production: Going Behind the Scenes in Spielberg's Jurassic Park and at Universal Studios Theme Park," *Genders*, 36, no. 53 (2002).
49 Balides, "Jurassic Post-Fordism," 144.
50 Thompson, "Inside the 'Jurassic World Live'."
51 F. Freitag, "'Like Walking into a Movie': Intermedial Relations between Theme Parks and Movies," *Journal of Popular Culture* 50:4 (2017): 707.
52 Balides, "Jurassic Post-Fordism," 155.
53 A. Liptak, "How Jurassic Park Led to the Modernization of Dinosaur Paleontology," *The Verge*, June 23, 2018 [Online]. https://www.theverge.com/2018/6/23/17483340/jurassic-park-world-steve-brusatte-the-rise-and-fall-of-the-dinosaurs-book-interview-paleontology. Accessed December 18, 2021.
54 Balides, "Jurassic Post-Fordism," 140.
55 P. Mu, "Sabah's Own 'Jurassic Park' Aims to Draw Tourists to Kiulu," *New Straights Times*, September 10, 2021 [Online]. https://www.nst.com.my/news/

nation/2021/09/726123/sabahs-own-jurassic-park-aims-draw-tourists-kiulu. Accessed December 18, 2021.

56 T. Mekeel, "15 Huge Animatronic Dinosaurs Coming to Dutch Wonderland's New Exploration Island," *LancasterOnline*, January 30, 2014 [Online]. https://lancasteronline.com/business/local_business/15-huge-animatronic-dinosaurs-coming-to-dutch-wonderlands-new-exploration-island/article_7626e694-8933-11e3-94aa-001a4bcf6878.html. Accessed December 18, 2021.

57 "Exploration Island: Where Dinosaurs Come to Life!," *Dutch Wonderland*, 2015 [Online]. https://www.dutchwonderland.com/things-to-do/attractions/Exploration-Island. Accessible December 18, 2021.

58 J. Rubin, "Dinosaurs Alive! on Adventure Island Opens Summer 2012 at Cedar Point," *InPark Magazine*, August 20, 2011 [Online]. https://www.inparkmagazine.com/dinosaurs-alive-on-adventure-island-opens-summer-2012-at-cedar-point/. Accessed December 18, 2021.

59 K. Moore, "Dino Roar Valley Opens in Lake George to Children's Awe," *Adirondack Daily Enterprise*, May 28, 2019 [Online]. https://www.adirondackdailyenterprise.com/news/local-news/2019/05/dino-roar-valley-opens-in-lake-george-to-childrens-awe/. Accessed December 18, 2021.

60 "The Immersive Tunnel Experience 'Jurassic War' Makes Its Debut at Cinecittà World," *RedRaion* [Online]. https://redraion.com/jurassic-war-cinecitta-opening/. Accessible December 18, 2021.

61 M. Overholt, "Jurassic Jungle Boat Ride Pigeon Forge: Tourist Trap or Beloved Icon?," *Smokies.com*, September 3, 2021 [Online]. https://www.thesmokies.com/jurassic-jungle-boat-ride/. Accessed December 18, 2021.

62 Liptak, "How Jurassic Park Led to the Modernization of Dinosaur Paleontology."

17

Family, Nostalgia, and Dinosaurs on Stage: *The Jurassic Parks*

Catherine Pugh
Independent Scholar, UK

Introduction

In a quiet moment before the chaos of *Jurassic Park* (1993) begins, John Hammond (Richard Attenborough) declares his intentions behind the park, explaining that he wanted to show spectators "something that wasn't an illusion. Something that was real, something that they could see and touch." Although a big-budget blockbuster such as *Jurassic Park* might seem an unusual choice for a stage production, theater's ability to be both real and illusion, to utilize both the physical and the imagination, encourages innovative performance that brings the fantastical to life. Theater, as a multisensory medium, is not limited to representation, allowing access to the absent, the incorporeal and the sublime. While the average performance space might not be able to accommodate life-sized dinosaur models or special effects such as CGI, international theater company Superbolt was able to bring dinosaurs to life on stage in their award-winning play *The Jurassic Parks*. Between 2016 and 2018, the company performed their play at festivals around the world. Set in the Lyme Regis Community Centre ("The Jurassic capital of the English coast"), the play follows the Park family as they hold a memorial for their deceased matriarch, including a screening of their favorite film to watch as a family: *Jurassic Park*. Unfortunately, the video cassette is missing, so the family pull together to act out the movie. What follows is a theatrical staging of the film using a bare stage, minimal props, and three actors, intercut with scenes of the estranged family going back through the mother's accidental death, parent's divorce, and other family tensions.

The Jurassic Parks must contend with the difficulty of staging the film to a theatrical audience, as well as integrating it with a seemingly completely disparate narrative. To achieve this, the play employs physical theater, comedy, music, mime, puppetry, and a dose of audience interaction to engage with the nostalgia of the film while creating a new and absorbing story. As well as navigating the challenge of transferring such a visually rich and ambitious film onto a small stage, the show offers debate on how this nostalgia is used in order to create a theatrical para-text that simultaneously honors and dissects the original. Despite being primarily played for comedy, The Jurassic Parks nevertheless expands and adapts Jurassic Park's themes of family and motherhood that are prevalent throughout the franchise. A key component in the success of the play is its ability to utilize nostalgia surrounding the film, both in depicting the film scenes and unraveling the story of the Park family. However, the nostalgic desires found within the film itself are reinterpreted through the play—for example, themes of recovering something that has been lost (particularly the longing for de-extinction), turning the clock back, motherhood, progeny, and found families. Discussing how—and why—the play focuses on the film's nostalgia and tensions concerning family allows for a detailed examination of these themes in the original film (something that notably continues in the franchise's sequels). A broken, grieving, and divided family, the Parks' impromptu show both exposes the fractures within their relationship and, ultimately, helps to heal them.

DIY Dinosaurs

As the audience enter the performance space, they are greeted by the Parks family—Terry Parks (Frode Gjerløw) and his teenage children Jade (Maria Askew) and Noah (Simon Maeder)—as they join the memorial for the children's mother, Madeline, who died a year prior after being hit by a truck. The family dynamic is tense; Terry and Madeline were divorced, while Jade (who addresses Terry by name rather than "dad") is about to leave to live on a commune in Scotland. While Terry and Jade at first appear indifferent to the film itself, Noah is excited to share memories of Jurassic Park with the audience; he stresses the importance it has to the family, putting emphasis on the fact that they used to watch it together both before and after the divorce. Madeline in particular enjoyed the film as she was a paleontologist, while the recording they plan to play is their own copy taped from the television, complete with 1990s adverts. The characters' open reminiscing about what the film means to them, as well as their ability to address the audience (who stand in for the people attending Madeline's memorial) allows them to talk about the film directly and invite nostalgic memories. Furthermore, after the family realize that the videotape is missing, Terry and Jade immediately begin to argue, before being interrupted by Noah as he starts to reenact the opening scene from the film. The enthusiastic and innocent Noah is the audience's portal into the fantasy world about to be created on stage; it is Noah who initially brings the sense of immersion and play into an increasingly stressful situation in a move very suggestive of a child's coping mechanism.

When asked whether the play is suitable for those unfamiliar with the source material, members of Superbolt have stated, "Of course, to get all the references, it does help to have seen the film .... But actually we have found that Spielberg's *Jurassic Park* is one of those classics where people remember the iconic moments—the trembling water, the *T-Rex* snapping at the children through the glass roof of a car, the velociraptors in the kitchen—even if they haven't seen the film in years!"[1] Part of the reason the play works is because the audience already knows the moments that are being referenced. This is not to say that an audience member who had not seen the film would be confused, only that greater pleasure can be derived from a shared knowledge of the original text, thereby allowing for pop culture references to become a shared language with the audience, such as "School councilor Muldoon" and, of course, the infamous Ian Malcolm (Jeff Goldblum) pose. This explicit nostalgia uses call-backs to the original film, while the sense of anemoia (a sense of nostalgia for something the subject has never actually experienced) is reiterated during numerous references to the 1990s (such as the use of 1990s songs, phrases, and adverts). Certain jokes and references may be missed on a first viewing, but nevertheless provoke pleasure when recognized. Some almost have an in-joke quality to them for the more film-savvy members of the audience, such as one of the flashback scenes involving a very young Noah freezing while eating (in an homage to Lex Murphy and her spoonful of jelly/jello) and Ellie Sattler (Jade) asking for help from the audience when lost ("follow the pipes").

Adapting a blockbuster film for the stage is a challenge even with a big-budget theater production, but Superbolt specializes in black box or festival theater, which usually demands a small stage and cast, minimal set, or props. *The Jurassic Parks* has a cast of three, few props, and no set aside from several plants upstage. From this, the company must create scenes from both *Jurassic Park* and the Parks' family history. While some of the re-enacted sequences are achieved by simply acting them out along with sound effects and mime, as the play continues the scenes taken from the film become increasingly complex. Moments which, in the film, require special effects and expensive sets are remade with minimal props, such as the *T-Rex*'s arrival signaled by a trembling glass of water held over a flashlight. Indeed, a significant amount of comedy comes from the hasty assembly and inventiveness of key moments as Terry, Jade, and Noah are forced to quickly improvise sometimes very complex scenes. For example, the kitchen scene where Lex (Ariana Richards) confronts the *Velociraptors* becomes a 2D fighting game, complete with a *Mortal Kombat*-style "Finish him!" Alternatively, lengthy scenes of dialogue from the film are reframed and/or conflated with real life, such as "Student councillor Muldoon" describing a trouble-making Jade in terms of the *Velociraptors*:

Muldoon: She made a dinner-lady cry. Called her a cow, ripped her to pieces. Jade is the reason the other girls can't eat outside anymore. She had them attacking the fences.
Terry: The electric ones?
Muldoon: No. This is a school.

One of the biggest (figuratively and literally) undertakings of this is, of course, reproducing the dinosaurs on stage, namely, the feature dinosaurs (the *Brontosauruses*, the *Triceratops*, the *Velociraptors*, and the *Tyrannosaurus Rex*). The company chose to do this by physically performing the dinosaurs on stage, rather than simply reacting to them. To avoid the repetition of simply imitating the dinosaurs, the company utilized their training from the Jacques Lecoq School in Paris, where they trained together. Lecoq's emphasis on precision and quality of movement (*qualité de mouvement*) demands a distinct and clear communication, where every physical action on stage must be easily understood. In a play where the characters have difficulty communicating with each other, this methodology becomes particularly pertinent; devising from a physical perspective first allows for words to be adapted into action. To complete their staging of the film, the characters must learn to speak—and listen— to each other. As the play continues, Terry, Jade, and Noah's physical performances become more complex and skilled as they gradually address the unspoken tensions within the family, in line with the audience's immersion into the world on stage. The infamous moment when Grant and Sattler arrive at the park and first see the *Brachiosaurus* is intentionally simple, with Noah picking up a surprised Jade while attempting a roar. Simon Maeder (Noah) explains:

The family at this point in the story are still getting into the telling of the film so we knew it couldn't be a showstopper moment. It was a transition. It represented the family crossing the threshold from memorial hosts, to film performers. Every dinosaur after that had to get more impressive. This culminated in an acrobatic lift and creative use of a backpack to recreate the infamous *T-Rex*. We had to get the characters to a point where they would believably do that, and that meant bringing the audience on the journey with us. Employing impressive physical acrobatics from the start would have diminished the impact of this dinosaur further down the line. But the basic form of me lifting Maria to create a dinosaur, was implanted in their heads as believable from the beginning.[2]

Using a combination of props, comedy, and physical theater, both actors and characters reform and embody the dinosaurs. For example, the sequence where the *Dilophosaurus* confronts and attacks Nedry is achieved by Jade performing as the dinosaur, delicately tiptoeing while copying the purring noises of the creature stalking Nedry (Terry). At the climax of the scene, Jade pounces on a terrified Terry as an unseen Noah hides behind her, using a flapping umbrella to recreate the *Dilophosaurus*' frills. As with other moments with feature dinosaurs in the play, the sequence works partly because of the performance (and clever use of props), and partly because the audience's knowledge of the original text essentially fills in the gaps. These sequences are recognizable from the film, but small touches or in-jokes enhance the narrative—and by extension, the nostalgia. Additionally, this technique allows for the scenes to be reframed, using the process of adaptation to the company's advantage. The *T-Rex* chase sequence is created with the aid of an empty backpack, co-opted to be the creature's head and mouth, while Noah carries Jade in an acrobatic lift to create the body and Terry is left to play the other characters in the scene. In contrast to Noah's poor attempts at roaring during the *Brachiosaurus* sequence, the *T-Rex*'s pre-recorded bellows are thunderous and blood-curdling. Despite the obvious peril on stage, the sequence is nevertheless played for comedic effect, including the use of the Blondie song "One Way or Another."[3] The enormity and terror of the scene cannot be directly portrayed on stage with the same effect as the film, so a scary, yet funny and tongue-in-cheek moment is created instead. Part of the pleasure of the show for the audience is the innovativeness of how iconic scenes are reproduced on a small stage; this sense of play—of acknowledging the constraints of the environment—becomes part of what makes the show successful as an adaptation.

Terry, Jade, and Noah are consistently played by the same actors, however; as they (Terry, Jade, and Noah) are portraying characters from their lives and from the film, they sometimes swap personas between (or sometimes during) scenes. Characters from the film are signified by often exaggerated physical and vocal tics in order to quickly and simply identify them to the audience: Malcolm's stuttering and pronounced "uh-uh" habit; Hammond's limp and accent; Muldoon's rigid posture, stilted speech, and gun. This allows any of the actors to play them at any moment; the audience can recognize which character is being portrayed even if the actor is swapped in the middle of a scene, keeping the narrative fluid.

Just as the characters become interchangeable, the play features interconnecting timelines, "where the past and present entwine like a strand of DNA."[4] Scenes of the Parks reenacting the film are intercut with flashbacks of their troubled family in reverse chronological order, starting with the week before the memorial and ending with Terry finding out that he and Madeline are expecting a second child. The switch from present to past is signaled through brief transition sequences of dinosaur herds as they move about the stage under cool-colored lights, accompanied by an acoustic rendition of the *Jurassic Park* theme played on guitar. Each herd movement is different, and suggestive of different kinds of dinosaurs, while remaining vague enough to represent the creatures without specifics.

Nostalgia in the play, therefore, functions within the family "past" scenes as well as the reenacted film "present," echoing Gizela Horváth's explanation of nostalgia types (utilizing frameworks by Svetlana Boym). First, restorative nostalgia "does not simply represent a desire for the past, but presumes a wish to experience it in the same form, to recreate it the way it 'used to be.'"[5] This kind of nostalgia idealizes the past, creating what Horváth terms "an enemy of progress—in the sense that it interprets progress as a distancing from the desired past."[6] *Jurassic Park* itself is primarily concerned with the problems of restorative nostalgia; Hammond sees only the wonder of the dinosaurs rather than the dangers of bringing them into a world ill-equipped both environmentally and sociologically. As Alan Grant (Sam Neill) notes, "Dinosaurs and man, two species separated by 65 million years of evolution have just been suddenly thrown back into the mix together. How can we possibly have the slightest idea of what to expect?" Here, nostalgia is made physical—along with its literal and figurative teeth—and dropped into a postmodern world. *The Jurassic Parks*, however, is more reminiscent of reflective nostalgia, where "the desire for the past is followed by a reflexive, critical attitude. Reflective nostalgia is aware of the selective and transformative mechanisms of memory (including collective memory) and distrusts the image it produces of the past."[7] While there is still desire for the past, the reflective framework lacks the idealization of restorative nostalgia, instead acknowledging that the past cannot—or should not—be brought back.

As the play's timelines continue to blend together, scenes of restorative nostalgia (the film scenes) are juxtaposed with those of reflective nostalgia (the Park's story); while the innovation and playfulness of the intertwining timelines encourages wonder and pleasure, there is an underlying sense of unease as life "finds a way" into the safe, nostalgic space on stage. An example of this occurs during the reenactment of the *Triceratops* scene, where Grant and his companions stumble across a sick dinosaur. Unlike the majority of the dinosaurs portrayed in the play, the *Triceratops* does not physically appear on stage. Instead, the actors' recreation of the iconic moment of Grant leaning against the animal accompanied by deep breathing sounds is enough to conjure the exact image in the spectator's minds. Noah begins to play a tune on a ukulele, with Jade soon joining in on a xylophone as her brother sings a child-like song about the *Triceratops* that is equally funny ("'bye, bye-'*ceratops*") and sad ("Now your tongue is so numb and your lungs are gasping for air"). As the song continues, the bittersweet moment is interrupted by a traumatic one, showing first Terry, then Jade, running through hospital corridors to a comatose Madeline. The timelines of the present (performing the film) and past (Madeline's death) blend together as the gentle, ingenuous song suddenly takes on darker and macabre connotations, the final verse ending with "I don't know if I'll ever get to see you again/But the fact that I've met you will always make me smile," followed by a pause before continuing onto the chorus. The lyrics gain a double meaning, while the sounds of breathing take on an eerie undertone. Staging the *Triceratops* as an invisible presence rather than directly represented by the actors allows the two timelines and moments of death to collide. The strained breathing of the creature suddenly becomes Madeline's; as the song ends, the sound of the ukulele plucking descends into the sound of her heart monitor on an otherwise silent stage.

The timelines begin to converge with increasing frequency and intensity, to the point where the family's flashbacks begin to interrupt the film narrative with no warning or transition, such as the mention of Hammond's flea circus momentarily morphing into a snapshot of a family outing at a carousel. This climaxes in an extended physical theater sequence where past and present violently collide. Set to a gentle, yet eerie, rendition of the "'Bye, Bye-'*ceratops*" theme and echoing sound effects, the bittersweet montage combines movements previously seen in the herd transitions morphing into memories of the Park family in happier times: taking photographs, surprising Madeline on her birthday, playing together. The sequence ends with the three actors embodying the crash that killed Madeline, smoothly moving together in unison as they slam on the brakes to the truck before blending into a scene of the remaining family sadly visiting Madeline's grave during a rainstorm. In the(ir) final moments, the dinosaurs return, only to look up as the cataclysmic fatal meteor draws near, tying together the two apocalyptic moments of the dinosaurs' extinction and Madeline's death.

Post-Humanism, Stage Bodies, and Dino DNA

The dinosaurs of the *Jurassic Park* franchise are simultaneously ancient and postmodern, but they are also arguably post-human constructs. They are not natural creatures; not only are they extinct creatures reanimated from discovered cells, but they are also not actual representations of dinosaurs. In *Jurassic Park* it is explained that the holes in the creature's DNA were patched with frog DNA (ultimately leading to the dinosaur's ability to change sex). Furthermore, the scientist Henry Wu (B. D. Wong) explains in *Jurassic World* (2015) that even the "natural" dinosaurs have been created based on what their audience expected to see, before going on to defend their more selective patchwork counterparts such as the *Indoraptor*: "you didn't ask for reality, you asked for more teeth." The dinosaurs are an amalgamation of real dinosaurs, other animals and human expectations; despite being animals, they are also strongly, genetically, influenced by humans.

This post-human dinosaur is introduced as far back as the original movie. Muldoon (Bob Peck) consistently warns that the *Velociraptors* are not simple animals; they have advanced cognitive and physical capabilities that put them on a par with humans. Unlike the other dinosaurs in the film, the threat of the raptors is in their animal nature (they want to kill and consume), their human-like behavior (opening doors) and their resulting uncanny nature (including the potential to change sex and breed). In *Jurassic World* and *Jurassic World: Fallen Kingdom* (2018), this is taken a step further, with the psychological and behavioral conditioning demonstrated with both *Velociraptor* Blue and handler Owen Grady (Chris Pratt) as well as the *Indoraptor*. While Blue's breeding and conditioning is initially presented as positive (she is made "more human" with the ability to show empathy), the reverse is true for the *Indoraptor*, who is presented as an unthinking animal that must follow its training and instincts. Ultimately, however, both dinosaurs become "too human." Blue cries tears when in pain and exercises choice, fighting for and then leaving the newly formed family of Owen, Claire Dearing (Bryce Dallas Howard), and Maisie Lockwood (Isabella Sermon) despite Owen's promises of care and protection. Although the *Indoraptor*'s obedience to training is ultimately its downfall, it demonstrates not only tactics and problem-solving, but also deception and even a mischievous side, toying with the sadistic hunter Wheatley (Ted Levine) by pretending to be sedated. The inverse relationship between dinosaurs and humans is also brought to life in the films through Maisie, a little girl made using the same cloning techniques as the dinosaurs. Like the dinosaurs, she is scientifically viewed as both a wonder and an abomination, empathizing with them to the point that she saves their lives by releasing them into the wild, completely altering the world's ecosystem, because "they're alive ... like me."

In *The Jurassic Parks*, human bodies are fluid almost to the point of augmentation, binding the humans to the dinosaurs; the actors are the Parks family, the film characters, the dinosaurs featured in the movie, the "wild" dinosaurs seen in the transitions and eventually an amalgamation of them all. The actors' embodiment extends beyond bodily boundaries into a post-human state. This is typical of Superbolt's work, in which characters do not only appear as themselves, but also "play" others, sometimes of different species. For example, in *The Uncanny Valley* (2012), the main characters ("the actors") are cyborgs and as such are not constrained by bodies or binaries. Therefore, the play is acted by humans playing cyborgs performing as humans as well as other, less evolved, cyborg ancestors. Much like the cyborgs that have almost crossed the uncanny valley and their older counterparts, one of the challenges for *The Jurassic Parks* actors is playing the herds of dinosaurs as well as the feature dinosaurs that appear in the film. The herds must project both the real and symbolic animal—recognizable yet vague enough to be any of a small number of species, accurate and memorable enough to incorporate movement yet not enough to interrupt the immersion of the experience. Instead of traditionally performed or reality-based dinosaurs, these herds have an intentionally artificial feel, with more precise, sharper, and angular movements. This more geometric interpretation sets the scene transitions apart from the main narrative. While the herds initially evoke confusion and laughter, their sudden interruptions are incorporated into the narrative to punctuate serious moments. The shock and strangeness of the transformation of both space and actors can be used to defuse tension. A particularly strained confrontation between Jade and Terry ends with the latter bellowing, "Well, your mum isn't here anymore!" swiftly followed by his comic transformation into a small, jumpy *Compsognathus* ("compy"). Conversely, these interruptions can underline the eeriness or uncanniness of a scene, particularly during the final movement sequence, where the distinct actions of the dinosaurs bleed into images of the family and the death of Madeline. This demands a post-human framework/performance. Rather than reacting to dinosaurs that are not physically there, the actors embody the creatures, introducing a playful element by creating them on stage through a combination of movement, sound, and props. The actors' movements reflect both dinosaurs and people; the stage body here must embody both human and nonhuman at different times and at the same time. Movements used to portray nonhuman creatures are later reintroduced and integrated into the final wordless physical theater sequence of the Park's family in happier times through to the mother's funeral, indelibly uniting both body and story.

Making Families

The play engages with academic analysis of *Jurassic Park*, such as Jade discussing the criticism of capitalism and the greedier Hammond's downfall in Michael Crichton's original novel,[8] as well as recalling her late-night talks with her mother ("Just two independent women talking together about *Jurassic Park* and the patriarchal hegemonization of society") and rewriting the lyrics to "Gangsta's Paradise"[9] in order to reflect feminist criticism of the film. Much like the film, the families and pseudo-families of the novel are dysfunctional and, as Laura Briggs and Jodi I. Kelber-Kaye point out, problematic in their failure to conform to white, heteronormative, middle-class ideals.[10] They note that "Crichton marks narrative problems to be solved through the improper gendering of women and girls, who take up masculine (read: professional) roles or are tomboys, dominating relationships with males,"[11] while families can be of mixed race or species, such as Ellie, Grant, and their dinosaur children.[12] Therefore, in the novel, "the closer the grouping comes to approximating a middle-class, racially/species homogenous, white American nuclear family with mom at home and girls in dresses, the better their chances for survival."[13] This continues in the film, where the survivors include the white, nuclear pseudo-family of Alan, Ellie (Laura Dern), Lex, and Tim (Joseph Mazzello), the children's grandfather and Malcolm (who, while unmarried, has children and in later films is revealed to be a loving, if absent, father). At the beginning of the film, Alan and Ellie, while a couple, are in dispute about their desire for children. Alan is adamant that he does not want children, and shows his unsuitability by terrifying a boy who doubts the danger of dinosaurs as well as ignoring Tim's enthusiastic pursuit. Ellie, on the other hand, does want children, and teases Alan by instructing Lex to ride in the same car because "it'll be good" for him. The children, Tim and Lex, are "improperly gendered,"[14] while Tim is scholarly, Lex is a tomboy. While in the novel it is Tim who has computer knowledge and is good at climbing, in the film this role is given to Lex (however, in the novel, Lex is more overtly a tough tomboy, carrying a baseball mitt and calling Tim a "sissy."[15] Therefore, "the work of the film's narrative becomes getting Grant to care for children ... the movie is as intent as the book in making nuclear families,"[16] with Grant and Sattler introduced as a couple in disagreement over whether to have children in direct contrast with the final scene where Sattler smiles as Grant embraces a sleeping Lex and Tim. The theme of restored or developing families continues throughout the franchise, including the latest instalment (at the time of writing), *Jurassic World: Dominion* (2022), which strenuously reinforces parent–child bonds in both biological (Blue and Beta; Maisie and Charlotte) and found families (Owen and Blue; Owen, Claire, and Maisie).

As Briggs and Kelber-Kaye note, "although it requires work to make Lexy and Tim into properly gendered children, it is also 'natural' in the sense that their 'right' gender emerges in response to stress; Lex whimpers, Tim takes charge," as oppose to the dinosaurs' "unnatural" or "monstrous" transformation from female to male.[17] In the film, Lex is ill-suited to the *Jurassic Park* environment even before the dinosaurs escape; she is a vegetarian and balks at the live goat being provided for food, she trips when walking across the park grounds, and she is wary about touching the animals. Once the dinosaurs are loose, she consistently makes bad survival decisions; shining the torch toward the *T-Rex*, screaming and panicking, almost strangling Alan when he tries to rescue her and refusing to touch the *Brachiosaurus* (and being sneezed on when she finally attempts it). The dynamic between Lex and Tim is somewhat paralleled in Jade and Noah. Jade is tough, angry, and closed-off, while Noah is the excitable, dino-loving, younger sibling. Noah is picked on, while Jade rules the girls at school with an iron fist. However, while the family is reunited by the end, they do not undergo the same "proper" re-gendering as Tim and Lex.

Briggs and Kelber-Kaye note the importance of the mother, along with "certain kinds of maternity" and the "natural" in *Jurassic Park*, while the contrasting father and "science" are ignorant, inadequate, and dangerous.[18] *The Jurassic Parks* subverts this dynamic; the science-minded, paleontologist mother is portrayed as the "good mother"; a nurturing caregiver who remembers her children's dietary requirements (like Lex, Jade is a vegetarian while Noah is lactose-intolerant) and delivers a forgotten lunch to the school, in contrast to the bumbling father who consistently forgets his son's dietary requirements, orders takeaways on school-nights (which Madeline would never allow), and forgets his daughter's dance school audition. Like the *Jurassic Park* scientists, men are shown as unnatural and insufficient at child-raising. Terry is ineffectual and ill-prepared; the *Jurassic Park* scientists underestimate their control and influence over their progeny. The mother, Madeline, is an indispensable character in *The Jurassic Parks* despite never appearing on stage. Her absence is palpable; not only are the audience ostensibly "gathered" for her memorial, but the flashbacks through family life all occur at significant moments where she is missing. In contrast to the film, in which ideals of motherhood run amok, the Park family are damaged by the mother's absence.

Initially, the Park family cannot communicate with each other. Despite the importance of *Jurassic Park* to the family, Terry demands that Noah go "out into the real world" and declares Madeline's memorial will be the last time that they watch "John Hammond and his little jungle adventure." He prefers to mumble to himself rather than dealing with difficult conversations and, when Noah tries to engage Terry in conversation about a possible ammonite "like mum always used to find," Terry cuts him off, dismissing the treasure as a "stupid rock." Noah uses *Jurassic Park* as a bridge to access memory and grief, as well as a method of communication (with increasing frequency as his character gradually regresses to a young child during the flashbacks). Terry's refusal to share that language or acknowledge those experiences further alienate him from his children. Taking part in restaging the scenes from *Jurassic Park*—and the resulting engagement with memory—allows him to regain that language and take part in family experiences again.

Jade, on the other hand, shuts herself off from her family, constantly listening to headphones and writing in her diary. Jade's way of expressing herself is through dance and music, performing routines to "Stronger"[19] and "Gangsta's Paradise." Terry is absent for her dance school audition and is unaware that she has switched dance partners, however, eventually both he and Noah are incorporated into the performances, completing the act as a family. When Jade addresses the audience directly, without her father and brother present, she is able to eloquently communicate her grief, but, like

Noah, must use the framework and language of *Jurassic Park* in order to be able to do so:

Jade: But, actually, like, life doesn't always find a way. And, personally, I think that's a really lame way of explaining chaos. It's more like, the world is really, really, really complex, and one tiny thing can have a massive impact. You know? Like, say, when you wake up one morning and you *don't* have an argument with your brother at the breakfast table, so you don't storm out the house and you *do* all have a really nice breakfast together. And then you do remember to pick up your lunchbox from the kitchen counter … And then, at lunchtime, your mum doesn't have to come to the school and bring you your lunch, because you haven't forgotten it. So, that truck that's driving really, really, really fast right by the school gates just keeps on going. … But, if one thing had changed, even a tiny bit, like, say, you *did* forget your lunch and your mum did have to come to the school to give it to you and she was crossing the road at the exact same moment when that truck was driving really, really, really fast…then your whole life would be changed forever. And, personally, I think that's chaos.

Terry's initial denial of the film equally denies Jade this language, and therefore the ability to express herself adequately. As a young child, she flatly responds "Who cares? He left us" when Terry separates from the familial home, invoking Lex's fear of abandonment throughout the events of *Jurassic Park*. Jade may experience a similar panic to Lex, but she cannot express it. Performing the de-extinction of the dinosaurs gives her access to communication, but also allows her to express the guilt and pain she has carried since her mother's death. Christy Tidwell speaks of the hopeful undertones of *Jurassic Park* through its "illustration of the possibilities of de-extinction, the process of returning animals from an extinct species to life."[20] In the same way that "de-extinction represents an opportunity for humanity to redress our wrongs,"[21] Jade wishes for a way to make amends, to change her actions from the day her mother died and, in so doing, bring her back to life. As the play continues, she is gradually able to engage with her grief and feelings of guilt, and, by extension, her family. Although she is initially reluctant to take part in the reenactment, she is eventually happy to share the stage with Terry and Noah, laughing as they interrupt her monologue in the guise of the infamous Mr. DNA. Ultimately, instead of leaving her father and brother for a commune in Scotland, she decides to stay, enthusiastically talking about a family meal that she had earlier rejected.

While Terry is not an unwilling father like Grant, or absent like Malcolm, he mirrors their inability to understand their children, reading Jade's phone and diary (later giving himself away by quoting it back to her), while forgetting her dance audition. Nevertheless, the heteronormative and complete family unit is restored at the end of the play. Jade agrees to stay with the family and supports her brother while Terry is able to comfort Noah rather than simply buying him presents to distract him whenever he is upset. Throughout the play, Terry, Jade, and Noah reenact the trauma of losing Madeline and of their family breaking down, allowing their grief to be expressed and exorcised. Concurrently, playing through the *Jurassic Park* family narrative allows them to begin to heal and come together; the story of Grant, Sattler, Tim, and Lex forming a chosen family is echoed on stage as three very different characters reignite their family bonds.

"You Can't Think Your Way Through This … You Have to Feel It"[22]

The Jurassic Parks relies on nostalgia, even when the audience are not particularly familiar with the original material. Nostalgia is invoked not only through the reenactment of the film scenes, but also through the family's own story, and it is the intertwining of the past and present that eventually allows the family to acknowledge their memories—both happy and sad—and be reunited. The bittersweet emotions of nostalgia texts are designed to evoke the same feelings as the original films alongside the time the spectator first saw them, usually considered to be "better," in that they are from a more innocent time in the spectator's childhood. Whereas the self-aware text invites the audience to engage in call-backs and in-jokes, prompting a collective and pleasurable nostalgia. The popularity of other 1980s–90s remakes and nostalgia-based texts set in the same period such as *Stranger Things* (2016–present), *The Fear Street Trilogy* (2021), or, indeed, the *Jurassic Park* franchise itself speaks to its appeal. However, care must be taken to move the narrative forward, avoiding the artistic stagnation of restorative nostalgia. In the case of *The Jurassic Parks*, the potential limitations of theatre's intimate space instead become an opportunity to re-engage with nostalgic memories, to reform spectacle and story from a different perspective. As Maeder explains, "theatre is a collaborative art. The images [from *Jurassic Park*] are all known to the audience already, so it was our job as theatre makers to make them see the dinosaurs in new ways, creating them in the minds of the viewers using the bare minimum of props and skills available to the actors and (more importantly) the characters."[23] The space where past, present, and future collide is filled with both wonders, humor, sadness, and unease. Like the Parks family and the *Jurassic Park* dinosaurs themselves, the past cannot be reclaimed, but it can be remembered.

Notes

1. "What Happened the Night Sam Neill (aka Dr. Alan Grant) saw the show and other frequently asked questions," *Superbolt Theatre*, 2015. https://superbolttheatre.com/superbolts-jurassic-park-what-happened-the-night-sam-neill-aka-dr-alan-grant-came-to-see-the-show-and-other-frequently-asked-questions/. Last accessed September 14, 2023.
2. Simon Maeder, email message to author, May 11, 2022.
3. Blondie, "One Way or Another," Track 2 on *Parallel Lines*, Chrysalis Records, 1978.
4. "The Jurassic Parks," *Superbolt Theatre*, 2015. https://superbolttheatre.com/jurassic-park/. Last accessed September 14, 2023.
5. Gizela Horváth, "Faces of Nostalgia. Restorative and Reflective Nostalgia in the Fine Arts," *Jednak Książki. Gdańskie Czasopismo Humanistyczne (Books Now. Gdańskie Humanistic Journal)*, no. 9 (April 2018): 145–56, 148.
6. Ibid., 148.
7. Ibid., 151.
8. Michael Crichton, *Jurassic Park* (New York: Random House, 1990).
9. Coolio featuring L.V. "Gangsta's Paradise," Track 3 on *Gangsta's Paradise*. Tommy Boy and Warner Bros., 1995.
10. Laura Briggs and Jodi I. Kelber-Kaye, "'There Is No Unauthorized Breeding in Jurassic Park': Gender and the Uses of Genetics," *NWSA Journal* 12:3 (2000): 92–113, 96.
11. Ibid., 96.
12. Ibid., 97. Incidentally, in *Jurassic World: Dominion* (2022), Grant and Sattler are romantically reunited and remain fascinated by dinosaurs either living (Sattler declares that "you never get used to it" when encountering a baby *Triceratops*) or dead (Grant has continued to dig up fossils because "palaeontology is a science, and science is about the truth"). However, despite being reunited with their "dinosaur children," they "parent" differently: instead of being "overwhelmed by the power of this place" in the original film, they take on responsibility for the future.
13. Ibid., 98.
14. Ibid., 91.
15. Crichton, *Jurassic Park*, 93.
16. Briggs and Kelber-Kaye, "There Is No Unauthorized Breeding in Jurassic Park," 104.
17. Ibid., 103.
18. Ibid., 94.
19. Britney Spears. "Stronger," Track 2 on *Oops…I Did It Again*, Jive Records, 2000.

20 Christy Tidwell, "'Life Finds a Way': *Jurassic Park*, *Jurassic World*, and Extinction Anxiety," in Jonathan (ed.) *Fiction and the Sixth Mass Extinction: Narratives of Loss* (Washington, DC: Lexington Books, 2020). 31–48, 36.
21 Ibid., 38.
22 Ellie Sattler to John Hammond, *Jurassic Park*.
23 Maeder, May 11, 2022. The author would like to thank Simon Maeder for his help and support with this work.

CONTRIBUTORS

Nathan Abrams is Professor of Film Studies at Bangor University, UK. He is the founding coeditor of *Jewish Film and New Media: An International Journal*, and he is also the author/editor of three books on Stanley Kubrick, including *The Bloomsbury Companion to Stanley Kubrick* (2021, with I. Q. Hunter), *Eyes Wide Shut: Stanley Kubrick and the Making of His Final Film* (2019, with Robert Kolker) and *Stanley Kubrick: New York Jewish Intellectual* (2018). He is currently working on a biography of Stanley Kubrick with Robert Kolker.

Carissa Baker is Assistant Professor of Theme Park and Attraction Management at the University of Central Florida in Orlando, USA. Her primary research focuses on narratives in the theme park space. She presents at academic conferences or themed entertainment industry events and publishes interdisciplinary work on theme parks. Baker has taught and researched in China in addition to having two stints as a visiting scholar at Breda University of Applied Sciences in the Netherlands.

Katie Barnett is Senior Lecturer in Film & Media Studies at the University of Chester, UK. Her research focuses primarily on representations of family and gender in American film and television from the 1990s onwards, with a particular interest in depictions of fatherhood, masculinity, and siblinghood on screen. She is the author of *Fathers on Film: Paternity and Masculinity in 1990s Hollywood* (2020) and is currently researching images of brothers and sisters in contemporary American cinema.

Ross Garner is Lecturer in Media and Cultural Studies at the School of Journalism, Media and Culture at Cardiff University, UK. His expertise concerns the spatial and material dimensions of media consumption. He is coeditor of the forthcoming edited collection *Pikachu's Transmedia Adventures* (2023) and is finishing the monograph, *Return to the Morphing Grid: Nostalgia, Licensing and Transmediality in the Neo-Saban Power Rangers Era* (2023). He is cochair of the SCMS Fan and Audience Studies SIG and one of the incoming editorial team for the journal *Popular Communication*.

Oliver Gruner is Senior Lecturer in Visual Culture at the University of Portsmouth, UK. His research focuses on American cinema and politics, often with a particular emphasis on the screenplay. He is the coeditor (with Peter Krämer) of *Grease Is the Word: Exploring a Cultural Phenomenon* (2019) and author of *Screening the Sixties: Hollywood Cinema and the Politics of Memory* (2016). He has had essays published in the *Historical Journal of Film, Radio and Television, Rethinking History, The Poster* and various edited collections.

James Kendrick is Professor of Film & Digital Media at Baylor University, USA, where he studies contemporary cinema. He is the author or editor of *A Companion to the Action Film* (2019), *Darkness in the Bliss-Out: A Reconsideration of the Films of Steven Spielberg* (2014), *Hollywood Bloodshed: Screen Violence and 1980s American Cinema* (2009) and *Film Violence: History, Ideology, Genre* (2009). He has published two dozen book chapters and journal articles, and he is also the film critic for the web site QNetwork.com.

Peter Krämer is Senior Research Fellow in Cinema & TV in the Leicester Media School at De Montfort University, UK. He also is a senior fellow in the School of Art, Media and American Studies at the University of East Anglia, UK, as well as a regular guest lecturer at the University of Television and Film Munich, Germany, Masaryk University, Czech Republic, and Palacky University Olomouc, Czech Republic. He is the author or editor of eleven academic books, including the BFI Film Classic *2001: A Space Odyssey* (2nd edition, 2020) and *United Artists* (co-edited with Gary Needham, Yannis Tzioumakis, and Tino Balio, 2020). He has published over eighty essays in academic journals and edited collections.

Tom Livingstone is a research fellow at The University of the West of England (UWE). His research focuses on emergent media with a particular interest in the impact of game engines on visual culture. He has published widely on film and digital media and his first book *Hybrid Images and the Vanishing Point of Digital Visual Effects* will be published by Edinburgh University Press..

Matthew Melia is Senior Lecturer in English Literature, Film and Media at Kingston University, UK. He is coeditor of *Anthony Burgess, Stanley Kubrick and A Clockwork Orange* (2022) and *The Jaws Book* (2020). He is the editor of *The Films of Ken Russell* (2021). Matt has contributed to a variety of publications, including *The Bloomsbury Companion to Stanley Kubrick* (2021), *Shadow Cinema: The Historical and Production Contexts* of Unmade Films (2020) and Reframing Cult Westerns (2020). In 2017 he convened the conference Ken Russell: Perspectives, Reception and Legacy, and in 2018 he co-convened the conference A Clockwork Symposium: A Clockwork Orange—New Perspectives. He is editor of the forthcoming special edition of Cinergie Il Cine e le Altre Arti, "Franchising Jurassic Park."

Ali Nabavizadeh is an assistant professor at the University of Pennsylvania School of Veterinary Medicine, USA. He has written numerous research articles on the anatomy, functional diversity, and evolution of feeding systems in large herbivorous dinosaurs and continues doing research on craniofacial anatomy in a broad range of extinct and living megaherbivores, including elephants. His interests in the portrayal of dinosaurs in film has also led to the publication of an article in the Natural History Magazine titled "Dinosaurs and Fantasia." He is also the lead author of the forthcoming book, An Illustrated Guide to Dinosaur Feeding Biology (2023).

Catherine Pugh is a writer and independent scholar with a PhD from the University of Essex, UK. Her research interests concern disability and mental illness, literary "madness," monsters, and horror landscapes. She has contributed to various collections including Slaying is Hell: Essays on Trauma and Memory in the Whedonverse (2022), Animal Heroes, Villains and Others: The Narrative Functions of Strange and Familiar Creatures in Film and Television (2022) and The Undead in the 21st Century: A Companion (2022), as well as online journals including Studies in Gothic Fiction and Aeternum: The Journal of Contemporary Gothic Studies.

Jennifer Schell is Professor of English at the University of Alaska Fairbanks, USA. Her specialties include North American literature, animal studies, Arctic writing, and environmental humanities. She is the author of "A Bold and Hardy Race of Men": The Lives and Literature of American Whalemen (2013) and has written numerous articles on ecogothic environmental themes, many of which involve endangered or extinct species (great auks, killer whales, polar bears, mammoths, megalodons, and Velociraptors).

Janet Staiger is William P. Hobby Centennial Professor Emeritus in Communication and Women's and Gender Studies at the University of Texas, USA. She particularly attends to questions about situated and historical authorship, audiences and reception, and positionalities of gender and sexuality. Among her books are Political Emotions (2010, coed.), Media Reception Studies (2005), Authorship and Film (2002, coed), Blockbuster TV (2000), Perverse Spectators (2000), Bad Women: Regulating Sexuality in Early American Cinema (1995), Interpreting Films (1992) and The Classical

Hollywood Cinema: Film Style and Mode of Production to 1960 (1985, coauthored).

Julie Turnock is Associate Professor of Media and Cinema Studies at the University of Illinois, USA. She is the author of *The Empire of Effects: Industrial Light and Magic and the Rendering of Realism* (2022) and *Plastic Reality: Special Effects, Technology, and the Emergence of 1970s Blockbuster Aesthetics* (2015). She has published on special effects, spectacle and technology of the silent and studio era, the 1970s, and recent digital cinema in *Cinema Journal, Film History, Film Criticism,* and *New Review of Film and Television Studies,* as well as several edited collections.

Ed Vollans is Teaching Fellow at the University of Leicester, UK. He is a former Bollywood journalist, member of the Creative Industries Federation, and teaches on advertising, promotion, audience, and game studies. His previous work explores the history of videogame trailers, the role of short-form digital promotion in publishing, and the industrial status of trailers in the arts. He is one third of the Watching the Trailer research project, which explores the attitudes to and the context of watching promotional trailers.

Daniel White is Lecturer of Musicology at the University of Huddersfield, UK, where he teaches on music for film and media, popular music studies, research skills, and performance. His doctoral research focused on the music of fantasy film franchises and their multimedia access points, and his book *Fantasy Film Music* will be published in 2023. He has also published widely on different aspects of this research, including an article in *Music, Sound and the Moving Image* on the opening sequences of the *Lord of the Rings* films and another in *InMedia* on music at *Harry Potter* tourist attractions. Other research interests include minimalist impulses in film music, the music of children's media, and the intersections of film music and fandom.

Allison Whitney is Associate Professor of Film and Media Studies in the Department of English at Texas Tech University, USA. Her research foci include the history of film technology, local film culture and oral history practices, sound studies, dynamics of race, class, and gender in film genres, and film studies pedagogy.

Linda Ruth Williams is Professor of Film at Exeter University, UK. She is the author of five books and contributed the chapter "Children as Bait" to *The Jaws Book: New Perspectives on the Classic Summer Blockbuster* (2020). She has also published on robots in Spielberg's films and on his representations of mothers and motherhood. She is the editor and coeditor of several volumes, including *Contemporary American Cinema* (2005). Linda was co-investigator of the AHRC-funded research project "Calling the Shots: Women and Contemporary UK Film Culture 2000–2015," and is now writing a book on women writer-directors in the British film industry. Since 2007, she has co-curated the Screenplay Film Festival in Shetland. Elsewhere, Linda has served as chair of the Edinburgh International Short Film Jury, cofounded the New Forest Film Festival, and has served as a jury member of the Strasbourg European Fantastic Festival and the Golden Trailer Awards.

INDEX

2001: A Space Odyssey (1968) 47
3D and 3D conversion process 2, 18,
    19 n.2, 86, 93, 122, 124,
    128 n.29, 263–75, 276 n.5
8 Out of 10 Cats Does Countdown
    (UK TV series) 75
9/11 250

Abrams, Nathan 16, 248, 256, 257
Abyss, The (1989) 8, 9
A.I. Artificial Intelligence (2001) 144,
    172, 190, 251
Airport (film series 1970–77) 49, 57
    n.25, 240, 241
Alive (1993) 245
Allen, Irwin (director and producer of
    disaster films) 166 n.13, 241,
    243–4, 253
Alligator (1980) 7, 224
Alpert, Rebecca 160
Al-Qaeda 250
Always (1989) 12, 185, 187, 245
Amblin Entertainment 6, 57, 58, 70,
    135, 138, 258 n.6
American New Wave 245, 247
Ancient DNA Newsletter 191, 193
Andromeda Strain, The (novel, 1969)
    11, 27, 28
animatronics 11, 24, 43, 115, 116,
    122, 140, 276 n.17, 296, 303–4
Apatosaurus 105, 206, 208
apocalypse 18, 170, 240, 251, 253,
    259, 317
Arendt, Hannah 162
Armageddon (1998) 49, 240, 246, 251
Armbruster, Karla 231
Art of the Deal, The (book, 1987)
artificial intelligence 249–51, 257

Aryan Papers (unmade Stanley Kubrick
    film) 157
atomic bomb 53, 163, 165, 242,
    251
atomic mutation 47, 242
Audissino, Emilio 75
augmented reality 132
Auschwitz 156, 159
Avatar (2009) 2, 19, 45, 48, 52,
    53–4, 295
Avengers: Age of Ultron (2015) 47
Avengers: Endgame (2019) 52

Back to the Future (1985) 44, 135
Bacon-Smith, Camille 133
Bakker, Robert (palaeontologist) 228
Balides, Constance 82–3, 86, 302, 304
"banality of evil" 162
banking systems 240
Barbasol can 248
Barker, Martin 133, 136
Barney the Dinosaur 277, 279, 286,
    287, 288, 290
Batman Returns (1992) 5
Battle at Big Rock (2019) 66 n.33,
    68–9, 132
Beast from 20,000 Fathoms, The
    (1953) 204, 242
Ben-Hur (1959) 49
Beyond the Poseidon Adventure (1979)
    241
Bhagavad Gita 165
Big Red (1945) 17, 224, 231–2
Biosyn 163, 175, 235, 252
Birds, The (1963) 57, 57 n.25
Birenberg, Leo (composer) 70–1
Blackgang Chine Family Theme Park
    (Isle of Wight, UK) 305

Blade Runner 2048 (2017) 92
blockbuster cinema 2–3, 5, 7–8, 14, 26, 33, 55, 86, 105, 108, 118, 126, 138–9, 185, 191, 192, 240, 244–5, 251, 264, 266, 289, 290, 301, 307
Blue the raptor 10, 81, 233–235, 297, 318, 320
Boesky, Ivan 174
Bogart, Humphrey 177
Bolan, Marc 158
Boland, Robert (psychiatrist) 194
"Bone Wars, The" 13
Boyarin, Daniel 160
"Boy-Dog" narratives 17, 231–6
Boys From Brazil, The (1978) 159
Bradshaw, G. A. 233
Breathed, Berkely 277, 285, 292
Bridge of Spies (2015) 251, 257
Bridge on the River Kwai (1957) 49
Brody, Martin (*Jaws*, Roy Scheider) 4, 187, 224
Browne, Michael W. 192, 194
Buhler, James 62
Burger King 140
Burian, Zdenk 203
Burton, Tim 11
Bush, George H. W. 175
"Butterfly Effect" 254

California 10, 12, 68, 157, 192, 193, 295
Calvin and Hobbes (comic strip) 279, 287, 289, 290
Cameron, James 8, 10, 21, 53, 116, 117, 127
"Camp Jurassic" (children's play area) 298
"Canopy Flyer" (rollercoaster) 16, 83, 84
capitalism 16, 81–94, 101, 165, 304, 319
Carter, Rick (production designer) 26, 31, 32
Casablanca (1942) 177
Chernobyl 248
childhood 28, 45, 75, 100, 103–6, 141, 177, 232, 323
chlorofluorocarbons (CFCs) 248

Chrysostom, John (Saint) 158
climate 49, 108, 190, 219, 248, 253
Clinton, Bill 180
Close Encounters of the Third Kind 27, 44, 187–9, 199
Code Blue (Michael Crichton screenplay) 28
commercial intertextuality 82–3, 85–7, 89–92
communism 248, 252
computer systems 241
Conan Doyle, Arthur 10, 45, 227
Congo (1995) 12
conspiracy theories 247
consumerism 15, 16, 85–9, 90, 175, 253
Corman, Roger (US film director and producer) 259 n.32
Costa Rica 30, 175, 252
Creative Artists Agency 28
Crichton, Michael 4, 6, 8, 11–14, 15, 21 n.26, 25–39, 44–6, 131–2, 134–6, 139–44, 146, 156–7, 165, 172, 185, 191–3, 242, 247, 254

D3D 86
Daily Mirror (UK Newspaper) 137
Danse Macabre (book, 1981) 195
Dante's Peak (1991) 240, 246
Davies, Derrick (website creator) 26, 31
Davis, Don (composer) 61, 64, 76
Dawn of the Planet of the Apes (2014) 48
De Jong, Caro 133
Dearing, Claire (Bryce Dallas-Howard, *Jurassic World*) 66, 72, 297, 298, 318
Debus, Allen 226
Deep Impact (1998) 49, 240, 251
Denson, Shane 119–20
Dern, Laura 3
digital cinema 9, 116, 119, 121, 269
digital dinosaurs 92, 113, 120, 122, 125

INDEX

digital effects 8–11, 16, 82, 89–94, 117, 126, 274
digital imaging 89
digital smoothness 113–26
digital technology 10, 85, 117, 118, 122, 123–6, 246
Digital Theater Systems 138
Dinosaur (2000) 205
dinosaur anatomy 203–20
Dinosaur Input Device (DID) 113, 123
Dinosaur Renaissance 204–5
dinosaur violence 223, 224, 225–31
Dinosaurs, The (Jim Henson TV series, 1991–4) 137
dinosaurs and dinosaurs across franchise 17, 18, 20, 22, 23, 24, 27, 30, 31, 35, 42, 43, 45, 46–50, 52, 57–60, 68, 75–8, 81–5, 86, 88, 90, 95, 97–113, 113–31, 203–223, 263–77
  Allosaurus 68, 217, 225, 227, 228
  Ankylosaurus 206, 212
  Apatosaurus 105, 206, 208
  Atrociraptor 217
  Brachiosaurus 6, 9, 59, 61, 65, 67, 73, 74, 105, 157, 173, 176, 199, 205, 206–8, 210, 289, 314, 315, 320
  Brontosaurus 82, 108, 203, 233, 314
  Carnotaurus 217, 305
  Compsognathus 30, 217, 219, 305, 319
  Corythosaurus 211
  Deinonychus 215
  Dilophosaurus 6, 171, 173, 176, 205 214–15, 248, 279, 299, 315
  Dimetrodon 218
  Dimorphodon 218
  Gallimimus 128 n.36, 214, 215, 228, 229–30, 252
  Giganotosaurus 217, 223, 231
  Hadrosaurs 207, 210–11, 227, 297
  Ichthyosaurus 226
  Iguanodon 211, 227, 305
  Lystrosaurus 218
  Mamenchisaurus 208
  Mosasaurus 5, 74, 81, 86, 218, 223, 231, 234, 297
  Nasutoceratops 68, 210
  Oviraptor 217
  Pachycephalosaurus 206, 211, 212
  Parasaurolophus 206, 207, 210–11, 305
  Plesiosaurus 225, 226
  Pteranodon 145, 218, 297
  Pterodactyl 108, 144, 225, 228, 233
  Pyroraptor 217
  Sinoceratops 210
  Spinosaurus 65, 144, 145, 217, 223, 230
  Stegosaurus 105, 108, 205, 212
  Stygimoloch 211–12
  T-Rex / Tyrannosaurus Rex 6, 8–9, 11–12, 35, 36, 37, 43, 62, 65, 81, 85, 89, 91, 92, 97, 98, 103, 107, 108, 113, 114–115, 135, 136, 145, 157, 159, 163, 164, 170, 172, 173, 173, 177, 179, 181, 205, 209, 210, 212–17, 223, 228–30, 231, 234, 245–6, 251, 251 254, 256–7, 268, 270, 272, 273, 274, 287, 289–90, 299, 301, 313–15, 320
  Therizinosaurus 217, 223
  Triceratops 6, 108, 171, 204, 205, 208–12, 227, 235, 296, 298, 314, 316, 317, 324 n.12
  Velociraptor/ Raptor 6, 7, 8, 10, 11, 14, 30, 35, 37, 62, 65, 67, 71, 72, 77 n. 19, 81, 88, 98, 101, 103, 106, 107, 108, 124, 128 n.36, 145, 157, 171, 172, 179, 205, 215–19, 223, 224, 228–9, 230, 231, 232, 233, 234, 246, 252, 254, 255, 256, 271, 273, 287, 289, 290, 296, 297, 298, 299, 300, 305, 313, 314, 318
"Dino-Soarin" (children's ride) 298
disaster cinema 239–48, 255–8
Disney, Walt 14, 32, 43, 204, 301
Disneyfication 252–3

Disneyland 42, 295, 296, 30
distribution 19 n.1, 99
DNA 2, 4, 7, 11, 34, 134, 135, 137, 162, 169, 186, 191–3, 219, 235, 242, 244, 250, 277, 315, 317–22
Doane, Mary Anne 84
Doctor Zhivago (1965) 49
Dodgson, Lewis (Cameron Thor) 163, 175, 252
Doherty, Amie (composer) 61
Dominican Republic 173, 252
Doonesbury (Comic Strip) 277, 285
Dr. Hobby (*A.I. Artificial Intelligence*; William Hurt) 189–191
Dr Strangelove, or *How I Learned to Stop Worrying and Love the Bomb* 10, 163
Dragon Teeth (2017 novel) 13
DreamWorks 140
Drinker Cope, Edward (palaeontologist) 13
Duncan, Jody 30, 82, 128 n.36, 237 n.17
Dutra, Randal (Stop Motion Animator) 116, 122, 123, 124, 125
Dyer, Richard 233, 290, 291

Eco, Umberto 302
ecosystems 53, 215, 219, 229, 230, 254, 318
Elliot (E.T.) (Henry Thomas) 189
Elsaesser, Thomas 6–7, 33
Embryonic Development and Induction (book, 1938) 159
Empire Strikes Back, The (1980) 122
Engel, Neil (creative director, Universal Studios) 19, 296, 299
ER (TV series) 11, 28
E.T. the Extra Terrestrial (1982) 7, 44–5, 52–4, 136, 137, 172, 187–9
event movie 1–8
evolution 67, 73, 83, 89, 90, 179, 181, 198, 213, 225, 249–50

existential threat 239–58
Exorcist, The (1973) 51
extinction and extinction events 46, 65, 92, 108, 186, 196, 212, 218, 228, 240, 305

Facebook 98–9
Faludi, Susan and 'domestic apocalypse' 170
Fantasia (1940) 204
Fantastic Beasts film franchise 49
Fight Club (1999) 119
"Flying Dinosaur, The" (theme park ride) 298
Four Horsemen of the Apocalypse, The (1921) 49
Frankenstein 17, 45, 57 n.23, 164, 186, 193, 194–200, 256, 257
Frayling, Christopher 193, 194
French, Phillip (*Observer* film critic, UK) 283
Freud, Sigmund 277–82, 288, 290, 291, 292–3, 293 n.10
Friedman, Lester D. 162, 163

Gaboury, Jake 89, 120
Gaffney, Dr. Eugene 194
Gennaro, Donald (Ferrero, Martin) 4, 17, 30, 34, 36, 160, 163, 170, 172–5, 176, 177, 179, 180, 213, 229, 252, 254, 273
Gertie the Dinosaur (1914) 10, 203
Ghettoization 158
Ghost in the Shell (2017) 92
Giacchino, Michael (film composer) 61, 65–9, 71, 73, 75, 77 n.19
globalization 242, 248, 251–3, 254, 257
Globe, Brad (Amblin Marketing and Licencing) 136
Godfather, The (1972) 51
Godzilla (1998) 47, 240, 251
Godzilla (2014) 47
Godzilla (*Gojira*, Japan, 1955) 205
Goldblum, Jeff 3, 75, 141, 155, 160, 161, 165

Goldeneye (1995) 140
Golem of Prague, The 164
Golems 164–5, 256
Gone With the Wind (1939) 49
Gothic, the 192, 195
Grady, Owen (Chris Pratt, *Jurassic World* Franchise) 81, 232, 297, 298, 318
Grant, Alan (Sam Neill) 4, 5, 9, 17, 29–30, 31, 32, 33–5, 36–8, 45, 59, 104, 105, 114, 160, 161, 162, 164, 169, 170, 173, 177, 178–80, 181, 196, 198, 199, 206, 207, 208, 213–15, 219, 233, 242, 252, 254, 255, 256, 270, 271, 272, 299, 301, 306, 314, 316, 320, 322–3, 324
Gravity (2006) 119
Gray (Ty Simpkins) 66, 81, 82, 87, 223, 234
Gremlins (1984) 48, 258 *n*.6
Gremlins 2: The New Batch (1990) 240, 258 n.6, 258 n.7
Grey, The (2011) 224
Grizzly (1976) 224
Grossberg, Laurence 102–3
Gulf War 248, 278
Gunning, Tom 18
Gurevitch, Leon 16, 88, 92

Hadas, Leora 136
Halloween (1978) 7
Hammond, John (Richard Attenborough) 4, 9, 14, 15, 26, 27, 28, 29–31, 32, 34, 35, 36–7, 38, 45, 59, 62, 64, 68, 81, 82, 142, 158, 160, 161, 162–4, 170, 172, 173, 174, 175, 176, 196–200, 207, 214, 219, 229, 242, 250, 252, 253, 254, 255, 256, 301–303, 304, 311, 315–17, 319, 321
Haraway, Donna 224
Harry Potter franchise (2001–11) 10, 47, 97, 295, 303
Harryhausen, Ray (stop motion animator) 204

Hasbro (toy manufacturer) 82, 140
Haskell, Molly (US film critic) 158, 159
Hayes, Craig (digital effects team) 117, 123, 124, 129 nn.42, 44
Heise, Ursula 236 n.3
Herman Melville (author) 45
Hess, Dr. Roberta (palaeontologist) 192
heteronormativity 100, 319, 323
high concept 3, 25, 98, 103, 143, 170, 244, 245
Higuchi, Russell (molecular biologist) 191–2
Hiroshima 53, 54
Hitchcock, Alfred (film director) 101
Hitler, Adolf 159
Hollywood and 'New Hollywood' 2, 4, 5, 6, 8, 11, 14, 25, 27, 29, 32, 38, 43–55, 74, 138, 141, 159, 162, 170, 178, 179, 181, 193, 239, 245, 247
Hollywood reporter (trade publication) 142
Holocaust, the 12, 13, 16, 156–9, 165, 251, 257
holograms 87, 90–3
Honeycutt, Kirk (journalist, Hollywood reporter) 142
Hook (1991) 12, 13, 26, 31, 33, 134, 185, 245
Hooper, Matt (Richard Dreyfuss, *Jaws*) 5, 187–8, 199
Horn, Dara (American novelist and essayist) 157, 159, 166 n.13
Hubris 4, 17, 45, 52–5, 165, 169, 176, 181, 190, 197, 242, 250, 253, 255–6, 266, 273
Hula Hoops (snack) 142

I, Robot (2004) 47
Icke, David 248
illusion 19, 36, 92, 115, 120, 241, 249, 265, 268, 302, 311
IMAX and IMAX 3D 18, 86, 264, 265–6, 267, 271, 274–5, 276 n.5

Independence Day (1997) 2, 14, 260, 240, 245
Indiana Jones Adventure (Disneyland) 296, 305
Indiana Jones franchise 47, 141, 159, 170, 177, 179, 220
Indiana Jones and the Last Crusade (1989) 12, 44, 187
Indiana Jones and the Raiders of the Lost Ark (1981) 187
Indiana Jones and the Temple of Doom (1984) 44, 177, 187
"Indominus Rex" (*Jurassic World*) 67, 71, 77 n.20, 81, 172, 217, 252, 297, 304
"Indoraptor" 217, 223, 231, 235, 318
Industrial Light and Magic (ILM) 8, 10, 89, 16, 113, 115, 116–17, 113, 122–123, 125, 126 n.4, 128 n.30, 129 n.43, 129 n.44, 138 n.36, 157, 245, 266
Innovation Centre (*Jurassic World*) 87, 90, 92, 93
internet memes 59, 61
Iron Man (2008) 120
"Isla Nublar Land" (Universal Theme Park) 298
Isla Sorna 63, 76 n.10
Island of Doctor Moreau (1896 novel) 45
"Islands of Adventure" (Universal Theme Park) 74, 297, 298, 303, 305, 306
Issac, Keith (Universal merchandising president) 137
It Came From Beneath the Sea (1955) 242

Jackson, Peter 115
Jarvis, Erich (neurobiologist) 233
Jaws (1975) 1, 4–8, 15, 11, 13, 14, 16, 27, 28, 44, 47, 51, 52, 53, 54, 57, 134, 135, 155, 156, 159, 162, 163, 170, 174, 175, 177, 181, 185, 187–8, 199, 200, 224, 229, 242, 244–6, 250–1, 256
Jaws 2 47

Jenkins, Eric 89, 93
Jenkins, Henry 300
jokes 18, 32, 277–94, 313, 315, 323
Jouhaneu, Jacques 193
Journey to the Beginning of Time, A (1955) 204
Journey to the Center of the Earth (novel, 1864) 17, 224, 226, 227, 236
Judgement Day (TV movie, 1998) 240
Jumanji (1995) 48
Jumanji: Welcome to the Jungle (2017) 48
Jungle Book, The (2016) 48
Jurassic Foundation 136
Jurassic Outpost (website) 20 n.23, 98
Jurassic Park (1993)
  adaptation 15–16, 25–43, 53, 71, 72, 85, 87, 93, 122, 131, 132, 137, 139, 143, 164, 165, 180, 194–6, 228, 245, 304, 311–24
  animatronics 11, 24, 43, 115, 116, 122, 140, 276 n.17, 296, 303–4
  artificial intelligence 249–51, 257
  Barbasol can 248
  blockbuster 2–3, 5, 7–8, 14, 26, 33, 55, 86, 105, 108, 118, 126, 138–9, 185, 191, 192, 240, 244–5, 251, 264, 266, 289, 290, 301, 307
  Box Office 2, 3, 5, 7, 12, 15, 19 nn.2, 4, 42–55, 134, 245
  chaos theory 14, 31, 35, 46, 161, 196, 254–5
  cinema of attractions 9, 18
  cinematography 83, 87, 93, 119, 157, 268
  commercial intertextuality 82–3, 85–7, 89–92
  consumerism 15, 16, 85–9, 90, 175, 253
  Costa Rica 30, 175, 252
  critical reception 3–7

INDEX

digital dinosaurs 92, 113, 120, 122, 125
digital effects 8–11, 16, 82, 89–94, 117, 126, 274
dinosaur violence 223, 224, 225–31
DNA 2, 4, 7, 11, 34, 134, 135, 137, 162, 169, 186, 191–3, 219, 235, 242, 244, 250, 277, 315, 317–22
environments and environmental catastrophe 13, 45, 52–5, 67, 85, 90–2, 105, 114, 193, 198, 219, 228, 241, 246, 248–50, 257, 299, 300, 302, 312, 315, 317, 320, 322
event movie 1–8
family 7, 27, 31, 35, 44, 65, 67–9, 137, 138, 162, 163, 171, 179, 180, 208, 224, 232, 250, 256, 279, 291, 298, 305, 307, 311–23
fandom and fan consumption habits 16, 97–109
female representation 5, 38, 54, 67, 101, 108, 158, 169, 171–2, 190, 219, 289, 320
fences and containment systems 62, 156, 164, 171, 229, 241, 251, 266, 271, 273, 297, 314
film premier 1, 1 n.1, 137, 191
final sequence 257
franchise 2, 7, 10, 15–18, 19 n.4, 43, 45–52, 59–94, 97–109, 127 n.22, 130–46, 150 n.73, 158, 170, 177, 206–20, 295, 296, 297, 298, 300, 304, 307, 312, 317, 320, 323
gates 62, 70, 71, 74, 114, 213, 299
genre and generic trends 6, 15, 17, 18, 47–50, 139, 156, 186, 225, 236 n.6, 239, 241
   exploitation cinema 7, 259 n.32
   horror cinema 3, 7, 67, 106, 142, 164–5, 186, 187, 191, 224, 236 n.3, 241, 251, 272, 278, 279, 289, 290–3, 294 n.17, 297

science fiction 11, 44, 93, 101, 107, 186, 203, 247–8, 250, 303, 306
war film, the 250, 256
Western, the 241
gift shop, the 15, 81–4, 85–6, 162, 252
"God Creates Dinosaurs..." 161, 171, 250
internet memes 59, 61
"Island Fanfare / Journey To the Island (score) 61–4, 66, 68, 69–73, 74, 76 n.4
Isla Nublar 29, 30, 34, 37, 62, 63, 66, 70, 72, 76 n.8, 162, 176, 178, 183 n.21, 243
Jewishness 16, 155–65, 188
jokes 18, 32, 277–94, 313, 315, 323
"Life Finds A Way..." 37, 53, 236 n.3, 250
logo 43, 63, 97–8, 107, 136, 300, 306, 307
marketing 1, 3–6, 15, 16, 33, 97, 103, 106, 127 n.16, 131–46, 170, 304
masculinity 5, 17, 169–85
merchandising 5–7, 15, 29, 34, 36, 38, 82–3, 86, 93, 98, 132–3, 134, 136–7, 139–41, 197, 252, 270, 289
musical world building (across the franchise) 59–81
nostalgia 19, 104–8, 141, 266, 311–24
opening sequence 6, 62, 63, 162, 229, 252, 267
paleontology 15, 17, 46, 98, 178, 180, 186, 192, 194, 203–20, 237 n.14, 276 n.5, 307
parenthood (including motherhood and fatherhood) 5, 28, 33, 34, 35, 53, 163, 164, 170, 172, 176–80, 186, 190, 204, 205, 232, 235, 244, 255, 278, 279, 288–9, 290, 302 306, 312, 313, 319, 320, 321, 322, 324 n.12
park infrastructure 229, 241, 254, 255, 256
park systems 254–6

340 INDEX

production (*see also* adaptation and script development) 8, 15–16, 18, 19, 27, 26, 27, 30, 31, 113–18, 121–6, 134, 135, 138–9, 155, 256, 263–4
promotion (including poster) 4, 43, 44, 131, 132, 134–9, 274–5
rating 4, 45, 137, 142
realism 9, 16, 116–18, 120–6, 127 n.11, 128 n.30, 187, 193, 266, 267, 268, 269
response from the scientific community 10–11, 17, 191–4
science and scientists 17, 29, 54, 158, 160, 161, 164, 169, 172, 185–91, 194–200, 219, 242, 307, 321
score / main theme 61, 62–75
security systems 162, 172
spectacle 107, 108, 136, 138, 161, 173, 199, 224, 227, 228, 229, 245, 247, 250, 252, 264, 266, 268, 272, 275, 304, 323
systems 62, 156, 164, 171, 229, 241, 251, 266, 271, 273, 297, 314
technology (production and diegetic) 9–10, 19, 19 n.2, 27, 53, 54, 55, 85, 89, 114, 115, 117–18, 118–21, 121–6, 138, 144–5, 164, 180, 186, 189, 192, 193, 228, 240–2, 245, 246, 249, 269, 275, 283
toys 2, 6, 34, 46, 61, 82, 85, 86, 88, 132, 133, 136, 141
trailer 133, 136, 138, 141–2, 145
T-Rex sequence 114–15, 159, 163, 164, 170, 213–14, 128 n.36, 273
twentieth anniversary 263, 275
West Indian Lilac 209
"Your scientists were so preoccupied with whether they could…" 36, 161, 198, 253, 269
"*Jurassic Park*—The Ride" 297
Jurassic Park III (2001) 2, 21 n.6, 46, 47, 50, 64, 66, 68, 97, 131, 132, 133, 139, 143–6, 210, 211, 212, 216, 217, 230
Jurassic Park IV (unmade film) 7, 20 n.23, 21 n.26, 258 n.25
Jurassic Park (Michael Crichton novel) 6, 8, 10, 11, 13–14, 15, 25–31, 36, 39, 44, 45, 131, 132, 134, 135, 137, 156, 165, 172, 179, 185, 191, 192, 226, 242, 246, 253, 254, 297, 299, 301, 319, 320
"*Jurassic Park* River Adventure" (theme park ride) 74, 298, 301
"Jurassic Park the Musical" 75
Jurassic Park: Behind the Scenes (walk through exhibit) 296
Jurassic Park: Operation Genesis (computer game, 2003) 73
Jurassic Parks, The (theatre production) 19, 311–23
Jurassic World (2015) 2, 5, 20 n.23, 46, 47, 50, 56 n.15, 56 n19, 67–70, 72, 74, 75, 78 n.41, 81, 82, 86, 87, 89–93, 99, 105, 172, 208, 210, 211, 218, 223, 233, 252, 298, 301, 303, 317, 318
Jurassic World: Aftermath (VR game, 2019) 87
Jurassic World: Alive (augmented reality game, 2008) 132
Jurassic World: Camp Cretaceous 2, 15, 50, 70–71, 132, 304
Jurassic World: Dominion (2022) 2, 19 n.4, 46, 47, 51, 64, 69, 132, 177, 208, 210, 211, 217, 218, 235, 245–6, 320, 324 n.12
Jurassic World: Evolution (computer game, 2020) 72, 74
Jurassic World: Evolution 2 (2021) 72
Jurassic World: Fallen Kingdom (2017) 2, 46, 47, 50, 66, 67, 68, 69, 87, 132, 169, 177, 183 n.21, 210, 212, 217, 234, 235, 297, 318

Jurassic World franchise 10, 15, 17, 61, 65–7, 106, 131, 132, 146, 210, 212, 216, 217, 218, 223, 224, 231, 232–6, 245, 246
"*Jurassic World*: The Ride" 74, 297
"*Jurassic World* Velocicoaster" (theme park ride) 74, 78 n.41, 298, 301

Kaiju 204, 256
Kalmus, Natalie 88
Karel Capek 45
Kellogg's (cereal brand) 142
Kendrick, Ben 264
Kennedy, Kathleen 143, 274
Keys (*E.T.*, Peter Coyote) 54, 118–19
King Kong (1933) 16, 45, 48, 63, 100, 113–18, 121, 172, 204, 227
King Kong (1976) 48
King Kong (2005) 48
King, Stephen 195
Knight, Wayne 3, 175
Koepp, David (screenwriter) 13–14, 15, 26, 31, 32–37, 38
Kokoro Dinosaurs (travelling exhibition) 137
Kong: Skull Island (2017) 48, 306
KP Foods 142
Kramer, Peter 27
Kripke, Saul 62
Kubrick, Stanley 128 n.33, 157, 158, 163, 250

Lacombe, Claude (Francoise Truffaut, *Close Encounters*) 188
Lacy, Mark 173
Laist, Randy 180
Lake Placid (1999) 224
Land Before Time, The (1988) 141, 205
Land that Time Forgot, The (1924) 17
Land that Time Forgot, The (1974) 204
Land Unknown, The (1957) 227
Last Action Hero (1993) 3
Lee, Ang 2
Legend of Isla Nublar, The (LEGO series, 2019) 2, 72

Legend of Tarzan, The (2016) 213
LEGO and *LEGO Jurassic World* 2, 15, 71, 72, 132, 159
Levinson, Barry 115, 129, 44
Lex (Ariana Richards) 5, 7, 33, 34, 35, 37, 88, 170, 172, 174, 175, 178, 179–81, 207, 208, 213, 215, 223, 229–30, 255, 271, 314, 320–3
Life of Pi (2012) 48
Lion King, The (1994) 7, 44
Lord of the Rings, The franchise, 2, 10, 16, 47, 115, 129 n.45, 133
Lorenz, Edward (scientist) 253
Los Alamos 65
Lost World, The (novel, 1912) 17, 45, 224
Lost World, The (1925) 20, 117, 224
Lost World: Jurassic Park, The (1997) 12, 13, 31, 46, 50, 63–4, 66, 69, 77 n.19, 97, 125, 131, 133, 139–43, 208, 210–12, 217–18, 230, 240, 246
Lost Worlds and Lost World narratives 17, 59–75, 224–5, 225–31
Lucas, George 44, 57 n.26, 244

Maat, Henk Pander 133
Maisie Lockwood (Isabelle Sermon, *Jurassic World* franchise) 233, 235, 318, 32
Malcom, Ian (Jeff Goldblum) 4., 5, 13, 15, 17, 18, 26, 28, 31, 34, 35, 38, 101, 160, 162, 169, 170, 179, 196, 210, 213, 219, 229, 242, 248, 250, 253–55, 257
Manhattan Project, the 165
Manovich, Lev (theorist of digital cinema) 92, 118–121
Margaritaville (chain brand) 81, 83
Mars Attacks (1996) 240, 257 n.7
Marsh, Othniel Charles (palaeontologist) 13
Marvel Cinematic Universe (MCU) 2, 120
Marx, Groucho 161
Masculinist Monster Myth 224

Masrani, Simon (Irrfan Khan, *Jurassic World*) 66
Matrix, The (1998) 16, 47, *119*
Matrix: Revolutions, The (2003) 47
Matsushita (Japanese electronics company) 4
mattering maps 101–9
Maus: A Survivor's Tale (1991) (graphic novel) 159
Mazzello, Joseph 208
MCA/Universal 6, 134, 137
McBride, Joseph 177, 187
McCay, Winsor (cartoonist) 203
McCreery, Mark (visual artist and creature designer) 122, 205
Meg, The (2018) 224
Men in Black (1997) 240
Mengele, Josef (Nazi Doctor and Eugenicist) 159
Menschlikayt / Mensch 17, 160, 161, 165
Mercedes-Benz 140
Metz, Christian 121
Millenium, The 10, 18, 86, 118, 170, 247–8
Millennium Bug 240–1
Mini Cheddars (snack) 142
Minority Report (2002) 189
Mitchell, W. J. T. 100, 108, 225
Moby-Dick (1851 novel) 45
Moby-Dick (1956) 48
Mohammed, Nick (comedian) 75
monsters, monster movie and monster theory 4, 5, 6, 14, 38, 142, 162, 170, 188, 191, 226, 236 n.6, 242, 246, 250, 256
Morris, Nigel 14, 28, 250
Morse, Janice 99
Mother Nature 52–5
MPAA 137
Muldoon (Bob Peck) 5, 171–2, 175, 267, 313, 314, 318
Munich (2005) 256
Muren, Dennis (visual effects supervisor, ILM) 8, 10, 117, 122

natural disasters 49, 57 n.25, 175, 240
Nazi Germany 158

Nedry, Dennis (Wayne Knight) 3, 17, 160, 162–3, 164, 170
Neill, Sam 17–18; 105
New York Times 10, 12, 159, 161, 186, 192, 193–4, 242, 288
newsweek 6, 180, 185, 186, 283, 284, 287
Nexis (media database) 46, 133, 278
Night Skies (unmade script) 7
Nightmare on Elm Street (1984) 290
Noble, Brian 106

O'Brien, Willis (stop motion artist) 204
O'Flinn, Paul 195
Old Yeller (1956) 17, 224, 231, 232, 236
One Million Years BC (1966) 227
ontological montage 92
ontology 118
opening sequence 6, 62, 63, 162, 229, 252, 267
Oppenheimer, J. Robert 164–5
Ornithischia 205, 209–12, 215
Ostrom, John (palaeontologist) 228
Outbreak (1995) 49
Outland (comic strip) 277, 285
ozone layer 248

paleontology 15, 17, 46, 98, 178, 180, 186, 192, 194, 203–20, 237 n.14, 276 n.5, 307
"Pandora: the World of *Avatar*" (theme park) 295
Pena, Jeremiah (composer) 73
Piranha (1978) *21*
Pirates of the Caribbean franchise 47
Planet of Dinosaurs (1977) 204
Planet of the Apes franchise 48, 57 n.25, 253
Plaza Cinema (Liverpool, UK) 1
Plumwood, Val 224
podcasts 16, 98, 166 n.13
Poinar Jr., Dr. George O. (palaeontologist) 192
Poltergeist (1982) 7, 187, 189
Poseidon Adventure, The (1972) 49, 57 n.25, 166 n.13, 240, 247, 251, 252, 254–5

Possession (1981) 3
post-cinema and post cinematic spectator 84–85, 89–94, 119
posthumanism 317–19
postmodernism 7, 302, 304, 316, 317
Predator 2 (1991) 240
promotional culture 83, 93
promotional software 144
"Protocols of the Elders of Zion" (anti-Semitic conspiracy theory, 1903) 247–8
"Pteranodon Flyers" (theme park ride) 298
Purse, Lisa 199

Quint (Robert Shaw, *Jaws*) 5, 14, 53, 54, 181

R.U.R. (Rossum's Universal Robots) (play, 1921) 45
race 100, 158, 159, 247, 320
rain 63, 136, 272–3, 273–5
"Rapids Adventure" (theme park ride) 298
"Raptor Encounter" (theme park exhibit) 297, 298
"Raptor Training School" (interactive exhibit) 298
Razorback (1984) 224
Read, Piers Paul (author) 245
Return of the Jedi (1984) 10
Richards, Ariana 7
Rising Sun (1993) 3
"Rites of Spring, The" (1913) 204
"River Adventure" (theme park ride) 73
Rogin, Michael 167
Rogue (2007) 224
Ross, Miriam 274
Rwandan Genocide 247

safety systems 162–3
Sally Forth (comic strip) 279
Sattler, Ellie (Laura Dern) 5, 9, 29, 30, 31, 32, 33, 34–35, 36, 37–38, 101–5, 160, 162, 171, 196, 198, 199–200, 206, 208, 218, 219, 250, 254–6, 296, 299, 313, 314, 320, 323

Saving Private Ryan (1998) 250, 256
Sayles, John (director and screenwriter) 7, 20 n.23
scale 9, 18, 114, 115, 119, 122, 170, 240, 245, 270–1
Schatz, Thomas 159
Schinder's List (1993) 12, 13, 16, 138, 155, 156, 157–9, 165, 250, 256
Schober, Adrian 174, 177
Schwarzenegger, Arnold 3, 174
Scotch Marmo, Malia (screenwriter) 13, 15, 26, 32–8
Sega 77 n.19, 140
Seinfeld (1991–98) 3, 162, 175
Seventh Voyage of Sinbad, The (1958) 48
Shaviro, Steve 85
Shay, Don 30, 82, 237 n.17
Shelley, Mary 45, 164, 186, 194, 195, 196, 200
Shining, The (1981) 7, 158
ShoWest '93 138
"Singularity, The" 249–51
Sony 4
specimen-spectacle-complex 106–7
spectatorship 84–90, 268–9
Spemann, Hans (Nazi scientist) 158–9
Spielberg, Steven (*see individual films*)
  adaptation and development 26, 27–32, 33, 35, 38, 135, 156, 192
  and George Lucas 44, 244
  and James Cameron 8, 53
  and UK opening of *Jurassic Park* 1, 19 n.1
  as director 11–13
  Box Office 44
  child casting 172
  collaboration 26, 27, 33, 34
  collaboration with Michael Crichton 7, 11–12
  creative power 136, 139, 140, 191
  debt to B movies 242, 243
  debt to the disaster movie 244, 246, 250
  digital development 8–11, 122, 245
  direction 229, 242, 263, 264, 274
  Hammond-Spielberg connection 34

Jaws and *Jurassic Park* 4–8, 155, 187–9
Jewishness 155–6, 159–65
Jurassic Park publicity 44
love of science fiction 186
Lyric cinema, Carmarthen 19 n.1
making *Jurassic Park* / *Schinder's List* at the same time 138, 156–9
prevents own children watching *Jurassic park* 4
producer 2, 143
producer 44, 124, 135, 144
promotion and marketing 135, 136
reluctance over *The Lost World: Jurassic Park* 139–40
Spielberg 'brand' 4, 11, 17–18, 27, 33, 38, 131, 132, 135, 244
Spielberg and Hammond parallels 9
Spielbergian motifs and themes 172, 173, 174, 177, 179, 180, 186, 187, 189, 198
star power / author status 137–8, 140, 142, 143–4, 264, 288
3D 266, 267, 273, 301
unmade films and collaboration with John Sayles 7, 21 n.26
Spiegelman, Art 159
Stallone, Sylvester 3, 174
Star Trek: The Motion Picture (1979) 47
Star Wars (1977) 1, 2, 51, 52, 122, 244
Star Wars franchise 2, 10, 44, 47, 53, 97
Star Wars: The Phantom Menace (1999) 266
"*Star Wars*: Galaxy's Edge" (theme park) 295
Stegosaurus 105, 108, 205, 212
Steiner, Max (film composer) 63
stereoscopy 263–4, 267–8, 270, 285
stop motion 10, 16, 74, 113, 115–77, 122–5, 126 n.3, 127 n.11, 129 n.50, 203–5
Stravinsky, Igor 204

subconscious 3D etiquette 263, 266, 275
Sugarland Express, The (1970) 5
Superbolt (theatre company) 19, 311, 313, 318
Swarm, The (1978) 241

Tan, Ed S. 104
Tarantino, Quentin 1
Tarzan (1999) 48
Tarzan 233
technothrillers 27
Ten Commandments, The (1956) 49
Terminator (1984) 8
Terminator 2 (1991) 3, 8, 10, 11, 47, 116, 118, 244, 245, 250, 251
Terminator: Salvation 47
Tetley Tea 141
Texas Chainsaw Massacre, The (1974) 290
Tim (Joseph Mazzello) 5, 7, 33–4, 35, 37, 164, 170, 172, 174, 175, 178, 179, 180, 181, 207, 208, 213, 215, 218, 223, 229–30, 255, 271, 272, 273, 320, 321
Tippett Studio, The 113, 116–17, 122
Tippett, Phil (creature designer) 10, 113, 122–5, 129 n.50
Titanic (1997) 5, 18, 44, 45, 59, 52, 53–4, 56 n.19, 224, 226, 251, 266
Total Recall (1990) 9
total cinema 117
Towering Inferno, The (1974) 49, 166 n.13, 240, 242–3, 244, 252, 254, 255
Toy Story franchise 88, 158
Toys (1992) 115, 129 n.44
trombone effect 267
Truffaut, Francois 188
Trump, Donald 174
Turkle, Sherry 302
Twister (1996) 49, 240
Twitter 98
typology of disaster 254–7
city fails, the 256

comic, the 257
historical 256
monster, the 256
natural attack films 256
"Ship of Fools, The" 243, 247, 255
war 256

UK Fan Studies Network 98
Universal Beijing Resort 298
Universal Studios Florida 297
Universal Studios Japan 298
Universal Studios Singapore 46, 74
unstable systems 49, 162–3, 241, 253, 254

V (TV series, 1984) 247
Valley of Gwangi, The (1969) 204
venality 17, 169, 172–6
victory 17, 178–80
Vietnam War 170, 188, 247
Vinge, Vernor (author and computer scientist) 249
virility 17, 178–8
virtual reality/VR 87–8, 93
Volcano (1997) 240, 246

Walking with Dinosaurs: The Movie (2013) 205
Wall Street (1987) 174
Walt Disney 14, 32, 301
war 48, 49, 159, 164, 165, 256, 306
Wasser, Frederick 244, 250

Watergate 170, 188
Wedding Banquet, The (1993) 2
Wells, H. G. 45
Westworld (1973) 11, 27
Weta Digital 115
Whale, James 194
When Dinosaurs Ruled the Earth (1977) 204, 268
When Time Ran Out (1980) 241
Where the Red Fern Grows (1961) 17, 224, 231, 232
Whissel, Kristen 270
Who Framed Roger Rabbit? (1988) 44
Williams, John 61–75, 157, 166 n.13, 243, 299
Williams, Linda Ruth 174
Willis, Bruce 174
Winston, Stan (and Winston studio) 8–9, 21 n.26, 116, 122, 125, 205
"Wizarding World of Harry Potter, The" (theme park) 295, 303
Wray, Fay 115, 172
Wu, Dr. Henry (B.D. Wong) 158, 159, 172, 197, 219, 297, 298, 317

X-Files: I Want to Believe (1998) 240

Yacowar, Maurice 239, 241, 243, 254–7
Young Frankenstein (1974) 47
YouTube 74, 78 n.41

Zach (Nick Robinson) 81, 82, 86, 87, 223, 233, 234

www.ingramcontent.com/pod-product-compliance
Lightning Source LLC
Chambersburg PA
CBHW070011010526
44117CB00011B/1505